William A. Douglass (Ph.D., anthropology, the University of Chicago, 1967) has published the following books relevant to this course: *Death in Murelaga: The Social Significance of Funerary Ritual in a Spanish Basque Village* (Seattle: University of Washington Press, 1969); and *Echalar and Murelaga: Opportunity and Rural Depopulation in Two Spanish Basque Villages* (London: C. Hurst; New York: St. Martin's Press, 1975). Relevant works that he has co-edited or co-authored include *Amerikanuak: The Basques of the New World*, with Jon Bilbao (1975; Reno: University of Nevada Press, 2005); *Los aspectos cambiantes de la España rural*, co-edited with J. Aceves (Barcelona: Barral Editores, 1978); *Beltran: Basque Sheepman of the American West*, and co-authored with Beltran Paris (Reno: University of Nevada Press, 1979).

Joseba Zulaika (Ph.D., anthropology, Princeton, 1982) has published the following books relevant to this course: *Terranova: The Ethos and Luck of Deep-Sea Fishermen* (Philadelphia: Institute for the Study of Human Issues, 1981); *Basque Violence: Metaphor and Sacrament* (Reno: University of Nevada Press, 1988); *Bertsolariaren jokoa eta jolasa* (Donostia–San Sebastián: Baroja, 1985); *Tratado estético-ritual vasco* (Donostia–San Sebastián: Baroja, 1987); *Ehiztariaren erotika* (Donostia–San Sebastián: Erein, 1990); *Del cromañón al carnaval: Los vascos como museo antropológico* (Donostia–San Sebastián: Erein, 1996); *Crónica de una seducción: El Museo Guggenheim Bilbao* (Madrid: Nerea, 1997), and, with William Douglass, *Terror and Taboo: The Follies, Fables and Faces of Terrorism* (New York: Routledge, 1996).

Basque Culture:
Anthropological Perspectives

Basque Textbooks Series

Center for Basque Studies
University of Nevada, Reno

This book was published with generous financial support from the Basque Government.

Library of Congress Cataloging-in-Publication Data

Douglass, William A.
    Basque culture : anthropological perspectives /
    William Douglass, Joseba Zulaika.
        p. cm. — (Basque textbook series)
    Includes bibliographical references and index.
    ISBN 978-1-877802-64-5 (paperback)
    ISBN 978-1-877802-65-2 (hardcover)
    ISBN 978-1-877802-66-9 (compact disk)
    1. Basques—History. 2. Basques—Ethnic identity.
3. Basques—Social life and customs. 4. País Vasco
(Spain)—History. 5. País Vasco (Spain)—Politics
and government. 6. País Vasco (Spain)—Social life
and customs. 7. Pays Basque (France)—History.
8. Pays Basque (France)—Politics and government.
9. Pays Basque (France)—Social life and customs.
I. Zulaika, Joseba. II. University of Nevada, Reno.
Center for Basque Studies. III. Title. IV. Series.
    GN549.B3 D68 2007
    306.0946'6--dc2

                                    2006036525

Cover photo: Xabier Irujo
Published by the Center for Basque Studies
University of Nevada, Reno /322
Reno, Nevada 89557-0012.

CONTENTS

Introduction

T HE PRESENT course on Basque culture is eclectic
in that it incorporates the experiences and perspectives of two social anthropologists with markedly
different interests and backgrounds. William Douglass
conducted field research between 1962 and 1964 on
the causes and consequences of migration in the villages of Aulestia (Murelaga), Bizkaia (Vizcaya) and
Etxalar (Echalar), Nafarroa (Navarra). Subsequently,
throughout much of his thirty-three-year career as
founder and director of the Center for Basque Studies of the University of Nevada, Reno, he studied
the Basque emigrant diaspora of the American West,
Australia, and several Latin American countries. He
has also published about Basque nationalism, and,
with Joseba Zulaika, on the subject of terrorism.

Joseba Zulaika studied his homeland's political
violence in the early 1980s. He also conducted ethnographic studies of transatlantic deep-sea fishermen, soldiers, artists, hunters, and versifiers. He has
analyzed the international discourse of terrorism and
worked on the history of Basque anthropology. More
recently, Zulaika's investigations have focused on
the city of Bilbao and on the Guggenheim Museum
project, in particular. He also contributes to current developments within Basque cultural studies.

The literature available in the English language
on the subject of Basque culture is both limited and
unrepresentative. This course is designed to employ
as its fundamental texts three works that are presently in print and one that is not. All encompass broad
areas of the Basque experience—Rodney Gallop's *A
Book of the Basques* (Reno: University of Nevada Press,

1998) and Mark Kurlansky's *A Basque History of the World* (1999; New York: Walker and Company, 2001) provide historical overviews of Old World Basques. *Amerikanuak: Basques in the New World* (1975; Reno: University of Nevada Press, 2005), by William A. Douglass and Jon Bilbao, describes Basque emigration and diasporic existence in several host countries.

In addition to these, Roger Collins's *The Basques* (Oxford: Basil Blackwell, 1990) is an excellent overview of Basque prehistory and the medieval world. Were they available in translation, Julio Caro Baroja's *Los vascos* (1949; San Sebastián: Bilblioteca Vascongada de los Amigos del País, 1999) and Philippe Veyrin's *Les basques* (Bayonne: Editions du Musée Basque, 1930) would constitute two other course texts. We recommend them highly to the student capable of accessing them in the original. The format of the following chapters will include suggested collateral reading (in English, whenever possible), as well. For additional bibliographic sources regarding any of the topics discussed in this course, consult the Web site http://basque.unr.edu and click on "Basque Database."

A WORD IS IN order regarding orthography. Prior to the creation of a unified Basque language (Euskara Batua) in the late 1960s, most of the literature on the Basque Country employed either Spanish or French renderings of its place names. In Spain, under Francisco Franco, the Spanish terms were the only legal ones. However, since the dictator's death in 1975, Spanish Basques have acquired considerable political autonomy, including nearly total control of their language policy. As we will see, there has been a concerted effort to resuscitate Basque and infuse its usage into all aspects of daily life. Consequently, in this text, whenever a place name first appears, we will provide both its Basque and

Spanish (or French) rendering and then subsequently employ the former—For example, "Bizkaia (Vizcaya)" with subsequent resort to "Bizkaia." The same is true of our employment of the Spanish name of Mondragón for the town known is Basque as Arrasate. We would note that in the case of Bilbo / Bilbao both terms are acceptable in Basque, and we have opted for the latter because of its international recognition. We would further note that prior to the codification of Euskara Batua, there was no standard Basque orthography, the varieties of written Basque further reflecting the several dialects of the spoken language. Consequently, use of certain terms in this text (which largely follows Batua) may differ (though not unrecognizably) from those in the assigned readings. For example, we employ *txerri puxkak* instead of *sherri pushkak* for "parts of the pig."

Finally, we emply the Basque pluralizer -k when pluralizing Basque, e.g. *baserria*, "farmstead" becomes *baserriak*, "farmsteads."

NB: What follows is more than a course outline and less than a textbook. It is certainly not intended as a publication in the traditional sense of a fully documented original contribution to knowledge and consequently should not be considered or cited as such. Rather, it contains the course notes that we have prepared as two instructors of a primarily anthropological (our discipline) treatment on Basque Culture presented and modified independently and sporadically by each of us over the past few decades (first given by Douglass in 1968). The sole intended use of this document is to facilitate and further the instructional mission of the Center for Basque Studies whether in the classroom or on the Internet.

As a set of course lecture notes, this document is not footnoted as a publication according to the classical scholarly standard, although in our required and suggested readings we attempt to invoke most, if not all, of the sources that either inform or complement our arguments. We also attempt to be explicit whenever we are advancing our own opinion regarding a particular subject.

Part One
Defining the Basques

I N CHAPTER 1, we begin by defining our subject
("the Basques") and our anthropological perspective regarding it. The latter requires consideration
of both the emergence of a specific Basque anthropology and its place within the general discipline.

Chapter 2 then situates our subject by describing both
the physical and human geographies of the European
Basque homeland, as well as the historical stereotypes
(both negative and positive) of Basques as held by others.

Chapters 3 and 4 regard Basque prehistory and biological and linguistic uniqueness—particularly the
many enigmas that they pose. At this juncture, we
are addressing the primordial foundations underpin-
ning Basque identity, both in the past and at present.

The Basque Country is central within the distribution of Europe's famed prehistoric cave art and contains many of the prime examples. Therefore, we
close Part One with the treatment in chapter 5 of the
various scholarly interpretations of both the purposes and the aesthetic properties of these artistic
expressions. We also consider briefly the influence
of the prehistoric art on the works of leading contemporary Basque artists—most notably, sculptors.

1 · Basque Anthropology

AS THE ETYMOLOGY of the term shows, anthropology purports to study all human activity and world-views, past and present, as well as the biological and psychological makeup of humankind. In a sense, then, of all the human sciences, anthropology is by far the most ambitious and eclectic. Indeed, critics claim that in purporting to study a little of every-thing, anthropology in reality studies little or noth-ing and therefore scarcely qualifies as a "science."

The sweeping universalistic and humanistic dimen-sions of the discipline notwithstanding, anthropology has also been regarded as the most particularistic of the human sciences. Anthropologists tend to parse the human experience into distinctive cultural and social configurations that, according to some contemporary critics, are then reified into cultures and societies—each representing a unique way of life, every one of which is equally valid and subject to evaluation only in its own terms. In this regard, it is fair to say that anthropology has been the bastion of cultural relativism. Indeed, it is not uncommon for the individual anthropologist to forge a strong (often romanticized) bond with a particu-lar group and then become not only its chronicler, but also an apologist for what he or she sees as "my people."

A particularly problematic aspect of this legacy has been the tendency of anthropological models to por-tray peoples and cultures in monolithic, homogeneous terms in which human actors are reduced to monads, rather than represented as persons. They become merely living expressions of a particular mindset, con-demned to acting out its cultural and social logics. In short, by essentializing human behavior into constrictive cultural configurations, ironically, the most universalistic discipline is also the most parochial.

What, then, of the present course on Basque anthropology? Obviously, we believe in the validity (existence, reality) of a social and cultural configuration that is sufficiently distinctive and distinguishable so as to constitute a "Basque people" as our object of study. Indeed, what follows might be regarded as a demonstration of the worth of such a subject position. The point is far from obvious or unchallenged. For some anthropologists (including Basque ones), as well as for historians and political scientists, the long-standing inclusion of the Basque homeland within the territories of Spain and France (with all of their corresponding "national" histories, cultural influences, and institutional arrangements) make "stateless" Basques little more than expressions of the overarching Spanish and French states. An analogy would be the status of Southerners or New Englanders in American life. We would argue that, even though at some levels both are principally expressions of "American" culture, each possesses its own anthropological interest precisely because it configures the identity, attitudes, and behaviors of a significant number of persons inhabiting a particular territory.

FROM OUR anthropological perspective, then, regarding Basque culture, the key question is not whether Basque identity is "invented" or even fabricated (as some claim), but rather how it has informed the worldview of at least some inhabitants of the Basque homeland in the past and how it continues to do so at present. We will also consider ways in which it has provided a sense of ethnic group solidarity to a sufficient number of Basque emigrants to allow discerning viable and persisting Basque diasporas in several host countries around the world.

Europe's mystery people
Two elderly siblings sharing childhood memories in the
baserri (farmstead) Buxungoborda of Etxalar, Nafarroa
(early 1960s).
Photo: William Douglass

Our approach will certainly be intellectually eclectic and omnivorous. Many of the topics of individual
chapters herein have already lent themselves to entire
courses within this series offered by the Center for

Basque Studies (e.g., Basque history, gender studies, economy, nationalism, etc.).

In devoting chapters to subjects such as history and economics, we may be straying beyond the confines of our discipline, but we do so mindful of the importance of disaggregating certain features that are normally embedded, and thereby obfuscated, within broader French and Spanish frameworks. Nor in providing the peculiarly Basque perspective regarding the local, regional, state, European, and world history of these features do we intend to privilege them over other interpretations of the same forces and events. Rather, we wish to provide the student with the slant that informs a Basque culturalist interpretation of the past, which, in turn, helps to sustain Basque identity in the present. In sum, we are concerned with the social and cultural significance of such Basque historiography, including ways in which it contests and is in turn challenged by alternative interpretations of history.

AT THE SAME time, we will concentrate more on the core concerns of our own discipline, or at least those of American anthropology—namely, what is called "the four-field approach." This approach deals with the interrelated topics of prehistory, linguistics, human biology, and culture. As we will see, there is much that is distinctive about Basques when viewed through the lenses of these subdisciplines. Finally, it should be noted that we are social anthropologists and are therefore more conversant with that fourth subdiscipline—culture.

During the latter half of the twentieth century, the designations "cultural" and "social" anthropology have largely become conflated and interchangeable when referring to the holistic study of the cultural and social distinctiveness of small-scale societies, more often than not of the non-Western variety (including minority groups enclaved within Occidental countries, such as Native Americans within the United States and Canada or Australian Aborigines). At the same time, such anthropology was as much a methodology as a model, in that it was expected that the anthropologist would reside for a significant period in the subject community (usually for at least a year) and become conversant with the language(s) of relevance to the research. Such residential longevity and linguistic fluency, referred to as participant observation, were felt to facilitate and culminate in an anthropological monograph reflective of a near-insider understanding of the workings of a particular society and culture.

HOWEVER, THERE are certain other challenges in applying the social anthropological gaze to our Basque subject. It might first be noted that while there is a Europeanist branch of the discipline, that is, there are anthropologists who study European peoples, there is a certain ambivalence within anthropology about these studies that stems in large part from the original formulation of anthropology as an Occidental enterprise focused on the study of (often colonized) non-Western peoples. For at least some practitioners, "real" anthropology is conducted in Africa or New Guinea, and not in Bizkaia.

At the same time, within Europeanist anthropology itself, there is the criticism that anthropologists have sought out exotic, marginalized peoples, whether they are marginalized socially,for example Gypsies, or physically—the isolated mountain village or island community. Furthermore, critics note that the first generation of Europeanists (from approximately 1940 to 1965) focused on what anthropologist Robert Redfield, in a classic work, dubbed "the little community"—the peasant or fishing village—to the exclusion of practically all of the vast social and cultural complexity of the European continent. Finally, a comment is in order regarding Basque anthropology, as distinct from the anthropology of the Basques. When William A, Douglass was conducting his research in Aulestia and Etxalar in the early 1960s, the Spanish term *antropología* referred almost exclusively to physical anthropology. This is not to say, however, that no one shared the anthropologist's interest in Basque culture and rural Basque society. To the contrary, those interested in various aspects of "traditional" Basque culture ranged from academic folklorists and ethnologists to enthusiastic antiquarians. The awesome centenarian figure of José Miguel de Barandiarán (1890–1991) may be cited as an example. While lacking an academic appointment per se for most of his extraordinarily lengthy and productive career, Barandiarán's interests (and those of his several disciples) ranged widely across all four of the anthropological subdisciplines. An ordained Catholic priest, he conducted innumerable archeological investigations, uncovering human skeletal material that prompted him to speculate regarding the racial characteristics of the Paleo-Basque population. He founded the journal *Eusko-Folklore* and encouraged its many collaborators (who were often parish priests in rural areas) to collect legends and folktales and to write descriptions of local "customs." This, in turn, implied careful documenting of Basque linguistic terminology, including dialectical variations.

THE MAIN THRUST of Barandiarán and his school was the collection (before they disappeared) of beliefs, traits, and artifacts, whereas thrust of social / cultural anthropology in the mid-twentieth century was to ascertain how contemporary little communities "functioned." That is, the subject community, treated for heuristic purposes as a largely timeless and self-enclosed social system, was regarded as a kind of organic whole in which each of the parts was assessed not so much in its own terms, but for its contribution to the functioning, maintenance, and reproduction of the system as a whole.

Among Barandiarán's many disciples stands the towering figure of Julio Caro Baroja (1916–95). In addition to his preoccupation with prehistoric themes, Caro Baroja immersed himself fully in the study of Basque history. While combining anthropology and social history, he authored more than a hundred books and innumberable articles on ethnology, linguistics, technology, ethnic minorities, violence, popular art, literature, and biography. A man of a liberal and humanistic disposition, a researcher of global historic processes, as well as the author of local ethnographic studies, and with an interest in material culture as much as in ideology, Caro Baroja was internationally the best-known figure produced by the Basque anthropological tradition during the dark period of Francoism. His work is indispensable for any student of Basque culture and society.

I N THE THREE decades since the death of Spanish dictator Francisco Franco, the Spanish Basque Country has evolved its own public and private university systems, which include anthropology departments. The term itself is now used more to designate social / cultural anthropology than the biological variety. The first generation of these new Basque anthropologists was trained abroad for the most part—Jesus Azcona in Germany, Teresa del Valle and Joseba Zulaika in the United States. Their students now constitute a new generation of autochthonous Basque social anthropologists, many of whom focus their research on Basque political and cultural issues. Finally, the ethnological and historicist legacies of Barandiarán, Caro Baroja, and their disciples persist, as well.

Lesson one

LEARNING OBJECTIVES
1. To understand the place of anthropology within the human sciences.
2. To recognize the several dimensions of anthropological investigation.
3. To understand the place of Europeanist anthropology within the discipline.
4. To understand the development of a Basque anthropology.

REQUIRED READING
Thomas J. Abercrombie, "Europe's First Family: The Basques," *National Geographic*, November 1995, 78–96.
Alberto Piazza, "Who Are the Europeans?" *Science* 260 (June 1993): 1767–68.

SUGGESTED READING
Jesús Azcona, "Notas para una historia de la antropología vasca: Telesforo de Aranzadi y José Miguel de Barandiarán," *Ethnica* 17 (1981).
———, "La escuela histórica de Viena y la antropología vasca," *Cuadernos de Etnología y Etnografía de Navarra* 43 (1984).
———, "On Time: Notes Regarding the Anthropology of Julio Caro Baroja," in *Essays in Basque Social Anthropology and History*, ed. William A. Douglass (Reno: Basque Studies Program, 1989).

Juan Aranzadi, *El milenarismo Vasco* (Madrid: Taurus, 1981).

Julio Caro Baroja, *Los Baroja* (Madrid: Taurus, 1978).

Angel Goicoetxea Marcaida, *Telesforo de Aranzadi: Vida y obra* (San Sebastián: Sociedad de Ciencias Aranzadi, 1985).

Luis de Barandiarán Irizar, *Jose Miguel de Barandiarán: Patriarca de la cultura vasca* (San Sebastián: Caja de Ahorros Municipal, 1976).

Teresa del Valle, "Visión general de la antropología," *Ethnica* 17 (1981).

Joseba Zulaika, *Del cromanón al carnival: Los vascos como museo antropológico* (San Sebastián: Erein, 1996).

WRITTEN LESSON FOR SUBMISSION

1. How would you explain the emergence of Basque anthropology within the broader context of European anthropology?
2. Describe some basic Basque themes that became the focus of attention for cultural anthropology.
3. Discuss the distinction between Basque anthropology and the anthropology of Basques.

2 · Situating the Basques
Physical and Human Geography

T HE BASQUE Country, or Euskalherria, is located in
the southwestern corner of France and north-central
portion of Spain, where the western spur of the Pyrenees
Mountains brushes the Cantabrian seacoast. It straddles
the present international frontier, which means that we
can speak of the French Basque and Spanish Basque
areas. The French Basque area, or Iparralde, is made
up of three regions: Lapurdi (Labourd), Behe Nafarroa
(Basse Navarre), and Xiberoa (Soule). There are four
Basque provinces within Spain: Nafarroa (Navarra),
Araba (Álava), Gipuzkoa (Guipúzcoa), and Bizkaia (Vizcaya).

GEOGRAPHY
Euskalherria is an extremely small geographical area.
From Baiona (Bayonne) in the north to Tutera (Tudela)
in the south, the overall distance is 160 kilometers, or
about 100 miles. From Maule-Lextarre (Mauleon) in
the east to Bilbao in the west, the distance is 170 kilometers, or slightly over 100 miles. The total territory
of the Basque homeland is about 20,000 square kilometers. It contains a population of approximately 2.5
million inhabitants. Iparralde has a small population of
220,000 persons occupying just 3,000 square kilometers
(1,158 square miles). This, plus the fact that the Spanish
Basque area, or Hegoalde, is heavily industrialized, while
Iparralde is not, means that the two regions play very
different roles within their respective countries. This difference in their scale and importance is reflected markedly in their political histories. Basque nationalism is
much more pronounced in Hegoalde (and particularly

in Euskadi, constituted by Gipuzkoa, Araba, and Bizkaia, but not Nafarroa) than in Iparralde.

The Basque Country is divided by the main ridges of the western Pyrenees, which run roughly from east to west. In the extreme eastern sector, the mountains reach a height of 2,504 meters, or 8,213 feet above sea level, at Mount Aneu (Anie). In the west, the two highest elevations are Aitzgorri and Gorbea, which are 1,544 meters (5,064 feet) and 1,475 meters (4,838 feet) above sea level, respectively.

IN NORTHERN Hegoalde, the landscape drops off sharply to the seacoast. The topography is extremely broken, with the hills reaching right down to the sea. There are a number of short, swift rivers that serrate the mountains with narrow valleys. In Bizkaia, the principal river is the Nerbioi (Nervión), which permits ocean-going vessels to penetrate as far inland as Euskalherria's largest city, Bilbao. In Gipuzkoa, there is the Bidasoa, which forms the French frontier for the last few miles of its journey to the sea. The only major rivers in Iparralde are the Errobi (Nive), which drains most of it, and the Adur (Adour), which enters the Basque Country just before reaching the sea, permitting vessels access to the largest French Basque city—Baiona. While, as a whole, the northern ecological zone is characterized by a mountainous landscape that may be regarded as the foothills of the main Pyrenees, the northern part of Iparralde opens out considerably into almost flat or undulating plains. The capital of Gipuzkoa, Donostia (San Sebastián), is a coastal city renowned for its spectacular seashell-shaped bay.

The climate in the northern ecological zone is what geographers refer to as maritime. The area is exposed directly to the influence of the Atlantic, which means that rainfall is considerable and the weather is unsettled

Nafarroa Behera   Zuberoa

Bizkaia Gipuzkoa Lapurdi

Araba Nafarroa

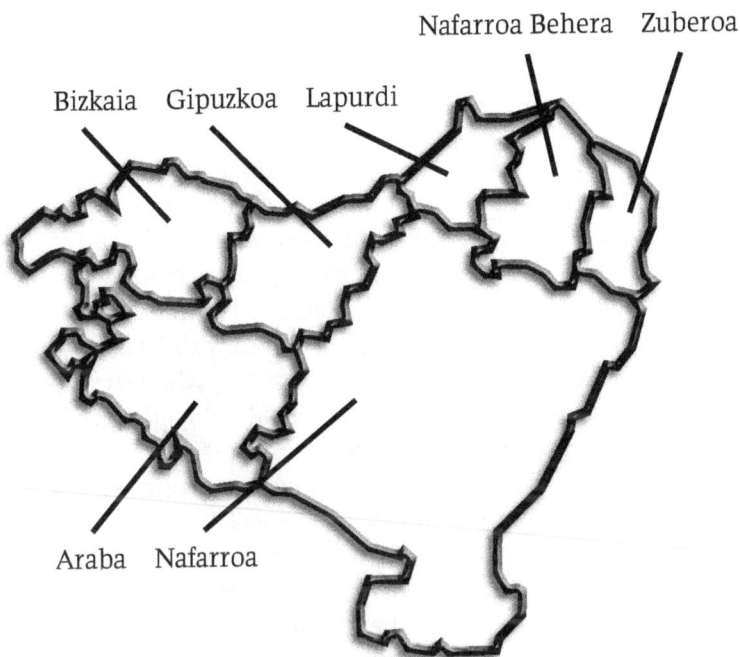

The seven Basque provinces

The territories of Lapurdi, Nafarroa Behera, and Zuberoa,
or Iparralde, are part of Southern France. Bizkaia, Gipuzkoa and Araba constitute the Basque Autonomous Com-
nmunity, one of the seventeen "autonomies" of post-
Francoist Spain. Nafarroa stands on its own as a separate
autonomous region.

---

and oftentimes violent. However, the temperature
extremes are rather moderate in that a maritime
climate has cool summers and relatively mild winters.
It seldom freezes, even during the winter months, and
when frost does occur, the temperature seldom dips
much below freezing. Snowstorms are rare events, and

many winters are altogether free of them. The rainfall is heavy, with the heaviest concentration in the late winter and spring, although no month of the year is entirely without rainy days. On average, it rains 230 to 250 days out of the year. With such a heavy rainfall, there is no need for irrigation, so agriculture is of the dry-farming variety. The natural vegetation is extremely lush, with deciduous forests of oaks, chestnuts, and beech trees (and, more recently, pines planted as a commercial timber crop). The forest floor is covered with ferns and undergrowth. Except for the late summer, when the area does have a tendency to dry out considerably, the landscape is always green and very picturesque.

The second, or what we might label the central ecological zone is the high mountain country. This is an area that is virtually uninhabited for the most of the year. Its two major economic activities are livestock herding in the summer months, when herders from surrounding foothill areas ascend to the high country with their sheep, cows, goats, and horses, and logging of the hardwoods, particularly beech trees. The climate is alpine. That is, there is considerable moisture, with a heavy snowfall and extremely low temperatures hovering at or below freezing for the most of the winter months.

THE AREA SOUTH of the Pyrenees, or the southern ecological zone, differs markedly from the other two. The landscape tilts away gradually from the high mountain ridges to the Ebro River in the south. The relatively open, flat country around Iruña (Pamplona), Nafarroa's capital city, famed for the San Fermín festival, and Gasteiz (Vitoria) (the capital of Araba) averages about 800 meters (about 2,500 feet) above sea level. The landscape is characterized by open plains covered with sparse vegetation. The climate is what geographers call continental, which means little rainfall and extreme temperature changes between winter and summer. Thus, in the winter months, the area is subject to heavy frosts, while in the summer, daytime temperatures soar into the nineties. In central Nafarroa, rainfall is about 700 millimeters (27.56 inches) annually, concentrated in winter and spring, which is sufficient to support dry farming. However, near Tutera, rainfall averages but 350 mm (13.78 inches), so agriculture requires irrigation.

HISTORICAL REPRESENTATIONS OF THE BASQUES

F OR AT LEAST two millennia, the Basques have established their presence beyond the precincts of their homeland, whether as legionnaires in the service of the Roman Empire, as Europe's first whalers in the North Atlantic, or as key players during five centuries of Spanish (and French) overseas colonial expansion.

During that time, popular images and stereotypes of the Basques have emerged. Rodney Gallop notes: "The mystery surrounding the origins and history of the Basque race, the difficulty of their uncouth tongue and the great reserve which they display in all their contacts with the outside world, a reserve to which is due, in all probability their survival as a race, have invested them with an air of remoteness and woven around them an atmosphere of romance."

This mysterious land, discovered by the Romantics, posed a challenging riddle pregnant with historical depth, occult prehistoric meanings, and even potential associations with lost or submerged continents yet to be discovered by science. According to Gallop:

On the shores of the Bay of Biscay, where the Pyrenees slope down to the sea, there lies a smiling land whose varied charm is made up of indented sea-coast, rugged mountain and green valley, rolling hills covered

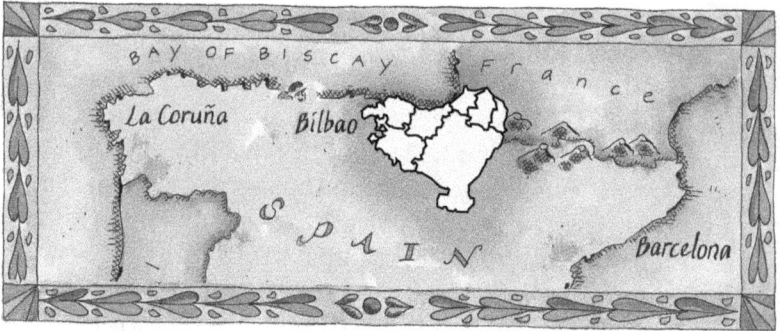

The Basque Country in Europe

The Basque Country is located on the Eastern side of the Pyrenees that divide Spain from France. It is open to the sea at the Bay of Biscay. Its historical territories are part of Southern France and Northern Spain. It is bordered by the regions of Aquitaine to the North, Asturias and Galicia to the West, Castile to the South, and Aragon and Catalonia to the East.

Base illustration by Jennifer Thermes.

---

with golden gorse and forests of oak or chestnut, trout-streams and maize-fields, shady lanes, sun-soaked vine-yards and apple orchards. From time immemorial this land has been inhabited by a mysterious race whom we call the Basques, but who call themselves *Eskualdu-nak*, and their land *Eskual Herria* or *Euzkadi*, a name which may, perhaps, be derived from the Basque word for "sun". There are few races on the face of the earth of whose origin so little is known, and who have exercised such a fascination over ethnologists and philologists of every nationality: "The most difficult problem presented by our history," writes Camille Jullian with hardly a trace of exaggeration, "is that of the origin of the Basques."

The riddle has left its traces even in the physiognomy of the Basque people, who are depicted as having several differentiating physical or phenotypical traits as evidenced by their skulls, facial features, blood types, and genome. The Basque language is non-Indo-European. Its origins and possible associations with other tongues are unknown. This combination of biological and linguistic uniqueness has led many scholars to proclaim the Basques to be Europe's "oldest race." (See chapter 5.)

BASQUE HISTORY is typically narrated as that of an independent and isolated people. However, Basques had extensive contacts and dealings with Romans and migrants and invaders. According to Gallop:

> Basque history, considered in its broadest aspect, is the history of the independence of the Basque provinces, and of their gradual submission, not so much to the countries to which they offered allegiance, as to the irresistible forces of time and progress. It resolves itself into the history of the *fueros* (charters), the traditional inheritance of the Basques from the Dark Ages and the warrant of their national independence, to which they clung for nearly a thousand years, and the final loss of which, when they had become a glaring anachronism, spelt the end of their independent existence and may eventually mean their extinction as a separate race.

Negative images of the Basques throughout history include the Vascones, depicted as brutal and ferocious pagans (fourth century A.D), and, as recorded in 1120 A.D., the Basques as a race speaking a strange language—real savages, as bloodthirsty and ferocious as the wild beasts with whom they live. The medieval pilgrim Aimeric Picaud describes Basques as "black, perfidious, faithless, corrupt, violent, savage, given over to drunkenness and evil-living." In the seventeenth century, the inquisitor Pierre de Lancre depicted Basques as prone to witchcraft because they drank too much cider. In the sixteenth and seventeenth cenuries, they were seen as cruel pirates and corsairs. Today, Basques are seen as terrorists.

Positive images, by contrast, initially revolved around Basques' exuberant behavior. The Roman chronicler Strabo relates that during the full moon, Basques danced and feasted in front of their dwelling places in honor of a nameless god. In 1528, Andrea Navagero recorded that "the people of this country are very gay and are quite the opposite of the Spaniards, who can do nothing save gravely. These people are always laughing, joking, and dancing, both men and women." René Le Pays, in 1659, wrote that "joy begins there [the Basque Country] with life and ends only with death." During the Romantic period, Wilhelm von Humboldt saw the "noble Basque" as noble savage. Basques also appeared in such heroic literary portraits as Pierre Loti's contrabandist Ramuntcho (1896) and Pierre Lhande's maiden Mirentchu (1911).

Gallop summarizes the Basque character this way: "loyalty and rectitude; dignity and reserve; independence and a strong sense of race and racial superiority; a serious outlook tempered by a marked sense of humor and capacity for enjoyment; deep religious feeling; and a cult of tradition amounting almost to ancestor-worship; all these correlated and directed by a deep-rooted simplicity and a courageous, objective view of life."

Lesson two

LEARNING OBJECTIVES

1. To acquire an overview of Basque geography.
2. To evaluate the historical images of the Basques.
3. To evaluate the Romantic rhetorics regarding the "mysterious" Basques.
4. To assess the information contained in social stereotypes and their limitations.
5. To understand the relevance of collective representations for social science.
6. To understand how narrativity exoticizes, while framing, our descriptions of cultures.

REQUIRED READING

Rodney Gallop, *A Book of the Basques*, (Reno: University of Nevada Press, 1970), 1–43.

SUGGESTED READING

William A. Douglass and Jon Bilbao, *Amerikanuak: The Basques of the New World* (Reno: University of Nevada Press, 2005), 9–20.

Mark Kurlansky, *The Basque History of the World* (New York: Walker and Company, 2001), 1–8.

Robert Laxalt, *A Time We Knew* (Reno, University of Nevada Press, 1990), 1–7.

WRITTEN LESSON FOR SUBMISSION

1. How much credence should we grant to these stereotypes of "national character"?
2. Do such stereotypes reveal more about the people described or about the writer (i.e. perhaps regarding Gallop's "British" values)? Has the folklorist fallen in love with his subjects?

3. Can entire cultures be described as "virtuous" or the opposite, as God-fearing or God-loving, or as lacking in imagination or sentiment?
4. How would you sift out the valuable information contained in such stereotypes, if any?
5. Can the Basques serve as a literary motif for various types of writing?

3 · Prehistoric Enigmas

IN CHAPTER 1, we drew an analogy between Basques within Spain and France and Southerners and New Englanders within the United States. Actually, a better American comparison might have been with the Hopi people of Arizona. After all, when invoking the culture of Southerners or New Englanders, the reference is primarily to variations on a (pre)dominant Anglo-American cultural theme easily documented in the historical record of European immigration transpiring between the seventeenth and early twentieth centuries. Furthermore, Southerners and New Englanders may manifest distinctive dialectical variation in their speech, but only as variation of a single, shared English language.

As English speakers, most Hopi also partake of this same linguistic heritage. As citizens of the United States, they also share with Southerners and New Englanders a common American culture, yet most Hopi are also bilingual in a language that does not derive from English's Indo-European linguistic origins. The Hopi, like the Basques, clearly did not originate in their present homeland, yet the where and the when (let alone the why) of the migrations of proto-Hopi and proto-Basques remain opaque prehistorical questions, rather than more translucent historical ones. (Parenthetically, we should note that the contemporary presence of a Basque ethnic group in Boise or Buenos Aires has a migration history that is comparable to and every bit as accessible as that of, say, the Irish element within Southern and New Englander culture.) We might therefore begin by considering the evidence adduced by various disciplines arguing for the uniqueness of the Basques.

First, there is the archeological record. Excavations at various sites in the BasqueCountry demonstrate that the ancestors of the modern Basque population have occupied the western Pyrenees for at least the past five millennia. A more liberal interpretation of the prehistoric record suggests that Basques may be descended directly from the cave painters of Lascaux in southern France and Altamira in northern Spain, and indeed, many magnificent examples of such art are found in the present-day Basque area. Such a view would suggest that the Basques have occupied their homeland for at least the past fifteen thousand years. Some investigators (particularly José Miguel de Barandiarán) have even suggested that Basques are the modern remnants of Europe's Cro-Magnon population, which would push the Basques' prehistorical baseline back to at least fifty thousand years ago. Whichever interpretation one chooses to accept, the archeological evidence places the Basque or proto-Basque population in the western Pyrenees prior to the second millennium before the Common Era, when there were invasions of Europe by Indo-European speaking tribes out of western Asia that created the bases for the major ethnic divisions of Europe as we know them today.

ANOTHER LINE of evidence of the relative uniqueness of the Basques regards certain features of their biological makeup, particularly their serological profile. Nevertheless, Basques are clearly Caucasians and therefore do not display sufficient biological differences to support unequivocally the contention by some physical anthropologists that they are racially distinct from other European populations. However, most investigators have argued that, at the very least, Basques have constituted a somewhat isolated genetic pool within Europe over a considerable period of time.

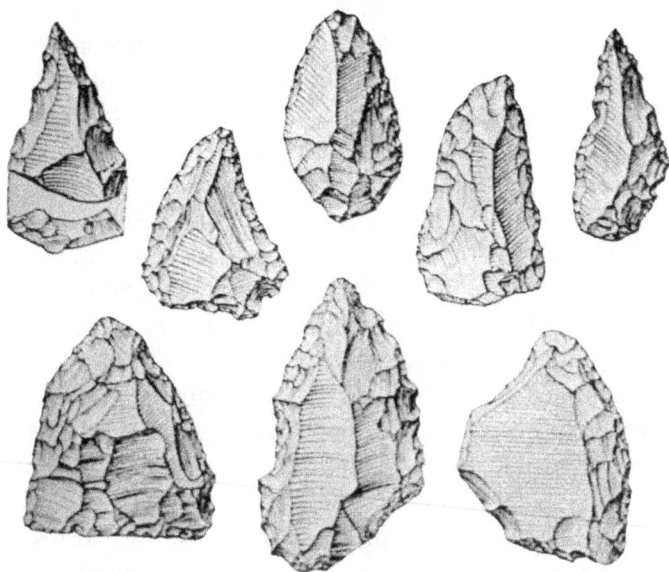

Earliest technology
Flint tools give us a rare glimpse of life in the Stone
Age. Mousterian-era lithic materials from Isturitz (Behe
Nafarroa). This is one of the richest Paleolithic sites in
the Basque Country.
Source: Jesus Altuna.

B Y FAR THE most telling evidence for the uniqueness of the Basques is the testimony of their language, or Euskara, as it is called in Basque. Euskara is
totally unrelated to the Indo-European languages of the
continent, a fact that has prompted philologists and
linguists to range far afield in search of a possible connections with other human tongues. Links with such disparate languages as Berber, Old Egyptian, Japanese, Iro-

quois, and other American Indian languages have been
posited, yet none have been demonstrated conclusively.
To date, for linguists, Basque remains the sole representative of its own language family. In chapters 4 and 30,
we will treat Euskara in greater detail.

The final line of evidence for Basque uniqueness is
their own self-concept. Basques refer to themselves as
Euskaldunak, or "speakers of Basque." Basques on both
sides of the French-Spanish frontier see themselves as
sharing a common cultural and linguistic tradition, one
that is quite distinct from those of the surrounding
French and Spanish cultures. Some Basques frame the
differences in terms of Basque racial, cultural, and moral
superiority. Regardless of such interpretations, the very
existence in the modern world of a discernible Basque
enclave in Western Europe after centuries of pressures
to assimilate into the wider structures of the Spanish
and French nations is a monument to Basque tenacity in
retaining their traditions and separate identity.

SUMMARIZING the results of the various lines of
inquiry that we have been pursuing, we find that
the prehistoric record tells us that the Basques have
remained *in situ* in their present homeland for at least
the past five thousand years and possibly for much longer, therefore making them the oldest identifiable ethnic
group in Europe. The linguistic evidence tells us that, at
least at the level of language, they are unrelated to any
other European group and, as far as is yet known, to
any other group in the world. The biological data indicate that, at a minimum, the Basques have developed
unusual blood-group frequencies, which is suggestive
of a degree of biological isolation from the surrounding European populations. And, finally, the Basques are
quite conscious and proud of their enigmatic position
within the ethnographic panorama of Europe and do all

within their power to maintain their cultural traditions and hence their uniqueness.

WHAT ARE the actual facts discovered by archeologists about Basque prehistory? Whereas there is little evidence in the Basque Country from the Lower Paleolithic, the Mousterian period in the Meso-Paleolithic (100,000 years ago) is better known. The cave of Lezetxiki is the main site. The humerus of a Mousterian woman was discovered there. In the cave deposits of that period, archeologists have found evidence of hunting activities, including the remains of bison, deer, wild goats, and wild horses, as well as those of two kinds of rhinoceros—one of them becoming extinct as recently as the last glacial period. Stone implements have also been discovered, as well as remains of animals that died of natural causes in the caves, such as bears, lions, leopards, and hyenas.

The cave of Isturitze contains another Mousterian deposit. Archeologists have surmised that for its inhabitants, hunting was the main mode of life—conducted from ambush and by driving the prey off cliffs. All of this hunting activity must have required some elementary form of social organization. Stone, horn, and bone implements have been found in this cave.

As to the lifestyle of the Upper Paleolithic (40,000–10,000 B.C.), hunting was clearly the principal activity. This can be ascertained from food-waste deposits, armaments, work implements, and other tools, art on walls and on objects, and the settings of the cave shelters themselves. A major deposit of this period was found in Santimamiñe. In this cave, 22 percent of the bones came from horses, 22 percent from bovines, 18 percent from deer, 15 percent from wild goats, and 9 percent from wild boars. In the cave of Isturitze, there are remains mainly of reindeer.

The old and the new

The people of the Pyrenees created some of the world's oldest and most striking works of art. Now its people enjoy modern times.

THESE PREHISTORIC people lived in cave shelters that had to be strategically placed for observing and controlling the passage of animals. The hearth was located at the rear of the main entrance hall; it was a circular hole sometimes surrounded by stones. Fire was a precious element. Animal skins were used to cover the body; needles for sewing have been discovered at the sites. Some objects were used as ornaments or amulets: perforated small shells, perforated small teeth, and quartz crystals. The presence of similar artistic styles and themes over large areas may reflect shared social relations beyond the family. Wall art suggests that the same animals that were hunted were also the objects of artistic and possibly religious concerns.

Around 10,000 B.C., the last glaciation ended. Very significant deposits of this Upper Paleolithic period can be found in the caves of Santimamiñe, Lumentxa, Bolinkoba, Ermitia, Urtiaga, Aizpitarte, and Isturitze. These caves are largely coastal and contain fishing artifacts (hooks, harpoons) and evidence that shellfish were now being collected.

THE INTERPRETATION given to such prehistoric facts can vary substantially. In the readings by William A. Douglass and Jon Bilbao and by Roger Collins, there are two samples of a general introduction to Basque prehistory that can be compared and contrasted.

One of the crucial challenges that any culture poses for its representatives is the interpretation of their own past. In the Basque case, a sense of prehistory is key to understanding much of Basque identity as expressed in present political attitudes. Today, the Basque Country is a developed, globalized, First World society, yet Basques cherish and invoke their prehistoric past. Archeology, anthropology, and art have played a significant role in its recreation. The activities of hundreds of Basque amateur archeologists and ethnographers reflect this passion for uncovering a unique prehistory and discerning its possible cultural continuities. Anthropological and artistic depictions of their prehistoric past have provided the

Basques with foundational myths of cultural uniqueness
that then anchor their contemporary identity as a people.

A distinction should be made between the actual archeological evidence and the significance ascribed to it. But
from the standpoint of its power to confer "meaning," it
is of minor relevance whether the prehistoric "facts" are
real or simply imagined. Furthermore, the archeological
"record" admits considerable interpretive latitude. After
all, prehistory is, by definition, lacking in the precision
afforded by written documentation. A degree of ignorance is inherent in the rendering of the prehistoric past.
It is a time that cannot be made fully present, and there
are essential components that cannot be captured by
recorded history. Such "deep memory" of the past must
rely heavily on symbolism. It privileges a higher order
of mythical time over the pedestrian one of the "merely"
historical. It renders history almost valueless, hopelessly
aleatory and insignificant. Given the claim that "we have
been here forever," the significance of recent political
events can seem trivial.

WHAT IS THE nature of *time*, or temporal continuity, in such prehistoric reconstructions? It
must be anchored in a mythical past; it has no anteced-
ent period that can somehow be used as one defining
parameter; it lacks elements of contextual relativity; and
comparison of it with the prehistories of others is all
but irrelevant. As is myth itself, this is "uncaused" and
"motionless" time. Yet such prehistoric cultural reconstructions define primordial Basque cultural authenticity and even posit the evolution of Basques *in situ*
in their present homeland, despite the evidence from
paleoanthropology that the human species first emerged
in Africa. There is also the biblical founding myth that
Basques were first differentiated ethnically (linguisti-

cally) at the Tower of Babel and then migrated from the Middle East to their present homeland.

Lesson three

LEARNING OBJECTIVES
1. To acquire an overview of Basque prehistory and history.
2. To consider academic debates regarding Basque prehistory.
3. To understand the relevance of their prehistory for contemporary Basques.

REQUIRED READING
Roger Collins, *The Basques* (Oxford: Basil Blackwell, 1990), 1–30.
Mark Kurlansky, *Basque History of the World* New York: Walker and Company, 2001), 18–26.

SUGGESTED READING
Jesús Altuna, *Lehen euskal herria* (Bilbao: Ediciones Mensajero, 1975).
José Miguel de Barandiarán, *El hombre primitivo en el País Vasco* (Donostia–San Sebastián: Beñat, 1934).

WRITTEN LESSON FOR SUBMISSION
1. To what extent (if at all) can we determine the origins of the Basques?
2. What cultural relevance does prehistory hold for the Basques?
3. What are the facts and what are the interpretations of Basque prehistory?
4. After all the scholarly debates, the final question of why the Basques exist in their linguistic and cultural

singularity still remains. Where do they come from?
What is the basis of their prehistoric memory? What
is the point of preserving a distinctive language and
identity?

4 · Euskara

As THE ONLY non-Indo-European language in Western Europe, Basque (or Euskara) is a linguistic island. This fact has made it the object of intense attention by scholars from many disciplines. The Basques' claim to their own culture relies heavily on this linguistic heritage.

Until the twentieth century (and then only partially and situationally), Basque had never been an administrative language in either Iparralde or Hegoalde. Rather, Latin and then the respective Spanish and French languages were the vernacular in which Eukalherria's official affairs were conducted. Consequently, Euskara was relegated to an inferior status. Indeed, between the sixteenth and eighteenth centuries in Spain, some opponents of the Basques questioned whether Euskara was a language at all and whether Basques could really communicate with each other in it. Others suggested that Euskara was corrupting and even diabolical. There came to be the exhortation "Speak Christian!"—by which was meant Castilian.

The Romantic savant Wilhelm von Humboldt was the first to underscore the uniqueness of Basque for the wider European audience. In 1799, he visited the Basque Country and became fascinated with both the people and their language. In his travel account, he drew invidious comparisons between Basques and Spaniards, depicting the former as morally superior. His obsession with Euskara persisted beyond his visit, and he continued to study it. Von Humboldt's investigations coincided in time (the early nineteenth century) with the fascination in the nascent field of linguistics with the connections of several European languages with Sanskrit, which led to postulation of both an Indo-European family of languages and evidence of the invasions of Europe by various tribes of its protospeakers. Von Humboldt underscored the non-Indo-European nature of Euskara and thereby laid the foundation for investigations regarding the possible connection between Basque and any other human language that continues to baffle scholars to this day.

THERE HAVE been multiple unsuccessful efforts at linking Basque with other languages. There are essentially two non-Basque linguistic families in Europe: the Indo-European cluster, which includes the Germanic, Hellenic, Romance, Slavic, Baltic, and Celtic languages; and the Uralic languages, which include Hungarian, Estonian, Finnish, and Lapp. Genetically and structurally, Basque is unrelated to either family, although it has borrowed vocabulary and grammatical forms from the former.

During antiquity and the Middle Ages, the distribution of the Basque language extended considerably beyond the present confines of Euskalherria. Basque place names occur to the north in the French Aquitaine, to the east throughout the Pyrenees, and to the south in the Rioja and Burgos.

The issue of the origins and potential relations of Basque with other languages has been a perennial topic for scholars. Among the dozens of linguistic comparisons between it and other tongues, two major hypotheses have received the greatest attention. Basque-Iberianism seeks to link Basque with the ancient Iberian language (of which only some inscriptions survive), which disappeared with the Roman conquest of the Iberian Peninsula. At one time, this theory enjoyed considerable support among linguists, but was ultimately abandoned. A related hypothesis, also abandoned, held that Basque

LINGVAE VASCONVM PRIMI-
tiæ per Dominum Bernardum Dechepare
Rectorem sancti michælis veteris.

Publishing in Basque

Title page of the first book published in Basque,
Linguae Vasconum Primitiae, by Bernard Dechepare (1545). It is a collection of religious and erotic
poems.

is related to North African languages such as Berber and the eastern languages once classified as "Hamitic."

The Basque-Caucasian hypothesis, the second major focus of research, has centered on affinities between Basque and the languages of the Caucasus region, between the Black Sea and the Caspian Sea. Although no irrefutable kinship has been demonstrated, certain similarities have been found. Renowned linguists have worked on this hypothesis; others have questioned its merits. Historical linguistics seeks cognates in the respective lexicons of two languages as evidence (or not) of their historical affinity. Given phonetic limitations on human speech patterns, any two human languages share a percentage of "coincidental" possible cognates. In the case of the languages of the Caucasus, there is considerable internal variation between separate language families and their subvariations. The comparisons with Basque have been made across this entire linguistic spectrum and may therefore reflect a cumulative effect, rather than a straightforward comparative one. There is also the problem that Basque itself subdivides into at least seven (or, according to some classificatory systems, more) "dialectical" varieties.

IN ANY EVENT, even if a linguistic relationship could be demonstrated between Basque and another human tongue, this would not necessarily establish the origins of the Basque language per se. Morphologically, according to René Lafon,

> Basque is a language in which words can often be analyzed without difficulty and in which the markers that are added to roots, to stems, and to other markers are clearly perceived. In other words, it proceeds by agglutination. Sometimes, however, the affixation of markers to roots, stems, and other markers has given rise

to phonetic changes, which have in turn given rise to unpredictable, irregular forms. But the comparison of dialects and the study of texts of various epochs sometimes make it possible to reconstruct forms older than those that are in evidence. (Lafon 1972, 1759).

Lafon conveys some sense of the grammatical complexity of the language. The following is a simple example of Basque grammatical agglutination:

etxe—the stem for "house"
etxe*a*—"the house"
etxe*ak*—"the houses
etxe*ra*—"to the house"
etxee*tara*—"to the houses"
etxe*an*—"in the house"
etxee*tan*—"in the houses"
etxe*tik*—"from the house"
etxee*tatik*—"from the houses"
etxe*ko*—"of the house"
etxe*koak*—"those pertaining to the house"

As in English, and unlike Romance languages such as Spanish and French, there is no grammatical distinction of gender in Basque.

THE BASQUE verb manifests extraordinary complexity: Its forms may contain up to four person markers. To grasp the structure of the verb, one has to distinguish between two verb classes having to do with transitive and intransitive. There is also a distinction between personal and impersonal forms. Furthermore, the personal forms can be simple and compound.

Regarding its lexicon, Basque has borrowed many nouns from other languages, including Celtic, Germanic, "Hamito-Semitic," but particularly Latin. It has also drawn extensively from the Romance languages (Spanish, French) and other neighboring languages, particularly Gascon and Provençal. The etymology of a large number of Basque names is unknown. As we have noted, there are various dialects in Euskara: Labourdin, Bizkaian, Gipuzkoan, and several varieties of the Nafarroan.

Finally, regarding persistence of Basque, Antonio Tovar concludes his work The Basque Language by stating:

> This wonderful preservation of the Basque from remote antiquity has made it most desirable that such a precious relic shall not be lost. In spite of the "modern way of life" and with no intention of making of Basque a new jargon alien to its inherent genius, the Basque mothers continue to teach their children that language ten thousand years old; and in the mountains there continues to resound through the villages and farms the mysterious idiom which leads directly back to the prehistory of Spain and the whole of southwestern Europe.

A large part of what is specific to human culture involves language and its vast capacity both to shape and to communicate perception and thought. The gift of a complex and well-ordered language is characteristic of every known human group. The morphologies of languages vary enormously, but it may be said that all grammars have the same degree of fixity.

LANGUAGE is the crucial and primary vehicle of cultural transmission. Despite the unique importance of language for the definition and expression of culture, it does not follow that there is a simple correspondence between linguistic form and the organization of the speakers' culture. The tendency of some scholars to see linguistic categories as directly expressive of overt cultural configurations is questionable. The cultural significance of language lies at a much more subtle level. This is partly because linguistic change is more conservative than cultural change. Furthermore, linguistic organization, largely because it is unconscious, tends to maintain itself indefinitely and resists the influences of cultural changes.

THE SPANISH linguist Antonio Tovar called Basque a "mysterious language, which defies the specialists and invites once and again the most unexpected comparisons; what we can say with all certainty is that the Basque Country where Basque is spoken is autochthonous and that it has preserved a primitive language under the most difficult circumstances. To realize the greatness of the achievement suffice it to say that Basque is the only surviving pre-Indo-European language in Europe.".

Lesson four

LEARNING OBJECTIVES
1. To gain an overview of the structure of Basque language.
2. To understand the historical and linguistic interests elicited by Euskara.
3. To understand the relevance of language to world view and a people's sense of heritage.

REQUIRED READING
Gorka Aulestia, "The Basque Language," in *Basque-English Dictionary*, (Reno: University of Nevada Press, 1989), a19–a65.

SUGGESTED READING

Euskaltzaindia, *Euskeraren liburu zuria / libro blanco del euskera* (Bilbao: Euskaltzaindia, 1978).

Joseba Intxausti, *Euskera, la lengua de los vascos* (Donostia: Elkar, 1992).

René Lafon, "Basque," in Thomas A. Sebeok, *Current Trends in Linguistics* (The Hague: Mouton, 1972), 1744–92.

Antonio Tovar, *Mitología e ideología sobre la lengua vasca* (Madrid: Alianza, 1980).

———, *The Basque Language* (Philadelphia: University of Pennsylvania Press, 1957).

Robert L. Trask, *The History of Basque* (London and New York: Routledge, 1997).

WRITTEN LESSON FOR SUBMISSION

1. What do you make of all this linguistic complexity?
2. Consider Euskara's linguistic insularity: How relevant or irrelevant is it for Basques?
3. Do you believe that language affects our thinking? If so, how?
4. How important (or unimportant) is the preservation of any one language in our globalized (and increasingly Anglicized) world?

5 · Prehistoric Art

THE TRANSITIONAL millennia from the last Ice Age, when the climate of the Basque Country was colder than today, the sea level lower, and the mountainous areas glaciated, are called the Magdalenian Period (18,000–11,500 B.C.). Fauna included bisons, bovines, horses, deer, hyenas, leopards and cave bears. Hunting, gathering and some coastal fishing were the means of sustenance. Suitable caves were used for shelter and were the venues for the famed prehistoric "cave paintings." The Basque Country is located midway between Europe's two most famous cave-painting sites—Altamira in north central Spain and Lascaux in southwestern France. The Basque area has many fine (if lesser known) examples of this art form.

There were two kinds of art: art on walls, called "parietal" art, and the art on objects, or "mobiliary" art. The latter presents great problems of interpretation: Was it instrumental, or expressive?

The specialists differentiate prehistoric art according to styles, materials, themes, techniques and associations. Thus, Ignacio Barandiarán distinguishes between: art as tools and implements, such as javelins, pointed objects, needles, and harpoons; art as suspendable objects; and movable "religious art" engraved on bones and stones

Among the motifs there are varied representations of animals or humans, as well as designs that are difficult or impossible to interpret. The figurative representation of animals in parietal art includes: deer, horses, bison, fish, goats, bears, and birds. According to the calculation of André Leroi-Gourhan, less than 10 percent of the objects include the human figure. Nonfigurative representations are divided into simple longitudinal forms;

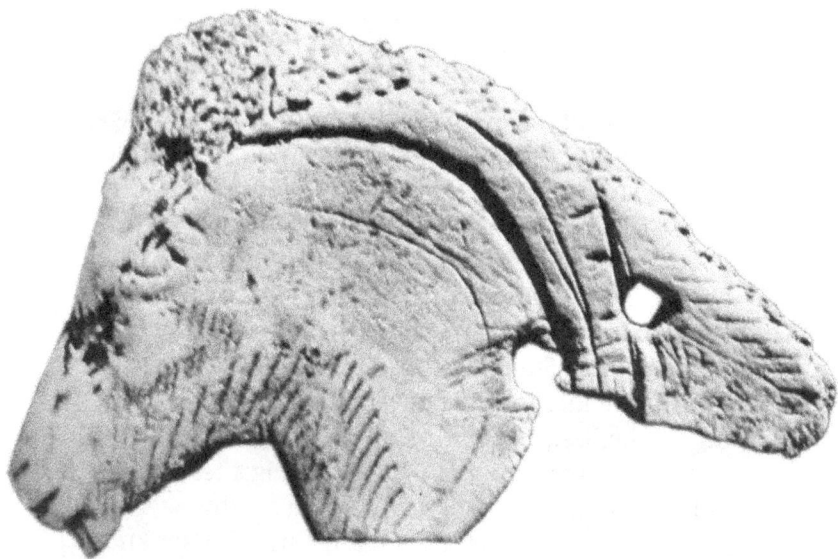

Magdalenian art
The image of a mountain goat carved on a horse bone found in
the cave of Isturitz (Behe Nafarroa).
Source: Jesus Altuna.

lineal forms embellished with teeth; zigzags; angular
V-shaped forms; X-shaped or star-shaped forms; arches;
composite rectilinear forms; closed forms: rhombs, triangles, and ovals; complex depictions of various shapes;
and forms determined by the function of the implement.
Of the 710 illustrations provided by Barandiarán, 98 percent are engravings and 2 percent are in relief.

AFTER A PERIOD of transition, the Mesolithic Age
began and lasted from 9,000 to 5,000 B.C. This was
a warm period and followed the last glacial age. New forests of birch and pine trees appeared, including beeches,
oaks, chestnuts, and hazelnuts. Arctic animals,

such as reindeer, the rhinoceros and the wooly mammoth retreated or disappeared. Besides hunting as a means of human sustenance, there is evidence of fishing and gathering. Changes in nutrition resulted from the disappearance of some animal species and the new fishing and gathering practices, but stone and bone implements remained similar to those of earlier periods. Art became more schematic than figurative; there were no longer parietal cave paintings. Given these modifications in lifestyle, important changes in the magical and religious beliefs must have occurred.

DURING THE Neolithic Age (5,000 to 2,000 B.C.), the warm climate continued. The main species of fauna were the cow, horse, deer, goat, roebuck, chamois, wild boar, fox, wildcat, and marten. The main quarry was wild boar and deer. There were sheep, as well (depicted in the caves of Santimamiñe), which indicates that animal domestication was under way, including that of animals that were previously hunted—the cow, the goat, and the horse. This probably entailed capture of the young after killing the adults or allowing them to return to the wild. The biological characteristics of the human population were similar to the present ones of the Basque population. In stone implements, old forms persisted and new ones appeared. There were now ceramics and vessels, as well as stone implements. Hunting was still the main occupation, but there also was fishing and the gathering of mollusks. The discovery of a stone grinder indicates that cereals were consumed. There was probably some kind of rudimentary navigation in small canoes. A great transformation of social and economic life occurred at this time. Cattle transhumance—the seasonal movement of livestock between mountain and lowland pastures— might also have begun at this time, which implied greater contacts between adjacent peoples.

The dolmens, prehistoric monuments consisting of several stone slabs placed in a vertical position, frequently forming a rectangle, then roofed with a horizontal slab, date from this period. More than four hundred have been discovered in the Basque Country. . They are believed to be funerary structures that may contain one or several corpses buried in succession. The axis of the building is always on an east-west line, the entrance being from the east, where the stones are usually smaller. Dolmens are situated in pastures and on hills. In the Basque Country, the region around Mount Aralar, a center of pastoralism, is a prime dolmenic area. Generally, the higher the elevation, the smaller and simpler the dolmens, which possibly reflects a basic geographical distinction between lowland and highland peoples in terms of socioeconomic development.

DURING THE Bronze and Iron Ages (1,500 to 800 B.C.) the climate was similar to the present one. Copper began to be used for arms and tools. We have many human skeletal remains from this period. There was an elaboration of mythical and cosmological beliefs that may have survived until the twentieth century. A significant religious change took place during this period: Most bodies were cremated. There were small population centers. Pastoralist and agriculturalist lifestyles coexisted. Other occupations appeared, as well, such as weaver, potter, and miner. Iron and wooden implements were common. Hundreds of cromlechs dating from this period have been found, as well as dolmens. A cromlech consists of circles of small stones. They are called "cromlechs" because they resemble the so-denominated megalithic art forms at Stonehenge in England. Actually, we are uncertain of their purpose. Some cromlechs surround a dolmen or tumulus. In some, the stones are equal in size, while in others there is a single dominant stone. They are situated in highly visible places and at crossroads. It seems their purpose was funerary, given the fact that ashes have been found inside them in some cases. Some menhirs—single upright monoliths—are also present in the Basque Country from this era. They have mythical names, and frequently they have symbols engraved on them.

Cave painting has given rise to considerable scholarly speculation. Paleolithic art, the mobiliary art of decorated harpoons and art on a reindeer bone, was discovered during the 1860s and 1870s. But the most sensational finding was Altamira's parietal cave paintings (1879). The main thrust of the subsequent investigations consisted initially in the establishment of a chronology and the quest for an explanation. Prehistoric people must have painted on bark, skin, wood and possibly on exposed stone surfaces, as well as in caves, but nothing remains of this fragile and perishable art. It is the sheltered parietal art that provides us with our evidence.

All scholars generally agree that the images in the caves reflect an ideology that is expressed in symbols associated with fertility and hunting. But there is disagreement as to why and how primitive humans could create such an advanced art. There are various theories, as summarized by Peter J. Ucko and André Rosenfeld, *Paleolithic Cave Art*.

ART FOR ART'S SAKE

CAVE ART MAY be simply ornamental and reflect abundance that provided a hunting population with plenty of leisure time. Prehistorians have found that even primitive peoples such as the Bushmen or Australian Aborigines, who had a difficult life, produced sophisticated parietal paintings. Similarly, the art of Paleolithic people must have had an essentially aesthetic function. In this view, Paleolithic art is no different from its modern counterpart. Initially, many authorities subscribed to this theory.

SYMPATHETIC MAGIC AND TOTEMISM

INFLUENCED BY Edward Tylor's and James Frazer's anthropological works at the end of the nineteenth century, as well as by Emile Durkheim's theory of totemism and society, whereby the former is deemed to be a fundamental religious expression in which the totemic animal and the clan naturally imply each other, in 1903 Salomon Reinach provided the first interpretation of Paleolithic art as evidence of beliefs in the efficacy of magic. He postulated that the paintings were expressions of hunting and fertility magic. His views were accepted by many. Basic to Reinach's thesis is that most of the Paleolithic representations were of animals with food value. One of his key points is that the images are situated in deep recesses with difficult access. These arguments challenged the idea of cave art as simply ornamental and aesthetic. According to this theory, all of the depicted pointed objects, such as a sharp stick over the image of an animal, have to do basically with homeopathic magic. If the Australian aborigines still employ it, the argument goes, such must have been the rationale of primitive humans. Furthermore, the Aborigines also paint in places with difficult access.

Abbé Breuil, arguably the most influential scholar of Paleolithic art, accepted the interpretation of cave paintings as expression of sympathetic magic. He became interested less in the "significance" of the art and more in the evolution of the various Paleolithic art styles. Like Reinach, he, too, relied on ethnographic comparisons. He also found the inaccessibility of the art to be a key feature. He invoked the "sanctuary"

Cromlech
This funerary monument was discovered in Oihanleku, Gipuzkoa. Such circular stone arrangements are common in the high mountain pasturages of the Basque Country.
Photo: Jesus Altuna.

---

analogy: "When we visit a painted cave, we enter a sanctuary, where, for thousands of years, sacred ceremonies have taken place, directed no doubt by the great initiates of the time, and introducing the novices called to receive in their turn the necessary fundamental instruction for the conduct of their lives."

AS MORE discoveries were made, Breuil had the advantage over Reinach of a larger database. He posited that rites associated with the paintings were also performed to ensure hunting success. When represented carnivores were discovered, Breuil assumed that totemism was at work, since here we have depicted

"again the qualities of a predator through its image."
That is, the hunter seeks to acquire the powers of the
successful carnivore by assuming its essence and identity. Breuil interpreted certain drawings in sexual terms,
their purpose being to promote fecundity. There are
examples of male animals pursuing females, and of obviously pregnant ones, as well. Breuil interpreted rooflike
designs—usually geometric—as representing dwellings.
(Others he regarded as animal traps.)

Fertility magic. Some interpreters of the cave paintings
have fixated disproportionately on fertility magic—fertility for humans, as well as for animals. They insist on
a sexual interpretation of a vast number of amorphously
indeterminate designs and animal representations. The
few female human figurines encountered are seen to be
mother goddesses. In this view, the Paleolithic world is
seen as dominated by the worship of a mother goddess
to which all Paleolithic art was ultimately related.

MORE RECENT WORK

ANNETTE Laming-Emperaire and André Leroi-
Gourhan refuse to admit the use of contemporary
ethnographic comparisons in interpreting European
cave art. They believe that interpretations must be based
on the internal evidence provided by the Paleothic art
itself. Leroi-Gourhan provided the first systematic analysis of the distribution of animal species in the caves. His
thesis has two points of departure: the frequency and
spatial distribution of animal representations in caves
and the analysis of designs and motifs

He notes that well over half of the animals depicted
are horses and bison. These, he concludes, must represent two coupled or juxtaposed images, "A" and "B,"
respectively, whereas other animals must have played
mere subsidiary roles. Calculating the frequencies in the

distribution of animals, he managed to allocate the caves into seven distinct regional types. For Leroi-Gourhan, the caves must have been systematically organized sanctuaries. Group "B" animals (bison and aurochs, a now-extinct large, wild ox) and women are found in the center of the representational field; group "A" animals are found in the margins (with the exception of the horse, which is also very commonly found in the central area). Thus, the basic thematic equivalencies are between man-woman and horse-bison. Leroi-Gourhan sees the whole of Paleolithic representations as the "juxtaposition," "opposition," "coupling," or "association" not of two groups of animals per se, but of the male and female principles.

THE SECOND part of his analysis concerns the interpretation of designs: Again "a" designs (lines, dots, etc.) represent the male, and "b" designs (ovals, triangles, etc.) represent the female. Group "b" designs are predominantly found in central areas, whereas group "a" designs are peripheral. He admits that the relationship between "a" and "b" designs and "A" and "B" groups is difficult to define clearly.

This is a thesis far beyond all previous interpretations. Gone are the significance of wounded animals, the inaccessibility of the cave site, animal traps, houses, the importance of food, and weapons. Now all is sexual symbolism whereby the Paleolithic painter sought to represent the male and female principles alone. Ironically, Laming interprets the same figures in exactly the opposite way from Leroi-Gourhan. For him, the male principle was represented by the bison, whereas the female one was represented by the horse. Both authors are convinced that Paleolithic art is the result of a very complex system of beliefs and practices, but they have arrrived at contradictory conclusions about it.

Megalith tomb
The dolmen of Sorginetxe (Arrizala) has a polygonal form. The chamber is composed of six slabs. The western exposure features an opening that serves as a window admitting crepuscular sunlight into the interior. It was discovered in the nineteenth century.
Photo: Jesus Altuna.

DEPICTION OF human hands provides one example of the contradictory nature of the several interpretations. Various authors interpret them by underscoring whether or not they were shown to be mutilated; whether the artist was left-handed or right-handed; whether they were the hands of men, women, or children; whether they were painted simply for aesthetic enjoyment; whether they were accidental imprints left by the artist while work proceeded on another representation;

whether there was any relationship between the hands and animal representations ("no doubt magical in origin"); whether they evidenced prayer to the mother goddess; whether female hands were accompanied by male signs; and whether female hands are found in central panels when other female signs are absent there.

AFTER REVIEWING all of these interpretations, do we really know anything for certain? We remain ignorant as to the use of the caves. Were they abodes, or simply ceremonial sites? Representations are often superimposed on one another. Does this mean that the real significance was in the execution, rather than lasting representation? Some are in inaccessible places. They are mostly of animals, hardly ever of humans. Why are certain animals depicted, and not others? The parietal art does not necessarily reflect human food consumption. The interpretations given by the authors may apply to aspects of the art. It is also possible that the painting was done for reasons that completely escape us.

Prominent contemporary Basque artists have engaged passionately in the recreation of their prehistoric artistic tradition. The following interpretation (2003) of the cromlechs by Jorge Oteiza, an internationally acclaimed sculptor, is a telling example:

> They [the cromlechs] are small stones forming a very private circle, very small, from two to five meters in diameter, with nothing inside ... Standing one day before one of these small cromlechs at the top of Mount Aguiña, struggling to understand it, I thought of my disoccupation of space, and suddenly I understood in its entirety what that circular void signified. It would not be easy to measure my emotion as I found a use for a statue that had been left unused for so many centuries. It coincided with the spiritual purpose of

the prehistoric sculptor of these cromlechs. It was
precisely my metaphysical sculpture from my recently
concluded experiments. The stones were not placed
from reality, but against it, from a metaphysical consciousness defined in space. Previously, in the figurative, the magical hunter from the Paleolithic period
controls the image of the animal (the bison history)
in his cave paintings from inside his material refuge.
Now, in the abstract, in this Neolithic cromlech, the
artist invents the habitation for his metaphysical root
in the precise external space of reality. Unamuno
would call it his intrastatue—his soul cupboard—his
intrahistory. Man has stepped outside of himself, outside of time. An aesthetic solution—religious reason—
for his supreme existential anguish.

Without this aesthetic calculus of the disoccupation
of the space, art has never achieved its spiritual des-
tiny. The development of an authentic contemporary
art along with a congruent definition of a new religious
architecture, depends on the urgent and enlightened
reformulation of a receptive art in the consciousness
of today's artist ... Every medium of communication
(communication with God in religious art) will have to
be reduced to pure receptivity, to spatial silence. Everything, we might say, must be reduced to cromlech, to
zero as formal expression. (pp. 324–330)

IN THE FINAL analysis, one important dimension of
the anthropologizing of the Basque past by archeologists and paleontologists has to do with the singular
significance of prehistoric art for contemporary culture.
Prominent avant-garde Basque artists, such as Oteiza
and Eduardo Chillida, have turned prehistoric art into a
crucial point of reference for their own purposes. Thus,
in the work of many Basque writers and artists, cultural

identity is expressed as emanating directly in an unbroken continuity from caves such as Santimamiñe, Ekain, and Lascaux. The power of this fiction of historical succession by which, as if belonging directly to the same cultural-historical reality, contemporary Basques are immediate successors of their prehistoric ancestors, cannot be overstated. It has been one of the major ploys and invocations in the creation of a Basque identity during the last several decades of cultural resistance to Spanish and French cultural and political hegemony.

B UT BESIDES Paleolithic paintings, Neolithic megaliths, and their remythifications, there is a strong component of neoprimitivism in Basque contemporary art, as well. This can be observed from Néstor Basterretxea's *Cosmogonies* to Augustín Ibarrola's *Forest Totems*, as well as in the works of Remigio Mendiburu, Mikel Angel Lertxundi, and others. (See chapter 35, "Modernist Art: Oteiza and Chillida"). The arborglyphs or tree carvings left by Basque shepherds in the American West might also be regarded as a folk version of such "totemic" art.

Lesson five

LEARNING OBJECTIVES
1. To explore the various interpretations given to cave paintings.
2, To consider the role of "primitivism" in modern art.
3. To understand the relevance of prehistoric art for contemporary Basque artists.
4. To evaluate the relationship of changing flora and fauna to human settlement.

REQUIRED READING

Morton Levine, "Prehistoric Art and Ideology," in *Readings in Anthropology*, ed. Morton H. Fried (New York: Thomas Y. Crowell Company, 1968), 708–24.

SUGGESTED READING

Jesús Altuna, *La cueva de Ekain y sus figuras rupestres* (San Sebastián: Sociedad de Ciencias Aranzadi, 1996).

Ignacio Barandiarán, *Arte mueble del paleolítico cantábrico*. (Zaragoza: Universidad de Zaragoza, 1972).

Jorge Oteiza, *Oteiza's Selected Writings* (Reno: Center for Basque Studies, 2003).

———, *Quousque tandem ... ! Ensayo de interpretación estética del alma vasca* (Donostia–San Sebastián: Auñamendi, 1963).

Luxio Ugarte, *Chillida: Dudas y preguntas* (San Sebastián: Erein, 1993).

WRITTEN LESSON FOR SUBMISSION

1. Why should art produced so long ago and under such different cultural conditions speak to us so intensely?
2. What do we learn about the nature of interpretation from these various theories about cave art?
3. What do you make of Oteiza's Basque "spiritual race"?
4. Have we advanced aesthetically from Lascaux and Ekain to Picasso?
5. What do we know about the processes of image formation and artistic creation? Do we know why people paint or sculpt nowadays? Can these motivations inform prehistoric art, as well?

Part Two
Basque History

THE EARLIEST written documentation regarding the
Basques derives from Roman chronicles and will be
considered in chapter 6. This evidence, as well as that
from Visigothic and Frankish early medieval accounts,
is fragmentary and often colored by the fact that it is
provided by the Basques' battlefield adversaries. By the
late Middle Ages (as treated in chapter 7), however, it is
possible to reconstruct the political history of the Basque
homeland. The Basques were under a single monarch,
Sancho el Sabio (1000–1035) and therefore constituted
part of a single polity for the first and only time in their
history. During the second millennium, several regions
within the Basque homeland coalesced into discernible
political entities, reinforced loosely by distinguishable
dialectical variations in their Basque vernacular. At the
same time, each was drawn into wider (non-Basque)
political orbits. The most enduring and important division was that between the Spanish and French spheres
of influence, formalized by the sixteenth-century recognition of their international boundary, which, at its western Pyrenean extreme, partitions the Basque homeland.

Chapter 8 regards Euskalherria's modern history down
to the commencement of the twentieth century, which,
while considering local vagaries, chronicles the steady
institutionalization of the distinction between Iparralde
and Hegoalde.

In chapter 9, we discuss the genesis and subsequent
development of the Basque nationalist movement.
Chapter 10 details the schism within the ranks of Basque
nationalists in the mid-twentieth century that produced
ETA (Euskadi 'ta Askatasuna, or Basque Land and

Freedom) movement, as well as the ensuing political violence.

We then contemplate the formation of an extensive Basque diaspora, or rather diasporas, through five centuries of emigration from Euskalherria to all of the world's inhabited continents. In chapter 11, the focus is on the Americas, particularly the so-called "southern cone" of South America (Argentina, Uruguay, and Chile), which, in terms of magnitude, received the largest contingents of Basque immigrants, and the American West, where, for more than a century, Basques were the region's sheepherders.

Finally, in chapter 12, we examine two lesser-known destinations of Basque emigration, Australia and the Philippines, as counterweight and antidote to the stereotypical views of Basques that developed in the United States (the romantic view that, as Pyrenean sheepherders, Basques naturally sought out the open ranges of the American West, the better to apply their Old World skills and predilections.) In Australia, the Basque immigrants' major occupational niche was that of sugarcane cutter in tropical North Queensland; in the Philippines, Basques constituted a colonial and business elite.

6 · Romanization

FROM THE time of the Pyrenean culture (circa 3000
B.C.) until the birth of Christ, the archeological
record sheds little light on developments in the northern part of the Iberian Peninsula. We do know that,
about the seventh century B.C., the Basques were subjected to pressure by other peoples from both the south
and the north. To the south, a people known as the Iberians appear to have expanded their territory, but as they
pushed northward, their advance was halted at the Ebro
River and in southern Santander. Farther to the east,
the Iberians were successful in occupying much of Alto
Aragón, and they even crossed the Pyrenees and entered
the Aquitaine in southern France. Consequently, it
appears that the Iberians were unsuccessful in penetrat-
ing the present Basque homeland to a notable degree.

From the north, there was pressure from the Celtic
tribes, that is, the ancestors of the Bretons, Welsh, Scots,
and Irish. The Celts were moving south, into the northern part of the Iberian Peninsula, and were particularly
successful in occupying parts of Galicia. However, it
appears that, on balance, they simply passed through
the Basque Country. The Celts did establish a few fortifications in the Pyrenees, and even some within Basque
territory. However, their influence on the surrounding populations appears to have been minimal and
extremely short-lived.

In the third century B.C., the Roman legions entered
the Iberian Peninsula and began the task of conquering
the whole area. The Romans met with differing degrees
of resistance, but, according to their own chroniclers,
the most difficult area to subdue was the north. The Cantabrian Wars lasted down to about 100 B.C., and the ulti-

mate Roman victory signaled the end to all resistance to Roman rule in Iberia. In about 56 B.C., the Romans succeeded in conquering the lowland areas of the Aquitaine, but not the high mountain regions (i.e., part of the present Basque homeland).

It would appear, then, that the Romans were very successful in subduing the area to the north of the Basque provinces, just as they managed to conquer the southern ecological zone of the Basque area, notably central and southern Nafarroa and much of Araba. The city of Iruña was established by the Romans as a garrison. They also built a fortification at Baiona. However, we find a minimum of Roman influence throughout the mountainous regions of the Basque Country. There are no out-and-out settlements and very few inscriptions or monuments. There was a major Roman road running from Dax to Orreaga (Roncesvalles) and on to Iruña— the main Roman arterial into the northwestern sector of the Iberian Peninsula. However, it would appear that the Romans were little interested in exerting direct control over the apparently wild and hostile mountain dwellers. Rather, they concerned themselves with maintaining security along the roadways and with protecting their garrisoned towns against possible attack.

THE HISTORIAN Julio Caro Baroja studied the nature of the organization of the administration of Iberia by the Romans in order to shed light on the degree of Romanization that might have transpired in the north. Administration was carried out by officials called "legates." The tribes—designated the Galaicos, the Astures, and the Cantabros—were governed by a single legate with two Roman legions at his command. This official was concerned with maintaining order among the most warlike people of the north. A second legate with one legion was in charge of of the area from the Cantabrian

Basque tribes during the Roman period

The map depicts the distribution of the main Basque tribes at the beginning of the Christian era. They were described by the Greek geographer Strabo and the Roman writers Titus Livy and Pliny the Elder.

Mountains to the high Pyrenees. A third legate ruled by his presence alone (in other words without troops) the area of the Ebro Valley down to the Mediterranean. This third area was the most highly Romanized and apparently the least troublesome. From this evidence, Caro Baroja deduces that the legate in charge of the Basque area was more concerned with fighting a holding action than with bringing the inhabitants under direct subjugation.

THE FACT THAT the Romans were well established in the southern Basque area (as far north as Iruña) gave this region a Latin character that persists down to the present. Also, much of the settlement patterning and organization of agriculture into estates, or *latifundia*, dates from the Roman period. Many an officer in the legions was rewarded upon retirement with a large *latifundium* in the area. Caro Baroja believes that the loss of the Basque language in the southern ecological zone actually began in Roman times. Thus, he sees the Basque language and culture being preserved in the northern area among the Karistios, Bardulians, and the northern Vascones, in part due to their isolation from Roman influence, whereas the southern Basque area became one of the most highly Romanized regions of Iberia. Caro Baroja also rejects the notion that in Roman times, Basque was spoken in areas outside the present-day Basque Country. In other words, he believes that Basque had already been lost in the high Pyrenees to the east and in the Aquitaine to the north.

Caro Baroja states that we simply do not have any information concerning Roman policy toward the Basque language. However, if we can take the example of how they acted elsewhere, we might infer that the Romans did all that they could to stamp it out in the areas where they held sway. Possibly the greatest leveler and the main means whereby the Basque language borrowed Latin loan words was through conscription of Basque speakers into the Roman legions. We know that many Basque-speaking soldiers fought throughout the Roman Empire. There was a Basque mercenary force engaged in the defense of Hadrian's Wall in Britain, for instance.

In sum, we find that the southern region of the Basque Country was highly Romanized and had Roman settlements with the full regalia of temples, baths, deities, and so on. However, the northern region, while nominally under Roman rule, received little direct influence. We may surmise that occasionally officials penetrated the north, and we do know that the Romans pushed some minor branches of their road system into the mountains and even established a few mines, such as at Oiartzun (Oyarzun), where we find the only Roman inscription in the entire province of Gipuzkoa. Again, the few inscriptions that do occur in the north are of very poor quality in terms of their Latin phraseology and refer to local or indigenous deities. This situation may be contrasted with the territories occupied by the Cantabros, Autrigones, and Astures, where the inscriptions are of better quality and much more numerous.

THE ROMAN period is quite important for the history of the Basque people in that it provides their historical baseline. The Roman chroniclers provide us with our first written accounts of the Basques. The single most important one is that of Strabo, a Greco-Roman historian who lived about the time of Christ. In his narrative, we see clearly that, although they could be divided into several tribes in terms of their lifestyles, the inhabitants of northern Iberia pertained to a single Cantabrian culture. The map of Ptolemy, another Roman historian during the second century A.D., shows these tribal divisions, but they should not be construed as ethnic distinctions.

Roman ruins
A wonderful example of a Roman structure built along
a trans-Pyrenean Roman road between Donibane (Behe
Nafarroa) and Orbaizeta (Nafarroa). It is felt to be both
a triumphal tower celebrating a Roman victory and a
boundary marker and was possibly erected by Pompey in
75 B.C.
Source: Jesus Altuna.

Thus we find a general cultural uniformity from Galicia
in the west to the high Pyrenees in the east.

STRABO DESCRIBES the lifestyle of the Cantabrians,
which he feels may be generalized to the surrounding areas. He tells us that when the Romans arrived in
the area, one of the mainstays of the economy was the
gathering of acorns, which were then made into flour.
There was some agriculture being practiced by the
women, who would raise oats for a type of beer, wheat
for bread, and flax for clothing. The men spent most of

their time in herding and warfare, but when the Romans conquered the area, they forced the Cantabrians to settle the plains and to engage in agriculture. This was done for political as well as economic reasons, since the sedentary population was much easier to control than were the high-mountain dwellers. The Cantabrians engaged in some pig and goat herding. There is no mention of cattle, although it is highly possible that they were present. There is little reference to hunting. Consequently, it appears that the Cantabrians' economy at the time of the Roman invasion was based on pastoralism, horticultural agriculture, and gathering. There is no mention of commerce, although it appears that some pieces of silver were exchanged.

A CONSTANT theme in the Roman accounts of the Cantabrians concerns their fanaticism and bravery in warfare. The Cantabrians were aware of poisons and used to make little containers in which to carry them into battle. If they were losing, the warriors committed suicide by drinking the potion. Strabo tells us that in the face of defeat, a father ordered his son to kill his mother and sisters so they wouldn't fall into Roman hands, and there were incidences of mothers killing their children.

The Cantabrians had a legal code. Sanctioning depended in part on the great respect accorded to elders, and it would seem that they passed judgment on lawbreakers. Some crimes (we don't know which) were punishable by death, and the condemned man was thrown over a precipice. One guilty of parricide was driven out of the tribe, a punishment that indicates that the Cantabrians had a strong sense of territoriality.

We have additional evidence of a type of tribal social organization. It appears that social groupings larger than the family were based on extended kinship ties. That is, kinsmen would coalesce around one of the members who assumed a degree of leadership and importance. Thus, a particular area might be occupied and ruled by a strongman, his allied kinsmen, and their families.

THERE IS SOME evidence, largely from Roman inscriptions, that there was a type of larger or regional political organization. One Roman inscription speaks of the Astures, who were constituted by the Zoelae and the Desconci; a similar inscription dealing with the Cantabrians speaks of the Cantabri, within which there were Orgenomesci and Pembeli. While these inscriptions would indicate that there was a conception of larger tribal divisions and, furthermore, that the individual tribes were differentiated internally, we do not know how the system operated. For instance, we are unclear whether the Zoelae and Desconci refer to equal subdivisions of one tribe or if we are dealing with a hierarchical structure such as a county within which there is a town. Similarly, we don't know at which point extended kinship relations plugged into the larger system of political power.

Strabo tells us that the Cantabrians had epic poetry and their own bards, who particularly eulogized battle victories. No trace of their work has been preserved. We also know that Cantabrians enjoyed dancing and feasting. They were heavy drinkers and had their own types of flute and horn.

Both men and women wore black frocks, in which they also slept. Men had long hair. Women wore theirs short until after marriage, at which time they would let it grow out and arrange it into the form of a phallic symbol to indicate their married status. Footgear was made from animal skins. Strabo even tells us a little about Cantabrian personal hygiene.

He further notes that they lived in clustered, round houses with walls that were joined together for defensive purposes. It is likely that the roofs were made of straw thatching. We also know that the Cantabrians practiced stone boiling as a cooking technique, heating stones in a fire and then dropping them into a vessel filled with liquid.

Strabo comments on their religion. Cantabrians worshipped at least one god who was like Mars, the Indo-European god of war. Frequent sacrifices of male goats, horses, and humans were made in his honor. The blood of sacrificed horses was consumed by the worshippers. Also, the Cantabrians organized war games and athletic contests held in the deity's honor. The moon was treated with a great deal of respect, if not in fact deified. There is a more recent suggestion of this practice among the Basques. *Illargi*, the Basque word for "moon," derives from "death" and "light" and is used reverently in Basque discourses. Finally, we know that the Cantabrians were great believers in augurs.

ONE OF THE most problematic bits of evidence provided in Strabo's account is his assertion that the Cantabrians were matriarchal. That is, inheritance was matrilineal in that property was inherited from the mother, and not the father; only daughters inherited; women "gave" spouses to their brothers—probably referring to the fact that women would provide their brothers with the economic wherewithal to marry; women worked the fields, while men mainly engaged in warfare; and the couvade was practiced—a custom found in some matrilineal societies whereby, during childbirth, the father of the child also experiences birth pains and is possibly confined to bed and treated as if he were the one giving birth.

The questions of whether or not the Cantabrians and, by inference, the Basques were indeed a matriarchal society is a thorny one. If we examine present-day

Basque culture, there is very little indication of matriarchal tendencies. Inheritance is not matrilineal, although
in some parts of the Basque Country women are not
excluded from inheriting ownership of farms. One
exception is a small area in Nafarroa where girls do
inherit, with the associated practice that the young men
in the village leave for the New World to make their fortune and then marry one of the heiresses of a farm upon
returning. However, this custom is clearly tied to later
historical circumstances.

THE QUESTION of the couvade is somewhat stickier.
Many books and encyclopedias today cite the Basque
people as one example of a society still practicing the
couvade. Yet we know that this is not the case. The con-
fusion stems from the fact that a French Basque writer,
Augustin Chaho, stated in his nineteenth-century book
Voyage en Navarre that the Basques practiced the couvade. Yet it is clear that Chaho was taking literary license
and was also influenced by Strabo.

Lesson six

LEARNING OBJECTIVES
1. To survey the first historical records regarding the
   Basque tribes.
2. To understand the significance of Romanization in
   early Basque history.
3. To understand the early economy and social organization of the early Basques.

REQUIRED READING
Roger Collins, *The Basques* (Oxford: Basil Blackwell,
   1990), 31–98.

SUGGESTED READING

Julio Caro Baroja, *Los pueblos del norte de la península ibérica* (Madrid: Aldecoa, 1943).

William A. Douglass and Jon Bilbao, *Amerikanuak: The Basques of the New World* (Reno: University of Nevada Press, 2005), 20–33.

WRITTEN LESSON FOR SUBMISSION

1. Describe the effect of Romanization on the Basques. How does this affect their image as an historically isolated people?
2. What does Strabo tells us about the Pyrenean tribes during Roman times?
3. Assess the allegedly matriarchal character of Basque society.
4. How does Rome's northern Iberian legacy support or refute the view that the Basque Country is an intrinsic part of the present Spanish and French states?

7 · The Middle Ages

THE ROMAN influence on Basques lasted from about 100 B.C. to the fourth century A.D. By about 250 A.D., a Christian bishopric was established at León-Astorga with nominal jurisdiction over the Basque area. Consequently, in the most Romanized territory, there were at least the beginnings of Christianization.

As the Roman Empire began to falter in the fourth century A.D., there were signs of trouble in the Basque territories. Accounts from the first part of the century refer to widespread banditry and, by century's end, the insurrection was on a tribal scale that was making travel impossible in the Pyrenees and parts of southern France. Finally, the cities were left isolated as islands of Roman influence amid a rebellious countryside. It was at this time that barbarian invasions from the north began. Near the end of the fourth century, Iruña was sacked, ostensibly by one of the outside barbarian tribes, but conceivably by the mountain-dwelling Vascones themselves.

The two major tribes of barbarians applying pressure from the north were the Visigoths and the Franks. In 419, the Visigoths conquered Toulouse in southern France and began their campaign to conquer all of the Aquitaine. They poured across the Pyrenees and, by the year 476 A.D., conquered much of Spain and were in possession of Iruña. In short, they supplanted the Romans in Iberia. This initiated a struggle of almost two centuries' duration between the Basques and Visigoths. It should be noted, however, that the invasion of the Visigoths created a political vacuum, since they did not seek to establish a rule similar to that of Rome. Instead, they in effect destroyed Roman authority without substituting anything in its place.

Paradoxically, this initiated a second period of Romanization among the Basques, this time among the mountain peoples of the north. Initially, they began to attack Romanized settlements in the south on a hit-and-run basis, with the raiders looting and then withdrawing back into the mountains. However, they later began to settle in the area, which brought them into contact with Romanized populations and eventually led to their Romanization, as well.

The people of the southern Basque areas were nominally under Visigothic sway, but the actual control of Iruña was exercised by the mountain peoples, and their influence extended as far south as the Ebro. This was the state of affairs through the sixth and seventh centuries A.D.—a period of regular hostilities between the Basques and Visigoths. In 711, King Rodrigo of the Visigoths was poised to attack Iruña when his attention was distracted by the invasion of southern Spain by the Moors.

THE STRUGGLES between the Basques and the Franks were less virulent and of shorter duration. Between 561 and 584, the Basques were allied with peoples in the Aquitaine against the Franks, who were pressing southward out of central France. The Basques and Aquitainians prevailed, but it would not be the Basques last brush with the Franks.

Meanwhile, the question of the Basques' opposition to the Visigoths had some interesting consequences for Basque history. The Visigoths were the prime carriers and champions of the Christian religion. The Basques continued to target them with such frequency as to earn them the reputation of being very warlike and devious. Furthermore, there is frequent reference in Visigothic sources to the fact that the Basques were treacherous in that they would sign treaties and then break them with surprise attacks. This resistance served to insulate the

Basques against the influence of the Christian religion. By the seventh century, most of Iberia was Christian, whereas Christianity had not even begun to penetrate the Basque area in any significant fashion. Medieval writers berated the Basques for their pagan beliefs and, in particular, for their faith in augurs.

SOME SCHOLARS suggest that as late as the eleventh century, the peoples of present-day Bizkaia and Gipuzkoa were totally ignorant of Christianity and those of Nafarroa, while ostensibly Christian, were strong believers in augurs. There is a document in Baiona, dated 890, that suggests an attempt was being made at that time to evangelize the mountain tribes. However, many missionaries were to lose their lives in the attempt. The medieval traveler Aymeric de Picaud, writing in the twelfth century, stated that the mountain people in the Basque area would prey on pilgrims heading for Santiago de Compostela—the tomb of Saint James and, after Rome, the most important destination of Christian pilgrimage. Hence, the church had practical reasons for subjugating the Basques.

The social historian Julio Caro Baroja states that there is no evidence of attempts to Christianize Gipuzkoa and Bizkaia in the ninth century and that the first ones date from the tenth. However, he believes that the full evangelization of the Basques actually had to wait until the fifteenth century. This would make the Basques the last people in Europe to embrace Christianity. Caro Baroja tells us that, as late as 1120, a bishop traveling through the Basque Country on his way to Portugal had to remove his clerical robes to ensure his safety. Caro Baroja also believes that the supposed legends concerning *gentiles*, or pagans, are based on a degree of historical fact. The *gentiles* were seen as extraordinary personages opposed to Christians, and the legends probably

Bridge in Baigorri, Behe Nafarroa
The Basque Country is on the famed pilgrimage route
to Santiago and therefore possesses many outstanding
examples of medieval Romanesque architecture.
Photo: Xabier Irujo

---

date from the period between the tenth and fifteenth
centuries, or when the Basque Country likely had mutually antagonistic Christian and pagan populations.

THE DEVELOPMENT of the Carolingian Empire out of
the Frankish tribes under the aegis of Charles Mar-
tel spelled new trouble for the Basques. In 768, Charlemagne assumed the throne and agreed to respect the
independence of the Basques. By this time, the Moors
had taken over more than half of the Iberian Peninsula and were pressing ever northward. Charlemagne
regarded them as a threat, so he decided to send an

expeditionary force across the Pyrenees to do battle near the Ebro. He negotiated an agreement with the Basques to move his army through their territory at Orreaga. The Franks were successful against the Moors, but, while returning home, old antagonisms were remembered. The Franks attacked Iruña and leveled its ramparts. As the main Frankish army withdrew through the Pyrenees, its retreat was covered by a rear-guard force under the command of a man named Roland. In the high mountains near Orreaga, the Basques fell on his force and inflicted a terrible defeat, killing Roland. This is, of course, the basic incident in the famous piece of French literature *Chanson de Roland* (The Song of Roland), in which the attackers are identified, erroneously, as Moors.

THE DEFEAT OF Roland lessened the pressure on the Basques from the north, but the incursion of the Moors into southern Iberia posed a new threat. The need for an organized military resistance against them provided the stimulus for a crystallization of alliances and the emergence of leadership that was to culminate in the formation of the Kingdom of Nafarroa. The first king was called Eneko Aritza, and he was from Baigorri (Baigorry) in present-day Behe Nafarroa. His successor was Sancho Garces, and it was under the latter that the Moors were soundly defeated in Nafarroa. The next king, Sancho Abarka, extended his sway to include all of Araba and Behe Nafarroa. In 844, the Normans attacked Baiona. The Normans were the descendants in northern France of Viking raiders. The Nafarroan king Sancho the First crossed the Pyrenees and drove out the Normans.

By 860, the Moors again were at the gates of Iruña, but were defeated and pushed back. Meanwhile, the Carolingian Empire to the north had weakened, and the French Basque area gained political autonomy under Duke

Sanche Menditarra, who established a dynasty that was to last down to 1058.

The greatest king of Nafarroa was Sancho Mayor (999–1035), who was successful in uniting all of the Basque area under his nominal rule. Sancho Mayor also ruled parts of Castile, Aragón, the Gascogne area, and the Toulouse region of southern France. It was during the reign of Sancho Mayor that we have the only period in history in which the Basque territories was under a single ruler. During Sancho's reign, the Kingdom of Nafarroa became the major Christian bulwark against the advance of the Moors into Southern Europe.

THE LAST Basque monarch of the Kingdom of Nafarroa was Sancho el Fuerte, who engineered the defeat of the Moors at Navas de Tolosa. This proved to be the turning point in the eight-hundred-year conflict between the Christians and Moors. After this victory, the Christian forces gained ground steadily until the last Moorish stronghold of Granada fell to the Catholic monarchs Ferdinand and Isabela in 1492.

Following the reign of Sancho Mayor, Basque history became divided between the area north of the Pyrenees, or the French Basque Country, and that to the south, or the Spanish Basque Country. This is because Sancho Mayor divided his kingdom among his sons; one retained the Kingdom of Nafarroa, one ruled Aragón, and a third ruled Castile. In 1076, Araba and Gipuzkoa became a part of the Kingdom of Castile while retaining a degree of local autonomy. During the twelfth century, these two provinces were returned to the Kingdom of Nafarroa but, in 1200, Gipuzkoa became permanently annexed by Castile, as was Araba in 1332.

Bizkaia retained its independence from the crown of Castile for a longer period. By 1224, a lord of Bizkaia ruled it, and his descendants continued to do so until

The defeat of Roland

Contemporary Basque sculptor Nestor Basterretxea's work Orreaga (or Roncesvalles) commemorates the destruction of Charlemagne's rearguard, commanded by Roland, ambushed in a Pyrenean mountain pass as it withdrew from Iberia.

Photo: Jill Berner

1379. The nature of the overlordship of the lord of Bizkaia indicates the degree to which local privileges were maintained and respected. Feudalism never gained a foothold in the Basque Country. Every male in Bizkaia was regarded as a freeman, and of noble blood, and all property holders were enfranchised. That is, the men of each village would elect a representative to a *juntas generales*, or general assembly, held in Gernika. These representatives would legislate the laws of the land. Their meeting was held beneath an oak tree, and the Oak of Gernika is reverently regarded by Basques down to the present as the symbol of their political liberty.

Of particular interest was the fact that the lord of Bizkaia was required to come to the reunion to swear to uphold the privileges of the people. No priests were allowed to attend the general assembly, hence, there was strict separation between church and state in an era when the church was the largest feudal landowner in Europe, and no lawyers were allowed to speak to the assembled, hence ruling out the possibility that a polished orator might put something over on the relatively uneducated legislators. The populace of Bizkaia remained immune from outside taxation and could be conscripted for uncompensated military service only if the campaign was to take place on Bizkaian soil.

IN 1379, the lord of Bizkaia, Juan de Haro, contracted a marriage that made him the king of Castile, thereby fusing Bizkaia and Castile under single rule. The custom of swearing to respect the privileges of Bizkaia continued in effect, and either the monarch or his or her representative made the trip to Gernika. The custom lasted down to the eighteenth century.

As the Spanish Basque area was brought under the influence of the Kingdom of Castile, there emerged a set of legal charters, called *fueros*, for each of the provinces.

These charters accorded the provinces a great deal of political autonomy, although the subsequent history of the Basque people is one of steady erosion of these ancient rights. Some of these, under the original charters, were the right to maintain a local governmental structure, freedom from taxation, freedom from arbitrary military conscription, freedom from outside tariffs, and the authority to exact their own tariff duties.

MEANWHILE, from the eleventh century to the fifteenth, Iparralde was subject to a different set of political and military pressures. Sancho Mayor established in the French Basque Country a countdom for his cousin, Lopez Sancho. Through aristocratic marriages, the area became attached to the Duchy of Gascony. In 1039, the last duke of Gascony died, and his holdings were annexed by the Duchy of the Aquitaine. In 1153, the daughter of the duke of Aquitania, the famous Eleanor, married Henry Plantagenet, who thus became duke of Gascony and the Aquitaine. In 1155, he inherited the throne of England. In 1169, Henry named his son, Richard the Lion-Hearted, duke of the Aquitaine. However, the Gascons and Basques refused to accept this foreign domination. In 1174, Arnaud, the son of the count of Lapurdi, revolted. Richard the Lion-Hearted attacked Baiona, took the city, and forced Arnaud to flee to Uztaritze (Ustaritz). In 1193, the last count of Lapurdi sold his rights to the English crown.

In 1295, the French king occupied all of Iparralde, but revolts by the populace in Baiona forced the French out of Lapurdi. In 1307, Count Auger de Miramont of Xiberoa, after many battles with the English, ceded his crown and fled to Nafarroa. So, by the beginning of the fourteenth century, all of Iparralde, with the exception of Behe Nafarroa, was under English rule.

This strong English presence in southern France
created a situation in which the Basque region was
to suffer due to the rivalries between the French and
the English crowns. In 1355, the Hundred Years' War
between England and France began. The son of the
English king, Edward III, known as the Black Prince, set
up headquarters in Bordeaux and Baiona. From these
bases, he conquered the whole of southwestern France.
However, in the fifteenth century, the tide was reversed,
and in 1449, Gaston IV of Bearn captured Xiberoa for the
French crown; in 1450, he occupied Lapurdi. The people
of the area agreed to sign away any claim to sovereignty
in return for respect for local charters, or *fors*, which
were comparable to the Spanish *fueros*. Thus, by 1451,
Iparralde, with the exception of Behe Nafarroa, which
remained part of the Kingdom of Nafarroa, was under
the French monarchy.

T HE PERIOD from the eleventh to the fifteenth centuries was characterized by a great deal of internal
strife in Bizkaia and Gipuzkoa. Throughout the area
there emerged a number of *jauntxoak*, or *parientes
mayores*, "big chiefs." Each came to dominate one of
the small valleys. He would gather about him a number
of kinsmen and retainers and then build a *casa-torre*, or
fortified house. The organization of such bands has been
compared to that of the Scottish clans. Each strongman
would then wage warfare against the others and on some
of the nearby towns. We have one glowing account of the
period, written by Lope de Salazar, called *Las bienandan-
zas y fortunas* (Good Adventures and Fortunes), which
describes the really hair-raising exploits of these bands.
The account is full of senseless attacks and ambushes, of
the slitting of the throats of women and children and the
burning of houses to the ground with their inhabitants
still inside. As early as the thirteenth century, there is

evidence of people not belonging to the bands joining forces in self-defense organizations called *hermandades,* or brotherhoods.

THERE WERE two by-products of the activities of the warring bands. First, they forced people to come together, and it is quite possible that many towns arose largely on the grounds that a larger population concentration afforded the beleaguered inhabitants with better defense. Second, the situation allowed rapid political inroads on the part of the Castilian monarch, since the monarchy tended to side with the *hermandades* and even provide them with a degree of military assistance.

By the fourteenth century, the malefactors had organized themselves into two broad divisions—the Oña-cinos and the Gamboinos—who were at war with each other, as well as with the rest of the population. In 1397, representatives of all the *municipios,* or towns, of Gipuzkoa came together to form the Hermandad of Gipuzkoa. After more than fifty years of intense struggles, it prevailed and, in 1456, most of the towers of the *casa-torres* were demolished. The struggles continued intermittently for another century, but, in 1559, the *parientes mayores* entered into a peace accord with the provincial government and general assembly of Bizkaia, thereby ending several centuries of internal strife.

While Castile was increasing its sway in the north, we should also note that the Basques were exerting influence on it. As the Moors retreated, they left behind many abandoned areas in the Castilian plains that were often recolonized by Basque people. Second, the Basques became famed for their literacy. There was an exclusively Basque college at the University of Salamanca that produced trained secretaries for the Castilian bureaucracy. Consequently, many of those holding administrative and

Weapon of mass destruction
A Sixteenth-century serpentine was flexible, easily
transported, and deadly. The late Middle Ages and early
Modern Age were periods of considerable violence and
warfare in the Basque Country.
Drawing by Albrecht Dürer

---

secretarial positions in the government of Castile were
Basques.

AT THIS POINT, we might take stock and summarize
what happened between the eighth and the fifteenth centuries in the Basque territories. In the early
part of the period, or about when Roland was defeated,
we have little indication that there was a widely developed Basque political structure. We still get the impres-
sion of peoples raiding out of the mountains in a fashion
not unlike that described by Strabo. However, there is

some indication that there was strong local control over areas such as that surrounding Iruña and, in fact, we might regard it as a kind of Basque city-state.

However, the Basque area was on the threshold of rapid and widespread political consolidation. The main stimulus for this development seems to have been the pressure from the Moors. By 1000 A.D., the Kingdom of Nafarroa had emerged as the last remaining Christian bastion in Iberia. The kingdom was also one of the major political entities in Europe. During the reign of Sancho Mayor, all of the Basque area and considerably more territory was consolidated politically under a single monarch.

As the threat from the Moors declined, the Kingdom of Nafarroa became atomized, due both to political realignments through marriage alliances and to partible inheritance in the royal families, as well to as the subsequent emergence of viable states to the south and north. Major dismemberment then transpired when Sancho Mayor divided Nafarroa, Aragón, and Castile among his sons. Later, Castile emerged as a power that annexed Gipuzkoa and Araba. Through marriage, the lord of Bizkaia assumed the throne of Castile, thereby fusing Bizkaia with the crown. To the north, sovereignty of Iparralde passed into the hands of the English monarchy.

So out of the ruins of the former unity under the Kingdom of Nafarroa, the present-day Basque provinces emerged, each with its separate set of charters (*fueros* in Spain and *fors* in France), guaranteeing a degree of local autonomy to the populace and preserving what were regarded to be its ancient rights. Thus, by the end of the fifteenth century, Araba, Gipuzkoa, and Bizkaia were controlled by the king of Castile, Lapurdi and Xiberoa, long under English domination, were recent annexations of the French throne, while the Kingdom of Nafarroa continued to maintain an independent, if greatly reduced existence, holding sway over present-day Nafarroa and Behe Nafarroa.

Then there is the question of feudalism. We have been speaking of lords, counts, dukes, and kings, which indicates clearly that there was an aristocracy in the Basque area. However, an aristocratic structure is to be distinguished from a feudal society in that the existence of the former is but one aspect of the latter. The basis of a feudal system is the estate on which there is a class of serfs—people who are bound to the soil. That is, the lords have life-and-death power over their serfs. In the Basque Country, as we have noted, there is no indication that this ever became a feature of aristocratic privilege. The noblemen had large estates—particularly in Nafarroa—and they were worked either by hired laborers or tenant renters. However, the residents on the estates remained freemen. This tradition, coupled with the fact that the Basque area was never under Moorish domination, has led to an interpretation by some that all Basques are born to nobility.

FINALLY, THERE is the question of lifestyle during the period. We know that in the southern ecological zone, agriculture was firmly established by Roman times, whereas the central and northern zones were pastoralist. During the period in question, we can assume that the southern zone remained agricultural, whereas we see the first real beginnings of agriculture in the north. For instance, religious documents making reference to the rural hamlet of Zubero in the village of Aulestia show that by the fifteenth century, at least eight of the present eleven farms were in existence. What's more, it would appear that the hamlet came upon the scene as a full-blown entity, rather than beginning with one or two households and then expanding gradually. This

Richard the Lion-Hearted
Statue in front of the British Houses of Parliament
commemorates one of the many outside leaders who
drew the Basques into different spheres of foreign
influence over time.
Photo: Craig Rairdin.

---

instantaneous hamlet form of settlement may have been
for defensive purposes in the unsettled times. This last
conclusion is further supported by the fact that a dis-
seminated farmstead form of rural settlement appeared

about the sixteenth century—or in a more peaceful historical period.

WHILE AGRICULTURE was becoming established in the northern ecological zone, we know that, along the coasts, there was already a fairly active maritime and fishing complex. Basques were famed for shipbuilding, as well, and it was a Basque-constructed and Basque-manned fleet that took part in the siege of the Moors at Sevilla in 1248. Basques were engaged in heavy maritime trade with Northern Europe. Donostia and Bilbao were major ports for exporting wool from Castile. In 1348, the Bizkaians established a house of commerce in Flanders (present-day Belgium). We also know that in 1351 and again in 1481, the Basques of Bizkaia and Gipuzkoa entered into treaty agreements with England to discourage piracy in the area and to facilitate commerce.

Basques were key innovators of maritime technology. According to the historian O. H. K. Spate in his work *The Spanish Lake*:

> Shipbuilding underwent a virtual revolution in the fifteenth century. ... Iberian builders, particularly those of Biscay, played an important role in this development, without which the Discoveries would not have been possible. ... Thus from about 1430 a bewildering variety of hybrids [ships] were developed, initially it seems largely by the Basques. ... The end result, the standard big ship for most of the sixteenth century was the carrack: three masts with a lateen mizzen, high castles (especially aft), and a large central cargo hatch. This was the *nao* of the Spanish *Carrera* and the *nau* of the Portuguese *Carreira* to the West and East Indies respectively. (p. 16)

While some have speculated that Basque fishermen
may have visited Terranova—the New World—prior to
the first voyage of Columbus, there is no real evidence.
Given fifteenth-century Basque activity in the North
Atlantic, the speculation is that Basque fishermen were
likely aware of the rich fishing grounds off the eastern
Canadian seaboard, but kept the information to themselves as a trade secret. While there is some plausibility
to the argument, its relevance really regards the question
of who were the first Europeans to "discover" the New
World. Its significance has been eclipsed by the incontrovertible evidence afforded by a recent archeological exca-
vation in Newfoundland of a short-lived eleventh-century
Viking settlement there.

At the end of the fifteenth and the beginning of the
sixteenth centuries, Basques participated fully in Spain's
"explorations." Columbus's flagship, the *Santa María*,
was possibly built in a Basque shipyard. It was captained
by Juan de la Cosa, sometimes called Juan Vizcaíno, and
had several Basques in its crew. Some believe that the
intrepid explorer may have learned about the New World
from a Basque mariner who had already sailed to the
New World.

Juan de la Cosa subsequently explored the coast of
northern South America (Colombia and Venezuela), and
he drew the first map of America (1501).

REGARDING RELIGION, we know that evangelization
of the Basque Country transpired largely during the
period in question and that by the end of the fifteenth
century, the Basque area was completely Christian. Two
factors in particular spurred the Christianization of the
Basques. First, as we have noted, the entire area was
brought under the control of the Kingdom of Nafarroa
and France, which was Christian by about the seventh
century. Second, the pilgrimage routes to Santiago de

Compostela passing through the Basque Country stimulated the construction of churches and monasteries built in Romanic architectural style, which served as way stations for the pilgrims.

By the end of the fifteenth century, there were five dioceses with jurisdiction in the Basque Country: Bayonne, which controlled Lapurdi, the Valley of Baztán (Nafarroa), and part of northeastern Gipuzkoa; Oloron, with jurisdiction over Xiberoa; Dax, which controlled Mixe; Pamplona, which ministered to Nafarroa and central Gipuzkoa; and Vitoria, which controlled Araba, western Gipuzkoa, and Bizkaia. Latin and subsequently Spanish, rather than Basque, were the cultured languages of administration.

FINALLY, WE might describe the social and political conditions characteristic of the Basque people in the fifteenth century. Feudalism was unknown. Consequently, there were no serfs, there was no obligatory labor, every man had the right to bear arms, and there was the right of assembly.Every inhabitant could hunt and fish freely, there was no death penalty, local affairs were administered through local assemblies, and the clergy enjoyed no special privileges. Family life was governed by local custom whereby women had equal status with men before the law and there was recognition that each farm holding was sufficient for a single family and hence should be passed on intact between the generations through the custom of selecting a single heir to the farmstead in each generation.There also was recognition that communities had the right to contract with other communities, even if such arrangements crossed political boundaries, thus, there were "transnational" agreements or *facerias* between adjacent communities in the borderland of France and Spain governing use of the mountain pastures between them. And there were also agreements between larger entities, such as a

treaty between Lapurdi, on the one hand, and Gipuzkoa
and Bizkaia, on the other, to the effect that they would
continue to maintain good relations even if Spain and
France were at war.

Lesson seven

LEARNING OBJECTIVES
1. To review of the various historical invasions experienced by the Basques.
2. To understand the process of Christianization of the
   Basques.
3. To trace Basque participation in the political history of
   Spanish medieval kingdoms.
4. To understand the historical context of Basque traditional laws and political institutions.

REQUIRED READING
William A. Douglass and Jon Bilbao, *Amerikanuak:
   The Basques of the New World* (Reno: University of
   Nevada Press, 2005), 33–51.
Mark Kurlansky, *The Basque History of the World* (New
   York: Walker and Company, 2001), 27–42.

SUGGESTED READING
Julio Caro Baroja, *Los vascos* (Madrid: Istmo, 1971)
Roger Collins, *The Basques* (Oxford: Basil Blackwell,
   1990), 99–179.

WRITTEN LESSON FOR SUBMISSION
1. Describe the Visigothic and Frankish invasions of the
   Basque region.
2. Discuss the historical encounter between the Basques
   and Charlemagne.

3. Was the Kingdom of Nafarroa a "Basque" kingdom? Argue both in favor and against.
4. How did the Basques participate in the political history of premodern Spain?
5. Assess the historical context of the Basque *fueros* and *fors*. Do they provide the Basques with a claim to legitimate "primordial" political sovereignty?

8 · The Modern Era

F ROM 1500 TO the present, the history of the Basque
Country became even more intertwined with those
of the Spanish and French nations. About 1500, Spain
and France were in the process of emerging as states,
and the discovery of the New World established a new
set of relationships, dependencies, and opportunities for
the Basque Country. These New World influences ranged
from the stimulation of shipbuilding and commerce, to
outlets for emigration, to the feedback of the ideas and
wealth of the returnees from the Indies, who would then
reestablish themselves in the Basque Country, often
building sumptuous houses, endowing religious and
public institutions, acquiring titles, and exerting influence over local politics. Other factors were possibly more
significant, such as the introduction into Basque agriculture of maize and the potato during the sixteenth century, some thirty-one years after Columbus's first voyage,
both of which were New World cultigens.

The period from 1451 to 1589 was one of almost constant warfare in the Basque Country. Nafarroa, in particular, was subjected to attempts to dismember it by the
crowns of both France and Castile. In 1463, Louis XI of
France and Henry IV of Castile tried to divide the Kingdom of Nafarroa between them. This touched off many
years of warfare. In 1512, the Castilians occupied Iruña
and Donibane-Garazi (St. Jean Pied-de-Port) in Behe
Nafarroa, and the Nafarroans agreed to union with Castile, provided that they be allowed to retain their *fuero*
and identity as a separate political state. Consequently,
Nafarroa was allowed to keep its parliament, its courts,
its own currency, its customshouses, and the exemption
of its citizens from forced military service outside the

limits of the kingdom. However, the king of Nafarroa was required to have as an adviser a viceroy appointed by the monarch of Castile.

Gipuzkoa, Araba, and Bizkaia retained their own *fueros*, as well as the right to hold their own assemblies to legislate local matters. They administered justice locally, although decisions could be appealed, in which event the matter went to Madrid. They had their own customs regulations, with checkpoints established at the Ebro River (as were the customshouses of Nafarroa), and their inhabitants were exempted from serving in the army outside of the Basque Country. These legal arrangements, which obviously accorded Basques a great deal of autonomy, were in effect in the Spanish Basque Country until 1839, when most Spanish Basques fought on the losing side in the First Carlist War.

THE NATURE of local government under the *fueros* differed somewhat from province to province. However, we can consider an example of how it worked. In Gipuzkoa, there was a strong democratic tradition based on the concept that all men are equal. There was a local municipal government elected by the male citizens. The town government named its representatives to the general assembly of the province, which met annually from July 2 to July 11. The last day was a festive affair in which the delegates themselves were required to perform an *aurresku*, a traditional Basque folk dance. All business had to be concluded by the last day. The general assembly met behind closed doors, and only its agreements (not its disputes) were made public. As in Bizkaia, priests could not serve as delegates, nor could lawyers, since the latter "were likely to foment discord which they could turn to their own advantage." The assembly was rotated annually among eighteen towns eligible to host it. This was a means of preventing any one community from monopolizing the proceedings. The king sent a representative, the *corregidor*, to the proceedings. However, he could not vote, and the general assembly could decide not to receive him.

In terms of executive power, the general assembly selected four of its members to serve as deputies of a *diputación* or provincial council. Each year, the site where the *diputación* was seated rotated among Azpeitia, Azkoitia, Tolosa, and Donostia. So Gipuzkoa did not have a capital city per se. Judicial power was exerted by the mayors of the villages, although decisions could be appealed to the Spanish Supreme Court.

FOR THE FRENCH Basque area, the period around 1500 A.D. was a trying one. In 1512, the English occupied Lapurdi. In 1521, the French attacked the area and laid siege to the Gipuzkoan town of Hondarribia (Fuenterrabia). Two years later, Spanish raiding parties burned several towns in Lapurdi. During the sixteenth century, Donibane-Lohizune (St. Jean de Luz) was burned to the ground on several occasions. In 1518, the French Basque area suffered a severe epidemic of the Black Plague.

During this time, the privileges of the French Basques were under attack. In 1514, the people of Lapurdi were required to produce a French-language version of the *fors*. In 1520, the *fors* of Xiberoa were written in the Bearnais language. Behe Nafarroa, of course, was operating under the *fuero* of Nafarroa.

At this point, the area entered into a period of religious wars. Protestantism took root in the Basque Country, particularly among persons of high social status on the French side of the Pyrenees. In 1559, the monarchs of Nafarroa converted. By 1569, Xiberoa was a Protestant stronghold, while Behe Nafarroa was largely Catholic. In 1569, the Catholics burned many towns in Xiberoa, and its inhabitants responded by sending a force against

Fortified dwelling
This fifteenth-century fortified house is the Jauregia Dorretxea (Tower Castle) in Donamaria, Nafarroa.

The region was incorporated into Castile in the sixteenth century. Royal order limited fortified stonework, which could be used as bulwarks against central authority. Many existing fortifications were modified by replacing the former stone tower with a wooden structure.

Photo: Xabier Irujo

Behe Nafarroa. Over the years, the Catholics gained the upper hand, but as late as 1631 there was a Protestant minister in Maule-Lextarre.

THE PROTESTANTS made little headway in Lapurdi, although there were some adherents in Baiona. In 1565, Phillip II of Spain used the excuse of the Protestant influence in Baiona to strip its bishopric of jurisdiction

in parts of Nafarroa and Gipuzkoa. This went a long way
toward making the emerging Franco-Spanish frontier an
effective divisive factor among Basques. By 1589, Behe
Nafarroa was removed from Nafarroa and became a part
of France.

I N SPITE OF the turmoil, the sixteenth century witnessed several cultural developments in the Basque
Country. Trade with and feedback from the New World
stimulated commerce. In 1545, a university was established at Oñati (Oñate) in Gipuzkoa. Also in 1545, Bernat
Dechepare's *Linguae vasconum primitiae* appeared as
the first work published in the Basque language. In 1571,
Ioannes Leiçarraga published the first Basque translation
of the New Testament.

In 1534, the Gipuzkoan Ignatius of Loiola (Loyola)
founded the Society of Jesus with the threefold purpose
of missionizing the new colonies, reacting against the
Protestant Reformation, and reforming the Catholic
Church from within. One of his early followers, the fellow Basque Francis Xavier, evangelized Japan and in 1552
was martyred in China. Both were subsequently canon-
ized saints of the church.

In sum, the sixteenth century in the Basque Country
was characterized by a great deal of strife and warfare,
but was a time of interesting religious, cultural, and economic development.

The seventeenth century witnessed the beginning of
major struggles for power between Spain and France. In
1615, there was an attempt to head off trouble through
marriage alliances between the crowns when the daughter of the French king, Henri IV, married the future
Spanish king, Phillip IV, and Anne of Austria, daughter
of Phillip III of Spain, married King Louis XIII of France.
The double wedding took place in the Basque Country.
However, the effort failed when, in 1636, the Thirty Years'

War broke out with Spain and France as opponents. Hostilities raged throughout the Basque Country, with many coastal towns besieged and burned on both sides of the frontier.

In 1659, a peace conference was held between the two countries on an island at the mouth of the Bidasoa River in the Basque Country. The Treaty of the Pyrenees was signed, which formalized the Spanish-French border. Again there was an attempt to solidify peace through a marriage alliance when King Louis XIV of France married Princess María Teresa of Spain in Donibane-Lohizune in 1660.

Despite the turmoil, this was a period of relative prosperity and internal peace in the Basque Country. There was rapid expansion of agriculture as farms were carved out of former wilderness. There was apparently great prosperity in the fishing industry, as well. In 1685, a cod-fishing fleet set sail from Pasaia (Pasajes) in Gipuzkoa for Terranova with forty-one vessels and 1475 men.

HOWEVER, THERE were two developments in the seventeenth century that cast a pall over the Basque Country, the erosion of local autonomy and the arrival of the Inquisition. The growing power of the respective governments of Paris and Madrid stimulated movement toward absolute monarchy and strong central government. Basque foral privileges came to be regarded as detrimental to the power of the state—particularly in matters of taxation and military conscription—and were increasingly subject to intense pressure. One common means employed by the monarchs was to grant titles and estates to favored persons, who then had the right to exact as many taxes in the Basque country as they were able—sharing the proceeds with the state.

In different areas, the erosion of autonomy occurred in different ways. Iparralde furnishes numerous examples.

Burial marker
Basque cemeteries were once adorned with elaborate
discoidal funerary stelae that have been interpreted by
some to be anthropomorphic.
Source: José Miguel de Barandiarán

During the seventeenth century, the French king provoked the outbreak of a civil war in Lapurdi in the 1650s
in order to to achieve a rapid revocation of Basque privileges. It was triggered when Louis XIV tried to name a
new bailiff for Lapurdi, replacing the lord of Saint Pée-
sur-Nivelle, who had traditional claim to the post. The
notary public of the town of Azkaine (Ascain) objected

and organized a group of followers who came to be
known as the Sable Gorris (Red Sashes), who clashed
with the Sable Xuris (White Sashes), supporters of the
king. The representative of the king in the area called an
illegal *biltzar* (the assembly of Labourd). It was illegal in
that the king's representative traditionally had no control over the proceedings, but was merely an observer.
The illegal *biltzar* fired the notary of Askaine from his
post. The Sable Gorris initiated attacks in order to free
members of their group who had been imprisoned. In
1657, the Azkaine notary was captured and executed.
This ended the struggle, but the province of Lapurdi was
forced to pay indemnification to the Sable Xuris. More
importantly, Louis XIV took advantage of the situation
to reorganize the *biltzar* in 1660. Thereafter, only the
king's bailiff, and not the syndic, who was elected by the
people, could convene the *biltzar*. Second, the proposals
of the syndic had to be approved by the king's lieutenant before they could be presented to the *biltzar*. Third,
the *biltzar* could meet only in Uztaritze and under royal
control. Fourth, the powers of the bailiff were enhanced.
Fifth, the mayor of Baiona (formerly elected) was now
named by the king. The post became hereditary and was
given to the Gramont family. Finally, the post of gover-
nor of Lapurdi was treated in the same fashion. Throughout the remainder of the century, there was agitation
against these measures, but they remained in effect.

IN BEHE NAFARROA, the seventeenth century also witnessed critical developments concerning the erosion
of autonomy. In 1620, King Louis XIII visited Pau to end
the religious wars. He issued the Edict of Union, which
declared the crown of Nafarroa to be united with that of
France. The edict tied the parliaments of Behe Nafarroa
and Xiberoa to the authority of the magistrate of Béarn,
thus removing local political control from Basque hands.

From then on, justice was dispensed to the Basque area from Pau. While the Edict of Union promised respect for the Basque *fors*, in practice, they were ignored. In 1632, there was an unsuccessful attempt to abolish Behe Nafarroa as a distinct political unit. By 1643, the Nafarroan currency was outlawed there. Through the remainder of the century, there was increasing French political domination of the area, accompanied by greater taxation.

Xiberoa was likewise submitted to Béarnais authority under the 1620 Edict of Union. Shortly thereafter, the king tried to set up a barony in Xiberoa for one of his former bodyguards. The new baron attempted to usurp control of the commons, the lands in each community that were owned collectively. This provoked armed reaction and, in 1661, a priest, Bernard de Goyheneche, alias Matalas, led a force of seven hundred men against the chateau of Maule-Lextarre, captured it, and abolished taxes. The government then sent an expeditionary force that ravaged Xiberoa, captured Matalas, decapitated him, and hung his head over the entry to the chateau.

So it is clear that, during the seventeenth century, Iparralde lost much of its autonomy. Indeed, after the border between Spain and France was fixed in 1659, the Basques were increasingly integrated into two separate political orbits. The French-Spanish frontier (although not formally demarcated with boundary stones until 1868) remains one of Europe's oldest and most stable borders. Since its creation, it has become increasingly necessary for many purposes to think in terms of a distinction between French Basques and Spanish Basques.

IN ADDITION to suffering greater integration into consolidating nation-states of France and Spain, the Basque Country also suffered from one of the more extravagant expressions of the Counter-Reformation: the Inquisition. During the seventeenth century, there were many sad instances of out-and-out witch hunts (see chapter 19). The Basques had a long-standing belief in witches, and the inquisitors found it easy to find persons willing to claim they had been bewitched and who were disposed to denounce others. The most tragic example was the proceedings held in Lapurdi under the direction of the fanatical French inquisitor Pierre de Lancre. De Lancre and his tribunal arrived in the area after many of the active adult men had set sail for the New World on fishing expeditions. Before the men returned, many dozens of women had been put to death as witches. The returning mariners drove de Lancre from the area.

BY CONTRAST, most of the eighteenth century was characterized by a fair measure of internal peace in the Basque Country. It was a period in which agriculture expanded greatly. By one estimate for the Spanish Basque area, the total amount of land under cultivation increased by one-third during the eighteenth century. Similarly, it was a period of industrialization. The iron mines of Bizkaia were exploited effectively, and there was a proliferation of small foundries throughout the Basque Country. Shipbuilding increased greatly at Baiona and in the Spanish Basque area, which, coupled with the demand for charcoal as fuel in the iron works, led to rapid deforestation. The cities of Baiona, Donostia, and Bilbao prospered due to trade with the New World. Baiona also became the home port of many pirates preying on the New World traffic of Spain and England. However, all was not rosy for the coastal areas. In 1713, the Treaty of Utrecht conceded Terranova to England— which curtailed the fishing rights of Basque coastal towns. In 1732, the fishing community of Donibane-Lohizune had a population of thirteen thousand persons, but, by 1783, it had declined to four thousand. The town had also become a pirates' nest.

From the point of view of political developments, we find evidence throughout the century of further attempts by the monarchs of France and Spain to infringe the traditional rights of the Basques. In 1717, the king of Spain attempted (unsuccessfully) to move the customshouses from the Ebro to the Pyrenees. The king again was ceding posts to favored persons, who were authorized to try to increase the taxation levied against the Basques.

FAR AND AWAY the most notable political developments of the century affected the French Basque Country: the French Revolution and its aftermath. For most French people, the Revolution was a welcome development, since it spelled the end of feudalism, terminated arbitrary taxation, curtailed the power of the clergy, and replaced absolutism with a constitutional monarchy. However, these benefits were less relevant for the Basques, since, as we have seen, the Basque Country had been free of classic feudalism and had a long-standing tradition of popular government. Therefore, the French Basques opposed much of the legislation of the Revolution and condemned its excessive anticlericalism.

In 1789, the revolutionary government convened its first meeting of parliament, or the Etats Generaux, in Paris and ordered all of the regions to send representatives. Xiberoa elected a delegation, but Behe Nafarroa refused to do so. Rather, the assembly of Behe Nafarroa met in Donibane-Garazi to reaffirm the ancient constitution of Nafarroa by rejecting the Edict of Union of 1620. It coined a new currency and declared Behe Nafarroan independence from France. It then elected a delegation to approach the central government to plead its case and demand respect for the ancient *fors*. In Lapurdi, there was agreement to elect a delegation to the Etats Generaux, and it was resolved to fight for recognition of the *fors*, as well.

Robespierre, the architect of state
Iparralde suffered greatly during the French Revolution
for defending its particular customs while resisting
the attempt to centralize France's political power and
homogenize its administration.

WHEN THE Etats Generaux met, one of the measures
it adopted was to strip the regions of France of
their ancient privileges. France was then divided into
departments that obliterated the old provincial divisions.
Thus, the Basque provinces were lumped with Béarn to
form the Département des Basses Pyrénées. All Basque
common law was declared null and void, and the laws

of the Revolution were henceforth applied equally to all French citizens.

These laws were particularly damaging to the Basques in the area of property relations. The legislators wished to break the economic hold of the feudal aristocracy throughout France and believed that the way to do so was to change inheritance practices to oblige equal division of a person's property at death among all of the legitimate offspring. This was a strategy for breaking up the feudal estates within a generation. However, applying the new law across the board threatened the existence of the single-family, small-scale farmstead so characteristic of the Basque countryside. This measure remains in effect to this day among French Basques, although they have become quite ingenious at circumventing it through simulated land sales between brothers and sisters and by other means.

A second area of concern to the Basques was a decision that all communal land was to become the property of the state. Basques rigorously opposed this, since Basque tradition vested control of the commons in the community, and the individual farmsteads were dependent on access to the commons. A number of (illegal) syndicates or corporations were organized in the French Basque Country as a means of retaining local control over the commons, and many of these arrangements continue down to the present.

THE FRENCH Revolution was strongly anticlerical. It resolved to abolish the three dioceses of Bayonne, Dax, and Oloron and to incorporate them into the single one of the Basses Pyrénées. This measure was opposed by the bishop of Baiona, who was forced to flee into Spain. The bishop of the Basse Pyrénées named clergymen for the Basque area, but when they arrived on the scene, they were poorly received. In many communities, the former clergymen continued to minister clandestinely, and many were arrested or forced to flee.

Another measure that caused deep resentment was the decision to strip many towns of their Basque name and rechristen them with a revolutionary one. For example, Itsasu (Itxassou) was renamed Union, and Luhoso (Louhossoa) was called Montagne-sur-Nive.

THE FRENCH Revolution provoked a strong reaction among neighboring countries and, by 1792, France and Spain were at war. The Basques were regarded by Paris as disloyal. The fact that many refused to be conscripted into the army supported this interpretation. The French also believed that the Basques were working as spies for Spain. Tribunals were set up in the Basque Country at Baiona and Donibane-Lohizune, which in a short time had guillotined sixty persons.

In 1793, there was a particularly tragic incident growing out of the hysteria of the day. The Revolutionary Committee of Donibane-Lohizune demanded that the entire population of the villages of Sara (Sare), Azkaine, and Itsasu be deported on the grounds that the people there were "putting on aristocratic airs" and forty-seven of their young men had deserted from the army. Over four thousand persons were rounded up and forced to march eighty kilometers north to the Landes area, where they were held in concentration camps. Families were broken up and, of the unfortunate four thousand, sixteen hundred died. The possessions of the deportees were pillaged. From Sara alone, over one thousand head of livestock disappeared. Subsequently, it turned out that many members of the Revolutionary Committee were tried for involvement in the thefts.

As the war with Spain wore on, the French Basques got into the spirit of the thing. Each area began to raise its own militia, and by the end of 1793, there were four

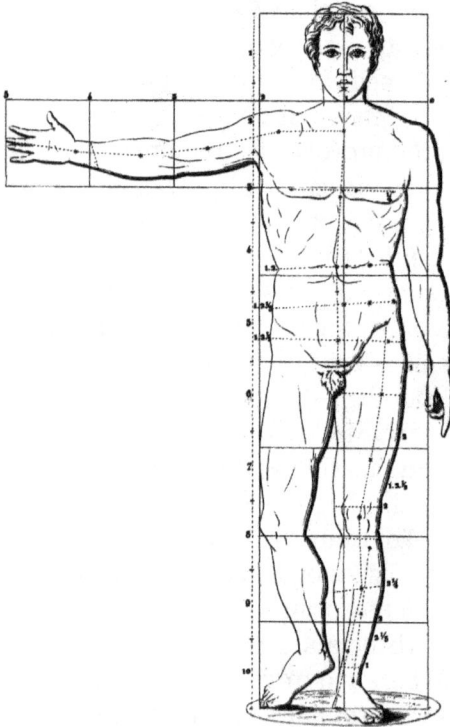

Measuring race

The discipline of anthropology began in Europe stimulated by the preoccupation with measuring human physical attributes as the foundation for classifying humanity according to races. From the outset, Basque physical and linguistic traits received considerable attention as the possible key to determining the proto-European type (i.e. the ancestry of the founding anthropologists themselves).

Johann Georg Heck: Heck's pictorial Archive of Art and Architecture.

French Basque companies in the field. France gained the upper hand, and, in 1794, French Basques helped capture Donostia. In 1795, both Iruña and Bilbao were taken.

At this point, there was serious consideration among Spanish Basques of joining France to unify the entire Basque Country under a single sovereign. However, the antireligious and strong centralist tendencies of the French government sobered proponents. In 1795, a peace treaty ended the war, and the French withdrew from the Spanish Basque Country.

WITH THE FALL of Robespierre in 1795, oppression of French Basques eased. Those in exile were allowed to return home. The tribunals were dissolved, and many churches reopened. There were some reprisals, because a few armed bands continued to roam the countryside. For instance, in 1796, a group of men entered the house of one of the former revolutionary officials and executed him.

In sum, during the eighteenth century, political events had minor impact in the Spanish Basque area, but in Iparralde, all semblance of Basque traditional rights as conferred under the *fors* was abolished.

The nineteenth century opened with renewed conflicts between France and Spain when Napoleon conquered the Spaniards. The beginnings of the Napoleonic Wars affected the French Basques indirectly, more in the form of conscription and higher tax rates than through of actual warfare in the Basque Country. The French Basque Country was still suffering from the excesses of the Revolution in that brigands made travel dangerous, there was an inordinate number of beggars, and there were many orphans. Also, education and the general state of welfare were in a shambles. The Revolution had stripped the clergy of their teaching role without providing a substitute. Agriculture had suffered greatly, and the number of livestock was reduced seriously, although the fact that it was an area of small proprietors protected the French Basque Country from famine.The Revolution and the subsequent war had destroyed what little industry there was, and an increase in Spanish tariffs cut the French Basque area off from Spanish markets. Similarly, the war had interdicted maritime trade and practically strangled Baiona. The fishing fleet was reduced to eking out a meager existence by catching sardines in coastal waters. On the other hand, the state of war provided ideal conditions for piracy and corsair activity. From 1793 to 1809, 106 corsair vessels were outfitted in Baiona alone, with local capitalists funding the ventures in return for a share of the booty.

WHILE THE beginning of the Napoleonic Wars affected the Basques only indirectly, the defeat of Napoleon was another matter. In 1807, Spain rose up against French rule, and between 1807 and 1810, three hundred and fifty thousand French troops passed through the Basque Country. When they were defeated, they retreated back through the Basque area, with their adversaries in hot pursuit. In 1813, the French were vanquished at Gasteiz, and the main force withdrew across the Pyrenees, setting up headquarters in Baiona. There was a rear-guard action between the French and the forces of the English Duke of Wellington that raged slowly across the Basque area, causing great hardship to the populace. By 1814, the Allies had crossed the Pyrenees, but then became bogged down in a siege of Baiona. On April 27, 1814, the Allied forces in France took Paris, but Baiona had still not fallen. However, with the defeat at Paris, Baiona's garrison soon surrendered.

Just as the eighteenth century spelled the end of Iparralde's privileges as conferred under the *fors*, the nineteenth century marked the demise of the Spanish Basque *fueros*. The events most instrumental in this loss of autonomy are known as the Carlist Wars.

The Carlist Wars in Spain ostensibly turned on a dispute over succession to the Spanish throne. In 1830, Don Carlos, brother of King Fernando, rebelled against the latter's attempt to install his daughter, Isabella, on the throne. Carlos maintained that, lacking a male heir, he, the king's brother, should become king. The dispute went much deeper, however, since Isabella was the champion of the liberal, anticlerical, centralist forces in Spain, while Carlos championed the cause of conservatism, Catholicism, and regionalism.

Predictably, the Basque Country was strongly Carlist, with the exception of urban areas such as Bilbao. After several years of warfare in which the Carlists enjoyed many initial successes under the leadership of their greatest general, Tomás de Zumalacarregui, who was killed in an unsuccessful siege of Bilbao, the Carlists began to lose and sued for peace. At the Convention of Bergara (Vergara) in 1839, the Carlists agreed to lay down their arms if the *fueros* were respected. The Liberals agreed, but once the war was over, they ignored the *fueros*, outlawed the local assemblies, tried to exact direct taxation, and attempted to conscript Basques into the Spanish army.

IN 1872, A NEW Carlist War broke out in the north and raged for seven years—once again the Basques were on the losing side. This time, no semblance of respect for the *fueros* was maintained by the government, and the customs posts were moved to the French frontier. Since the Second Carlist War, the *fueros* have applied only in the limited areas of transmission of property between the generations and dowry payments, and even then are applicable only in parts of Bizkaia and Nafarroa. Araba and Gipuzkoa lost all vestige of foral privileges.

However, down to the Spanish Civil War of 1936–39, the Basque provinces were allowed a degree of economic freedom under *conciertos económicos*, or economic pacts. Under this arrangement, the provincial government raised taxes locally, maintained its own budget for services such as highways and schools, and made a single annual lump-sum tax payment to the Spanish state. Its amount was negotiated periodically. Thus, the state still could not tax Basques directly. However, after the Spanish Civil War, all of the Basque provinces except Nafarroa (which sided with Franco) lost this privilege.

THE POLITICAL history of the French Basques from 1815 to the present, by comparison, is relatively uneventful. The area underwent some economic development and progress in the field of education. It continued to oppose the increase in central authority, but, particularly in the twentieth century, the French government has intervened in almost every facet of local life with its welfare programs. Not only have rural areas received services such as electricification, there is a family fertility subsidy plan that benefits French Basques greatly. Consequently, Iparralde receives more from the government than it pays in taxes. This has fostered dependency on Paris.

Lesson eight

LEARNING OBJECTIVES
1. To survey the broad outline of Basque history from the sixteenth to the twentieth centuries.
2. To understand the historical background of the administrative differentiation between the French and Spanish Basque Countries.

3. To trace the political subordination of Basque territories to the French, English, and Spanish dominions.

REQUIRED READING

Marianne Heiberg, *The Making of the Basque Nation* (Cambridge: Cambridge University Press, 1989), 11–44.

Mark Kurlansky, *The Basque History of the World* (New York: Walker and Company, 2001), 65–79, 103–125.

SUGGESTED READING

Rachel Bard, *Navarra: The Durable Kingdom* (Reno: University of Nevada Press, 1982).

Fernando García de Cortázar and José María Lorenzo Espinosa, *Historia del País Vasco* (San Sebastián: Editorial Txertoa, 1996).

William A. Douglass and Jon Bilbao, *Amerikanuak: The Basques of the New World* (Reno: University of Nevada Press, 2005), 61–67.

WRITTEN LESSON FOR SUBMISSION

1. In light of the information provided by the course to this point, discuss the extent to which we may conceive meaningfully of a single Basque tradition and people.

2. Conversely, to what extent should "Basques" be viewed distinctively as "French" and "Spanish" Basques?

3. Situate Nafarroa both within and outside of Basque history.

9 · Basque Nationalism

ONE CAN hardly talk about Basques without raising the question of nationalism, a movement that is over a century old in the Basque Country. During the last five decades, Basque resistance to Madrid's authority has constituted one of Europe's most virulent ethnic nationalisms. What follows is a brief overview of some basic topics.

First, there is the issue of historical precedent. Both ardent Basque nationalists and their Spanish or French nationalist counterparts find a charter for their views in the history of the region. The Basque nationalists claim that, for millennia, Basques have fiercely defended their freedom against any possible invader—including the Romans, Visigoths, Franks, and Moors. Their critics argue that the Basques were never a unified political entity and, indeed, only once and briefly lived under a single rule (the Kingdom of Nafarroa between 1000 and 1035 A.D.). Rather, the region was characterized by a fragmented political history in which the different traditional Basque areas were alternatively duchies, small kingdoms, or simply districts within larger political frameworks. At times, Basques were even battlefield adversaries.

The nub of the issue turns on the interpretation of the laws, the *fueros* in Spain and *fors* in France, that we considered in chapter 8. These ancient statutes, whose origins are lost in the mists of time, spelled out local political privileges and processes, questions that became increasingly relevant in the late Middle Ages as the Basque areas were drawn into the orbit of the emerging Spanish and French nations. According to the Basque nationalists, the *fueros* are ancient, almost sacred, charters antedating political alliances with Spaniards and the French. When such alliances were forged, the Spanish and French monarchs were forced to recognize them as the laws of the land and as the repositories of local political independence in the Basque Country. The centralists dispute this interpretation and regard the *fueros* as a list of privileges conceded by the monarchs as an incentive for the Basques to enter into a wider political federation. As concessions, they were subject to revocation.

This debate is unlikely ever to be resolved to everyone's satisfaction, since Basques, Spaniards, and the French all imbue their interpretations of foral law with a kind of mythical significance. However, it is fair to say that under the foral system, the Basques enjoyed enormous political autonomy from the late Middle Ages to the eighteenth century. Again, the details are complicated, differed regionally within the Basque Country, and are subject to interpretation. However, if we look at Bizkaia as an example, we find that it had one of Europe's oldest democracies under foral law. As we have noted, each valley elected a male representative to a general assembly held periodically beneath an oak tree in the town of Gernika in order to legislate the law of the land. Each new Spanish monarch had to come personally or send a representative to Gernika to swear to respect the Bizkaian *fuero*. John Adams and William Wordsworth both later wrote with admiration about this primitive democracy, ensconced in an isolated corner of an otherwise largely feudal Western Europe.

As NOTED IN chapter 8, by the late eighteenth and early nineteenth centuries, the Basque foral political system was under centralist assault in both France and Spain. The modern Basque nationalist movement was born out of the Carlist conflicts in Spain, or, more accurately, out of the profound disillusionment in the aftermath of defeat in the Second Carlist War. The Basque provinces, and particularly Nafarroa, had been the main staging area for Carlism, and throughout the nineteenth century constituted the backbone of the movement. This penchant for Carlism reflected a strong conviction on the part of the Basques that the best means of protecting their political autonomy was to control the reins of government in Madrid. If the Basques' adherence to the Carlist cause constituted rebellion against the leadership in Madrid, it was not tinged with separatist overtones. The two Carlist Wars represent recourse to violence in order to effect change within the political life of the Spanish nation.

THE WARS, which were largely fought in the Basque provinces, not only decimated the countryside, as we noted in chapter 8, but encumbered the population with huge debts in the forms of war retributions and left a standing army of occupation. They also created a climate of intimidation aimed at undermining Basque culture, exacerbated by a massive migration of workers and their families into the Basque Country from other areas of Spain. Therefore, by the end of the nineteenth century, Spanish Basques were faced with the fact that with stunning rapidity they had lost the *fueros* and their leadership, and their culture was under assault in the homeland.

It was out of this climate that modern Basque nationalism was born. The movement was essentially the product of an urban environment and was led by urban people, particularly from Bilbao and Donostia. By the beginning of the twentieth century, both Bizkaia and Gipuzkoa were undergoing rapid industrialization, a development that attracted to them a large influx of Spanish laborers. Consequently, Basques were becoming a minority in their

Sabino de Arana y Goiri (1868-1903)
Founder of the contemporary Basque nationalist movement, Arana defended the rights of Basques to retain
their political privileges, ethnic distinctiveness and linguistic uniqueness in the face of the leveling influences
of industrialization of the Basque Country.

---

own urban centers, and the Basque language was heard
but rarely on city streets.

SABINO DE ARANA y Goiri, a young Bilbao native, was
the father of modern Basque nationalism. He
launched the movement by authoring virulent attacks
on Spanish institutions and Spaniards. He delighted in

the fact that Spain was in the throes of losing most of
her overseas possessions, and when Cuba fell to American forces during the Spanish-American War, Arana
was arrested for sending a congratulatory telegram to
President Roosevelt. In his book *Bizkaya por su inde-
pendencia* (For Bizkaian Independence), Arana called for
the outright independence of the Basques while decry-
ing the evident process of Castilianization of the Basque
Country. He invented the new term "Euzkadi" to refer to
an independent Basque nation and designed its flag. He
advocated the expulsion of all French and Spanish people from Basque soil. He coined pejorative terms to refer
to non-Basques and laced his writings with a racist view
that Spaniards are inferior beings, while the Basques
are the most ancient pure race remaining in Europe.
He railed against intermarriage with non-Basques, a
position that Miguel de Unamuno was to denounce as
"absurd racial virginity."

ARANA STRUCK a responsive chord among some
sectors of the urban middle classes, students, and
the Basque clergy. His ideas, however, met with considerable apathy in the rural areas and with outright
hostility from most Basque industrialists, who feared
retaliations against the Basque Country by the central
government. Arana's personal career was both hectic
and short-lived. As the prime mover in the movement,
he would found a journal or a newspaper from time to
time, publish a few issues, then suffer official censorship and, periodically, imprisonment. Arana's activist
following was always relatively few in number, but it is
obvious that he was verbalizing the frustrations of many
in Bizkaia. In 1898, he was elected a representative to the
provincial government. He was to die shortly thereafter.

While Sabino Arana provided the movement with its
martyr, he also created its organization and programs. In

1893–94, he laid the groundwork for a new political force in the Basque Country called the Partido Nacionalista Vasco (PNV), or Basque Nationalist Party. About 1893, he wrote the principles of the party from a Bizkaian viewpoint and with the philosophy of "Jaungoikoa eta Lagi Zarra" (God and Old Laws).

WITH THE DEATH of Sabino Arana in 1903, the formative stages of Basque nationalism were completed. From 1903 to 1921, the movement gained in strength and local political respectability, particularly in Bizkaia, where, in 1918, the Basque Nationalist Party gained control of the *diputación,* or provincial government. From the outset, there was a polemic within the ranks of the nationalists concerning the degree to which Basque separatism was an attainable or even desirable goal. A strong faction agitated for return to the foral system of government within the Spanish nation. The nationalists also took a great deal of interest in international developments in Europe, particularly the growing tendency to give the grievances of European ethnic minorities a serious airing. In 1916, the Basque nationalists sent a delegation to the Conférence des Nationalités in Lausanne to press Basque political claims.

During the first two decades of the twentieth century, there was a notable cultural revival in the Basque Country, in part stimulated by nationalism. The Basque nationalists sponsored numerous folk festivals, competitions between *bertsolariak* (versifiers), and athletic contests involving traditional Basque sporting events. In a different vein, the movement sponsored serious scholarship, notably in the area of archeological excavations, the collection of folklore, Basque linguistics, the ethnography of rural life, and the sociology of urbanization and social problems in the industrial zones. Scholarly journals such as *La Revista Internacional de Estudios Vascos*

Anticipating the Spanish Civil War
King Alfonso XIII of Spain, exiled in April of 1931,
general Primo de Rivera (helmeted) and general
Millan del Bosch, who later took part in the military
coup led by general Francisco Franco, on parade.

---

and *Eusko-Folklore* were founded. These efforts were to
culminate in 1919 in the First Congress of Basque Studies.

THE POWER base of the Basque National Party was
to remain urban, but the message began to rely
heavily on the use of rural symbols as a means of invoking traditional values. Since the rural areas were the last
remaining strongholds of the Basque language and had
received considerably less of an influx of non-Basque
populations, the nationalists laced their speeches with
praise for the farming way of life and the independent

and honest character of the Basque farmer. It is not surprising that an urban nativist political movement would opt for rural symbolism. It might be argued that the brute effects of the urban environment on the maintenance of Basque culture had become too obvious for anyone to hope to reverse the trend. It might also be argued that the nationalists were in part simply verbalizing the frustrations of too rapid urbanization, a kind of back-to-nature and traditional-values reaction.

IN ANY EVENT, the Basque Nationalist Party enjoyed some initial successes before being forced underground in 1921 under the dictatorship of Primo de Rivera. With the new climate of political freedom that swept Spain with the advent of the Republic in 1931, however, the Basque Nationalist Party was able to surface on the national scene. A major development was the transfer of control within the party to its younger, more active members. By 1931, the first generation of Basque nationalists from the days of Sabino Arana had aged, and under the repression of Primo de Rivera, many of its members had become disillusioned. However, in 1931, a new dynamism emerged under the leadership of José Antonio Aguirre, a twenty-seven-year-old lawyer, industrialist, and former president of the powerful youth organization *Acción Católica* in Bizkaia. Aguirre and other young members of the leadership core successfully campaigned for election to the Spanish *Cortes*, the parliament in Madrid. The first generation of Basque nationalists had laid the foundations for a Basque cultural revitalization and achieved local political gains. The second converted the movement into a serious and respectable factor in Spain's political life.

By 1931, the Basque Nationalist Party had wrested control of the electorate in Bizkaia and Gipuzkoa from the formaerly dominent Carlist Party. The Basque delegates to the parliament in Madrid began to clamor for home rule. In June 1932, a congress was held in Iruña to discuss adoption of a statute of autonomy. The Nafarroans rejected the plan by a narrow vote, while the delegates of the other three provinces adopted it. In 1932, the statute was approved by a plebiscite in the three provinces of Araba, Gipuzkoa, and Bizkaia. The only province that it failed to carry was Nafarroa, which remained Carlist in political orientation, although even there, Basque nationalism was making some inroads.

T HE REPUBLICAN government in Madrid, however, failed to act on the plebiscite, despite the fact it had already granted a statute of autonomy to Catalonia. Many Basque nationalists believe that the Republican government, always suspicious of the Spanish church, distrusted the Basques for their traditional clericalism. The Basques' demand for direct relations with the Vatican posed a major obstacle to granting of the statute.

In any event, the Spanish Civil War began in 1936, and the beleaguered Republican government hastily granted the Basques their autonomy in order to retain their loyalty. In October of that year, Aguirre, then the leader of the Basque delegation to Madrid, was named president of the Basque government. Most of Nafarroa and Araba had already fallen to the forces of General Franco, but the provinces of Gipuzkoa and Bizkaia prepared for war, fielded an army, issued passports and a currency, and sent out diplomatic missions to foreign countries. The first Basque government represented a coalition of political forces that included Spanish Republicans, Socialists, and Communists. However, Basque nationalists held the key posts, including the presidency.

The effort was to be both painful and short-lived. The Basque army was outnumbered and underequipped, and the Basque provinces, along with Asturias and Santander, were cut off from the remaining Republican-held areas of Spain. Within nine months, Basque resistance collapsed, and the Basque government was in exile in Paris.

The aftermath of the Civil War was extremely difficult for the Basque Country. An occupation army remained behind, all Basque-language publications were prohibited, and it was made illegal to speak the language in public. Persons with activist records in the Basque Nationalist Party were tried, some of them receiving prison sentences and others being executed. Therefore, at the conclusion of the Spanish Civil War in 1939, those Basque nationalists remaining in Spain were either in prison or paralyzed by fear. Thousands of nationalists were in exile in France, and many were emigrating to join relatives in the Basque diaspora, notably in Latin America. The coalition Basque government continued to operate in Paris, where it propagandized against the Franco regime. The Basque Nationalist Party was headquartered in the French Basque area, where most of its efforts were directed toward assisting refugees to become established locally or to emigrate. Exiled Basque political leaders residing in Latin America directed their efforts to radicalizing local Basques. They enjoyed considerable success and were able to found anti-Franco political journals, notably in Buenos Aires, Caracas, Santiago de Chile, and Mexico City.

A FURTHER BLOW to Basque nationalism came in the form of the German invasion of France. Aguirre and other members of the Basque government were forced to flee out of fear that the German authorities would extradite them to Spain. Thus, during the Second World War, much of the leadership of both the Basque government and the Basque Nationalist Party fled to Latin America. Aguirre and some key figures settled for a period in New York City, where they lobbied the U.S.

government and the nascent United Nations for official recognition of Basque political sovereignty.

At the conclusion of the Second World War, euphoria swept the movement, for Franco's days appeared to be numbered. In the eyes of the international community, he was identified with Hitler and Mussolini. The community of nations boycotted Spain both politically and economically, and exiled Spanish political groups gained new respectability, since they would likely dictate the political future of the Spanish nation. The leadership of the Basque nationalists returned to France and planned the details of their resumption of power. However, Franco proved to be considerably more resilient than anticipated. He turned Spain in upon itself, declaring that the nation would get along without the rest of the world. The years from 1945 to 1951 were particularly difficult. Spain was still smarting from its terrible Civil War, and the imposed economic and political isolation precluded its participation in the Marshall Plan and frustrated most of its own efforts to recuperate.

In 1951, the United States, pursuing a Cold War policy of containment of Communism, approached the Franco regime with a request for air bases. Franco exacted in return diplomatic recognition and massive amounts of economic and military aid. The American pact spelled the beginning of the end of Spain's isolation. Recognition by the United States provided Franco with a modicum of international respectability; correspondingly, Spanish resistance groups, such as the Basque nationalists, suffered a serious blow.

THESE DEVELOPMENTS produced profound disillusionment among the Basque nationalists. The movement was no longer the heir apparent to political authority in northern Spain, but rather was relegated overnight to the status of an outlawed utopian dream. By this time,

Identity
Two rural men conversing in Basque in the company
of their dogs. At the turn of the 20th century, the new
Basque nationalist movement became the dominant
ideological force in the rural areas.
Photo: Joyce Laxalt

---

the aging process in the leadership ranks was becoming
apparent. The second generation of Basque nationalists,
accustomed to exercising real political power during
the Spanish Republic and the few months of Euzkadi's
existence, now found themselves in the position of ini-
tiating a new process of politicization at the grassroots
level—a task that would have to be carried out in the face
of almost impossible odds. What's more, the leadership
had become increasingly conservative and more given
to moderation in its actions. Its financial support was
derived almost exclusively from businessmen and professional persons who were ambivalent regarding total
commitment to revolutionary activities. The decade of

the 1950s was therefore characterized by decay and inde-
cisiveness in the leadership ranks. Some died (Aguirre
himself in 1960), and others simply withdrew from what
they regarded, with much bitterness, as a lost cause.

At the same time, the seeds of schism were bloom-
ing within the ranks of the nationalists. By 1954, the
leaders of the Basque Nationalist Party were concerned
with revitalizing its youth group, Eusko Gaztedi (Basque
Youth), known as EGI. Young persons were encouraged
to become involved in propagandizing by distributing
clandestine literature, writing political grafitti on walls,
and placing Basque flags throughout the Spanish Basque
area. The first sign of schism appeared when a faction of
EGI rejected this moderate course of action in favor of a
hard-line approach. This group founded a new organization known as ETA, which was openly separatist and
which announced through its literature that violence on
the part of the Franco regime would be met by violence.

ALTHOUGH COUCHED in the same nationalist sentiment, the relationship between ETA and the PNV
has been fraught with tension and at times open hostility. The use of terrorist means by ETA has been the main
bone of contention. After Franco's era ended in 1975,
during the post-Franco democracy, the PNV became
again the main Basque political force. In 1978, a new
democratic constitution was passed in Spain, but with
the approval of only one-third of the Basque electorate.
The following year, the Basque Statute of Autonomy
was approved by the majority of the Basques. Under its
provisions, Basques of Euskadi have their own Eusko
Jaurlaritza, the Basque government, with a president,
parliament, taxation system, police force, media, and
university system.

Lesson nine

LEARNING OBJECTIVES

1. To understand the historical context in which Basque nationalism was born.
2. To understand the central ideological tenets of the movement.
3. To understand the roles of Sabino Arana and the Basque National Party in Basque nationalism.
4. To assess the centrality of Basque nationalism in contemporary Basque politics.

REQUIRED READING

James Jacobs, *Hills of Conflict: Basque Nationalism in France,* (Reno: University of Nevada Press, 1994), 1–38.

Stanley Payne, *Basque Nationalism* (Reno: University of Nevada Press, 1975), 61–86.

SUGGESTED READING

Javier Corcuera, *Orígenes, ideología y organización del nacionalismo vasco, 1976–1914* (Madrid: Siglo XXI, 1979).

Marianne Heiberg, *The Making of the Basque Nation* (Cambridge: Cambridge Univeristy Press, 1989).

WRITTEN LESSON FOR SUBMISSION

1. Consider the historical precedents for and against Basque nationalism.
2. In which ways was Arana's nationalism rooted in an "old" tradition, versus being a recent "invention"?
3. Can the genesis and history of Basque nationalism be understood without reference to the French and Spanish states?

4. Is Basque nationalism monolithic, or does it allow
   for variations regarding the use of violence, religious
   belief, cultural pluralism, and so forth?

10 · Basque Political Violence
and the International Discourse of Terrorism

D URING THE early part of the 1960s, ETA was
considerably less activist than its platform promised. The new movement was anathema to the Basque
Nationalist Party, which continued to monopolize the
sources of financial support for Basque nationalism. ETA
became increasingly desperate and initiated a series
of robberies in the Spanish Basque provinces. It tried
to intimidate some of the contributors to the Basque
Nationalist Party, eventually imposing its own "revolutionary tax" under threat of violent retaliation. The early
1960s also witnessed the beginning of ETA violence in
the form of bombings that were carefully planned as
warnings that would not take human lives.

Throughout the 1960s, the rift between ETA and the
Basque Nationalist Party deepened. For ETA activists,
the leaderships of both the Basque Nationalist Party
and Basque government-in-exile had grown old and
were locked into a kind of marriage of convenience with
the Franco regime. That is, in return for a measure of
tolerance of their propaganda activities, the established
Basque Nationalist Party and Basque government-in-
exile had renounced violence as a legitimate means of
attaining their goals, while at the same time hedging
on the question of total separatism. Conversely, the
leadership of these more established Basque nationalist
entities viewed ETA as an upstart whose activities were
both immature and ill timed. The greatest fear in Basque
Nationalist Party circles was that ETA would bring down
the full force of the Franco regime on the Basque provinces, or, by virtue of committing atrocities, would alien-
ate the Basque masses from the cause of Basque nationalism.

The Gernika legacy
Hitler's *Lufwaffe*, on Franco's request, bombed
Gernika. 'Your fight in Spain was a lesson to our
opponents,' were the welcoming words by Hitler to
the pilots who destroyed Gernika. Churchill added:
'Guernica was an experimental horror.'

The early 1960s were characterized by a parallel, but
largely independent acceleration of resistance among
Basque clergymen. In part encouraged by a growing concern within the Catholic Church for strong stands on the
issue of human rights, many young clergymen in Bizkaia and Gipuzkoa began to confront their bishops and
engaged in public denunciations of what they regarded
as the perpetration of cultural genocide against their
parishioners. Thus, in 1960, 339 Basque priests signed
a document of protest calling for a papal investigation

of the Basque question. In many respects, the challenge from the clergy was a more serious problem for Franco than that of the Basque political organizations. Good relations with the Spanish church and the Vatican constituted one of the keystones of the policy of the Franco regime. In return for church support, Franco made a number of concessions, including paying the salaries of Spanish priests and allowing the church disciplinary control over the clergy. Consequently, the vociferous priests had to be treated circumspectly and were in a position to take public stands that were unthinkable for the most ardent Basque-nationalist layman.

THE DECADE of the 1960s was therefore characterized by an acceleration of Basque resistance on two fronts—the secular and the clerical. On the civil front, ETA increased its activities, notably armed holdups and bombings, to the point that by the mid-1960s, it had the strongest claim to leadership of Basque-nationalist activism.

By 1968, the first deaths since the Spanish Civil War and its aftermath plagued Basque nationalism. ETA members and Spanish police were dying in gun battles. In 1968, ETA assassinated Melitón Manzanas, the chief of police of Gipuzkoa. The response from Madrid was the imposition of martial law in the province. This was quickly extended to Bizkaia. The police rounded up hundreds of suspects, including many dissident clergymen. The Basque Country was awash with rumors and accusations of police brutality and torture. Subsequently, a military tribunal, in what came to be known as the Burgos Trial, convicted several persons of the Manzanas assassination, imposing capital punishments. However, due process was so patently violated that it triggered a massive international protest that forced the Franco government to commute the sentences.

Further exacerbating the division between it and the Basque Nationalist Party, ETA turned sharply to the left of the political spectrum. Its propaganda became increasingly laced with the notion that the free Basque state or Euskadi should be established on Marxist-Leninist principles. In point of fact, during the 1970s, ETA itself splintered into at least two factions over the issue of whether the primary goal was Basque nationalism as a narrowly defined local issue or Basque nationalism as a facet of the wider struggle of the oppressed peoples of the world. The internal debate within ETA over socialism as the future political platform for the Basques clearly alienated many members of the Basque Nationalist Party.

However, the schism between ETA and the Basque Nationalist Party during the Franco years should not be exaggerated. There was relatively broad-based sympathy for ETA as the most effective tool against the Spanish state, even among those who were too ambivalent or fearful to declare their open support for it. ETA operatives pursued by the police frequently reached France along better-established Basque Nationalist Party networks. Indeed, the existence of ETA gave the party additional leverage in its negotiations with Madrid. It could invoke the specter of the radical and violent threat posed by ETA to argue for concessions by Spain to the more moderate mainstream of Basque nationalism.

FRANCO'S DEATH in 1975 changed the Spanish political equation completely. Despite some setbacks and the constant fear of a new right-wing coup, the nation moved swiftly from dictatorship to democracy. In the new political climate, the varying forces were able to test their strength in both the local and parliamentary elections. Thus, a new era of opportunities and pitfalls was initiated for Basque nationalism. Of particular importance had been the decision by the Spanish parliament to set aside a centralist model for the nation in favor of a system of regional autonomies. The various parts of the country were able to constitute themselves into autonomous regions, each with its own leadership largely in charge of local affairs. Certain regions, designated *territorios históricos* (historical territories) in recognition of their marked ethnic uniqueness, have been granted special privileges. The two most prominent examples are Catalonia and the three provinces of Araba, Bizkaia, and Gipuzkoa.

THE PROCESS OF devolution of powers, which began in the late 1970s, is still not complete. However, in the Basque case, since 1979, the three Basque provinces have constituted the region of Euskadi. The new regional Basque government adopted the Aranist flag, elected a parliament and president, and established its own ministries. It has assumed control of the primary and secondary schools, launched a university system, created a police force, established economic development agencies, and created Basque-language media, including a Basque television channel and a radio station.

While these gains are more than modest, in themselves they pose in stark terms the question of which Basque nationalist model is to be adopted, and by whom, and which provides the historical background for the ongoing violence. It is in the new climate of democracy, with tolerance for regional autonomy, that unresolved contradictions within Basque nationalism come to the forefront. The issues may best be posed as a series of dilemmas.

The first dilemma concerns differences concerning the degree of political integration with Spain versus Basque national unity. It manifests itself in at least four dimensions. First, there are splits among Basques between those favoring Spanish national unity versus Basque national sovereignty, as well as between the autonomists and the separatists. Such divisions are reflected in the political parties, which can be grouped broadly into the two categories: the Spanish-oriented versus Basque-oriented and the Basque "moderates" versus the "radical" nationalists. The approximate division of electoral strength during the democratic period has been about 55 to 45 percent in favor of the Basque nationalists and, within their ranks, the Basque Nationalist Party has managed to maintain a slight majority with about 28 percent of the overall vote, whereas the various parties that have acted as political arms of ETA typically have captured about 10 to 15 percent.

A second dimension of the political integration dilemma is the question of Nafarroa. We may recall that Basque nationalism began in Bizkaia and found a strong echo in Gipuzkoa. It was much less successful in Araba. In Nafarroa, a former independent kingdom in its own right and the bastion of Carlism, Basque nationalism met with considerable suspicion and opposition. However, the Basque nationalist vision incorporates Nafarroa into a unified Euskadi. Basque nationalists were therefore chagrined when the Nafarroans opted to constitute themselves into their own autonomous region within post-Franco Spain.

THE THIRD dimension of the political-integration dilemma is the fact that the Basque government must negotiate its powers and budgets on two fronts simultaneously. There is, of course, the constant negotiation of power with Madrid. In fact, some of the transfers of functions that were agreed upon statutorily, social security being paramount, have yet to be effected. Consequently, the whole process has been drawn out and contentious and frequently produces exasperation and bitterness on both sides. But at the same time, the relationship

The war of the flags
In the summer of 2006, in Lesaka, Nafarroa, the traditional emblem of the chains of Nafarroa (on the left) hangs from a balcony side by side with the Basque ikurriña (flag) designed by Sabino de Arana. Both were displayed (but not hung from the flag pole reserved for the Spanish flag in order to avoid flying the latter symbol).
Photo: Xabier Irujo

---

between the Basque government and its provinces has proven a difficult one, as well. Each of the three provinces has its own government or *diputacion*; each has a lengthy foral tradition and a jealously guarded sense of historical uniqueness. Since the Basque government receives most of its resources from funds made available by the individual *diputaciones* on a voluntary basis, at times, provincial interests may clash with regional ones.

Finally, the fourth dimension of the political-integration dilemma is posed by the French Basque Country. Although Basque nationalist sentiment is on the increase there, support remains in the single digits, and it is difficult to foresee a possible union of French and Spanish Basques. Political reality notwithstanding, the irredentist Basque-nationalist agenda demands an independent Basque state that includes Nafarroa and Iparralde, irrespective of the desires of their respective electorates.

The second dilemma posed by recent developments regards the issue of social integration. For the past century, or since the beginning of the industrialization of the Basque Country in the late nineteenth century, the in-migration of non-Basque Spaniards into the Basque Country has far exceeded the natural increment of the populace. At the same time, there has been considerable depopulation of the rural districts, the traditional bastion of Basque culture. It is therefore common to speak in terms of "the two communities." At times, there is considerable tension between them. This nonnative Basque community is a potential target of opportunity for the Spanish-oriented political parties, particularly since it might also be mobilized along social class lines. Still, many nonnative Basques have come to espouse and identify with Basque nationalism, even providing ETA with some of its most dedicated operatives.

ALL OF THIS points to a third dilemma faced by Basque nationalists, that of the cultural integration of Euskadi. For most Basque nationalists today, the persistence of Basque culture is equated with the survival of the language. The Basque government is committed to a major effort to foster it in the educational system, the media, and the civil bureaucracy. In a society in which only about 25 percent of the populace speaks Basque, such policies have created a degree of resentment, the critics questioning their cost-benefits return.

It is against such historical, social, and political background that ETA continued its campaign of violence throughout the 1980s and 1990s. ETA is responsible for more than eight hundred deaths; the Spanish police forces are responsible for about two hundred deaths. During the mid-1980s, Spain's Socialist government organized the state terrorist group, GAL, which killed twenty-seven Basque refugees in southern France. The practice of state torture has been routinely denounced by organizations such as Amnesty International.

DURING THE 1990s, a new generation of radical nationalists became involved in the practice of *kale borroka*, or urban warfare, against the Spanish state and against Basque as well as Spanish political parties. Although not strictly classifiable as "terrorism," the street violence of nationalist youth, perceived as the future recruits of ETA, created unprecedented levels of social anxiety. The work of anthropologist Begoña Aretxaga has focused on the political culture and the social dynamics of this new generation of violent activists, one that was born in a democratic regime and perpetrated its activism despite the growing opposition to it within both Spanish and Basque societies. For Aretxaga, the problem of terrorism is complicated in the Basque case by the fact that it does not so much denote a particular kind of violence as it constitutes an overdetermined discursive and performative site. It is a field that condenses a variety of social anxieties—such as the redefinition of Basque identity and the Basque nation within the global system, the definition of the state in a country constituted by autonomous ethnic regions, and the status of democracy vis-à-vis the persistence of illegal state violence in the form of torture and paramilitary assassinations.

Responses and threats

The political struggle between Spain's central government and ETA militants is nearly half a century old. While hundreds of people have died in the conflict, it is also a war of words. Here ETA spokesmen disguise their identities while giving a news release.

Source: Francisco Letamendia, Euskadi: pueblo y nación *(Donosti / San Sebastián: 1990).*

THIS NEW form of youth violence emerged in conjunction with the disclosure of the involvement of the Spanish government, the then-ruling Socialist party, and security forces in the assassination of Basque separatists under the cover of a paramilitary group called GAL (Grupos Antiterroristas de Liberación—Antiterrorist Liberation Groups). This operation became known in the mass media as the state's "dirty war." There was furthermore the emergence of a Basque police force ready to employ innovative technology and techniques, such as street video surveillance, hoods to disguise officers' identities (and hence avoid accountability), and its own secret police. In turn, nationalist youths resorted to alternative technologies, such as hand-held radios and the networking through the Internet, as ways to combat state control. They also resorted to the use of their own hoods while rioting and to bombing police vehicles with Molotov cocktails.

As described by Aretxaga, the rioting techniques and technologies of control transformed the political culture into a ghostly space in which both state violence and youth violence were at once all-pervasive and impossible to locate within a single structure, organization, or site. Mirroring stories about the violence of both sides circulated through different social channels, creating a social reality of fear where the boundary between the real and the fantastic became impossible to distinguish.

ARETXAGA´S RESEARCH determined that the nationalist youth movement is a highly contradictory formation, at once deeply anti-authoritarian and rigidly dogmatic in its nationalist ideology, borrowing from transnational culture, yet deeply entrenched in local networks. These tensions are expressed in the relations that these nationalist youth have with other groups within the nationalist movement, including the more radical ones. Even the latter have often opposed the youngsters' sabotage tactics. An example of this conflict surfaced during ETA's cease-fire (1998–99), when the leadership of the radical nationalist movement unsuccessfully asked the nationalist youth to stop their *kale borroka* in order to facilitate the peace initiative. The response was more or less 370 attacks carried out during the period, prompting the Spanish Ministry of the Interior to label the youth violence as "low-intensity terrorism." Its persistence informed the state's refusal to accept ETA's representation that violence had been suspended. The question that interested Aretxaga was not only how nationalist youth perceives and reacts against a state, but also how the perception and fear of these youngsters by state officials as actual or potential terrorists delineates state forms of violent intervention that then reinforce and encourage additional *kale borroka*.

There were also significant changes in the political thermostat during the late 1990s. When, in the summer of 1997, a Popular Party town councilor from the town of Ermua, Miguel Angel Blanco, was kidnapped and executed, massive demonstrations against the murder brought millions of Basques and Spaniards into the streets. Ordinary people lost the fear of publicly airing their revulsion for ETA. A social and political movement emerged from those events, known as "The Spirit of Ermua." As never before, terrorism was seen as an international stain on all Basque nationalists. It was a turning point.

ONE YEAR LATER, a second major shift transpired. In September 1998, all Basque nationalist parties, various social movements, and even the Spanish party called The United Left signed a document that became known as the Lizarra Agreement. Within days, ETA announced a cease-fire that lasted for fourteen months. The document invoked the model of the Irish peace process. In simple terms, it called for ETA to stop armed activity and proposed that the Basque political parties, as the sole representatives of the democratic electorate, find a solution to what nationalists see as the impasse to their legitimate aspirations. In practical terms, the agreement implied that the moderate Basque nationalists, rather than conducting politics as usual with the Spanish state, would take the demands for sovereignty made by ETA's followers more seriously. It is not entirely clear what such claims would entail, but for most nationalists, the result would probably be embodied in something like the right of self-determination. Sovereignty or self-determination may differ from full independence, although the latter remains the stated goal for a significant minority.

FOR MOST Basques, terrorism against democratic Spain had become so abhorrent that ETA's cease-fire created a sense of euphoria. Furthermore, the sudden unity among the nationalists, leaving aside decades of bitter internal enmities, signaled the possibility of a working majority in the Basque parliament. This made Madrid nervous. The interior minister declared that the cease-fire was a "trap." Months went by, and nothing transpired on the negotiation front. The Lizarra forces staged in vain huge demonstrations demanding political concessions, such as the transfer closer to home of Basque political prisoners dispersed in the remotest parts of Spain. More ominously, street violence by pro-ETA youths became daily news. The police continued arresting people allegedly associated with ETA. After eight months of cease-fire, it was reported that a meeting had taken place in Switzerland between the representatives of the Spanish government and ETA. But the real news came a few months later: French police had arrested the young woman who had been one of ETA's two negotiators. The arrest, they claimed, was the fortuitous result of a traffic violation. Accustomed to the close collaboration of the French and Spanish police forces, most Basque nationalists needed no explanation. It was akin to the Irish Republican Army's spokesman Gerry Adams being "fortuitously" arrested by the British police. There was not even an echo of these events in the international media. And there were no more meetings, of course. Soon ETA was back in action.

By this juncture, the Popular Party's government in Madrid, under José María Aznar's leadership, had essentially severed its ties with Eusko Jaurlaritza. During his first term in office, Aznar had been forced into a pact with both Catalan and Basque nationalists in order to form the coalition government that ended the long-standing rule of the Socialist Party at the level of Spanish state politics. In the subsequent election, Aznar's party gained sufficient seats in the Spanish parliament to eschew its dependence on its ethnonationalist partners. The Partido Popular continued a somewhat shaky collaboration with the Catalans, but struck a confrontational attitude toward the entire spectrum of Basque nationalists. Indeed, it became increasingly clear that depicting both Eusko Jaurlaritza and the Basque Nationalist Party as sympathizers, when not outright supporters, of ETA's terrorism was emerging as the PP's main electoral strategy on the Spanish national scene. Aznar even refused to return Basque President Juan José Ibarretxe's telephone calls.

THERE WAS also a rather broad-based assault by the Spanish judiciary on Basque cultural and political institutions. The only Basque-language newspaper was closed and its editorial staff imprisoned. The radical left Basque political party, Batasuna (roughly equivalent to Ulster's Sinn Fein) was outlawed. When the leadership of the Basque parliament refused to expel the democratically elected members that represented Batasuna, arguing that to so do would destroy utterly the Basque parliament's integrity and independence, its president and executive committee were criminally indicted for their refusal and faced prosecution that might lead to their imprisonment.

Meanwhile, the Basque parliament asked President Ibarretxe to inform it of the details regarding (the

The condemned
The military trial of the six defendants (left to right:
Eduardo Uriarte, Jokin Goristidi, Xabier Izko, Mario
Onaindia, Xabier Larena, and José María Darronsoro)
accused of being ETA's perpetrators of the assassination of Gipuzkoa's chief of secret police, Melitón
Manzanas (August 2, 1968). They were all given death
sentences. The trial triggered an international protest and pleas for clemency from heads of state and
the Vatican. The sentences were commuted and the
prisoners subsequently freed after Franco's death.
Source: Francisco Letamendia, Euskadi: pueblo
y nación *(Donosti/San Sebastián: 1990)*

obviously strained) relations between Eusko Jaurlaritza
and Madrid, requesting as well a proposal for a plan of
action. In 2002, Ibarretxe complied, putting in play for
the parliament's deliberation possible modification and
eventual approval a document that came to be known as
the "Plan Ibarretxe." It called for a new political arrangement under which Euskadi would be in a relatively voluntary or free association with other Spanish regions
within a single Spanish state. Under the plan, the
Basques would relinquish a claim to absolute political
sovereignty in return for relative political independence.

The Plan Ibarretxe was vilified by all of the Spanish
political parties, both within and outside the Basque
Country. Under the Spanish Constitution, for such a

proposal to acquire legal effect required the approval of the Spanish *Cortes*. However, Ibarretxe had announced his intention to submit whatever plan that emerged with the Basque parliament's approval to a popular (if not legally binding) referendum of the Basque electorate. This prompted passage of a law in the Spanish *Cortes* that, in such an eventuality, would have resulted directly in Ibarretxe's imprisonment for several years.

Such was the state of affairs in early 2004 as Spain prepared for national elections in March. According to all of the polls, the PP was favored to win, largely due to an anti-Basque / anti-terrorist campaign that seemed to have defused the popular discontent with Aznar's decision to place Spanish troops in Iraq and the perception that the Aznar government had mishandled a major oil spill off the Galician coast. The only real question regarding the pending election was whether it would confer upon the PP the absolute majority that would facilitate even more its domestic and international agendas.

HOWEVER, ON March 11, a few days before the election, there was a series of coordinated lethal bombings at Madrid train stations during the morning rush hour that produced more than two hundred fatalities. While a stunned nation attempted to process the events, the Aznar government immediately attributed the attacks to ETA, despite considerable evidence to the contrary. Unfortunately for the PP, enough of the facts emerged (the culpability of Muslim fundamentalists who were retaliating against Spain's involvement in Iraq) before the election to trigger anti-PP demonstrations throughout Spain. Aznar was voted out of office, to be replaced by the Socialist leader José Luis Rodríguez Zapatero.

Since assuming power, Zapatero has demonstrated a willingness to seek compromise with both Basque and Catalan nationalists. He is clearly attempting to accommodate greater regional autonomy without completely compromising Spanish national unity. It is obviously a difficult political balancing act (particularly given the PP's harsh criticism as the party of the opposition), and the negotiations have been tense. However, there is now dialogue, with channels of communication between Gasteiz and Madrid. Ibarretxe was even invited to present his plan to the Spanish *Cortes* (where, predictably, it met with a cool reception), and the charges against the leadership of the Basque Parliament were dropped.

REGARDING ETA, the events and the discourse of global terrorism have once again overtaken it. After the attacks of September 11, 2001 and the War on Terror declared by President Bush, ETA remains the only Western European "terrorist" group, to the chagrin of a significant majority of Basques. The Madrid bombings on March 11, 2004, added to the sense that "old" ethnonationalist violence such as ETA's was now a thing of the past. If, in the international context of the twentieth-century revolutionary wars of liberation in Cuba, Algeria, and elsewhere, the initial campaign of anti-Francoist violence had been deemed liberationist and legitimate, the new post-9 / 11 global war on terror undermined the acceptance of ETA's violent historical protagonism. Zapatero announced his willingness to negotiate with ETA if it would first renounce violence. In March of 2006, the organization did so and as of this writing (July 2006) is currently engaged in negotiations with the Spanish government. The Ulster model, whereby the decades-long conflict in Northern Ireland has seemingly been resolved through compromises, and the commitment of the IRA to pursue its political goals as part of a democratic rather than violent process clearly informs the present attempts to resolve the Basque question. Stay tuned!

Lesson ten

LEARNING OBJECTIVES
1. To survey the genesis and history of ETA.
2. To analyze the political and moral dilemmas posed by political violence.
3. To identify the ritual and mythical aspects of recent Basque violence.
4. To trace the trajectory of Basque nationalists from freedom fighters to terrorists.
5. To situate Basque nationalism in the international discourse of terrorism.

REQUIRED READING
Joseba Zulaika, *Basque Violence* (Reno: University of Nevada Press, 1988), 74–101.
————, and William A. Douglass, *Terror and Taboo* (New York: Routledge, 1996), 31–63.

SUGGESTED READING
Cyrus E. Zirakzadeh, *A Rebellious People: Basques, Protests, and Politics* (Reno: University of Nevada Press, Reno, 1991).
Robert P. Clark, *Negotiating with ETA: Obstacles to Peace in the Basque Country, 1975–1988* (Reno: University of Nevada Press, 1990).

WRITTEN LESSON FOR SUBMISSION
1. How would you characterize the main differences between the Basque Nationalist Party's nationalism and that of ETA?

2. From an ethnographic perspective, how would you mediate, or refuse to mediate, the existence of competing interpretations of the violence in the Basque Country as "revolutionary" or "terrorist"? Are there clear criteria to distinguish one from the other, or does it depend mostly on the political context?

3. How do the writings regarding terrorism by journalists, politicians, anthropologists, novelists, and terrorism experts differ?

11 · Basque Emigration and Diaspora
The Americas

I N THE AMERICAN West, the Basque immigrant is
equated with the sheepherder. As the stereotype goes,
the Basques herded sheep in their Pyrenean homeland
and consequently were either recruited or came of their
own accord to the American West to herd sheep once
the opportunity became available. Like any stereotype,
this one is only partly accurate. So let us consider a brief
overview of the history of Basque emigration, a history
that encompasses several centuries and embraces the
four corners of the globe.

From earliest recorded times, there is evidence that the
excess population of the Basque Pyrenees sought opportunity elsewhere. Roman chroniclers tell us of Basques
serving in the Roman legions. During the Middle Ages,
the Basques were heavily involved in sea traffic in the
Mediterranean and Atlantic waters, and they established
trading missions in England and the Low Countries. As
Spain emerged as an imperial power in the fifteenth century, Basques commonly served as mercenaries in places
such as Sicily.

However, the real explosion in Basque emigration
came when Spain discovered the New World. Indeed, as
we have seen, Basques were instrumental in the discovery. The first New World colony failed due to schism
between the Basques and non-Basques left ashore by
Columbus during his first voyage.

Basques subsequently provided many of the explorers,
administrators, and clergymen to Spain's New World
enterprise. They were prominent in the ranks of Cortez's
forces and bore the main brunt of the thrust into present-day northern Mexico and the American Southwest.
The first archbishop of Nueva España was the Basque

Juan de Zumárraga. Basques founded the mining districts of places such as Zacatecas and Fresnillo. Much of northern Mexico was christened "Nueva Vizcaya," with its capital of Durango named for Zumárraga's natal town in Bizkaia.

From the outset of the colonial enterprise, The Basque Country was viewed as a prime source of permanent colonists, as well. In 1511, the Spanish king ordered his agents to recruit emigrants in the mountains of Gipuzkoa, where "there are many inhabitants and few resources, so that workers will go out to those parts."

Seafaring was another vital service provided by the Basques to the colonial enterprise. According to the historian John Lynch, between the years 1520 and 1580, fully 80 percent of the movement of goods on the American run depended on Basques vessels and ships' crews. Individual Basques were key players during the sixteenth century in several New World venues and undertakings. Juan de Zumárraga introduced the first printing press to the New World. Fray Francisco de Vitoria defended the humanity of Native Americans at a time when they were considered to be subhuman and therefore candidates for enslavement. He is the acknowledged founder of international law. Domingo Martínez de Irala founded Asunción (Paraguay), and Juan de Garay was the founder of Buenos Aires, as was Bruno Mauricio de Zabala of Montevideo.

IN THE NEW World itself, the Basques were particularly successful in commerce. This was so much the case that at several times and in several places they were denounced for controlling an area's economy. In Santiago de Chile, this included the import-export trade and in San Luís de Potosí the silver mines, while in Venezuela, the Royal Gipuzcoan Company of Caracas emerged as the de facto government. In such cases, the Basques

Ethnic cuisine
This sign of a Basque restaurant in Bakersfield, California, employs the twin symbols of Old-World folk costume and dancing and the New-World occupation of sheep husbandry while projecting the fame of Basque cuisine.
Photo: William Douglass

were so prone to act in ethnic group terms and were so successful at protecting their interests that they triggered anti-Basque violence. Several Basques were killed and others were driven from Potosí by irate non-Basques, and in Caracas, royal troops had to be sent in to quell a rebellion by a mob shouting "Long live the king; death to the Basques."

THE EXAMPLES could be multiplied, but these suffice to show that throughout the three centuries of the existence of Spain's New World colonial empire, Basques were prominent in the ranks of the mercenaries, missionaries, mariners, and merchants. Indeed, they were disproportionately represented in the ranks of the colonial elite.

The political and economic clout of the Old World–born colonists ended, of course, with the New World independence movements that began in the early nineteenth century. Some of the most prominent figures in these revolutions were of Basque descent—including Augustín de Itúrbide in Mexico, Simón de Bolivar in northern South America, and José de San Martín in the Río de la Plata region. In Cuba, Puerto Rico, and the Philippines, the Basque colonial elite persisted until the end of the century, when Spain finally lost these colonies in the Spanish-American War.

The liberation of the colonies did not, however, end Basque emigration to Latin America. The new nations of South America, particularly Argentina and Uruguay, had vast territories and few inhabitants. They therefore encouraged immigration from Europe, and from Spain in particular. The first half of the nineteenth century was an especially difficult period in the Basque Country, because the area was rocked by both the Napoleonic Wars and the First Carlist War. There were therefore many refugees anxious to try their lot in a new country.

Many thousands of Basques left for southern South America.

This emigration represented a cross section of Old World Basque society. It included intellectuals, lawyers, doctors, and skilled workers. It also included a large segment of peasant farmers. The educated found it possible to secure employment in the population centers, but the unskilled were forced to the outer fringes of European civilization, where they became pioneer settlers. Basque peasants quickly gravitated into sheep raising under frontier conditions. Range was plentiful and could either be settled, where unclaimed, or rented or sharecropped when held in vast tracts by Argentine *estancieros*, or ranchers. Sheep raising presented an ideal prospect under such circumstances, since their flocking tendency made it possible for a herder and his dog to care for a thousand animals without the expense of fencing. A man could move with his charges, adjusting to seasonal changes on his range. This nomadic lifestyle made it possible for the immigrants to acquire assets with minimal or no capital investment in such things as land, fencing, and buildings. Consequently, by the middle of the nineteenh century, there were hundreds and possibly thousands of small-scale Basque sheepmen in Argentina and Uruguay.

THERE WERE some fabulous success stories. A French Basque, Pierre Luro, for example, became a legend in Argentina. He entered the country penniless, and by the time of his death, he owned almost one million acres, three hundred thousand sheep, and one hundred thousand cows. He was one of the richest men in the country. During his lifetime, he was said to have brought over more than two thousand Basques, whom he employed and then provided with their own livestock and working capital. Luro was not alone, since a list of the fifty largest landowners in Argentina in the second half of the twentieth century includes twelve Basques.

One could develop a similar scenario for several other Latin American countries. Notably, the ones with significant Basque populations are Chile, Argentina, Uruguay, Venezuela, Peru, Cuba, and Mexico. In Argentina alone, by one estimate, today Basques and their descendants constitute more than one million of the nation's thirty million inhabitants. In contrast, the most conservative interpretation would place their number at no more than one hundred thousand. The Basques of Latin America also constitute an important economic, social, and political elite that is all out of proportion to their numbers. In addition to some of the wealthiest ranchers and industrialists of the region, many Latin American presidents and dictators have been of Basque descent. Consequently, to be Basque today in Latin America is to have a special identity that is displayed and sometimes manipulated for political and economic purposes. This is in sharp contrast to the situation in the American West, where until recently, Basques maintained a low profile and were largely ignored, when not denigrated, by their non-Basque neighbors.

WE MIGHT, then, turn to the question of Basque settlement in the American West. There were, of course, precursors of the modern Basque immigrants in the region. Since California and the American Southwest were part of the Spanish empire, Basque explorers and missionaries visited the area. In 1598, Juan de Oñate was the first to establish a permanent European colony on what would become U.S. soil—in the present state of New Mexico. Somewhat prophetically, he brought with him the first sheep to be introduced in the United States. Several of the governors in California during the Spanish and Mexican periods of that state's colonial history were

Basque. However, there is little or no continuity from this Hispanic baseline carrying over into the Anglo or American period of the region's history.

Rather, the two beginnings of the modern Basque presence in the American West date from the days of the California Gold Rush. We have noted that, by the mid-nineteenth century, there were thousands of Basques in southern South America who were drawn from modest Old World backgrounds. While, as we have seen, many were to carve out brilliant New World successes, the majority had little intention of remaining permanently. Rather, most hoped to spend a few years acquiring sufficient savings to return to Europe to buy a farm or start a small business. When news of gold in California reached Chile and Argentina, the rush was on. The two South American nations were better situated for the race geographically than was Europe or even the eastern United States. Many South American Basques opted to try their luck.

OF THE BASQUES who first entered the mining camps, many quickly became disillusioned and left the mountains for the coastal districts. In Southern California, they found agricultural conditions that were not unlike those of southern South America. Consequently, several acquired sheep and either leased land from ranchers or went out to the margins of European settlement.

The few Basque sheepmen of the 1850s quickly multiplied into several hundred by the 1870s, as the established immigrants sent back to Europe for kinsmen and fellow villagers to employ as herders. The newcomers tended to work for their benefactor for a few years, took their wages in sheep, and eventually hived off in search of new range. In this fashion, the Basque sheepmen

The liberator
Simon Bolivar (1783–1830) led several independence
movements in South America. He freed Venezuela,
Colombia, Ecuador, Peru and Bolivia (named after
him). His ancestors came from the Basque town of
Bolivar, Bizkaia.

---

proliferated over much of Southern California and
pushed into the Central Valley region, as well.

THERE WAS one notable ecological difference between
California and South America. In the pampas, the
outfits were reasonably sedentary in that the terrain
was one unending plain. In California, desert valleys
were flanked by high mountains. The Basque sheepmen

quickly developed a pattern of transhumance, in which the herds wintered on the valley floors and summered in the high-mountain pastures. As competition for suitable range became more intense, the nomads sometimes wandered over several hundred miles during the year.

This pattern of transhumance proved to be adaptable to most of the arid regions of the American West. Thus, by the 1880s, itinerant Basque sheepherders had spread across Arizona, New Mexico, and Nevada. In the 1890s, they penetrated southern Idaho. During the first decade of the twentieth century, they were present in Utah, Wyoming, Colorado, Montana, and eastern Washington.

Consequently, within little more than half a century, the Basque sheepman became ubiquitous throughout the open-range livestock districts of the American West. Whether as operators of an itinerant band, employees of such an operation, or hired herders for a ranch-based property, Basques had become the esteemed herders on Basque and non-Basque-owned outfits alike. This group reputation for skill and dedication to herding made the Basques one of the prime architects of the region's sheep industry. At the same time, their very success in the competition evoked considerable hostility.

THE ITINERANT sheep bands, "tramps" to their detractors, operated on the premise that everyone had equal access to range on the public lands on a first-come basis. While legally correct, this interpretation ignored other realities. Wherever there was sufficient water to sustain permanent settlement, ranch-based cattle and sheep operations appeared, established primarily by American citizens. The ranchers exerted a de facto claim to the public lands contiguous to their holdings and forged understandings accordingly with their settled neighbors. The appearance of the itinerant sheep band threatened such arrangements, and the resulting

confrontations provided copy to the newspapers and litigation to the courts. While blown all out of proportion
in Western fiction and Hollywood depictions, there were
isolated cases of violence and even death.

Consequently, then, although the Basque itinerant
operators were technically within their legal rights to
graze everywhere on the public lands, as a group, they
were both hated and virtually without political power.
Few were even U.S. citizens, and no American politician would risk alienating his ranching constituency
by defending the foreign interlopers. Consequently, as
political pressure mounted, there began to emerge a
patchwork of local legislation aimed at hampering the
itinerants. A favorite was the so-called three-mile-limit
law, which prohibited grazing stock within three miles
of a rancher's fence line. Since this effectively extended
local jurisdiction over federal lands, such laws were regularly declared unconstitutional.

HOWEVER, ON another front, the ranchers made
greater progress. By the turn of the century, the
American frontier was all but closed, and there was
growing concern over the effects of overgrazing on the
public lands. The settled ranchers therefore found an
ally among the environmentalists of the day as both
pushed for creation of the national forest system. During
the first decade of the twentieth century, vast tracts of
the public lands were set aside as forest reserves. Grazing was still to be permitted, but under carefully regulated conditions. Rights were allocated by local boards
consisting of settled ranchers. The applicant had to own
private ranch property, and its livestock-carrying capacity determined the grazing allotment on the public range.
Aliens were ineligible to apply. There was little doubt
regarding the target and scapegoat of the exercise. By
1909, newspapers througout the open-range districts

Riding the range
Two mounted herders with sheep hooks patrol a
lambing ground in spring to assist ewes having difficulty
giving birth.
Photo: Richard Lane

carried headlines such as "Basque Sheepmen Are
Excluded from Reserve."

THE SUCCESS of their detractors in excluding the
Basque itinerants from the public lands proved to be
only partial. In fact, in many areas, it only exacerbated
the situation. The forest reserves encompassed only the
higher, timbered sections of what had formerly served
the itinerants as summer range. However, in some areas,
particularly in much of Nevada and parts of Oregon and
Idaho, there were treeless mountain ranges that were
sufficiently high to provide some summer grazing. The
itinerants, then, began to concentrate around places

such as Steens Mountain, near Burns, Oregon, or Diamond Mountain in eastern Nevada. Within a short time, the situation was indeed critical. By one account, on Diamond Mountain, there were no fewer than seventeen sheep outfits, and the laggards had to wait until the wee hours of the morning to water their animals at the scarce springs.

It was not until 1934 that the question was resolved when the Taylor Grazing Act brought the remainder of the public lands under the jurisdiction of the Department of the Interior to be administered by the Bureau of Land Management. Again, the Basques were instrumental in triggering the legislation. The bill's author, Congressman Edward Taylor, was from Colorado. The western part of his state had become a favorite summering area for Basque itinerants, and Taylor was under considerable pressure from his voting constituents.

THE TAYLOR Grazing Act spelled the end of the era of the itinerant Basque sheepman. A few bought ranch property, became citizens, and acquired their own grazing allotments. Others went to town and established small businesses. Most simply sold out and returned to Europe.

Meanwhile, there were other developments that were affecting the Basque colony of the American West. During the 1920s, U.S. immigration laws were tightened considerably as the nation questioned the wisdom of allowing continued massive immigration. There was a distinctive bias against southern Europeans in the new quota system. The French nationals' quota remained high, so the essentially French Basque population of California and of parts of Nevada, Colorado, Wyoming, and Montana was little affected. However, in 1924, the Spanish nationals' quota was set at 131 persons annually.

Text continues on page 166 ►►

United States Basque Population 1980, 1990, 2000

State	French Basques		Spanish Basques	
	1980	1990	1980	1990
Alabama	36	24	0	44
Alaska	10	37	33	38
Arizona	152	53	199	298
Arkansas	34	20	0	21
California	3,619		3,813	3,508
Colorado	341	148	168	110
Connecticut	36	22	64	64
Delaware	18	0	0	7
Dist. Of Columbia	22	0	12	16
Florida	201	117	315	334
Georgia	87	11	59	27
Hawaii	10	19	4	29
Idaho	221	166	600	353
Illinois	422	49	66	75
Indiana	94	55	48	0
Iowa	260	20	24	8
Kansas	92	10	18	24
Kentucky	81	11	15	15
Louisiana	133	73	57	38
Maine	22	2	0	21
Maryland	51	60	48	45
Massachusetts	34	37	80	73
Michigan	145	7	28	47
Minnesota	110	24	8	15
Mississippi	7	4	2	0
Missouri	164	27	18	10
Montana	116	66	6	46

For notes see page 166

Basques		Total Basques		
1980	1990	1980	1990	2000
46	14	82	82	107
62	170	105	245	276
749	965	1,100	1,316	1,655
39	63	73	104	71
8,098	12,227	15,530	19,122	20,868
446	679	955	937	1,674
120	233	220	319	262
3	6	21	13	12
29	21	63	37	180
343	738	859	1,189	2,127
77	90	223	128	282
55	121	69	169	175
3,511	5,068	4,332	5,587	6,637
165	321	654*	445	533
18	135	160	190	168
40	31	324	59	50
50	36	160	70	146
36	68	132	94	55
65	115	255	226	354
28	13	50	36	57
148	163	247	268	339
187	227	301	337	383
158	162	331	216	306
102	91	220	130	195
20	24	29	28	64
61	114	243	151	180
268	357	390	469	564

Continued on next page

Continued from previous page

State	French Basques		Spanish Basques	
	1980	**1990**	**1980**	**1990**
Nebraska**	2707	0	6	0
Nevada	371	472	915	776
New Hampshire	3	0	0	0
New Jersey	98	72	134	143
New Mexico	87	63	83	61
New York	202	131	508	242
North Carolina	57	16	48	6
North Dakota	25	0	0	0
Ohio	207	33	31	15
Oklahoma	21	0	5	23
Oregon	369	172	224	298
Pennsylvania	138	23	14	13
Rhode Island	5	0	44	0
South Carolina	24	4	31	14
South Dakota	50	0	7	8
Tennessee	34	2	4	14
Texas	159	98	170	238
Utah	129	148	134	261
Vermont	0	0	0	0
Virginia	168	19	72	59
Washington	124	145	306	154
West Virginia	78	0	5	0
Wisconsin	189	8	5	8
Wyoming	155	146	103	21
TOTALS	11,918	6,001	8,534	7,620

For notes see page 166

Basques		Total Basques		
1980	1990	1980	1990	2000
41	45	2,754	45	85
2,092	3,592	3,378	4,840	6,096
29	53	32	53	158
265	319	497	534	643
291	378	461	502	600
716	927	1,426	1,300	1,252
31	97	136	119	330
0	11	25	11	39
85	155	323	203	230
84	82	110	105	126
1,660	1,787	2,253	2,257	2,627
68	214	220	250	278
40	24	89	24	23
14	30	69	48	76
5	22	62	30	64
16	75	54	91	145
558	912	887	1,248	1,691
610	1,013	873	1,422	1,361
28	2	28	2	34
112	325	352	403	575
704	1,471	1,134	1,770	2,665
23	9	106	9	8
49	85	243	101	98
241	435	499	602	869
22,686	34,315	43,140	47,965	57,793***

Notes on the Basque population table

* There is a compiler's discrepancy of one French Basque in the 1980 Illinois count.

** The results for 1980 are final official tallies provided by the Census Bureau. They clearly incorporate a coding error whereby an (unspecified) ethnic group in the Midwest was counted as "French Basques." Note the huge discrepancy for French Basques reported in 1980 in Nebraska (2,707) versus in 1990 (0). If the results are revised with this error in mind, the national total of French Basques in 1980 may be reduced by about 4,000 persons and the national total for all Baques declines from 43,140 to approximately 39,000.

*** Includes 187 Basques in Puerto Rico. It was not until the 2000 census that Puerto Rican ancestry totals were reported within the overall national count. It should be noted that due to the overall small number of Basques in the United States, the Census Bureau decided not to disaggregate the French Basque, Spanish Basque and generic Basque categories within the 2000 census.

▶ Text continued from page 161.
This effectively blocked entry of Spanish Basques and profoundly affected the largely Bizkaian colony of Idaho, Oregon, and northern Nevada. Furthermore, by this time, most of the herders were Spanish Basque, so there was a clear potential for a labor crisis in the sheep industry as men retired, died, returned to Europe, or turned to other occupations. The problem came to a head during the Second World War, when most sectors of the American economy experienced a shortage of manpower. The situation was particularly acute in a sheep industry, in which wages were traditionally low.

Stepping into the future
Basque children and their teacher dancing at a Basque
festival in Ketchum-Hailey, Idaho, October 15, 2006.
Dance is a key marker of ethnic identity and cultural
transmission among diaspora Basques.
Photo: Xabier Irujo

DURING THE war years, Congress began to pass a
series of what came to be known as sheepherder
laws. There were a number of Basques in the American
West who had jumped ship and had made their way to
the sheep districts, where they were herding as illegal
aliens. The sheepherder laws were individual pieces of
legislation introduced by a Western senator or congressman legalizing the status of one or more of the illegal
Basque aliens in his district. In this fashion, between

1942 and 1961, 383 men received permanent residency in the United States.

Such an approach was cumbersome and scarcely able to address the labor crisis of an entire industry. Consequently, political pressure mounted to exempt Basque herders from the immigration quota system. The pro-Basque stance was spearheaded by Nevada's Senator Pat McCarran, an ex-sheepman himself. The irony is that McCarran was coauthor of the McCarran-Walter Omnibus Immigration Bill, which, except for providing special treatment for sheepherders, was a highly restrictive and xenophobic piece of legislation. McCarran continued to introduce legislation favoring the importation of herders. A rancher's group, the California Range Association (which subsequently became the Western Range Association) was authorized to recruit herders in Europe. The men were offered a contract that set the salary, specified conditions of employment (such as health insurance and vacation provisions), and determined the length of their stay.

D URING THE early years of the program, the herder was required to leave the United States after three years, thus precluding him for qualifying for permanent residency, though he could then return for more three-year sojourns. In the early 1970s, this was liberalized to allow herders to apply for permanent residency after completing one contract. They could remain in the United States with the freedom to work at any job. However, by this time it was becoming a moot point, since the Spanish economy had improved to the degree that few young men were interested in the rustic lifestyle and relatively low wages of the herder occupation. Consequently, during the 1970s, the typical herder of the American West was more likely to be Mexican or Peruvian than Basque. Of the fifteen hundred herders employed by the Western Range Association in 1970, well over 90 percent were Basques. Of the seven hundred and fifty herders under contract in 1976, about one in six was a Basque. The contract herder program thus brought several thousand Spanish Basques to the American West, although the majority did not settle there permanently.

UNDOUBTEDLY, the single most important social institution among Basque-Americans was the boardinghouse or Basque hotel. Once a few itinerant sheepmen and employed herders became established in a particular place, a Basque hotel in the area's servicing center was sure to follow. Cities such as Los Angeles and San Francisco and major towns such as Reno, Boise, and Bakersfield developed Basque hotel districts. There was also a sense in which the hotels were stitched together into a regional network through which an intending herder could find employment and a retired one a place to while away his golden years.

Usually established by an ex-herder and possibly his Basque-American wife, the Basque hotel provided the Old-World–born herder with his ethnic haven. Should a man be laid off during the winter, when two sheep bands were consolidated into one for about five months under the care of a single herder, the hotel was his home. The hotelkeeper (or the hotelkeeper's spouse) served as translator on shopping trips or on visits to a doctor or dentist. While out on the range, a man might leave his best suit of clothes at the hotel. If he returned to Europe for a visit (usually of several months' or even years' duration), he might store his rifle, saddle, and bedroll in the basement of his favorite hotel.

For established Basque-American ranchers in the district, the hotel was a place to charge their ethnic batteries. There, the New World–born individual could

Continued on page 172 ▶▶

Passage

Prior to the late nineteenth-century, passage from
Europe to the Americas was fraught with danger and
discomfort. Shipwrecks and deadly disease were distinct
possibilities during an ordeal lasting several weeks.

The invention of the steamship revolutionized travel between the continents, introducing safety and speed while largely reducing illness to the seasick variety. *From Jim Harter:* Transportation: A Pictorial Archive

▶ Continued from page 169.
practice his or her Basque, dine family style (at a long
table) with the boarders, and learn about the European
homeland from them. Some ranchers kept their children
at a Basque hotel during the school year, and a woman
about to give birth might stay there while awaiting the
event. The hotel also hosted baptismal feasts, birthday
parties, wedding celebrations, and wakes. It held dances
at which bachelor herders might meet and mingle
with Basque-American spinsters. The hotelkeepers
were also prone to send back to Europe for unmarried
women willing to work as domestics or in the kitchen—
few remained unmarried for long after arriving in the
American West. In these fashions, the Basque hotel was
instrumental in the formation of an enduring Basque-
American identity and community.

IN RECENT YEARS, and particularly since the sharp
decline in the herder population, the hotels have
been transformed into restaurants featuring famed
Basque ethnic cuisine. With the staff possibly dressed in
folk costume and the walls adorned with both Old World
and New World Basque memorabilia, the hotel is now a
showcase of Basque culture for the uninitiated.

During the late nineteenth and early twentieth centuries, except for the hotels, there were practically no
Basque ethnic institutions or group manifestations in
the American West. The real burst of organizational
activity is more recent. Passage of the Taylor Grazing
Act and the growing sheepherder crisis of the 1940s did
wonders for the group's image. The hated Basque itinerant sheepman was gone, and Basque and non-Basque
outfits alike were anxious to hire the esteemed herders.
Then, too, the herding occupation came to be viewed differently. The United States became increasingly urban,
and Americans began to romanticize simpler lifestyles.

The independent herder became the object of positive articles in the popular press. Basque ethnic pride and a growing willingness to display one's ethnic heritage began to emerge. In more recent times, this was fueled by Americans' renewed fascination with their ethnic "roots."

To cite but a few landmarks in the emergence of a Basque-American collective identity, we might note the founding of the social club Euskaldunak, Inc., in Boise in 1949. By 1951, the group had its own building, complete with bar and banquet facilities. In 1957, Robert Laxalt, son of a French Basque sheepherder, wrote his epic work *Sweet Promised Land*. It detailed his father's return visit to the Basque Country after decades in the American West. The work provided Basque Americans with their literary spokesman while introducing their group history to a wider American public that was largely ignorant of it. In 1959, there was another critical development. A Sparks, Nevada, casino owner married to a Boise Basque decided to sponsor a national Basque festival. A committee consisting of both French and Spanish Basques was formed and worked on the project for several months. The two-day festival was a huge success and was attended by about six thousand people from throughout the American West. Many went back to their home areas and founded Basque clubs and festivals of their own.

An important development was the creation of the Oinkari dance group in Boise in 1960 by a group of young Basque-Americans who visited the European Basque homeland and learned several dances. In subsequent years, the Oinkaris performed at many Basque festivals throughout the region, which stimulated several local Basque clubs to form their own dance groups. The Oinkaris were also ambassadors of Basque culture,

appearing at the Seattle World's Fair in 1962 and representing Idaho at the 1964 New York World's Fair. Subsequently, they performed at Expo '70 in Montreal and the
1974 Spokane World's Fair.

By the early 1970s, there were more than a dozen
Basque social clubs throughout the American West, and
several of their representatives met to form NABO, North
American Basque Organizations, Inc. This provided
Basque-Americans with a regional organization capable
of organizing summer music camps (*udaleku*) where the
children could learn dance and to play the traditional
txistu (flute). NABO also sponsors the American tours
of European Basque performing artists and organizes a
national championship for *mus*, a Basque card game.

BEGINNING IN the 1990s, every five years, Boise
Basques have organized Jaialdi, a weekend-long multifaceted series of cultural events. Attracting as many as
thirty thousand attendees, it is easily the biggest Basque
"happening" in the United States.

Prior to 1980, it was impossible to know the number of Basque-Americans in the United States. The U.S.
Census counted U.S.-born Basques as "American," and
the Old World–born were censused as either "Spanish"
or "French" nationals. Beginning with the 1980 census,
however, a sampling of respondents were asked to specify their ethnic ancestry if they so chose. The table below
reflects the results of an approximation of the Basque-
American population by state in the last three censuses.
It further disaggregates the results into "French-Basque,"
"Spanish-Basque" and simply "Basque" identities
specified by respondents. Interestingly, there are some
Basques in every one of the fifty states. California has far
and away the largest community, followed by Idaho and
then Nevada. While totaling only about fifty-seven thousand individuals in 2000, the Basque-American com-

munity seems to have experienced growth of about 25
percent over the past twenty years, despite the fact that
during this period there has been practically no Basque
immigration into the United States.

Lesson eleven

LEARNING OBJECTIVES
1. To understand the nature and extent of Basque emigration to the Americas.
2. To encounter the emigrant's experience in the host
   societies.
3. To evaluate the consequences of migration on Basque
   culture and identity.

REQUIRED READING
William A. Douglass and Jon Bilbao, *Amerikanuak: The
Basques of the New World* (Reno: University of Nevada
Press, 2005), 177–246.

SUGGESTED READING
William A. Douglass, "Santi's Story," in *Portraits of
Basques in the New World*, ed. Richard W. Etulain and
Jeronima Echeverria (Reno: University of Nevada Press,
1999), 141–54.
Jeronima Echeverria, *Home Away from Home: A His-
tory of Basque Boardinghouses.* (Reno: University of
Nevada Press, 1999).
Richard Lane and William A. Douglass, *Basque Sheep-
herders of the American West: A Photographic Docu-
mentary* (Reno: University of Nevada Press, 1985).
Robert Laxalt, *Sweet Promised Land* (New York: Harper,
1957).

Beltran Paris, as told to William A. Douglass, *Beltran: Basque Sheepman of the American West* (Reno: University of Nevada Press, 1979).

Gloria Totoricagüena, *Basque Diaspora: Migration and Transational Identity* (Reno: Center for Basque Studies, 2005).

Carmelo Urza, "Basque Ethnic Identities: Old World and New World Expressions," in *Solitude* (Reno: University of Nevada Press, 1993),71–89.

Nancy Zubiri, *A Travel Guide to Basque America: Families, Feasts & Festivals* (Reno: University of Nevada Press, 1998).

WRITTEN LESSON FOR SUBMISSION

1. What are the geographical and social conditions that for centuries have prompted Basques to emigrate?
2. Outline the differences between Basque emigration to South America and to North America.
3. How would you describe the transformation of Basque culture and identity from their European homeland expressions to their diasporic manifestations.
4. Are Basque diasporic identities any less relevant than nondiasporic ones in the contemporary world? Are hyphenated Basques any less "Basque" than those of the mother country?
5. Discuss the ironies reflected in the encounter between "Old World" and "New World" Basques during the dedication of the national monument to the Basque sheepherder in Reno, Nevada.

12 · Basque Emigration and Diaspora
Asia And Oceania

D URING THE sixteenth century, Spain emerged as
the phalanx of Europe's exploration of the world
and as its quintessential imperial and colonial power. As
we have noted, Basques were Spain's main mariners and,
as such, played a disproportionate role in the voyages of
discovery, the subsequent secular and religious imperial
administrations, and development of the several colonial
societies and economies.

Regarding the exploration of the world, we need only
consider the role of Basques in what were arguably the
three key voyages in the configuration of Spain's imperial hegemony. In chapter 7, we mentioned Basque
involvement in Columbus's seminal first voyage of discovery in 1492. The second key expedition was that of
Ferdinand Magellan, beginning in 1519. The Portuguese
mariner Magellan is often regarded by historians as the
first individual to circumnavigate the globe. In fact, he
was killed in the Philippines, at which point a Basque
from Getaria (Guetaria), Gipuzkoa, Juan Sebastian de
Elkano (Elcano), assumed command. Magellan began
his epic journey with five vessels and 265 expeditionaries drawn from throughout Europe, of whom 28, or a
disproportionate more than 10 percent, were Basque.
On September 6, 1522, 22 bedraggled survivors reached
the Andalusian port of Sanlúcar de Barrameda, having
established Spain's claim to southern South America
and parts of Asia. Emperor Charles V received Elkano
and rewarded him with 500 ducats and the right to incorporate into his family escutchen an image of the globe
bearing the inscription "Primus Circundedisti Me" (You
were the first to circle me).

Primus circumdedisti me
Statue of Juan Sebastian de Elkano, first circumnavigator
of the globe, in his natal town of Getaria, Gipuzkoa.
Photo: Xabier Irujo

IN 1525, THERE was another Spanish expedition
to the Orient in which Elkano served as second-in-
command. Four of its seven vessels were constructed in
Bizkaia, and of the 450 expeditionaries, at least 21 were
Basque. (More might have been, since the crew lists we

have are incomplete.) This time it would be Elkano who would die (of scurvy) in the mid-Pacific. Accompanying Elkano as his personal page was a bright seventeen-year-old fellow Basque, Andrés de Urdaneta. During the expedition, Urdaneta acquired intimate geographical knowledge of the Philippines and the Moluccas, the fabled "Spice Islands," as well as competency in some local languages, which prepared him for his critical role in Spain's subsequent third monumental expedition to the Orient in 1564.

BY THE MID-SIXTEENTH century, hostilities and competition with Portugal had all but precluded for Spain a secure eastward trade across the Atlantic and Indian Oceans with the Orient. Consequently, the Spanish crown became interested in establishing a Pacific sea route between Nueva España (out of the port of Acapulco) and the Philippines. By that time, Urdaneta was an Augustinian friar living in Mexico City. Viceroy Luis de Velasco offered him command of an expedition to the Philippines, the main objective of which was to discover the still-elusive navigational knowledge that would facilitate the return voyage. (Lacking expertise regarding currents and the seasonal variations in prevailing winds, all previous attempts to sail from the Orient to the Americas either had failed or had lasted for many months.) At first, Urdaneta was reluctant, preferring instead to explore northern Asian waters or possibly even the South Pacific in search of a rumored Terra Australis—the undiscovered southern continent. However, he was eventually ordered by his superior to accede to the king's and viceroy's wishes.

The other key figure in the Philippines venture was Urdaneta's fellow Basque countryman and relative Miguel López de Legazpi. Legazpi was a government official and well-to-do businessman—and hence in a position to commit considerable personal wealth to the enterprise. His involvement attracted investment from other Nueva España Basques, as well. The expedition sailed on November 20, 1564. Its 350-man contingent was laced liberally with Basques, including Legazpi's grandson and Urdaneta's nephew. Of the six Augustinian friars who were intending to evangelize the Philippines, four were Basque.

URDANETA AND Legazpi had a royal charter admonishing them to colonize the Philippines. They spent the next year laying the foundation for what proved to be the most enlightened policy of any Spanish colony. Europeans attempting to enslave the natives were punished, and it was mandated that the Christian faith be taught in the indigenous languages.

In 1565, by first sailing considerably north, Urdaneta discovered the prevailing winds and currents that provided an efficient eastward sea route back to Nueva España. He thereby founded what came to be the port of Acapulco's lucrative Asian trade, based on the annual arrival of the "Manila Galleon."

For more than three hundred years, until the eve of the twentieth century, the Philippines remained a Spanish colony. Manila became a significant European trading enclave in Asia, particularly in the commerce with China. Basques played key roles in the administration and economic development of the islands. Over time, several became landowners, often owning sugar plantations in the rural areas. In 1785, a group of powerful Basques residing in Madrid formed the Philippines Company, which came to dominate the colony's trade with Nueva España and the Spanish metropolis until eclipsed by nineteenth-century rebellions in the islands.

Nineteenth-century developments in Spain, particularly the Carlist Wars, stimulated Basque emigration to the Philippines. Some settled the land, others organized and / or served in the merchant marine of the interisland trade. Then there was the activity of José Oyanguren, a Gipuzkoan Basque from Bergara. In 1847, he was charged with exploring, pacifying, and settling the rebellious Muslim territory of Mindanao. Once established there, he named the island Nueva Guipúzcoa and its capitol town Bergara (present-day Davao).

In the 1850s, the port and province of Iloilo also attracted a Basque contingent and ultimately emerged as the second most important focus of Basque settlement in the islands, after Manila. It was here that important Manila-based Basque companies, such as Ynchausti and Company, which controlled half a dozen large sugar plantations and a fleet of more than twenty vessels in the interisland trade, opened branches. Iloilo had Basque-owned businesses of all kinds and a number of Basque hotels and boardinghouses, as well.

BASQUES FROM the four Spanish Basque provinces were present in the islands. The most numerous were the Bizkaians, due to the fact that the opening of Philippine ports to international trade attracted seamen—captains, pilots, and shipbuilders. The second most important group were the Nafarroans, who were involved in trade and in the planting of abaca (sometimes called "Manila hemp"), coconuts and, later, sugar. The third group was the Gipuzkoans, involved in exploration, as was Oyanguren and his friend Joaquín Urquiola (from Gaviria / Gabiria) on the Island of Mindanao, or in trading, as was José Joaquín de Ynchausti from Zumarraga, who founded Ynchausti and Company. (His partners were Nafarroans: Joaquín Elizalde, Marcelino Valentín Teus, and others.) The Arabans were less numerous, being mostly involved in government administration and later in their own businesses, for example, the Ayala family. A handful of French Basques also settled in Manila.

BASQUE TRADING companies in Manila—such as Otadui, Marcaida, Matia and Menchacatorre, and Orbeta—specialized in importing European goods and agricultural machinery. However, it was in shipping that Basques were to excel. Before the opening of the Suez Canal, several ships, with names such as the *Bella Vascongada, Bilbaino, Aurrera, Alavesa, Neurea,* and *Unzueta,* plied the Liverpool-Bilbao-Manila route, as well as the Cadiz-Manila run. The Larrinaga Company, a Basque trading company established in Liverpool plying the Liverpool–New York and Liverpool-Havana runs, opened offices in Manila, as well.

After the inauguration of the Suez Canal in 1865, Basque immigration into the Philippines increased. The Second Carlist War created refugees. Furthermore, many young men with some schooling in business administration were brought out by the Basque companies involved in agriculture or trade. By this time, the same companies were buying foreign steamships or constructing ships for interisland commerce. They employed such a number of Basque merchant marine officers that over 90 percent of the captains and pilots in the interisland trade and on the Singapore-Manila and Hong Kong–Manila runs were Basques. So were many of the port officials of Manila, Legazpi, Cebu, and Iloilo.

The Spanish-American War (1898) did not greatly affect the majority of Basques in the islands. Some families, such as that of Ruiz de Luzuriaga in Negros, were very involved in the independence movement against Spanish control of the area, but most stayed out of politics. In fact, American occupation gave a new impetus to Basque immigration. Young Basque males who wanted

Embarques de Azúcar

Ofrecemos otra vista del Espigón donde podemos contemplar las operaciones de embarques de azúcar para los Estados Unidos.

Exporting Cuban sugar to the United States
Basques played key roles in every aspect of the Cuban sugar industry and came to constitute an ethnic elite within Cuban society. Today many of its members reside in the greater Miami area or Europe.
Photo: *Gordejuela*, March 22, 1947

to avoid military service in Spain could join their kinsmen in the Philippines.

ON JULY 31, 1909, the feast day of the Basque patron saint, Saint Ignatius of Loiola, some Basques of Iloilo founded the Euzkeldun Batzokija, the first Basque nationalist club in the Philippines. The board of directors was formed by two Bizkaians, one Encartado (from western Bizkaia), and one Nafarroan. The club was located in the Hotel Bilbao, and the membership collected money to help Basques in distress to pay their hospital bills or their way back to the Basque Country. Every year, the association celebrated Saint Ignatius's day with a mass in Basque, followed by a banquet with singing and dancing in the Hotel Bilbao. This religious feast day was observed in the Basque communities of Manila, Legazpi, and Cebu, as well.

During the Second World War, Philippine Basques were active in guerrilla warfare against the Japanese. A limited account of such effort by Bizkaians is found in a book by Higinio Uriarte entitled *A Basque among the Guerrillas of Negros*.

SINCE ABOUT 1950, there has been an exodus of Basques from the Philippines to Australia, Latin America, the United States, and Europe. Those who remain are likely to send their children to Europe or to the United States to be educated. Some return to take care of family businesses. However, it is easy to detect a certain nervousness among today's Philippine Basques. The independence of the islands ushered in a period of unrest and clouded the future of a European population enclaved in an Asian world.

Had Urdaneta managed to sail successfully in search of the fabled Terra Australis, Basque history in the antipodes would likely have differed considerably. As it turned out, the coast of the southern continent was first explored extensively by the Dutch seafarer Van Diemen and then by the Englishman James Cook. It was the voyages of the latter, in the second half of the eighteenth century, that brought Australia into the European orbit as an English colony. As is well known, for much of its early years, and particularly during the first half of the nineteenth century, Australia was a colony of the penal kind.

After 1850, Australia entered a more normal European settler phase driven by agricultural development of the coastal fringe and mining booms in the interior. A handful of Basques entered the several Australian colonies in search of opportunity in both sectors. Their arrival was highly idiosyncratic, rather than a part of an organized or patterned emigration, such as that of the Basque sheepherders in the American West at this same time that we considered in chapter 11. The typical individual Basque immigrant was a mariner who reached Sydney while serving on a merchant ship, possibly based out of Callao (Peru) and who then decided to jump ship and remain in Australia.

The foundation of a discernible Australian-Basque community dates from the first decade of the twentieth century. By that time, there was a substantial sugar industry on the northeastern littoral, extending for nearly two thousand miles from temperate New South Wales to tropical North Queensland. In the latter, sugar plantations were in operation by the 1870s, staffed mainly by dark Kanakas or Pacific Islanders whose indentured status and working conditions bordered on slavery. As the several Australian colonies evolved toward single nationhood within the British Commonwealth, achieved in 1901, Queensland came under intense pressure from the others to repatriate its nonwhite Kanakas. By 1907, it had pretty much done so.

BEGINNING IN 1891, the desperate cane growers turned to southern Europe for a possible "swarthy" substitute for the Kanaka fieldworkers. (The British conventional wisdom of the day declared whites to be unsuited for manual labor under the tropical sun.) Initial recruitment focused on northern Italy. There was

Missives and missiles
Basque political refugee from the Spanish Civil war,
Andrés de Irujo, founder of the Editorial Ekin of Buenos
Aires. His publishing concern was the only source of
Basque works during much of the Franco dictatorship
(given its censorship of Spanish publishers). Irujo once
stated (to Douglass), "I consider each book to be my
bullet aimed at the dictator!"
Photo: María Elena Etxeberri (Irujo's widow)

---

also an abortive plan to recruit in Bilbao. In 1907, 104
Catalans from the Barcelona area embarked for Australia's sugar districts.

IN ABOUT 1910, some Basque mariners from Lekeitio
jumped ship in Sydney, heard about the cane-cutting
opportunity in the north (probably from Sydney Catalans), and made their way to Ingham, North Queensland.
Between 1910 and 1930, this foothold grew into a Basque
presence as some cutters acquired sugar properties of

their own and sent back to Europe for kinsmen and fellow villagers. The "new chums," as they were called, formed their own cane-cutter gangs of eight to ten individuals (usually bachelors or married men whose spouses remained in Europe) that circulated among several farms. It was highly lucrative employment for dedicated workers, since the pay was on a piece-work basis. The men lived in farm barracks and kept pretty much to themselves. By then, Italian was the lingua franca of the industry, so most Basques learned it, even before acquiring a smattering of English. As "southern Europeans," Basques shared in the joys of the Italo-Australian community (church, taverns, dances, social events, and even intermarriage) while suffering its sorrows (the prejudice of many Anglo-Australians against Latin "wogs" and "dagoes").

The major downside to cane cutting was its seasonality. Thus, the men who remained in the sugar districts remained unemployed (or underemployed) for roughly half a year. There emerged a practice whereby three or four would purchase a car together and travel south to pick fruits and vegetables in rural New South Wales and Victoria. Some drifted to Brisbane, Sydney, and Melbourne. Most returned north for the sugar season, but a sufficient number remained behind to form the basis of small Basque enclaves in urban Australia.

DURING THE Second World War, Australia interned most of its Italians as presumably dangerous enemy aliens. Nevertheless, after the conflict, and given the country's near miss of experiencing a Japanese invasion, Australia underwent a dramatic shift in its immigration policy. Alarmed by the "Yellow Peril" posed by a crowded Asia to fourteen million whites occupying a continent as large as the lower United States, Australia instituted a pro-immigration policy designed to increase the national population by 1 percent per annum. Since this goal could evidently not be achieved by limiting recruitment to the most acceptable British Isles and then to northwestern continental Europe, immigrants from Southern and Central Europe were required, as well. By the mid-1950s, Queensland's sugar growers were again recruiting workers in Italy with Australian governmental approval. However, in the wake of the Marshall Plan, the Italian economy underwent a miraculous recovery, so it proved difficult to recruit and then retain a sufficiency of Italian cane cutters. (Cutters of every nationality were prone to leave the harsh conditions and hard work of cane harvesting and either resettle in a city or return to Europe with their savings.)

By then, Basques had the reputation of being excellent and reliable cutters, and Spain, under the internationally ostracized Franco regime, lagged behind the rest of Europe's postwar recovery. So, in 1958, the sugar growers sent a recruiter to Bizkaia. Eventually, 712 men left for Australia in three shiploads—labeled "Operation Emu," "Operation Eucalyptus," and "Operation Kangaroo." The Australian and Spanish governments, as well as the Catholic Church, also collaborated in recruiting at least one planeload of Basque spinsters, ostensibly for domestic and factory work, but also in the hope that they would marry Basque cane cutters, establish families, and thereby solidify their husbands' commitment to the sugar industry.

SINCE BASQUES are not censused as such, and there was a considerably larger number of Spanish nationals in Australia, it is impossible to state with accuracy the size of Australia's twentieth-century Spanish Basque population. (There are practically no French Basques in the country.) We might estimate that there were as many as two thousand Basques in Australia by the mid-1960s, probably the community's demographic high-water mark. By then, the harvesting of sugar was becoming mechanized, diminishing exponentially the industry's demand for manual labor. A few Basque cane cutters pooled their savings and purchased the expensive mechanical harvesters, but the era of the Basque sugar worker in Australia was pretty much over.

Many returned to Europe, while some resettled in urban Australia, infusing new blood into the Melbourne and Sydney Basque colonies. In 1964, the Basques of Melbourne rented a facility and established a club called Gure Txoko (Our Corner). In 1966, Sydney Basques followed suit, actually managing to purchase a building (later retrofitted with a small handball court or *frontón*) for their own Gure Txoko.

THE CLUBS serve as focal points for periodic reunions and banquets, as well as for picnics and excursions for their memberships. Both observe Aberri Eguna, the Day of the Fatherland, a Basque nationalist holiday. Both celebrate Saint Ignatius's feast day. Both clubs receive assistance in the form of grants from the Basque government's Ministry of Foreign Affairs. They have sent a joint "Australian" delegation to each of the three week-long Congresses of Basque Collectivities in the World sponsored by the Basque government and held in Vitoria-Gasteiz in 1995, 1999, and 2003. In this fashion, Basque-Australians have met representatives of the North and South American Basque diasporas.

Today, the Internet permits Basques worldwide to access a kind of virtual Basque Country. Consequently, the relations of diasporic Basques are no longer exclusively with the European homeland, but are maintained with each other, as well. Nevertheless, in Australia, the Basque clubs struggle to survive in the face of the recent rapid decline in the numbers of Basque-Australians, which is due to several factors. First, there is no longer a specific occupational opportunity or niche comparable to cane cutting attracting Basque immigrants. Today's Basque immigration in Australia is quite comparable to that of the late nineteenth century, that is, it is characterized by the entry of a few individuals with idiosyncratic motives. Second, with the death of Franco in 1975 and the subsequent democratization of Spain, many Basque families who were either political or economic refugees in Australia have returned to their European homeland. Finally, the pioneering generations have aged and undergone mortality's natural thinning of their ranks. Today, there may be fewer than five hundred Basques and their descendants in all of Australia. The prognosis for the future of the Basque-Australian diaspora is unfavorable.

In sum, at present there is little transatlantic Basque emigration, whether to the Americas or to Asia / Oceania. Rather, today, the intending Basque migrant is likely to select a destination within Spain or the European Union. In point of fact, there are now large Basque clubs in Madrid and Barcelona, as well as incipient ones in Paris, London, and Rome. There are no longer internal barriers to young Europeans seeking education or employment in one another's country. One can only assume that we are witnessing at present formation of new Basque diasporas, ones that promise to eclipse the older ones with the passage of time.

Lesson twelve

LEARNING OBJECTIVES
1. To analyze Basque elitist activity within Spain's Asian colonial enterprise.

2. To analyze the recent Basque labor emigration to Australia.

REQUIRED READING

Marciano R. de Borja, *Basques in the Philippines* (Reno: University of Nevada Press, 2005), 7–29, 58–74.

William A. Douglass, "The Basques of North Queensland, Australia," in *Homenaje a Francisco de Abrizketa / Frantzisko Abrizketa'ri Omenaldia*, ed. Román Basurto (Bolibar, Sociedad Bolivariana del País Vasco), 443–66.

SUGGESTED READING

William A. Douglass, *Azúcar amargo: Vida y fortuna de los cortadores de caña italianos y vascos en la Australia tropical.* (Lejona: Servicio Editorial de la Universidad del País Vasco, 1996).

WRITTEN LESSON FOR SUBMISSION

1. Compare and contrast the North and South American Basque diasporas with those of the Philippines and Australia.
2. Speculate about the capacity of the Internet to sustain Basque identity outside the European homeland.

Part Three
Traditional Lifestyles and Worldviews

A^S NOTED in chapter 1, in recent years, Europeanist anthropology has been criticized for focusing its gaze on the backwater "little communities" in island and mountainous settings far-removed from the mainstream of Western civilization. The depiction is more accurate regarding the formative years of Europeanist anthropological interest. Basque anthropology, and particularly its Anglophone dimension, is no exception. It was during this period that William A.Douglass worked in Aulestia (Bizkaia) and Etxalar (Nafarroa) (1963–65), Davydd J. Greenwood examined the decline of agriculture in Hondarribia (Gipuzkoa) (1969), Sandra Ott conducted fieldwork in the Xiberoan mountain shepherding village of Santa Grazi (Saint Engrâce) (1976), and Joseba Zulaika revisited as a scholar his natal community of Itziar (Gipuzkoa) (1979–81). In this section, we will consider the results of this and other research regarding two Basque traditional lifestyles—fishing and agriculture.

Chapter 13 examines the history of Basque fishing, with particular emphasis on one community—Lekeitio (Bizkaia). The anthropological dimension regards the attempt to elucidate the ways in which an overarching economic activity configures the social, cultural, political, and religious life of the community.

Chapter 14 considers the organization of the farmstead (*baserri*) and neighborhood (*auzo*) of the Basque peasant village. Reflective of social anthropology's structural-functional emphasis of the mid-twentieth century, the subject is treated in holistic terms and underscores the features of local life and world view that make the Basque peasant village emblematic of what Robert Redfield characterized as the "little tradition" (as opposed to the "great tradition" of any—and in our case, Occidental—civilization).

Chapter 15, compares and contrasts different aspects of traditional fishing and agricultural ways of life—particularly regarding their respective worldviews.

Chapters 16 through 20 shift the focus from the little community per se to certain kinds of thematic topics germane to the "traditional" worldview. Chapter 16 examines the (former) relationship between the sexes regarding courtship and marriage in rural Basque society. Chapter 17 regards Basque views toward animals, both domestic and wild, particularly as expressed by hunters and in the running before the bulls (and subsequent bullfight) during Iruña's famed festival of San Fermín.

Chapter 18 examines Basque mythology. After analyzing Basque folklore, legends, and myths, Rodney Gallop concluded that, as reflected in these cultural beliefs, Basques constitute a "living museum" of wider Western European patterns. The same can be said for Basque witchcraft, the subject of chapter 19. In every regard, the Basque witch is of the familiar "Halloween" variety (old crone, black cat, flight with a broomstick).

In chapter 20, we examine folk religious beliefs as reflected in funerary rituals of Aulestia and apparitions of the Virgin Mary at Ezkioga (Gipuzkoa), both of which place Basques firmly within the tradition of European Marian devotion exemplified by the better-known events at Fatima and Lourdes.

13 · Fishing the World
and the World of Fishing

ACCORDING TO some accounts, Basques were Europe's first whalers. By at least the eighth or ninth century, there is evidence of whaling towers constructed along the Basque coast. They were manned by lookouts, and when a whale was spotted, the whalers put to sea in long boats to pursue the quarry. If they were successful, they towed the whole carcass back into port and rendered the blubber into whale oil. The oil itself was the household petroleum of the continent, lighting Europe's night lamps. It was therefore a major trade item for the Basques and drew them into European commerce. There was a Basque maritime fleet and shipbuilding complex along the Basque coast, an industry that was favored by the stands of native oak in Euskalherria, which could be used for masts and ship bottoms, and by a local iron industry, which supplied the fittings and armaments of military vessels. Whale oil, however, provided the critical commodity to Basque maritime commerce. Its importance is further underscored by the fact that the coats of arms of many of the Basque coastal communities bear the imagery of whales and whaling.

Since the Basque coast had few natural harbors, and since those it did have required protection from the fierce storms and wave action of the Cantabrian Sea, much of our earliest evidence of the fishing complex regards the construction and repair of seawalls and wharves. In the village of Lekeitio, for example, in 1486, a man was leased the port facilities for a five-year period on condition that he extend the new wharf and seawall. Such private solutions, however, seemed to be ineffective. In 1552, the fishermen's *cofradía*, or brotherhood, petitioned the bishop of Calahorra for permission to fish on certain religious holy days on condition that the proceeds from the catch be used to repair the port facilities. In 1607, a new clause was added to the municipal code of Lekeitio that required that one-third of the proceeds of the sale of the tongues of whales captured in Cantabrian waters be given to the church and two-thirds devoted to the repair of the port facilities.

In 1829, given the state of disrepair of the port of Lekeitio, the fishermen's brotherhood and town authorities agreed to a tax on wine. The members of the *cofradía* were prohibited "from leaving the town under any pretext with the sole object of drinking wine, must, or other beverage, whether as a group or as individuals" under pain of four reales for the first offense, eight for the second, and an appearance before a judge who would apply a discretionary sentence for the third.

A S THE DEMAND for whale oil increased, the Cantabrian Sea became depleted of its migratory cetacean population. In fact, some experts believe that in the face of intense whaling pressure, the mammals changed their migratory routes and began to avoid the area. Whatever the case, the Basques began to travel afar in pursuit of their quarry, ranging into the North Atlantic to Spitzbergen Island in northern Scandinavia. They were the acknowledged experts in the field. In the early sixteenth century, when the English decided to become involved, they contracted with Basque whalers to teach their crews their whaling techniques and the habits of the various species. Basques were also in the forefront of naval design as it became increasingly necessary to build vessels that could traverse the high seas and transport the cargo back to Europe. Prohibited by the European powers from establishing land-based rendering works in Spitzbergen and Terranova, the Basque whaling industry developed the technology to render blubber onboard ships, thereby becoming the precursor of more modern nineteenth-century and twentieth-century whaling operations, which are only now ceasing in light of the worldwide save-the-whales campaigns.

One might point out an interesting sidebar reflected in the history of whaling. For English-speaking readers, the classic work on the subject is Herman Melville's *Moby-Dick*, regarded by many critics as the great American novel. Melville was an assiduous student of whaling history, and his book alternates between a fictional narrative and an exposition of whaling technology, techniques, and history. After citing some ancient Greek, biblical, and even Hindu references to whales, Melville attributes the Dutch with having initiated the whaling industry in the sixteenth century, which later became dominated by the English, who, by Melville's time, had themselves been coopted by the ubiquitous Nantucketers of his novel. Melville makes no reference whatsoever to the Basque whalers of yore, an omission that underscores the extent to which knowledge easily becomes encapsulated in distinct and scarcely overlapping intellectual traditions—in this case, that of the Hispanic world, on the one hand, and the Anglo-American one, on the other.

AN AS YET unresolved question germane to the Atlantic expansions of the Basque whaling complex is that of chronology and, by implication, the possible Basque role in the discovery of the New World. It is clear that at some point, Basque whaling interests extended their operations far enough to the north and west to discover the rich fishing banks off Terranova. Basques had become involved in extensive cod-fishing operations by the early sixteenth century in Terranova waters. Were they there prior to the voyages of Columbus? Possibly. As yet there is no incontrovertible evidence to favor the theory, but the magnitude of operations there in the

Ample allusions
Insignia of the Euskal Erria Basque Center of Montevideo, Uruguay. The design—which incorporates such Basque traditions as the "seven provinces," the tree of Gernika, "God and the Old Laws" (symbolized by resplendent cross over a mountain peak), whaling, industry and agriculture—was conceived by Florencio Basaldua with the collaboration of Sabino de Arana. It was adopted formally by Euskal Erria on March 30, 1912. *From the collection of Alberto Irigoyen.*

---

early and mid-sixteenth century suggest that it is at least plausible. In any event, by the mid-sixteenth century, the volume of maritime traffic stimulated by the fishing interests in the North Atlantic was greater than that on the sea lanes to Spain's entire American colonial empire.

For the next two centuries, Basques (both Spanish and French) contested the Terranova codfishery with the Bretons and the Portuguese. Actually, each group had its favored haunts and pretty much respected the others' claims. A document of a notary public in the Bizkaian town of Lekeitio, signed in 1583, gives some insight into the extent to which fishing excursions to Terranova were internationalized. It is an agreement signed by a French Basque fishing-vessel owner that outlines the terms whereby nine young men from nearby Irelegy would sail to Terranova for the upcoming summer season. They received monetary advances against their one-third share in the anticipated catch.

BY THE LATE seventeenth century, France, under Louis XIV, recognized the value of the fisheries and extended its territorial claims from French Canada to embrace the Terranova fishing banks. This was the first concrete attempt to claim European sovereignty in an area that for nearly two centuries had been left to the whims of the various sojourning fishing fleets. That is, the fishermen visited its waters only during the summer months and abandoned their facilities to return to Europe every winter. There was therefore no permanent European settlement in the area.

The French claim did little to alter the status quo, because there was no serious attempt either to control the activities of foreign fishermen or to exclude them altogether. However, in 1713, as a result of the signing of the Treaty of Utrecht, sovereignty over the area was transferred to England. The treaty called for respect of established rights of access by Spanish and French fishermen, insofar as they could be verified. At the same time, the English passed legislation reserving the fishing privileges for English nationals. The English authorities engaged in stringent interpretation regarding verification of traditional rights under the treaty. Despite numerous protests and attempts by the Basques to demonstrate their presence in the area "from time immemorial," Basque fishing interests lost their access to Terranova. In 1758, twelve Basque vessels set out for the area, backed by a royal decree from the Spanish monarch declaring to be legal their intent to enter the traditional fisheries. Eleven of the vessels were confiscated by English authorities, and it required two years of litigation to release those seamen with Spanish citizenship. French Basque vessels in the fleet were detained indefinitely, since England and France were at war.

The importance of the Terranova fisheries was clear to the English from the outset. Although dependence on whale oil was in decline, salted codfish had become a major trade item between Great Britain and the Catholic countries of the Mediterranean. It should be remembered that in Catholic countries, it was prohibited to eat meat on Fridays and during the forty-day Lenten period. In fact, by the mid-eighteenth century, English salted codfish was the second most important trade item, after textiles, entering the port of Bilbao.

MEANWHILE, in 1760, William Pitt the Elder ordered the English ambassador in Madrid to remain intransigent during the negotiations over Spanish access to Terranova, noting that the New World fisheries were "the principal base of the maritime power of Great Britain." Consequently, Basque fishing interests were never successful in recuperating their New World grounds. In fact, the matter, along with others, subsequently became a cause for war between Spain and England.

The *cofradías*, or brotherhoods of fishermen, were themselves an interesting historical feature of the Basque fishing complex. We have information regarding the Brotherhood of Saint Peter in Lekeitio, which might

Fishing port of Elantxobe, Bizkaia
While some Basque fishing villages have natural harbors,
note the sheer coastline on which Elantxobe perches and
the man-made seawalls that provide the only shelter for
its small fleet.
Photo: William Douglass

---

have been founded as early as 1381 and which was
clearly operative by 1457. According to one sixteenth-
century document, the brotherhood was founded in
order to protect the citizenry against incursions into
the town by armed bands of the two warring factions—
the Oñacinos and Gamboinos—that were contesting
control of the Basque countryside. Be this as it may,
the brotherhood quickly assumed several regulatory
functions with respect to fishing. By the mid-sixteenth
century, it met regularly to discuss and approve rules.
The members elected a *mayordomo*, or official, whose
job it was to apply the regulations and deal with other

authorities. By the eighteenth century, the Brotherhood of Saint Peter was age-graded. That is, in assembly, the preferential voice and votes were given to the eldest boat owners, then to the second eldest, and so forth until all were heard. Boat owners were the only members allowed to serve as or vote for the *mayordomo*. Outsiders were excluded from the proceedings until they had resided in Lekeitio and gone to sea out of its port for a minimum of six years.

The *mayordomo* had the power to exact fines in the name of the *cofradía* for such things as disturbing the peace. He could also levy the ultimate sanction of preventing a fisherman from going to sea for a period of time or, in extreme cases, could ban him from fishing altogether.

By the eighteenth century, the *mayordomo* received an annual salary and one percent of the total catch of all participating boats. A man who was elected *mayordomo* had to post a bond, in effect guaranteeing from his own resources his honesty in office. Four men were elected by the boat captains to serve as councilors and to monitor the books. None of the four could be related within four grades of kinship to the *mayordomo*. Should an elected *mayordomo* refuse or be unable to post bond within twenty-four hours after the election, he was disqualified from holding office, and a new election was held. Once annually, at the end of June, the *mayordomo* held a public meeting at which he presented an accounting of the year's expenses.

AFTER IT WAS determined who was to be *mayordomo*, the brotherhood went in procession to his house on the eve of Saint Peter's Day with the chest containing the documents of the organization. There a dance was performed, including the *kaxarranka*, in which a male dancer danced on the document chest suspended on the shoulders of other members. According to local tradition, in Lekeitio, the dance dates from 1521. It seems that the *cofradía*, along with many others, had been defrauded by persons ostensibly raising funds for the Holy Crusades. The brotherhood complained to the monarch, who issued an order restoring its losses and warning potential defrauders not to solicit support from it. In celebration, the brotherhood instituted a festival and dance ritual. Originally, three men assumed roles during the procession. One, dressed as Saint Peter, stood on the chest as it was carried through the streets, while the other two, dressed as Saint Andrew and Saint John, walked alongside. By the early seventeenth century, the ritual was a source of considerable controversy between the fishermen and both the local religious authorities and the bishopric. On several occasions, the church tried to ban it, but it was held anyway, with or without the traditional participation of the local priests. It seems that the church viewed the ceremony as a profanity, given that laymen dressed as apostles blessed the crowds as believers fell to their knees. In the words of one ecclesiastic in a criminal complaint filed in the seventeenth century against the fishermen:

> They do certain rituals and vain ceremonies, taking in procession, and with pomp and solemnity, a chest in which it is said there are the mariners' documents, carrying the chest on their shoulders through the public streets of said town, and on it there is a man dressed in pontifical vestments, giving blessings, and another two men dressed in the capes and gowns of the church, thereby mixing together ornaments and things that pertain to the divine cult with profane ones, and causing thereby much scandal and causing the many foreigners, the French, the English, the Flemish, and oth-

ers who are in that town for the festivities and because
it is a seaport, to think badly of our holy religion and
also of many people of that town and region.

BY THE NINETEENTH century, the dispute seems
to have been resolved. Saint Peter no longer perched
atop the chest. Rather, he was replaced by a male dancer
in top hat and tails. On its way from the house of the
former *mayordomo* to that of the incoming one, the
procession passed before the effigy of Saint Peter. There
the dancer performed the *kaxarranka*. He did so again
before the house of the incoming *mayordomo*.

The intertwining of the sacred and secular, however, was evident from the outset of the brotherhood's
existence. Several religious duties and devotions were
written into the rules. For example, anyone joining the
cofradía was required on doing so to confess and take
communion as a sign that he was in God's favor, and a
statute of the organization, dated 1691, states that during
the festivities of Saint Peter, every member had to go to
confession and communion and that all were to attend
a Mass said on behalf of the souls of deceased members.
All were then to participate in the procession with the
proper religious decorum. There were other feast days in
the year, as well, on which members were required to go
to confession and take communion.

It was further ordered that if anyone learned that a
member was ill, he should inform the *mayordomo*, who
was then obliged to visit the patient. Should he be found
in a state of need or want, the *mayordomo* was to decide
on the amount of assistance the brotherhood would
afford the afflicted member. In the event of the death of
a member, all of the others were to come to his house
to accompany the corpse to the church and also to lend
comfort to the deceased's closest relatives.

Furthermore, the *cofradía* agreed to sponsor a religious festival on Saint Andrew's Day, attending as a body the Mass in the town's main church and giving to the priest a customary offering. One of the brotherhood's officials was required, as was the tradition, to kiss the priest's hand.

A MAJOR CONCERN of the brotherhood was for the safety of its members. It was one of the functions of the *mayordomo* to direct, with signals from a watchtower, the dangerous crossing of the bar by the boats into the harbor during bad weather. If he was deemed by the boat owners to be unskilled in this task, he was required, at his own expense, to hire an acceptable substitute.

The brotherhood maintained a guard in the watchtower who was proposed by the *mayordomo* and approved by the boat owners. The guard was informed in great detail of his duties so that he could not claim ignorance in case of failure to perform them.

The brotherhood also elected two individuals called *señeros*. The *mayordomo* proposed the names of the candidates, and the boat owners voted for or against them. At that time, the salary to be paid to them was also determined. Each *señero* served for one year. He received a third of his salary upon being elected, a third after six months, and the final third on completing the year. The *señero* began service on November 11, or Saint Martin's Day.

The *señeros'* main charge was with the fishermen's safety. It was up to them to "observe and understand the weather, tides, and surge of the sea and in this manner to determine the opportune moment at which to set out to sea for fishing." It was also their job to determine before dawn each day whether the fleet should leave port. If the decision was positive, they dispatched *llamadoras*,

The mighty cod

"The Basques, unlike the Vikings, had salt, and because fish that was salted before drying laster longer, the Basques could travel even longer than the Vikings. They had another advantage: The more durable a product, the easier it is to trade. By the year 1000, the Basques had greatly expanded the cod markets to a truly international trade that reached far from the cod's northern habitat."

Kurlansky, Cod: A Biography of the Fish that Changed the World, 21–22.

---

or young girls, who went to determined areas within the fishermen's quarter to shout out the wake up call "Gora Jaungoikuaren ixenian!"—"Get up in the name of God!" Any man failing to answer the first call was fined two reales. If he failed to answer a second call, he was fined

four reales and prohibited from participating in that
day's catch on his boat.

If the *señeros* were unable to decide whether or not the
fleet should chance it on a particular day, they sent word
to all the boat owners, who had to come to the watchtower immediately or send an acceptable representative.
If a boat owner failed to comply, he was fined two reales.
At the watchtower, the *señeros* would state their reason-
ing and listen to the opinion and arguments of the boat
owners. There was then a secret vote in which balls
were placed in one of two compartments of a box made
especially for the purpose. The result was binding on
everyone, requiring the entire fleet either to set out or to
stay in port. This practice prompted the German traveler
Wilhelm von Humboldt, who visited Lekeitio in 1801, to
characterize the town as a "small fishermen's republic."

Once the boats were at sea, if the *señeros* noted a
change in the weather or that some boats were prudently
setting sail for home because of changing conditions,
they ran up a sail as a sign to the others. Each then signaled back whether its crew felt it proper to return to
port. The *señeros* tallied the vote. The remaining boats
had to remain in place until the outcome was determined or pay a fine of thirty reales. All them had to
abide by the collective decision if it was to return to port.
If, however, the majority wished to continue fishing, dis-
senters were free to return home of their own volition.

THERE WAS A distinction between fishing in *altura*,
or on the high or open seas, and in *bajura*, or the
coastal shallows. Apparently, part of the fleet was likely
to be engaged in both. If the high-seas fleet decided to
return to port and on the way in the weather improved,
the *señeros* could oblige all to resume fishing in the
coastal waters or pay a fine to the *cofradía*.

The watchtower guard also had control over the fleet's actions. It was his duty to observe the surging of the sea and tides in order to ensure safe reentry of the boats. If, in his opinion, conditions at the mouth of the port were deteriorating to a dangerous degree, or if the wind from the interior picked up to the point where it might be difficult to come into port against it, he lit a fire with smoky materials in order to send a signal to the fleet. Boats on the high seas had to begin the return journey immediately. Those fishing in *bajura* could continue until the boats from the high seas reached them. Then they had to head for port or pay a fine of two hundred reales.

If the fleet was in peril, all of the schoolchildren, along with their teachers and a priest, would go to the Church of San Juan to chant litanies to God and the Blessed Virgin to intervene on behalf of the imperiled men. They took with them bread baked on Christmas Eve. They cut a cross into each loaf with a knife. Each child then kissed the cross and recited an "Our Father." The bread was broken into pieces, which were thrown into the sea, along with oil from the lamps of the hermitage of San Juan. In gratitude, the *cofradía* sponsored a festival for the children on the feast day of Saint Andrew, at which time each child was given bread and cheese.

IT WAS ANOTHER duty of the watchtower guard to be constantly vigilant for signs of big prey, such as whales, swordfish, and sharks. When he spied something, he would run up a banner on a flagpole that was visible to all, located on a hill above the town. He would send smoke signals to the fishermen at sea. Those planning to pursue the prey would return at once. Not all did, however, because only some households had the necessary truss used for suspending its share of the kill. In fact, in order to pursue such quarry, a boat had to be certified by all of the *cofradía*'s elected officials as

Living on the land
This baserria is located in the Goiherri (highlands)
of the province of Gipuzkoa. The baserria is the basic
economic and social institution of Basque rural society; therefore, it has also been the main repository of
Basque language and traditional culture and, as such,
it has merited the attention of much ethnographic
work by linguists, folklorists and anthropologists."
Photo: Xabier Irujo

properly equipped. If it failed to pass an annual inspec-
tion, its crew was prohibited from sharing in the considerable benefits of a whale kill.

THE DIVISION of the catch was itself governed by
tradition. The harpooners of the first and second
boats to wound the animal received a fixed portion. The
details were extremely complicated and varied over time.
The sharing was also conditioned by whether or not

only one whale was involved. However, according to one document from 1550, each boat could carry a maximum of six men. The first boat to wound a whale got a quarter of the head and tail as its reward. If the animal was large, a maximum of nine more boats could participate in the sharing, and if small, five boats. They received among themselves three-quarters of the value of the head and tail, shared equally.

If anyone was injured in the pursuit, his medical expenses were deducted before the distribution of shares. The cost of broken or destroyed equipment (a frequent occurence) was not taken into account. Each of the participating crews paid one share to the *cofradia* to help it meet its expenses. The watchtower guard was also compensated for spotting the prey. If there were disputes over who first harpooned the whale, they were adjudicated by the two eldest men in the *cofradia*.

DISPUTES APPEAR to have been common and were of considerable concern to the fishermen. In fact, they often transpired between crews from different towns. In the mid-seventeenth century, the *cofradias* of Lekeitio and Ondarroa signed an agreement. It seems that it was common for both fleets to spot and attack a whale, creating an anarchical situation when it came time to divide the catch. In fact, so many people were involved that, at times, the share of each became insignificant. It was therefore agreed that once a whale was wounded, the first harpooner's *cofradia* had exclusive right to it, unless it had clearly escaped from the initial pursuit. In the latter event, the whalers from the other town could intervene. Also, if the first harpooner needed help, and his *cofradia* mates were not available, but those of the other town's cofradia were, he could ask for assistance from them and then let them share in the catch. The agreement also established a boundary between the fishing fleets of the two towns.

Despite this accord, the problems continued. Whales lightly wounded by one town often made it to the precinct of the other before dying. The two towns also accused each other of trespass on several occasions, a seventeenth-century version of what has continued to echo as a modern problem. There were also several occasions on which the Lekeitio *cofradía* denounced their Ondarroa rivals to the royal authorities for fishing practices that were viewed as excessively damaging to the fishery. One example is a document of Lekeitio's Brotherhood of Saint Peter dated January 8, 1776. It accuses the inhabitants of Ondarroa of using "pernicious implements" and of night fishing, which together were destroying the lobster stocks, as well as those of the local sardine fishery.

Regarding the division of the catch for other forms of fishing, there were also traditional arrangements. One eighteenth-century document specified that in sardine fishing, the boat owner received one-half of the catch, with the remainder shared among the crew. If the owner failed to sail himself, he had to pay a captain to go in his stead. A share was paid to the auctioneer in the port. He and the owner were expected to share equally the costs of providing the boat crew with wine and food while at sea.

THERE WAS considerable care taken regarding the nightly fish auction, which was held under the watchful eye of the *mayordomo* and the *señeros*. They exercised quality control over the sea-bream harvest, grading the catch. In fact, the *mayordomo*, the two *señeros*, and the watchtower guard all had a right to a sea bream of any catch up to thirty-six fish. Above that quantity, the lucky boat had to pay an additional two bream to be divided among the four officials. Two boat owners also presided over the sale of the sea bream and were given wine in return for their services. The duty rotated among the boat owners, and the two men on duty represented the interests of the other owners at the sale. There was concern over requiring that the fish caught by the fleet be processed through the local auction. There was a fear that Lekeitio fish would be taken to another port or sold to buyers on the high seas. Stiff fines were exacted for such behavior.

One eighteenth-century document sheds light on the range of Lekeitio's market for its catch. It states that Lekeitio's lobster were in demand in the Kingdom of Nafarroa, but not "like the other species [that are desired] in Castile and other parts."

IN SUM, WE find that, by as early as the Middle Ages, a small Basque coastal village with a few thousand inhabitants was actually thoroughly embedded in national and international commercial networks. A young man from Lekeitio might be a globe-trotting mariner in the service of Spanish or foreign maritime interests, or he might be on naval service for the Spanish monarchy. Just as likely, he was a seasonal fisherman off Terranova. Then, too, he might be a member of the Brotherhood of Saint Peter, fishing local coastal waters for a catch that was in part shipped to Iruña, Madrid, and beyond. In short, at least from the perspective of Lekeitio, globalization is scarcely a late-twentieth-century phenomenon.

Lesson thirteen

LEARNING OBJECTIVES

1. To understand the historical significance of fishing and seafaring for Basques.
2. To analyze the small universe of Lekeitio (Lequeitio)—a Bizkaian fishing community.
3. To understand the cultural and diasporic consequences of fishing for Basque society.

REQUIRED READING

Mark Kurlansky, *Cod: A Biography of the Fish that Changed the World* (New York: Walker and Company, 1997), 17–60, 92–106, 177–89.

SUGGESTED READING

Felipe Barandiarán Irizar, *La comunidad de pescadores de bajura de Pasajes de San Juan (ayer y hoy): Estudio antropológico* (Oihartzun: Litografía Danona, 1982).

William A. Douglass and Jon Bilbao, *Amerikanuak: The Basques of the New World*, (Reno: University of Nevada Press, 2005), 51–57.

Mark Kurlansky, *The Basque History of the World* (New York: Walker and Company, 2001), 43–64.

WRITTEN LESSON FOR SUBMISSION

1. Discuss the role of Basque fishermen in the discovery and development of the New World's fishing industry.
2. To what extent was fishing in Lekeitio a collective versus an individual enterprise?
3. Using the Basque case, discuss how fishing and seafaring reflect a relationship between local and international politics.

14 · *Baserri* and *Auzo*

TRADITIONAL Basque agrarian society is anchored in the institution of the *baserri* farmstead. It has been a favored object of study by folklorists and anthropologists. Although its present economic relevance is fairly negligible, its historical and cultural significance are far greater.

The Basque *baserri* farmstead is a physically discrete land unit, which is to say that it is composed of a dwelling located roughly in the center of its combined land holdings. For the Basque peasant, there is a strong correlation between the farmstead and the peasant family. Ideally, a *baserria* is capable of being worked by a single family while providing it with a satisfactory living.

On both moral and economic grounds, it is felt to be wrong to dismember a *baserria*, either by selling a part of it or by dividing it among several heirs. Consequently, in each generation, a single heir to the farm is selected by the owner and spouse from among their offspring. In many parts of the Basque Country, the selection is determined by male primogeniture, that is, the eldest son inherits. However, there are many exceptions. What is important is that a single heir be selected, marry, and continue residing on the farm. The siblings of the selected heir are expected to leave. Traditionally, there were several alternatives open to them. They could marry onto nearby farmsteads, enter religious life, migrate to an urban area, or emigrate abroad.

A key condition of being named heir to the farm is that one contract marriage and thereby provide at least a strong prospect that the family line on the farmstead will continue into the next generation. So formal or legal ownership of the farm is transferred to the heir(ess) only

at the time of his or her marriage. The newly formed
couple and the retiring former owners are then expected
to form a coresidential unit, that is, they will continue
to live under the same roof. Therefore, the ideal form of
rural domestic group organization in the Basque Country is what social scientists call the "stem family."

THIS SINGLE-HEIR transmission of ownership and the
stem-family form of social organization on fixed land
units means that, ideally, over time, there is neither an
increase nor a decrease in the number of farming households in a particular village. And in fact, the territorial
stability of the system is indeed startling. In Etxalar, for
example, many of the farmsteads on the ground today
may be traced back through written documents to as
early as the fourteenth century.

The immutability of the *baserria* is therefore viewed
by the peasants themselves as the mainstay of the rural
society. Each farmstead has a name, which is equally
unaltered over time. The actors take their social identity
from their house name, rather than from their surname.
Jesus Damboriena of the farm Buxungoborda is referred
to by his fellow villagers as "Buxungobordako Jesus" or
simply "Buxun." This identification has prompted one
observer to declare that in Basque society there are no
people—only *houses*.

Not only do persons receive their social identity from
their house name, they are expected to subordinate all
personal interest to the well-being of the household as
long as they remain in residence. The active married
male, called the *etxekojaun*, or "lord of the house," and
the active married female, the *etxekoandre*, or "woman
of the house," are the prime authority figures within
the family. They control all of the household's economic
resources and are partly in control of the economic desti-
nies of the unmarried members. This is true in that the

Hauling hay
To this day, in parts of the Basque countryside, many
agricultural activities remain unmechanized. In this
photo, taken in the early 1960s in the auzo Zubero of
Aulestia, Bizkaia, an etxekojaun used donkey-power to
drag a loaded hay sled from his meadow to the stable in
his dwelling.
Photo: William Douglass

active married couple must provide dowries to all departing members (both male and female), their nature
and amount being at the discretion of the donors. This
nearly total dependence on the *etxekojaun* and *etxekoandre* means that unmarried members, even though they
may have attained physical maturity, are regarded by the
society as social dependents, a fact reflected in the terms
used for bachelor and spinster—*mutil zahar* and *neska
zahar*, "old boy" and "old girl." In the event that the
heir's sibling remains unmarried, he or she has a right
to remain in the household, although subordinated

entirely to the authority of the *etxekojaun* and *etxekoan-dre*.

THE BASQUE *baserria* has considerable social and economic independence. In the traditional society, the ideal living situation was said to have been the extremely isolated farmstead where a family met all of its own needs, living life in harmony and free from outside interference. The word *baserri* reflects this, since it derives from *baso* (wilderness) and *erri* (settlement).

In fact, the isolated farm is a prime cultural symbol of Basqueness, in romanticized form even for urbanites. In the nineteenth-century folk song "Ikusten duzu goizean," the words of the first stanza underscore this attitude:

> Ikusten duzu goizean
> Argia hasten denean
> Menditto baten gainean,
> Etxe ttipitto aintzin xuri bat
> Lau haitz ondoren erdian
> Xakur xuri bat atean
> Iturrino bat aldean
> Han bizi naiz ni pakean.

> Lift your eyes to see
> At the break of day
> Set upon a hill
> A little house, shining white
> Set amid four oaks
> With a small spring nearby
> And a white dog in the doorway
> There I live in peace.

Until the turn of the twentieth century, the farming way of life was a great source of pride for the rural populace. *Etxekojaun* or *etxekoandre* were the most respected roles in the rural society. The peasants would speak disparagingly of the miserable living and working conditions of the urban populace and point with pride to the fact that they were their own bosses. All of this changed rapidly in the twentieth century. The industrialization and urbanization of the Basque Country have led to improvements in urban life and have reversed the roles. It has become more prestigious to work in industry, and the peasant has come to be regarded as backward and brutish. This loss of prestige was one of the major factors contributing to a rural exodus or flight from the land. However, even today, the interpretation of the *baserri* way of life as desirable from a moral standpoint lingers.

The average *baserria* has about ten hectares, or twenty-five acres, divided among arable fields, meadows, and mountain lands. The arable land is where crops such as corn (and in some areas, wheat), root crops (such as turnips used for livestock feed), potatoes (used in both the human and livestock diets), and the household vegetable garden are grown. In short, the arable land is what is plowed for cultivation and what produces a variety of crops.

THE MEADOWS provide the hay reserves and green forage for the livestock. They play a very important role in the household economy, since the worth of the farm is based on its cow-carrying capacity. These lands also contain orchards of apple trees, pears, peaches, plums, cherries, figs, walnuts, and chestnuts, all of which enter the human and animal diets.

The mountain lands are made up of three elements—forests (which provision the household with firewood, nut crops, and building materials), fern lands (which provide the bedding for the stabled livestock, which is then used for fertilizer) and rough pasturage (which provides grazing, in particular for sheep).

Plowing
Formerly fields in Aulestia were prepared for seeding
by turning the soil with a simple plow pulled by a pair
of milk cows. Note the steep slope of the field, a factor
which complicated the farmer's task. Over time the top-
soil migrated to the bottom of the slope and had to be
carried manually back up the hill.
Photo: William Douglass

THE TYPICAL *baserria* has only a little over one hectare
of land in cereal production, and its meadows are
only slightly larger. This means that on the ten-hectare
model *baserria*, almost 70 percent of the land is of the
mountainous variety, while the more extensive, labor-
intensive agricultural operations are carried out on little
more than three hectares.

The distribution of the three types or zones of cropping is not haphazard. The fields where the most labor
is expended are located closest to the farmer's place of

residence. This is the arable land, which requires annual plowing, harrowing, fertilizing, planting, weeding, and hand harvesting. It also tends to be the most level. The meadows are the next closest zone of cropping to the dwelling. They require less labor input during the year, since they need not be plowed. However, each meadow is scythed off as many as four or five times annually, and the green fodder and dried hay must be transported to the dwelling to feed the stabled livestock. The third zone of cropping, the mountain land, requires the least amount of labor input throughout the year. The major activity here is the annual scything of ferns to be dried and carted to the dwelling for use as animal bedding. This is done each autumn and for a period of three or four weeks is the main activity of the family. However, for the rest of the year, the mountain lands are visited infrequently in search of firewood or to check up on the pigs and sheep that are allowed to graze there without close supervision. Each household supplements its own mountainous land with access to the forests and pastures of the village commons.

THE PEASANT experiences time cyclically and seasonally. The agricultural cycle begins in the spring. In late April, the cereal lands must be prepared for the annual planting of a corn crop. By mid-May, the land is ready for seeding. In early August, turnips and other forage plants are seeded. In September, the corn plants mature. By early October, the beans ripen. In November, the ears of corn are stripped from the bare stalks and carted to the household. In December, the fields are cleared of the corn stalks. Throughout late autumn, the turnips and forage crops begin to produce. The potato patch is prepared in March.

The *baserri* dwelling is equally reflective of the institution's economic and social self-sufficiency. It is a three-storied structure, although there is some architectural variety in this regard. The first floor is the entry and an area where four or five milk cows are stabled permanently, except when used briefly for spring plowing. The stable also contains the pigsty. Adjacent to the building are a poultry run and a lean-to for the winter protection of the household's thirty or so sheep. A flight of stairs leads to the family's living quarters. In addition to the two or three bedrooms (unheated) there is the *sukalde* (place of fire), or kitchen, which serves as the focus of daily life, and a *sala*, or living room, which is used only on formal occasions.

The centerpiece of the kitchen is the low hearth, raised but a few inches above the floor. It is where food is cooked in pots suspended over an open fire. It is also where the family used to while away the dark winter evenings, possibly recounting the day's events, singing, or telling folk tales while roasting chestnuts, shucking corn, or carding wool. Until the mid-twentieth century, the only illumination was from candles made from the *baserria*'s own beeswax. Indoor plumbing was also a late-twentieth-century innovation.

THE *SALA* is its own special world. Dominated by a formal dining table, it is used but rarely, on ceremonial occasions. These might include a banquet for kinsmen returning from nearby cities to celebrate the village saint's annual feast day or a dinner to welcome back a family member who emigrated to Argentina or Idaho decades earlier. It is also where the open coffin of a deceased household member is displayed before being carried by pallbearers over the traditional *il bide* (death road) that links every *baserri* to the village church. Formerly, each *baserri* had its own sepulture, a rectangle on the church floor where women from the deceased's household would observe the ritual cycle of the customary year of mourning.

The walls of the *sala* are a veritable family museum. They are adorned with the photographs of several generations of householders, often taken on formal occasions such as baptisms, christenings, and weddings. They may be supplemented as well with exotic images of an uncle playing the Basque card game *mus* in a Mexico City Basque club or another dressed as a working cowboy and astride his horse on the range of some Nevada ranch.

UNTIL ABOUT 1900, as we've noted, the main emphasis in the rural economy was on household self-sufficiency. That is, ideally, the domestic group or family was expected to meet all of its needs without recourse to purchases in the marketplace. This was obviously impossible, although, in fact, it was approximated on the Basque *baserria* to an amazing degree. The diet around 1900 was extremely simple, consisting of soups, porridges, milk and milk products—and very little meat. Vegetables that have subsequently become quite popular were almost unknown, including potatoes, tomatoes, lettuce, carrots, beets, string beans, and so on. The three main staples were chestnuts (eaten roasted or ground into a mash for soups), cornbread, and beans. All of these items were produced on the farm. The main beverages were milk and apple cider—both from the farm. The only recourse to the store was for salt, some sugar, chocolate, coffee, and occasional alcoholic beverages. However, even here we are dealing with very infrequent purchases of a small quantity consumed on special occasions. Other items produced on the farm for the diet were honey, used as a sugar substitute, fruits, and some meat. The major meat source came from the annual killing of a pig and curing of the meat. It was then used sparingly throughout the year to lend flavor

---

and sustenance to stews and porridges, but was rarely eaten by itself. Chickens were kept, but both the hens and eggs were usually sold.

Self-sufficiency was apparent in other activities. Furniture was manufactured on the farm, and all repairs to the dwelling were done by the householder. Even eating utensils were carved from wood. Footwear was made from the skins of animals. Each household grew a small patch of flax and manufactured linen clothing and bedding, literally from the seed through the finished product. The sheep provided wool, which was used for stockings and bedding. Most of the tools for agriculture were built on the farm, including wooden plowshares. Chemical fertilizer for the fields was produced by building ovens and burning limestone to reduce it to powder. The only dependence on store-bought implements was for hardware such as nails, metal tools, and cooking vessels.

THIS PICTURE of extreme self-sufficiency was altered profoundly during the twentieth century. Basque peasants, like everyone else, aspire to the material benefits available in the modern world, and we might even suppose that the proximity of urban-industrial areas in the Basque Country has made them aware of such benefits more quickly than in other European peasantries further removed from such influences. By the 1960s, the diet was much more varied, and there was increased dependence on store-purchased foodstuffs. No one ate *talo* (cornbread) any longer. Wheat bread was purchased in the local bakery daily. Apple cider was seldom made, and the daily beverage became purchased wine. Chickens and eggs were consumed in great quantities. Pigs were still killed for home consumption, but people also ate beef purchased in the local butcher shop and fish

Essentials
Traditional music on drum and flute played at a
Basque event in Montevideo (Uruguay) in the early
twentieth century. The figure of the txistulari is central
to Basque music folk performances.
Photo from the collection of Xabier Irujo

brought inland from the seacoast. Canned goods were being consumed with ever-increasing frequency, and fresh fruits grown elsewhere, such as oranges, were often purchased. There was a much wider variety of garden vegetables consumed, which were both grown on the farm and purchased locally. Clothing was rarely manufactured on the farm any longer. Footgear was purchased in the stores, and wooden eating utensils were no longer made on the farm.

IN SUM, throughout the last several centuries, the *baserria* farmstead was the primary institution of rural society. The term refers simultaneously to a dwelling (*etxe*), an ecological unit (the three zones of land use), the socioeconomic unit (farmstead and stem family), a mode of life (peasant versus urbanite), and a symbol of Basque tradition.

In Basque rural society, the *baserri* households are arranged into an administrative division, or *auzoa*, which contains from ten to thirty-five farmsteads. While each *auzo* is a named unit and territorially discrete, there is no corresponding internal political structure, unlike the *barrio* structure in parts of Spain and Latin America. What constitutes a neighborhood varies from one village to another. In Aulestia, every *auzo* has a name and a patron saint and is a corporate body regarding maintenance of its own roads and public utilities. In Santa Grazi and Etxalar, each household defines the limits of its own neighborhood. Its two main characteristics are the permanence of neighbor relationships and dyadic reciprocity between neighbors.

Within the householdcentric *auzoa*, neighborhood ties and obligations constitute the primary networks of social and economic relations, including the special relationship that a household maintains with its closest or "first" neighbor (geographically defined), the relationship that the household maintains with three or four of the physically most proximate households, and the relationship that the household maintains with all other households within its *auzoa*.

The physically nearest household is called *auzorik urren* ("the first neighbor"), in Aulestia, or *lenbizikoate* ("the first door"), in Etxalar. Traditionally, every household depended on another for first-neighbor obligations. The first neighbor was the initial outsider to be informed whenever there was a crisis. If a member was taken seriously ill, the first neighbor was notified and would then dispatch someone to get the doctor. In the event of a death, the first neighbor notified the priest and civil authorities, arranged for the funeral and coffin, and contacted relatives of the bereaved. During the early days of bereavement, the first neighbor assumed the domestic and agricultural chores in the stricken household. The importance of the first-neighbor relationship is eulogized in refrains and reflected in the common statement that it was more important to be on good terms with one's closest neighbor than with a brother.

SANDRA OTT describes a prime example of the first-neighborhood relationship in her analysis of blessed bread. In Santa Grazi, the *etxekoandre* attended Mass in the village church and then brought home two candles for use in the household and two loaves of bread blessed by the priest. One of the loaves was intended to circulate throughout the village "for the living," from first neighbor to first neighbor as tangible sign of social solidarity. The other loaf was consumed at home. The circulating bread was transmitted serially in a clockwise direction among the households. The bread giver on the left gave to the bread receiver on the right. The loaf was handed over with the words "our seed." Meanwhile, the strongest funerary obligations between two households circulated from right to left (a relationship referred to as "first, first neighbor"). Since there were ninety-nine *baserri*ak in Santa Grazi, it required about two years for the blessed bread to complete its trip around the *ungüru* (circle).

The second network of *auzo* relations implicates the three or four geographically most proximate households in a close neighbors' network of moral support and labor exchange that is mutually reciprocal with respect to the defining household. In the event of a death, the close neighbors play a prominent role in the funerary proceedings. Close neighbors assist one another with certain agricultural tasks, such as hand plowing, lime burning, and corn shucking, which are easier or more pleasant when carried out with the assistance and in the company of others. When a household slaughtered a pig, it would send *txerri puxkak* (pig parts) to its closest neighbors. This constituted a form of primitive banking and a hedge against spoilage in a traditional society that lacked refrigeration. One parceled out perishable meat too abundant to be consumed expeditiously by a single family in the expectation that one's close neighbors would return the favor when they processed their pig.

FOR THE *baserria* household, the *auzoa* as a whole bounded another of its social networks. A representative of every *auzo* household was expected to "visit" a member *baserri* experiencing birth / baptism, marriage, illness or death. The *auzoa*, when constituted as a corporate body, also carried out *auzolan* (*auzo* work), communal projects such as road maintenance. Any household lacking a suitable member for the task had to find a substitute or pay a fine.

In many regards, then, ties between neighbors in rural Basque society were both dense and intense. However, the obligations are prescribed so formally by the distribution of *baserris* on the ground that one easily understands and discharges his or her social obligations with a minimum of personal affective commitment. It is thus scarcely an exaggeration to suggest that in rural Basque society, "houses" indeed were more important than "people."

SINCE THE mid-twentieth century, however, there has been notable decline in the number of Basque *baserriak*. In large measure the abandonment of farmsteads, or their transition to something other than subsistence agricultural enterprises (for example, as the modernized residence of people commuting daily to a factory job in a nearby town), is largely attributable to the "consumer revolution" of a globalized world. We will return to this topic in chapter 27.

Lesson fourteen

LEARNING OBJECTIVES
1. To understand the primary rural socioeconomic institution of the *baserria* or farmstead and its role within Basque traditional culture.
2. To analyze Basque peasant life as a cultural universe.
3. To understand the relevance of neighborhood relations in the rural Basque social universe.
4. To analyze the economic and cultural dilemmas of Basque peasants in a globalized world.

REQUIRED READING
William A. Douglass, *Echalar and Murelaga: Opportunity and Rural Exodus in Two Spanish Basque Villages* (New York: St. Martins Press; 1975), 18–49.
Sandra Ott, *The Circle of Mountains* (Reno: University of Nevada Press, 1993), 63–81, 117–30.

SUGGESTED READING

William A. Douglass, "The Famille Souche and Its Interpreters," *Continuity and Change* 8, no. 1: 87–102.

Miren Etxezarreta, *El caserío vasco* (Bilbao:Iker, 1977)

Davydd J. Greenwood, *Unrewarding Wealth: The Commercialization and Collapse of Agriculture in a Spanish Basque Town* (Cambridge: Cambridge University
Press, 1976).

WRITTEN LESSON FOR SUBMISSION

1. Discuss the institutional components of the *baserria*
   itself and its relations within the *auzoa*.
2. Summarize the essential factors of economic production in the traditional *baserri / auzo* economy.
3. How does life on a *baserria* and in an *auzoa* differ
   from that in an American suburb?

15 · Contrasting Traditions
Peasants and Fishermen Compared

IN THE Basque Country, as in much of rural Europe, fishing is an alternative to agriculture, rather than its complementary lifestyle. This is true even though the coastal community may well contain agricultural-ists (*baserritarrak*), as well as *arrantzaleak* (fisher-men), since the two sectors represent markedly distinc-tive ways of life. Such economic segregation has been reported in Wales and Scandinavia, and is clear in the Basque case, as well. Davydd J. Greenwood, in his mono-graph on the death of agriculture in the town of Hond-arribia, for instance, discusses the economic strategies employed there without practically any reference to the fishing complex that is a large part of the local economy.

It should be noted that the labor-intensive periods in fishing and agriculture largely coincide. That is, both are at their peaks during the spring-to-autumn period of the year. This fact alone may account in large measure for the economic compartmentalization of the two popula-tions. There is also a certain social discrimination, as well, in that the fishing population is viewed as *kaletar-rak* (dwellers of the street), rather than fellow *baserri-tarrak* (*baserri* people). They are viewed by the farmers as urbane townspeople living in crowded conditions in fishing *barrios* with a lively social life and the kind of involvement with one's neighbors that is anathema to *baserri* dwellers.

The fishing *barrios* of the coastal towns are densely populated, with people living in apartment buildings. The ground floors are given over to myriad small busi-nesses and taverns. When in port, the men engage nightly in the *txikiteo*, or bar hopping, with their friends. The *baserritarrak* thus describe the fishing

The Basques and the sea
The fishing fleet of Donibane-Lohitzune (St. Jean de Luz), Lapurdi, is Iparralde's largest. Farming and fishing constitute the two main occupations in the Basque traditional economy. Despite their geographical and social proximity trough residence in the same towns, the mentalities of farmers and fishermen are starkly different. Throughout history, Basque have been known for their maritime ventures.
Photo: Joyce Laxalt

population as loud, precocious, and obnoxious. In Bizkaia, for instance, the figure of the native from the fishing town of Bermeo is invoked as the stereotype of a crazy person. For their part, the fishermen characterize the farmers as suspicious, backward, and brutish. In Lekeitio, for instance, if the children spotted a farmer

walking down the street, they would pursue him with taunts of:
> *Baserritarra*
> *Tirritarra*
> *Jan belarra*
> *Bota uzkarra!*

> *Farmer*
> *Neener, neener, neener*
> *Eat grass*
> *Pass gas!*

In short, there seems to be a qualitative difference in the social life of the two groups. There is also a sense in which there is strong segregation of the sexes, but not in terms of the traditional Mediterranean pattern, with its chaperonage and overtones of honor and shame. Rather, fishing requires that fathers be absent from the family for extended periods of time. There is therefore a sense in which wives lead an independent existence while serving as the main authority figures within the family. Women usually control the purse strings and set the priorities for the domestic unit. In fact, in Basque society, one way of characterizing a domineering woman is to say that she is from Bermeo.

THERE ARE other ways in which the imagery of the independence of the fishwife is underscored, as well. Traditionally, it was she who traveled from the coastal village to the city to sell her husband's catch. Songs such as "Desde Santurce a Bilbao" and "Kattalin" are the Basque equivalent to the Dubliner song "Molly Malone," extolling the figure of the lone woman peddling her wares in a cruel world, surviving by her grit and wits.

Another manifestation of the social segregation of the fisherfolk is their pronounced tendency toward

endogamy. As one informant put it to William Douglass,
"only a fisherman's daughter could marry a fisherman."
The implication was that the family norms and lifestyle
of those who fish differ so markedly from those of the
surrounding population that a person would have to be
socialized into them from an early age.

IN CONTRADISTINCTION to the assertive, self-confident
fishwife, we might juxtapose the figure of the husband. Absent for part of the year and strongly oriented
toward his fellow fishermen, even when on shore, he
is practically a bit player, if not a stranger, in his own
household. In fact, there is a sense in which the lifestyle
leads to personal irresponsibility, at least with respect to
child-rearing duties and self-centeredness.

We might mention one incident to illustrate the
point. When Douglass was doing fieldwork in Aulestia, his dearest friend was Don Emilio, the local parish
priest. Don Emilio was from Lekeitio and hence knew
many fishermen well. A dish of particular renown in
the Basque Country is *marmitako*, a stew made with
fresh tuna. It is standard shipboard fare for the fishermen while at sea. Don Emilio extolled its virtues and
promised to arrange a tuna barbecue and *marmitako*
to introduce the anthropologist to both his friends and
their dish. One day he received word that that evening
he and Douglass were invited to a *marmitako* to be organized expressly for them in Mendexa (Mendeja), a small
village near Lekeitio. They arrived at dusk, and about
twenty men were in the midst of the lively preparations.
After a wonderful meal, everyone lingered until one or
two in the morning over the brandy, cigars, and singing.
Finally, a few of the men began to excuse themselves
and slipped away. The anthropologist later learned that
they had all arrived in port that day after several weeks
absence, had spent the afternoon unloading the cargo,

then prepared the *marmitako* and were scheduled to leave the next morning for another stint at sea. Those who slipped away wanted a few hours of conjugal visit.

A further point is the importance of fishing within the worldview of Basque society as a whole. As with the case of traditional agriculture and the *baserria*, fishing carries a symbolic load within Basque culture that is all out of proportion to its demographic and economic significance. It might be argued that seafood is central to Old World Basque cuisine, with particular emphasis placed on dishes employing hake, codfish, tuna, sea bream, sardines, anchovies, and squid. Hence, news about fishing is a front-page item in the Basque press and even serves as a kind of barometer of the citizenry's collective sense of well-being. Above all, dire news that the catch is down or that more fishermen are giving up the lifestyle create considerable uneasiness, a kind of concern over "what will we eat?" in the vox populi that is simply absent when there are equally poor harvests of vegetables or when the price of meat increases.

JUST AS WITHIN the farming complex, we can discern both individualist and collectivist tendencies within fishing. Regarding the individualism, there are instances, such as in Hondarribia, in which each boat is owned by a single family and goes out just a short distance from port on a daily basis. In this case, the unit of economic exploitation is a family enterprise not unlike that of the *baserria*. Each family cooperates with others at certain levels, but is largely on its own. Its success or failure depends on luck and its own efforts. There is some evidence, however, that at least traditionally there was a system whereby the luck factor was spread out among several participating families. For instance, in past times, if, while fishing, a boat got into a school and was observed by less fortunate crews, the latter could rush to the scene.

If they shouted "partners" before the nets were hauled in, they were allowed to share in the catch. This seems to have been a way of spreading the risk in a context in which an extended run of bad luck could spell disaster for a family. It is also a means of banking resources and effort that is not unlike the *txerri puxkak* network in the rural *auzoa*.

In his book *Terranova*, Joseba Zulaika analyzes the fishermen's ethos (their culturally standardized emotions) framed by three basic settings in their lives: the home, the sea, and the foreign port. It can be said of a fisherman that, from the moment he leaves home, he is emotionally "returning" to it.

The fisherman develops a strictly dichotomous world between sea and land. It is framed in terms of oppositions: The sea is a workplace; the shore is the "life" from which he departs and to which he must return. The stay at sea is temporary; the shore is more permanent. The sea is experienced as a "prison" in which emotional deprivation reigns; the shore is the place where emotional needs are satisfied. The sea is the place of uncertainty; the shore is security. At sea, luck is everything; on shore, security, particularly personified in one's family, is all.

THE FISHERMAN has to pay an enormous psychological toll for his long months of isolation: He has difficulties in adapting to life on shore after his return, and his children develop largely without his presence and influence. Yet he cannot do without the sea, the nets, the seductive play with luck. His dilemma consists in that his thoughts turn homeward while he is at sea, but when at home, he anticipates the next voyage. He therefore experiences continuous distancing, even alienation, from present circumstances—no matter what they are. In a foreign port, the fisherman can display a double

Gregorio Elizalde and Marcelina Esandi
Typical wedding photo replete with formality and
decorum taken in Estella, Nafarroa at the turn of the
twentieth century.
Photo from the collection of Xabier Irujo

---

sexual standard: It is totally inadmissible that his wife should have affairs while he is away fishing, but it is "understandable" that he should visit prostitutes while in a foreign port. The double standard corresponds to a definition that differentiates relations with a prostitute as mere substitute sex. His infidelity in a foreign port and infidelity at home are also differentiated. The former is tolerable, the latter is not. In the required reading, Charlotte Crawford provides interesting insight into the fishermen's family life viewed from the women's perspective. Note the marginalization of the men in the women's descriptions. Accordingly, while maintaining the ideal of the authority of the husband, in fact "women maintain a position of dominance within the family sphere." In a world in which men's and women's activities are highly compartmentalized and autonomous domains, the women make the basic decisions concerning family purchases and initiatives while keeping the husbands informed of what is going on.

THERE IS ONE clear difference between the worlds of peasant agriculture and fishing: their distinctive concepts of luck or chance. Peasant agriculturalists are vulnerable to the vagaries of excellent and poor harvests due to a season's weather. The crop in one part of a village can be leveled by a localized summer's hailstorm that misses other fields within the same community. A cow can sicken and die, potentially a devastating loss for the affected *baserria*. In the readings regarding the *baserria* and the *auzoa*, we considered the social and ritual mechanisms designed to protect or cushion afflicted households from such devastating eventualities. Such risk management is played out within a worldview that sees harvests as a generally reliable and predictable return on hard labor expended over time, rather than as driven by highly erratic good or bad short-term fortune.

A fisherman, however, is confronted, first and foremost, with chance. There are huge fluctuations in the catch of a single day. It may surpass that of the following two weeks. The basic framework of a fisherman's worldview regarding the sea includes the notion that hard work is the means to the catch, but, unlike the lot of the peasant agriculturalist, there is no cause-and-effect relationship between willingness to work and outcome. Fishermen also believe that there is a gap between the human and the natural orders that cannot be bridged by sheer effort alone. Rather, much depends on chance, a probability that is categorized as luck—"good" or "bad." Thus, there is a sense that it is the fisherman who, by means of his luck, rather than his dedication, mediates between the two otherwise unbridgeable orders.

Luck can be defined variously according to cosmology (when natural resources become accessible for human action), logic (when potential fishing possibilities become actual realities), philosophy (the arbitrary causation that governs the world), psychology (the regulation of human expectations), economy (profit through a combination of the natural and technical orders), emotion (the need to support one's family), and the social (the legitimization of the fishing way of life).

THERE IS A sense in which "good" luck just happens, while "bad" luck can sometimes be ascribed to human shortcomings, such as technological failures or poor application of technical expertise, as when those in command miscalculate when and where to fish. The fishermen's own team leader has the greatest responsibility (and culpability) in such matters. He is the prime mediator who, if he cannot guarantee good luck, should at least avoid bad luck. The worst eventuality of all is "no luck." Superstitious beliefs and practices are the antidotes to

---

the absence of luck. There is an imperative to search out the hidden causes of this void.

Lesson fifteen

LEARNING OBJECTIVES
1. To analyze the similarities and differences between the two "traditional" Basque lifestyles—agriculture and fishing.
2. To consider the extent to which mentalities are formed in reaction to basic occupations.

REQUIRED READING
Joseba Zulaika, *Terranova: The Ethos and Luck of Deep-Sea Fishermen* (Newfoundland: ISER, 1981), 65–94.
Charlotte Crawford, "The Position of Women in a Basque Fishing Community," in *Anglo-American Contributions to Basque Studies: Essays in Honor of Jon Bilbao*, ed. William A. Douglass, Richard H. Etulain, and William H. Jacobsen, Jr. (Reno, Nevada: Desert Research Institute Publications on the Social Sciences 13, 1977), 145–52.

WRITTEN LESSON FOR SUBMISSION
1. To what extent are people affected by their geography? Are Basque "character," culture, and migration affected by the land and sea?
2. To the degree that occupation fashions a mentality, would we expect to find significant differences in outlook between Basque fishermen and Basque peasants?
3. What can we learn from the worldview of deep-sea fishermen?

16 · Character
and Rural Basque Sexual Mores

THIS CHAPTER might also have been entitled "Sex Ambivalence in Traditional Rural Basque Society." "Rural" because what we are about to say pertains primarily to insights gained from anthropological fieldwork in rural communities conducted half a century ago. Sexual mores in the urban Basque context are not of central concern here, although we do believe that there is some carryover. "Traditional" because in the last forty years, the Basque Country, like much of the rest of the Western world, has experienced a sexual revolution. "Ambivalence" because we will argue that there was an inconsistency regarding sexual matters that led to considerable tension within rural Basque society. That is, there was a tradition of sexual permissiveness coexisting side by side with one of Europe's most puritanical complexes of sexual mores.

To introduce the topic properly, it is well to contrast Basque traditional sexual mores with those of neighboring peoples. As we have seen, there is a sense in which Basques are culturally a non-Latin people enclaved in the Latin world of Southern Europe. This is particularly apparent in the attitudes toward sexuality. While it is an oversimplification, let's consider in broad outline the two components of the famed Southern European double standard, or what might be called its "Don Juanismo," the cultural centrality of the macho figure of Don Juan. Typically, males were permitted considerable sexual latitude, indeed were almost exhorted to premarital and even extramarital sexual conquests as a demonstrable sign of manhood. Sexual bravado with one's male friends was required to the point where the timid or unsuccessful man might even invent sexual adventures to

Pello and Maite kissing in Altzuza, Nafarroa.
An open sharing of affection in the "New Age" of gender relations.
Photo: Xabier Irujo

---

recount to his male companions. Conversely, women were expected to be the bastions of sexual virtue. Premarital chastity and strict fidelity within marriage were demanded of them. Indeed, a family took its honor from the reputation of its female members, which made fathers and brothers the custodians of wives, daughters, and sisters. The fallen woman was a constant literary theme and cuckoldry one of the most explosive social situations imaginable. In the world of the Mediterranean male, the most telling insult that one man could level at another was that of being a cuckold—a *cabrón* in Spanish or a *cornuto* in Italian. Within the legal system, avenging one's dishonor for the sexual digression of a spouse or female family member was a legitimate male plea for clemency in murder cases. By the same token, the publicly indiscreet female was the object of great derision. The young girl believed to have engaged in sex relations all but forfeited her chances of marriage. She was also likely to be disowned by her family, ending up as a domestic servant, a prostitute in some distant city, or in a convent as a repentant nun.

THIS SYSTEM, of course, displays inconsistencies of its own, different from those of the Basque Country. If Don Juan must seduce women in order to make his reputation, yet ensure the chastity of his sister and daughter, then who is available for Don Juan to seduce? In one sense, it might be said that the system couldn't work without Swedish tourists. We are not just being facetious, because in the female Swedish tourist we are invoking the image of the outsider; the woman *without* a father and brothers for all practical purposes.

Much more could be said about Don Juan, who, as often as not, is Don Pepe—the beleaguered father of a family and henpecked husband of a domineering wife. However, we raise the stereotype only to use it as a foil against which to view the Basque situation. In contrast to the foregoing Latin complex, in rural Basque society, there was no pronounced double standard for men and women, and family honor was not seen to turn on the question of female chastity. We do not mean to suggest that premarital sex was particularly encouraged or dismissed, but, once publicly acknowledged, it did not lead automatically to either forced marriage or destruction of the future marital prospects of the exposed woman. At the same time, however, there was a considerable reticence about sexual matters in both men and women alike. This inconsistency is at the core of the ambivalence about sexual matters in Basque society. While more leeway was permitted both sexes in terms of sexual behavior, sexual behavior itself was not seen as something that could be discussed or even mentioned.

CONSIDER THE ethnography of courtship and marriage in Etxalar or Aulestia in the early 1960s. We might begin by noting that in any Basque village of the time, there was considerable public segregation of the sexes. Boys went to one school, girls to another. In church, there were men's and women's segregated seating sections. The taverns were primarily male venues, although women were not rigidly excluded. One might note that, in the 1960s, all three taverns in Etxalar were owned and operated by women, which was not regarded to be morally compromising or reprehensible. Indeed, all three women raised their small children in the midst of tavern life. Young adolescent men had their religious sodality and hunting groups; young women had their Hijas de Maria, their Daughters of Mary sisterhood. Sexual indiscretion by a young person of either sex resulted in expulsion from the respective religious association, the Basque equivalent of the scarlet letter.

The formal context for young people to meet and mingle was the weekly dance held in the village square on Sunday afternoon and evening. Sometimes the young people collected money to pay an accordionist; sometimes the town officials made the arrangements. The dance would begin at dusk, usually with all the young men gathered at one end of the plaza and the women at the other. After a while, young girls would begin to dance with each other. Most of the boys remained in their own tight little cliques, nervously exchanging banter and horseplay. Toward evening's end, a few young men worked up the courage to ask a girl to dance. Few were accomplished or even seemed to enjoy the dancing in which the couple embraced. There was more spontaneity and release when the accordionist broke into the strains of the *jota* and the dancers could disengage and "perform," rather than touch each other.

Once the formal dancing was over, say about eleven o'clock, the young people dispersed, and the practice of *neska laguntza*, or "accompanying a girl," began. That is, in marked contrast to Mediterranean society, there was no chaperonage of young women, and many of the girls lived as much as an hour's walk away on a mountain *baserri*. If a young couple were beginning to be interested in one another, they would make no show of it in the plaza. If he danced with anyone, it would be with girls other than his intended. However, under cover of darkness, he would wait for her at the edge of the village nucleus and walk her home. Over time, the relationship might become sexual and would be hidden from close friends and family. Even once it was known that two people were going together, there was considerable avoidance of the topic.

IN THE HOUSE where the anthropologist was staying, the eldest daughter had been dating a young man for five years and was in the final stages of preparing for her wedding. One day, shortly after he had learned about it, the anthropologist and her father were standing in the plaza as the young man passed by. Douglass greeted him, but her father turned his back. The young man moved away quickly. When asked if he disliked Carmen's suitor, the father blushed and said that no, he was a fine young man, but no one in the household had mentioned the relationship to him, and he preferred it that way.

This lack of explicitness in sexual matters often took extreme forms. For instance, once a couple decided to marry, they had to receive obligatory premarital instructions from the priest. For a while, the anthropologist lived next door to the priest in Etxalar and observed a young woman arrive with a chicken, telling anyone in earshot that it was a gift from her family to the priest. She would go inside. Half an hour later, her fiancé would arrive furtively, and presently they would leave separately. However, at some point the relationship had to be made public. The church required that on three Sundays prior to the wedding, the banns of marriage be announced at Mass. When the priest first announced the engagement during the sermon, a buzz went through the congregation—a sort of "I didn't even know they were going together" exclamation that rippled through a community of fewer than one thousand persons in which everyone knew everyone else pretty well.

Then there was the question of the ceremony. While some of the weddings were held in the village church, more frequently, the couple went with close friends and relatives to a distant religious sanctuary such as the monastery of Aránzazu in Gipuzkoa. The couple would be married far from the public scrutiny of their neighbors, go on their honeymoon, and then return to the village with as little fanfare as possible to assume their new role as married adults.

NOT UNCOMMONLY, the bride would be pregnant before the wedding ceremony, a fact of considerable chagrin for the priest, but one that elicited surprisingly little comment from the congregation. The ethnographer José Miguel de Barandiarán has suggested that in the French Basque village of Sara, there was trial marriage to demonstrate the fertility of the couple. While not a consciously stated objective, such a practice would certainly be consistent with the social-structural imperative of turning over ownership and nearly full authority within the *baserria* to the designated heir(ess) at his or her marriage. There was danger in deeding over the property to a barren couple and thereby threatening social

Wedding in Agoitz, Nafarroa (2002)
Much of today's typical Basque wedding is identical to
that characteristic of Catholic ceremony throughout
the Occidental world. However, note that in departing
the church the couple passes under a flowered archway
held aloft by dancers in folk costume.
Photo: Xabier Irujo

continuity on the farmstead. In any event, premarital pregnancy had the function of terminating what were often seemingly interminable courtships. In Etxalar, there were several cases of courtships lasting for ten years or more.

This raises the related questions of the high mean age at marriage in rural Basque society, the high rates of spinsterhood and bachelorhood, and the frequency of arranged marriages. Along with rural Ireland, the rural Basque Country manifested Europe's most extreme example of delayed marriage. It was not unusual for men to marry in their late thirties, with women marrying only somewhat earlier. This practice can also be explained as part of the stem-family system of social organization, since the heir really was able to marry only when the elderly were prepared to relinquish legal control of the *baserria*. However, it also reflected a certain fear of sexuality and its responsibilities. This seemed clear in the high incidence of celibacy. It was not uncommon for two male and one female siblings to reside together on a farm after the death of their parents, thereby permitting all three to avoid marriage. A nephew or niece might be brought in and raised by them as heir or heiress in the next generation.

THERE WAS ALSO a prevalence of arranged marriages. Again, one might invoke a social or economic rationale. For instance, there existed in Etxalar and Aulestia a greater than chance incidence of cousin marriage, which could be interpreted as a means of consolidating property in a particular family line. However, it was also employed by desperate parents to coax a shy son or daughter out of his or her shell. For example, the forty-year-old, only-child son of one family in Aulestia finally consented to marry his aging first cousin—his parents' argument being "you know her already, you don't have to do anything more than show up at church."

Indeed, this underscores the extent to which marriage was felt to be as much an economic and social arrangement as a question of romantic predilection—if not more so. Matchmaking by professionals has long characterized rural Basque society. In 1960, the going rate for anyone who could find a bride willing to marry a farmer was one cow. Oftentimes such matchmaking brought people together from different towns and even provinces, with the actual parties to the union taking the step as virtual strangers. The emigrant diaspora also provides many examples of arranged marriages. A herder in the American West, a cane cutter in Australia, or a meatpacker in Argentina might send for a "mail-order" bride, possibly after having been "introduced" by her fellow-immigrant brother.

CONVERSELY, THERE were many examples of lengthy family separation. In Aulestia, there were several women with husbands in the United States herding sheep or in Australia cutting cane. During the second half of the twentieth century, married men signing contracts to herd sheep in the American West faced a minimum three-year separation. There was a man from Aulestia who had signed five contracts, spending six months to a year at home between sojourns in the American West and fathering a child on each trip back. He returned permanently after twenty years, but had a difficult adjustment to family life.

We might mention an extreme case from Aulestia that highlights many of the points we have been making. A sheepherder returned to the village after forty years' absence and moved into his sister's household. His eldest niece was a beautiful girl and was engaged to a popular young man. The uncle was quite wealthy

Three musicians playing folk music
While today Basque culture is at the cutting edge of
universal contemporary musical trends, there remains
considerable commitment to folk traditions. This performing group, Aizkorbe, Sagastibeltza and Eskudero, is
from the San Fermín (Nafarroa's patron saint) ikastola
or Basque language school.
Photo: Xabier Irujo

---

by local standards, and his sister coveted his money.
The old man took a fancy to his niece, and the mother
ordered the young girl to marry him. Public sentiment
ran high against the marriage, and the priest denounced
it. The young girl was desolate. Her desperate young
fiancé signed a herder's contract and left for the United
States, in part to get away from the situation, but also

in the hope of saving enough money to satisfy the girl's mother. All he succeeded in doing was removing himself as the uncle's rival. The old man was in ill health; the mother became fearful he would move out or spend his money foolishly before dying and leaving it wisely to her daughter. She brought relentless pressure to bear, and the young woman finally consented to the union. The wedding was set secretly for five o'clock in the morning in the village church, so, presumably, it would be a fait accompli before the village awakened. However, as luck would have it, the groom had had a falling out with his best friend a few days before. The friend knew about the pending wedding and happened to live in a house with a balcony overlooking the church. Consequently, on the morning of the ceremony, as the couple walked out of the church, he took his revenge by firing off skyrockets from his balcony to publicize the girl's cruel fate.

THERE IS A literature regarding sexual mores in the Basque Country. The most notable work is by the ethnographer José M. Satrústegui. He examined the situation in a number of Nafarroan communities and found much evidence that is consistent with the foregoing description. First, Satrústegui noted the tremendous difficulty that both men and women had in even discussing the topic of sex. One of his female informants, when speaking with a female interviewer, could answer questions only if she first closed her eyes. There was great timidity and even shame regarding pregnancy, and sometimes married women found it difficult to confide their state to their own mothers until it became a physical impossibility to hide. Men were even more reticent than women to talk of sex and did so only with great embarrassment. One man confided to the anthropologist that he had never disrobed before his spouse, preferring to confine his sex life to total darkness.

Regarding the difficulty of proposing marriage and conducting courtship, Satrústegui cites the cases of men asking their mother to convey their proposal to a prospective wife. There was also an indicated day (March 1) in one Nafarroan town specifically set aside for matchmaking. Two notary publics set up shop to make the legal agreements and ran a service akin to the multiple listing in today's real estate market. That is, while the young people attended a festival, their parents lined up to check out the proposed dowries and the property of prospective spouses, as well as any other personal background information they could obtain. The two sets of parents would sign a marital agreement in the morning and then introduce the young couple to each other that afternoon.

ANOTHER THEME running through Satrústegui's work—and one that helps explain the Basque reticence about acknowledging sexual behavior—is the role of the clergy in fomenting a fanatically puritanical view of sexuality. This point may be developed by placing it in historical context. The theological view of human sexuality present in both rural Basque and rural Irish culture was highly influenced by Jansenism, a movement that was founded in the seventeenth century by a Belgian priest named Jansen. He and a group of disciples in a monastery near Paris espoused an almost Calvinistic brand of Catholicism. They denied the existence of free will, maintained that human nature is basically corrupt, and claimed that Christ died to save the select few, rather than all of humankind. There were two consequences that flowed from this philosophy. The clergy ruled, railing against human weakness, particularly warning against dangers of the flesh. And the individual was obliged to act as if he or she were saved in order to convince himself or herself and others that this was indeed

the case. Hence, there was great emphasis on ascetic living and religious formality. There was, then, the perception of an aloof and stern God who appointed the clergy
as the watchdogs over frail humanity.

Jansen was ultimately declared a heretic and excom-
municated. His disciples went to Ireland and became
a moving force in Irish monasticism. Jansen himself
took refuge at a seminary in the Basque Country under
the aegis of his major disciple, the bishop of Baiona.
There he helped form a generation of Basque priests.
Shortly before his arrival, both the Spanish and French
Inquisitions had conducted extensive witchcraft trials
in the Basque Country and had condemned many of the
accused to death. The testimony turned on *akelarreak*,
or witches' Sabbaths, in which black Masses and sexual
orgies, including copulation with the devil, were supposed to have transpired in many Basque villages. (See
chapter 19.)

THE TRIALS HAD spread great fear throughout the
area and had obviously softened it up for the puritanical message of Jansen and his followers. This initiated a nearly tyrannical dominance by an authoritarian
clergy obsessed with sins of the flesh. The bishops were
constantly issuing edicts against such things as corn-
husking bees, where young men and women might work
and socialize together. In one eighteenth-century edict,
the bishop of Iruña ordered that a dog should be able
to pass between any two persons engaged in dancing. A
nineteenth-century edict gave rise to a "handkerchief
dance" in which the circled participants held on to the
ends of the cloth, rather than touching hands. On one
occasion, the bishop of Iruña simply mandated a fine
of fifty ducats for anyone caught dancing. Parish priests
regularly threatened to expel girls from the Daughters
of Mary organization for it. Satrústegui tells of the time

in one village in which, during a dance, the priest rang
the death dirge from the church tower, thereby forcing
everyone to stop and bless themselves. It happened three
times, and one young man come running to ask who
had died. The priest answered, "Common sense, my son,
common sense." Musicians were regarded by the clergy
as evil, and priests referred to the accordion as *infernuko
auspoa*, or "the bellows of hell."

FEMALE DRESS was another preoccupation of the
priests. The bishop of Iruña issued an order that
before a woman entered a church, her sleeves must
reach her wrists. As recently as 1943, a woman was
denied Holy Communion because her dress exposed her
knees, and another suffered the same fate for approaching the altar rail wearing lipstick. In the 1960s, one priest
maintained a collection of women's bathing suits in his
sacristy and required any woman contemplating buying beach wear to examine the ones he deemed acceptable. These examples could be multiplied. However, we
should also note that, after the Ecumenical Council of
Pope John XXIII in the early 1960s, the clergy in the
Basque Country changed considerably, though generational differences remained. One still can not help but
wonder how the priest with the collection of bathing
suits might have felt about today's topless bathing on
some Basque beaches.

Of course, none of the above suggests ambivalence.
Rather, it reflects a rigid system of puritanical sexual
philosophy. However, there is evidence that suggests
that it was superimposed on a very different sexual
worldview, one that has been largely defeated, but not
entirely destroyed. We are referring to the fact that there
is another discernible strand within Basque sex history in which the matter was dealt with explicitly and in
permissive fashion. Drawings of Basque female dress

from the sixteenth century include headdresses, which varied from village to village. They were worn by married women and were a phallic symbol meant to declare their status publicly. In some of the medieval literature from Western Europe, Basques are described as sexually promiscuous. The first Basque-language book, published in 1545 by Bernat Dechepare, a pre-Jansen parish priest, contains highly erotic verses. While such attitudes clearly retreated before the subsequent Jansenist assault, to this day there is a sense in which the people retain greater tolerance in sexual matters than do their priests.

IN SUM, DESPITE all the sermons about the infamy of bastardy, the magnitude of the indiscreet Basque girl's fall from grace is not nearly as great as in the surrounding Latin cultures. We might close with an example from Etxalar, where a particularly autocratic priest was scandalized at the birth of an illegitimate child. The mother had taken a job in a nearby city and left the infant with its grandmother. When Don Justo demanded that the baby be sent to an orphanage in Iruña to remove the public shame, he was driven into the street by the irate woman, who shrilly told him to stay out of her affairs. She raised the boy as her own son. This scarcely squares with the broader Mediterranean world's link between female virtue and family honor.

Lesson sixteen

LEARNING OBJECTIVES
1. To analyze rural Basque sexual attitudes.
2. To Analyze the contrast between Basque sexual mores and "Latin" ones.

REQUIRED READING

Rodney Gallop, *A Book of the Basques* (Reno: University of Nevada Press, 1998), 44–68.

SUGGESTED READING

José M.Satrústegi, *Comportamiento sexual de los vascos* (San Sebastián: Txertoa, 1981).

Teresa del Valle, et. al., *La mujer vasca* (Barcelona: Anthropos, 1985).

WRITTEN LESSON FOR SUBMISSION

1. Compare the rural Basque sexual mores described above with American attitudes during the same period.
2. Does the recent evolution in Basque sexual mores diverge from or reflect changes within the Occident? Discuss.

17 · A Basque Bestiary
From Wild Boars to Tame Pigs

WITHIN ANTHROPOLOGY, some of the best ethnographic work has been devoted to the study of animals. One can cite such examples as E. E. Evans-Pritchard's Nuer cattle, Claude Lévi-Strauss and his binary birds, Gregory Bateson and his dolphins, Clifford Geertz and his Balinese cocks, Roy Rappaport and his Thsembaga pigs, Marvin Harris and his Indian sacred cows, and James W. Fernandez and his Asturian donkeys. Whether regarding sacrifice, play, social dynamics, ritual, taxonomy, material determinism, Neolithic revolutions, or simply metaphor, anthropologists often invoke animal imagery. What is an animal? The answer to that question can be most revelatory of a culture's worldview.

In many of the world's cultures, the definition of humanity is in opposition to animality. As we noted in chapter 5, when considering prehistoric art, since at least the Magdalenian period in the Basque area, there was a fascination with the enigma of the animal "other." The millennia-old activity of hunting, and more recently animal husbandry, both underscore the singular relevance of animals in the Basque experience. There is a basic distinction to be made between wild and domesticated animals that have learned to adapt to human contact and command. The domestication of animals had crucial economic consequences and amounted to what is known as the Neolithic Revolution. Until the invention of agriculture and animal domestication, hunting (along with gathering) provided all subsistence. Although contested today by animal-rights groups, hunting is still widely practiced in many societies. In some respects, the hunter invokes the image of the liberated wild man, unfettered by the constraints of civilization. The culture

Wild boar
The wild boar or basurde (forest pig) stands at the apex
of the game animals targeted by Basque hunters.
From Donald R. Rice: Animals, a picture sourcebook.

---

of hunting is of particular interest because it organizes
the senses and emotions in primordialist terms.

IN RURAL BASQUE society (and for many urbanites as
well), there is nearly an obsession with hunting
among males. Whether pursuing birds (including the
song varieties, but particularly wild doves and snipes),
rabbits and hares, or particularly the favored big-game
animal, the wild boar, hunting is a rite of passage—the
means for both acquiring and then expressing masculinity. In rural Basque society, to be famed as an expert
hunter is most prestigious indeed.

We have both had occasion to study certain Basque hunting practices—Zulaika analyzed the boar hunt in Itziar, while Douglass wrote about an ancient form of netting migratory doves in Etxalar.

Curiously, while hunting is commonly framed in solitary terms—the contest between a hunter and his quarry—in fact it is a quintessential social activity. Indeed, in Basque society, whether expressed through the informal groups of fellow hunters or the formal hunting societies of urbanites, hunting is a prime context for male bonding. The hunting of boars requires teamwork among several hunters (and dogs); the netting of doves in Etxalar entails the intricate coordination of several hunters, each of whose right to participate is passed down through the generations within the same household.

IN THE BOAR hunt, the semiotics are characterized by traces, vestiges, smells. The hunter is guided only by the quarry's tracks. Such signs are transitory and impermanent. They cannot be "mapped," although the skilled hunter must have an imaginary one that anticipates the beast's erratic moves.

When the hunter is accompanied by a dog, information regarding the quarry is transmitted mostly through smell. No information could be more invisible than odor. It is a form of communication that preexists imagery. Indeed, concrete images of the beast are missing during the hunt and are but brief and fleeting at its conclusion. The image is reserved for the ultimate encounter, made final in the form of the trophy. Its presence marks the end of the hunt. It can also be the vivid imagining of what might have been had the quarry not escaped. So in hunting, we are immersed in a dichotomized world of pure signs (absence or presence), rather than one of gradated images or concepts. The hunter perceives and processes endlessly the animal's signs, but

hardly ever its image. A Basque hunter may spend fifteen years pursuing wild boars without ever having seen
one. Hunting therefore consists in conflating the distance between the hunter's mental image and that of the
real beast. It is nurtured as well by the "near miss," the
all but successful hunt gone awry through fate (the shift
in the wind that reverses the flow of odiferous information from the hunter to the hunted, the missed shot,
etc.).

ODORS, THEN, rather than words, images, or maps,
are what inform the hunt. The dogs perceive the
web of smell left behind by the wild beast, which is then
communicated through barking. The hunter imagines
smell as an invisible substance, yet something very real
and concrete, not just an ephemeral or deceptive sign. Of
course, the smell does not admit any visual representation, but it does require the presence of the animal emit-
ting the odor. It is then transmitted by the wind, another
invisible index. There is a sense of contagion to smell.
This is basically metonymic communication, not meta-
phoric.

His enormous gaps in knowledge force the hunter into
divinatory thinking and guesswork. Ritual notions of
"passage" and symbolism become crucial to him. Interpretation is essential to guesswork. Scarcity and plenty
("plenty of nothing") are essential to hunting. That is,
the hunter's spirits are nourished by the capacity of his
imagination to populate a seemingly vacant landscape
with game. The symbolic knowledge of divining and
believing compensates for the absence of factual knowledge and for only sporadic success.

In the Basque worldview, animal symbolism regarding
hunting versus domestication reflects notions of order
versus chaos. The "wild boar" becomes the "dirty pig."
Dirt is essentially disorder, and hunting therefore

becomes an activity that "cleans up" the forest, that rids it of its chaotic element. It establishes the clear separation between wilderness and civilization, nature and culture, animality and humanity. Hunting conditions the subjectivity of the hunters. They refer to the final moment of the hunt as "emotional" or "ecstatic," even to the point of being trance-inducing.

The *Palomeras*, or dove hunt of Etxalar, which is famed throughout the Basque Country, dates from at least the sixteenth century. Each autumn, during the month of October, more than a dozen villagers man posts to intercept flocks of doves migrating through the Pyrenees from their summer range in Central Europe to their winter grounds in Africa. Six fine-meshed nets are suspended between tall posts at the summit of a low mountain pass. They form the focal point of the two arms of a V constituted by a line of towers flanking both sides of the canyon leading to the pass. Once a flock of birds is sighted, the hunters exchange information on their movements, signaling with a white rag attached to a stick. As the doves pass a post, the hunter launches a whitened wooden disc, approximately the size and shape of a ping pong paddle, above their flight.

THE OBJECT simulates a bird of prey, forcing the birds to dip to tree-top level—their normal defense when so attacked. Ideally (although much can go wrong), the flock is "controlled," that is, forced to maintain a low flight pattern until reaching the summit, where a last skillful throw of the decisive disc forces them into the nearly invisible trap. The net is then released and falls to the ground. A concealed hunter pounces immediately on the enmeshed birds and dispatches them by biting them in the back of the neck. (Rodney Gallop, possibly reflecting his English sensibilities and squeamishness, notes that "little can be called sporting in the methods used for slaughtering the pigeons which cross the Pyrenees in migratory flight" and brands the hunt as "the annual massacre.")

THE HUNT HAS become commercialized in several fashions. The kill (which is actually a tiny percentage of the total number of migrating birds) fetches a high price in restaurants throughout the Basque Country— thereby constituting one of its traditional seasonal dishes. Today, the daily hunt attracts hundreds of spectators, whose presence fuels a local tourist economy (souvenirs, meals), albeit briefly. Finally, blinds behind the nets are auctioned off to wealthy urbanites (at thousands of dollars each), who thereby obtain the privilege of shooting at the birds that elude the nets—the majority. The proceeds from the auction are a significant source of revenue for the municipality.

In chapter 14, we noted the extent to which the lives of humans and animals have been intertwined in rural Basque society. Virtually every traditional household had several cats for rodent control and a dog (or several) for herding livestock, including pigs. Cows and pigs were stabled in the first floor of the *baserria*, meaning that Basque farmers truly cohabited with their livestock. Poultry, rabbits, and bees, as well as possibly burros and horses, would round out the typical *baserri*'s menagerie. In the traditional agricultural economy, with its emphasis on self-sufficiency, each species served multiple functions. A sheep supplied meat, milk for cheese making, and wool for clothing and bedding. A cow might be milked daily, but was also yoked with another periodically to pull either a cart or a plow. In short, in many fashions, animals were not simply passive charges to be raised for sale or domestic use, but were also integral to the household economy's production process. In this regard, the intimacy between humans and animals in

Dove hunt
During autumn of 1963 in Etxalar, Nafarroa, a dove
hunter prepares to launch a wooden missile designed
to simulate a raptor to force a flight of doves into the
camouflaged nets.
Photo: William Douglass

---

traditional rural Basque society was pronounced and
assumed the form of partnership.

WHILE IT MIGHT be tempting to frame such intimacy
in domestic terms, there is more to the story. Periodically, of all the domestic livestock, all but the cows
were allowed to lead nearly feral lives. Sheep spent most
of their time unsupervised in the mountains. (With the
extinction of bears and wolves throughout most of
Euskalherria, they have had no natural predators.) Even
pigs were turned out in the autumn to graze on the nut
crop and then had to be be rounded up in a fashion that
is at least an echo of the boar hunter's "cleaning up" of

the forest. The farmer's periodic trips to the mountains to check up on his sheep, pigs, and horses have a degree of the liberating feel of the hunt. For that day, he would be free and in pursuit of an elusive quarry.

THE TRADITIONAL rural Basque worldview placed a premium on *indarra*, physical strength and endurance. This is something that must be demonstrated, rather than simply asserted. While not an exclusively male trait, it is more a metaphor of masculinity than of feminity. It is particularly prone to expression through sports. Animals can display *indarra* just as readily as humans. Thus, just as rural Basque sports include contests between woodchoppers, weightlifters, weight carriers, scythers, runners, rowers and tug-of-war teams, they also includes ram butting and tests in which oxen compete to see which can drag an enormous block of stone the furthest distance.

Then, too, certain animal-related events have punctuated the *baserria*'s social life. The unusual visit to the distant livestock fair might be the farthest afield that a man would travel from his *baserria*, and his most memorable experience, in ten years. The livestock fair of Gernika is attended every Monday by farmers from an extensive hinterland, who frequent the local taverns and restaurants at midday and then attend an afternoon professional *pelota* or *jai alai* match, possibly wagering on the outcome, before returning home. Then there is the significance of a *baserri*'s annual pig slaughter, arguably one of the year's major social events, detailed in the reading assignment, Mark Kurlansky's "Postscript: The Death of a Basque Pig." Finally, there is the bull, which arguably occupies a liminal space between the feral and domestic realms. When it was still undomesticated, the bull appeared frequently in Paleolithic cave paintings. Fascination with bulls as the most powerful of the domesticated animals is ancient within Occidental culture, particularly within its Mediterranean expression. Ancient Egyptian art is replete with images of the bull. For the classical Greeks, the sacrifice of a bull was the ultimate offering to their gods. The frightening Minotaur (half man, half beast) was the progeny of the union between a bull and a goddess. It inhabited the labyrinth of Minos or Crete and demanded human sacrifices (Athenian) until slain by Theseus. Minoan art informs us of the spectacle wherein nimble youths would vault over the horns of a charging bull. Roman coins with bull effigies have been found in the Basque Country. The bull was regarded as the symbol of vitality or life itself and was sacrificed regularly at the weddings of Spanish monarchs, and, of course, Spain seemingly invented the bullfight—called "the festival of lights."

Near Itziar is the mountain hamlet of Lastur—famed for its ferocious feral bulls. In Itziar, as in many other Basque villages, a feature of the annual patron saint's day festival is the *encierro*, or "enclosure." The church square is fenced, and a young bull is released within the circle. Young men from Itziar test their mettle by challenging the bull, running obliquely before it. Occasionally, someone is injured. (At the *encierro* that we happened to attend together, a young man's ear was nearly torn off.) However, it is all more reminiscent of Minoan bull leaping than the Spanish bullfight.

THE TWO FORMS conflate in Iruña's famed festival of San Fermín—a week-long celebration in which each morning the six bulls destined for that afternoon's bullfight (*corrida*) run through the streets of the city. Anyone is free to run before the bulls (there are fatalities), and later there is an *encierro* in the *plaza de toros* in which young bulls are challenged, much as in the event at Itziar. The afternoon's bullfight is Spanish and, like in all others, results in the deaths of all six bulls at the hands of professional *toreadores*.

THANKS TO Ernest Hemingway, the San Fermín festival (and particularly the running of the bulls) has become a world-renowned media event and attraction for international tourism. He experienced Iruña in 1923 and fell in love with the city and the Basques. His return visits there and to Donostia and Hendaia (Hendaye) were frequent. Portions of his novels *The Sun Also Rises* and *A Moveable Feast* are set in the Basque Country. Hemingway, the angler, provides descriptions of Hegoalde's trout fishing, which he often experienced in conjunction with San Fermín festivities. He was also an *aficionado* of bull fighting. So, just as Lévi-Strauss tells us that animals are "good to think," for Hemingway, bulls were "good to write."

We might conclude, however, with another view of the San Fermín festival—a more ethnographic one. While conducting fieldwork in Etxalar in the early 1960s, Douglass had one of only two private cars in the village—a Volkswagen Beetle. He was encouraged by several of his informants to attend the festivities in their capital city, and, of course, to take them along. Interest was particularly high because Lopene had entered the competition of the livestock fair.

Lopene was a corpulent bachelor in his mid-thirties. A livestock buyer by day, at night, he used teams of contrabandists to smuggle horses from Spain to France, where they were slaughtered for human consumption. In a given year, Lopene moved literally thousands of horses across the international frontier, which formed part of the Etxalar's municipal boundary, as well, providing supplementary employment to most of the village's households. Lopene was a bon vivant and generous to a fault, frequenting (scrupulously) all three village taverns and inviting one and all to a drink.

Douglass arose in the dark, collected his three companions, and arrived in Iruña about daybreak. They went straight to the lower city, where the livestock fair is held. The fair was physically well removed from the tourist haunts, the route of the bull running, and the *plaza de toros*, but for rural Nafarroans, his companions, the fair was the *real* event. To everyone's delight, Lopene was prominent in the parade of the contestants in the best-of-breed competition. He had won the blue ribbon for his superior pair of oxen.

AFTERWARD, LOPENE joined his fans (us) for a mid-morning snack, and then everyone scattered to make the purchases demanded of them by their spouses as quid pro quo for assenting to their husbands' escapade. By early evening, we excursionists were homeward bound, having never mentioned (let alone experienced) the bull running, *encierro*, or *corrida*. It was then that Douglass observed, to everyone's enormous merriment, "But, wait a minute, I have never seen an ox in Etxalar!" The anthropologist's naiveté proved to be the perfect capstone to the perfect day—Lopene had smuggled the pair of oxen into Nafarroa from France for the competition, and the prized pair were already on their way to their home north of the Pyrenees.

Lesson seventeen

LEARNING OBJECTIVES
1. To understand the role of animals in traditional peasant society.
2. To examine hunting as an occupation and a cultural complex.

3. To analyze the interdependence that an occupation may create between the senses of hearing, speech, touch, and smell and cultural premises.
4. To analyze the bull complex in the Basque bestiary and its literary recreation by Hemingway for an international audience.

REQUIRED READING

José Ortega y Gasset, *Meditations on Hunting* (New York: Scribner and Sons, 1972), pp. 27–37; 51–61; 101–112; 126–143.

Mark Kurlansky, "Postscript: The Death of a Basque Pig," in *The Basque History of the World* (New York: Walker and Company, 2001), 352–59.

SUGGESTED READING

Ernest Hemingway, *The Sun Also Rises* (New York: Scribner, 1954).

James W. Fernandez, "Persuasions and Performances: Of the Beast in Every Body ... and the Metaphors in Everyman," *Daedalus* 101, no. 1: 39–60.

Joseba Zulaika, "Ehiza: The Hunting Model of Performance," in *Basque Violence: Metaphor and Sacrament* (Reno: University of Nevada Press, 1988), 187–207.

WRITTEN LESSON FOR SUBMISSION

1. Discuss the distinction between the wild and the domesticated as a human behavior paradigm.
2. Elaborate the differences between primary senses (touch and smell) and secondary ones (speech, vision) and point out their social implications.
3. How would you distinguish between the running of the bulls or enclosure—*encierro*—as play and the deadly spectacle of choreographed sacrifice of the bull?

4. What does the extraordinary appeal of Hemingway's literary imagery say about the power of animal metaphors and about his readership?

18 · Folklore and Mythology

W E MIGHT say that folklore is the literature of preliterate societies—an oral and usually dramatized means of transmitting a cultural legacy in social contexts with no (or little) dependence on the written word. The corpus of Basque "folk" expressions, including tales, songs, and dance, is extensive and is the subject of the reading assignments in Rodney Gallop's *A Book of the Basques*. In chapter 31 we will consider *bertsolaritza*, another vehicle for transmitting cultural legacy verbally, rather than by means of writing.

There is a certain relationship between folklore and mythology. Both originate in orality. Both seek to entertain (i.e., to hold an audience's interest), rather than simply to inform. Both may ultimately be transcribed and then become the objects of scholarly study. Indeed, such research has determined that a certain (limited) number of themes inform both the folktale and myth cross-culturally. There is, however, a sense in which myth is both more ancient and more serious. Myth is also a kind of longstanding folk tale, oftentimes elevated to the status of founding myth and / or morality tale.

What follows is a summary of the Basque mythic figure Mari's story, constructed from José Miguel de Barandi-arán's work.

1. Mari was a young girl who disobeyed and was then cursed by her mother. As a result, the enemy of mankind took her to his underground abode, whence she rules over storms and droughts. She is also queen of the genies that inhabit the earth.
2. Mari is a plural and an omnipresent figure. She lives in numerous caves. All of the significant ones

throughout the Basque Country are occupied by and named for her.

3. When she makes herself visible, she is usually seen in the form of a woman surrounded by fire and flying from one cave to another. A tremendous noise precedes or follows her aerial journey. Her other guises are those of a horse, crow, vulture, heifer, tree, blast of wind, white cloud, or rainbow. The effigy of a flame or a fireball is also frequent in her flights, and that of the moon, as well. But whatever form she assumes, she is always a woman.

4. Mari is extremely beautiful and wealthy. She has immense treasures in her caves. She is surrounded by golden objects—combs, cups, candlesticks. There is a toad at the bottom of some of her golden cups. If stolen, her golden canteen explodes. Likewise, her golden candlesticks are transformed into toads when taken out of the cave. On at least one occasion, she gave as a gift a piece of charcoal, which was then turned into gold on being taken from the cave.

5. While her name is Mari, she is usually referred to as Señoria [Lady] or Dama [Maiden], followed by the name of the nearest mountain or cave inhabited by her. Some of her other names are Yonagorri [The Red-skirted One], Gaizto [Bad, Naughty], and Arpeko Saindua [The Cave Saint].

6. Mari has a husband name Maju, a minor personage who appears in forms similar to hers. A violent storm follows their encounters. Sugaar [He-Snake] is a personage identified with Maju: He plays a historic role in the foundation of the House of Bizkaia—its first lord, Jaun Zuria, was begotten by him [Sugaar] while sleeping in his dreams with a Scottish princess.

7. Some legends allude to Mari's marriages with mortals. According to one of them, she has seven children that

Fearing the supernatural
The Catholic Church often commissioned art depicting graphically the dangers to humans posed by otherworldly creatures. In this stonework on the entrance to the church of Iribas, Nafarroa, (thirteenth century) monsters devour obviously terrified persons.
Source: Xabier Irujo

---

she does not baptize. On one occasion, when her husband attempts to take her and the children to church, Mari flees to the cliffs of Murumendi [one of her dwellings] surrounded in flames and exclaiming: "My children for heaven, and I now for Murumendi." Some myths refer to Mari's two daughters; others to but one. She has two sons named Atarrabi and Mikelats—the former good, the latter evil.

8. Besides her numerous servile terrestrial genies, Mari usually has in her underground service a young girl also called Mari. The reasons given for this

unfortunate girl's condition are varied: In return for a favor, there is a mother's fulfillment of the promise of offering her daughter to Mari; a daughter may be cursed by her mother for disobedience or for spending too much time combing her hair; or simply Mari obtains a little girl who she carefully educates for several years and then releases, offering her a handful of gold.

9. Mari is often seen sitting by the fire in her cave's kitchen and having her hair done. Some have observed her combing her hair in the sun at the entrance of her cave. Another of her common activities is spinning. In one representation, she spins balls with golden thread, winding the skein with a ram's horns providing the reel. She is also seen undoing the wool. Once she was observed combing her hair mounted on a ram. When asked why she scrubbed her face with its left foot, she answered paradoxically: "Because today I am going to Nafarroa to cut hay with a sickle."

10. Mari forges storms. In each part of the Basque Country, their origin is attributed to Mari's nearest cave dwelling, from which she sends the tempest. At such times she is frequently seen flying in the form of a horse.

11. Mari rewards people's faith in her powers. She helps those who have recourse to her and will hover over the head of someone who has called upon her three times. When she is asked for advice, her oracles are esteemed to be true and useful. These powers were used in the fourteenth century when Diego López de Haro [the most important figure in Bizkaia's medieval history] was mysteriously released in Toledo [some 400 kilometers south of the Basque Country]

from imprisonment by the Moors and then carried home on Mari's horse.

12. There is still a cult devoted to her. The harvest of anyone who gives Mari an annual offering will be spared from hailstorms. The gift that most pleases her is a ram. Shepherds and entire villages go to her caves to make supplications: If, during them, Mari is inside the cave, that year it will not hail in the area; if she is absent, however, then hailstones will fall, destroying the harvest and injuring the livestock. Sometimes the priest of the village will join the procession and celebrate a Mass at the threshold of the cave, praying for Mari's mercy. There is an annual pilgrimage to the cavern of Arpeko Saindua [one of Mari's abodes] in which a stalagmite that represents a petrified shepherdess associated with Mari is the object of veneration and prayer.

13. When visiting one of Mari's dwellings, a set of rules must be observed: 1. She must be addressed as *hi* ["you" in the familiar form, as opposed to the respectful formal one]. 2. The visitor must leave the cave oriented in the same way that he or she entered: If one entered face forward, then one must retreat by stepping backward. 3. The visitor must always remain standing when inside the cave.

14. Mari is nourished by the negative principle or "the no." When asked by a shepherd where she obtained her good cider, she answered: "This cider was made with the apples dedicated to the no."

15. She punishes lies, theft, pride, boasts, breaches of promise, disrespect, and refusal to lend needed assistance. Her most frequent punishment is to deprive the culprit of something. Her most dramatic scourge is the hailstorm. The sickle is the symbol of Mari's protection against lightning, itself one of the phe-

FOLKLORE AND MYTHOLOGY · 273

nomena under her control. Celebration of masses
and magical conjurations are the only defenses
against her wrath.

16. A typical punishment is to force the penitent to sift
flour and bran together endlessly with a *baia* [sieve]
or to require that he or she carry water in a bot-
tomless bucket—impossible tasks. Thus, Atarrabi
was forced by the devil to sift all the flour from the
bran in his copious storeroom: an interminable job
because both passed with equal ease through the
sieve. The devil, who certainly did not have excessive
confidence in his pupil, asked constantly, "Atarrabi,
where are you?" Atarrabi had to reply, "Here I am."
But then the pupil taught the sieve to answer "Here
I am" to the devil's questions. Once, when the devil
was some distance away, Atarrabi began to walk
backward out of the storeroom, the sieve continued
to give the oft-repeated reply, "Here I am." As soon
as Atarrabi had one foot outside the door, he was
observed. The devil sprang forward, but it was too
late: Atarribi was beyond his master's jurisdiction.
Only his shadow remained inside the cavern, and it
was captured by the devil. There are certain obvious
similarities in the story with the escape of Ulysses
from the cave of the Cyclops.

As is the case with foundational myths, Mari's story
is concerned with matters of form, pattern, mental
process, communication, organization, and differentiation. These are some of the key topics cryptically presented by the mythical narrative.

From point one we see that it deals with basic social,
moral, natural, and cosmological dichotomies and
their mythical inversion: humans versus the spirit

world, surface versus underground, rainfall versus droughts. There is also an initial breach (the first transgressive "no") of a key social tie—the mother / daughter relationship.

Point two brings up issues of naming, classification of place, the singularity and plurality of geography, locality, Mari.

Point three presents us with a flying lady. She bridges basic natural oppositions—up and down, aerial / underground, vertical / horizontal, near / far. There are various codes to describe her: gender, female; visual, visible / invisible; sound, preceded and followed by loud noise; color, red fire, white cloud, dark cave; animality / humanity; geometrical forms: sickle, moon, ball, globe ...

Point four underscores Mari's entitlements: royalty; beauty; wealth. There are unexpected transformations within and outside her mythical realm: Charcoal becomes gold, gold becomes toad, golden cups with hidden toads. [In chapter 19 we will examine the connection between toads and witchcraft, toads and folk medicine, and the image of a toad in a person's left eye as the mark of a witch.]

The fifth point has to do with naming of place, entitlement, character.

In the sixth point, Mari's sorry male counterpart is characterized by formal irrelevance and an animal code (snake), storm, and a legendary role.

The seventh point surveys a plethora and plurality of marriage forms and family patterns (seven children, two sons, two daughters, single daughter), baptized / unbaptized, going or not to church, flying to the Christian heaven versus flying to Mari's mythical one (Murumendi), good versus evil.

Brewing up a storm
Here witches use their supernatural powers to create a
storm that devastates fishing and agriculture.
Source: Olaus Magnus: Historia de gentibus septentrion-
alibus, *(Rome, 1555).*

Mari (and her own reproduction); mythical reward
with gold.
   Point nine describes Mari's activities: combing hair,
spinning balls of golden thread onto a ram's horns,
hygiene.
   Point ten depicts Mari as cosmological agent: She is
the source of storms.
Point eleven underscores her positive moral properties: She rewards faith, her advice and oracles are ben-
eficial, she can be faithful and useful.
   Point twelve addresses Mari's cult: the annual offering, particularly of a ram; supplications; and annual
pilgrimage.

Point thirteen lists the rules governing visits to Mari: 1. She is addressed in *hika* (thou) (which in Basque is deictically singular) rather than the plural *zuka* (respectful "you" like the French *vous*); 2. the visitors observe the same orientation when departing the cave as upon entering; 3. The visitor never sits down inside the cave (vertical up / down movement is ruled out). Sitting is Mari's prerogative.

In the fourteenth point, there is nourishment by negativity, "the no." There is a crucial relevance of this bounding negative principle in formal terms, whether in Freudian or cybernetic theories. In logical terms: An initial negative limit is required for serial multiplicity to take place.

Point fifteen considers Mari to be the moralizer who punishes transgressions. More than the single property of Christian dualism between good and evil, she embodies both simultaneously.

Finally, there is the impossible task of sifting with a sieve (*bai*), which in Basque means "yes," as well. The crucial issue is one of classification. There is the paradox of classification of immovable movement, "Here I am." The affirmative is the equivalent to a sieve that fails to discriminate between two different substances and thus produces indeterminacy instead of classification.

IN SUMMARY, the myth presents us with basic mediation between yes and no, left and right, empty and full, horizontal and vertical, life and death, and so on. It privileges the female, left, void, moon, absence, and circularity. There is a "fugue of the senses" in that auditory, visual, tactile, gustatory, and olfactory codes are employed to convey information. The basic classificatory system is expressed by ideas that are taken from logic, language, social organization, and the senses, as well as from the zoological and botanical orders.

WHILE CONDUCTING research in Aulestia in the early 1960s, Douglass witnessed an extraordinary inter-generational exchange regarding the subject of Mari. An elderly man recounted the properties of Anbotoko Dama, a Mari figure who resided in the cave of Anboto, but who had another residence near the chapel of Santa Eufemia on the summit of a local mountain. He noted that people have seen her flying between the caves and sitting next to a pool of water, combing out her long hair. When his nineteen-year-old son made fun of him for such beliefs and asked if his father had actually ever seen Mari, the answer was, "Only once while herding sheep in Idaho. She flew by horizontally, trailing flames behind her." A somewhat sobered son replied, "If that really happened, then how can the Catholic Church's teachings be right?".

Lesson eighteen

LEARNING OBJECTIVES
1. To consider Basque folk tales, songs, and dance ethno-graphically.
2. To review the corpus of traditional mythology centered on Mari.
3. To consider how mythology reflects rites of passage.
4. To evaluate the cryptic cultural rules that represent Mari's antagonism to Christian ideology.
5. To examine the premise of "nourishment by the nega-tive."

REQUIRED READING

José Miguel de Barandiarán, "Legends," in *A View from the Witch's Cave*, ed. Luis Barandiarán Irizar (Reno: University of Nevada Press, 1991), 95–127.

Rodney Gallop, *A Book of the Basques* (Reno: University of Nevada Press, 1998), 95–127, 109–37, 160–77.

SUGGESTED READING

Resurrección María de Azkue, *Euskalerriaren yakintza*, 4 vols. (Zarauz: Itxaropena, 1968).

José Miguel de Barandiarán, *Diccionario de mitología vasca: Obras completas*, (Bilbao: La Gran Enciclopedia Vasca, 1972), vol 1.

Wentworth Webster, *Basque Legends: Collected Chiefly in the Labourd* (London: Griffith and Farran, and Walbrook and Co., 1877).

WRITTEN LESSON FOR SUBMISSION

1. Are Basque folklore and mythology alternative or complementary ways of viewing the world?
2. How would you relate the prevalence of female characters in Basque mythology to the rest of the culture? Does it imply Basques are "matriarchal"?
3. Mari appears to mediate all sorts of spatial, social, and cultural transitions. Can they be ranked according to their significance?

19 · Witchcraft

Julio Caro Baroja provides a historical summation of the belief in witchcraft since Greco-Roman times:

> There is documentary evidence of the existence over a period of centuries of the belief that certain women (not necessarily always old ones) could change themselves and others at will into animals in classical times; that they could fly through the air by night and enter most secret and hidden places by leaving their body behind; that they could make spells and potions to further their own love affairs or to inspire hatred for others; that they could bring about storms, illness both in men and animals, and strike fear into their enemies or play terrifying jokes on them. To carry out their evil designs these women met together after dark. The moon, night, Hecate and Diana were the deities who presided over them, helping them to make philters and potions. They called on these goddesses for aid in their poetic conjurations, or threatened and constrained them in their spells when they wanted to achieve particularly difficult results.
>
> Apart from these powers, the women who were believed to attend such meetings were supposed to be experts in the manufacture of poisons and also in cosmetic arts; sometimes they were used as go-betweens in love affairs. (*The World of the Witches*, 39–40).

DURING THE thirteenth century, the theologian Canon Dollinger thought of the witch as a monstrous product of the imagination dreamed up by narrow-minded lawyers and theologians in the service of temporal authority. In later centuries, learned people

Auto-da-fé
In the early sixteenth century, the Basque Country was
targeted by the Inquisition for investigation of witchcraft.
Those who failed to establish their innocence in an auto-
da-fé were burned at the stake.

---

came to believe that the witch had real diabolical powers. A historical controversy developed between those
who contended that actions attributed to witches (and
most particularly their covens) were real and those who
maintained that belief in witchcraft was simply errone-
ous, when not the outright fabrication and manipulation
of interested parties.

THE FORMER viewpoint prevailed and, by the early
fourteenth century, the Inquisition was established
to expose and then punish persons in the thrall (or service) of satanic forces. The mandate covered all heresies,
but alleged that witches were prime targets. They were

believed to attend sinister nocturnal Sabbaths or black masses in which Satan was the celebrant. During the fourteenth century, those accused of witchcraft were tried by inquisitional courts. After such an auto-da-fé, those found guilty were executed publicly by being burned at the stake.

By the late fifteenth century, there was a genuine European witch craze. *Summis desiderantes affectibus*, a papal bull issued by Pope Innocent VIII in 1484, deplored the spread of witchcraft in Germany and authorized two Dominican inquisitors to extirpate it. In 1486, they produced an encyclopedia of demonology, the *Malleus maleficarum*. The two documents complement one another. Did this campaign against witches solve the problem? Quite to the contrary. The more fierce the countermeasures, the more ubiquitous witches seemed to become.

BASQUES WERE to figure prominently in these developments. In 1466, Gipuzkoa sent a petition to King Enrique IV of Castile asking for the eradication of the witches. In 1500, there was a case against witches in Anboto (Bizkaia), who were alleged to be worshippers of Satan incarnated as a he-goat. Around 1527, the inquisitor Avellaneda uncovered three covens of witches; one attended by 120 persons; another by 100; and the third by more than 200. The whole area was thought to be infested with witches who allegedly renounced God and his laws in return for temporal wealth offered by the devil. The imprint of what looked like a toad's foot in the iris of a person's left eye was taken to be a sure sign of the witch.

Bishop Juan de Zumarraga was appointed as inquisitor in Bizkaia in the early sixteenth century. He spoke Basque and was considered lenient. (Usually inquisitors did not know the native language.) A particularly prominent figure was Pierre de Lancre, appointed by the French king in 1609 as inquisitor in Lapurdi. According to Caro Baroja, he was a typical lawyer obsessed with the desire to uncover criminal activities and a person who accepted religion as the sole basis for the penal code. He did not like the Basques and thought that there were plenty of geographical, moral, and cultural reasons why Satan should have chosen the Basque Country as the focal point of witchcraft in Europe. He wrote: "The people of Labourd, bad tillers of the ground and worse craftsmen, had little love for their country, their wives and children, and since they were neither French nor Spanish, they had no established pattern of behavior to follow." One point that particularly irritated de Lancre was that women acted as sacristans of the churches. This was particularly shocking to him in view of their notorious reputation for loose living, unfaithfulness, and immorality.

DE LANCRE'S writings established the Basques as Europe's quintessential practitioners of witchcraft. He had a striking propensity for mixing realistic and fantastic elements in his accounts. For example, de Lancre believed that the fact it rains a lot and the storms are violent during the autumn in the Basque Country was due to the work of the witches. Through intimidation, he elicited the confessions of girls and boys between the ages of five and twelve who attested that they had attended witches' covens after flying through the air to get there. They became airborne after rubbing on their bodies ointments made from toads.

The church's own ritual was said to serve as the model for the witches' "Sabbath." There were black or satanic masses. The devil officiated, and, at a critical moment, the faithful, rather than kissing the celebrant's ring, kissed Satan's anus. De Lancre relied on the depositions of children, the elderly, and individuals whom he had tortured. From his incorrect transcriptions of names, it is evident that he barely knew Basque. Also, de Lancre relied on a foreign surgeon living in Baiona, who became quite adept at detecting a witch by sticking a needle into a suspect's bandaged eyes. If there was an insensitive spot, guilt was established. The only difference between de Lancre's superstitions and those of his unfortunate victims was that his were overlain with a veneer of learning. He believed himself to be a victim of the devil, as well.

THROUGH HIS investigations, De Lancre identified no fewer than three thousand suspected witches, which, given Lapurdi's sparse demography, represented a significant percentage of the population. Scarcely a family remained unaffected, and many fled across the Spanish border. The refugees included priests, although de Lancre detained and accused of collaboration seven prominent ones. Given the sensational nature of the subject and the graphic accounts of the refugees from Lapurdi, it is scarcely surprising that an infectious mass hysteria broke out almost immediately in the mountain villages of northern Hegoalde and Nafarroa. By 1610, village priests were conducting their own investigations into the possibility of witchcraft among their own parishioners, again relying on the accounts of children. Some were probably sincere, while others were opportunistic in denouncing suspects to the jurisdictional Inquisition based in Logroño. In retrospect, it is also clear that the craze allowed some vindictive persons to settle old scores by denouncing their adversaries as witches. Once denounced, the accused entered the realm of catch-22. If one admitted to being a witch, she (or he) could be reconciled with the church. If one proclaimed innocence, however, the classic test was the dunking chair. She (or he) was immersed underwater. If the person drowned, then innocence was evident; if not, then guilt was established, and the lying witch was then executed by being burned at the stake.

The auto-da-fé of 1610 in Logroño against the witches of Zugarramurdi (Nafarroa) became particularly famous. The Inquisition was compelled to take action, pressured by civil authorities following a wave of public panic. Nearly three hundred people were under suspicion of witchcraft, not counting children.

The information gathered by the inquisitors during this trial suggests that there are remarkable similarities between these witchcraft activities and certain cults of classical antiquity. Witches allegedly proselytized for new recruits; there was the taking of vows (consisting of formal renunciation of Christianity); the novice was marked in the left eye's iris with the sign of a toad; the initiate was given a toad as guardian angel. Children, rather than being willing participants, were lured to the Sabbath. There was an internal hierarchy: novices, neophytes, initiates of several grades, and, finally, senior sorcerers and witches.

THE ACTS committed by members of the witches' sects were: causing storms; casting spells on crops, animals, and people; vampirism and eating the flesh of the dead; and assuming animal forms. Eighteen of the accused in Logroño were reconciled with the church; seven others refused to confess and were burned to death. Effigies of five others who had died before the auto-da-fé was held were burned, as well.

One theologian of the epoch, Pedro de Valencia, had several theories to explain witchcraft. There was the possibility that the Zugarramurdi meetings assembled evil people in order "to commit fornication, adultery, or sodomy." Thus, there was nothing supernatural about them.

The ritual kiss
Alleged Basque witchcraft practices were but a part of a witch craze that swept across much of western and central Europe. Here Satan's disciples line up to kiss his posterior.
Source: R.P. Guaccius: Compendium Maleficarum *(Milano, 1626).*

He compared the witches' Sabbath to the bacchanals and the Dionysian mysteries of antiquity. Alternatively, there was the possibility that a pact was indeed made with the devil, but everything that was said to take place at the covens was only a trance or dream induced by Satan with ointments and other substances. Or perhaps everything was real, down to the last detail. This opinion was particularly dangerous when combined with the second hypothesis, since it made accusations of innocent people possible.

Valencia favored the first theory: that men and women came together for illicit pleasure. Caro Baroja wrote of Basque peasants caught up in the witch craze: "They were cut off and protected from the world outside by their strange language, and so they still clung to the same conception of the world as their forefathers, a view of life rooted in antiquity, full of mystery and poetry and even, at times, humor. Witchcraft and magic were still very much realities for them."

The inquisitor Antonio de Salazar stands out as a great historical figure. He was one of the three judges who presided over the 1610 trials of Logroño. He reached the conclusion that the majority of the alleged acts never occurred. His activities between 1611 and 1620 were instrumental in framing the investigation of witchcraft in an entirely new and different fashion. He held the view that the majority of the declarations and accusations were imaginary.

AS STUDIED BY Gustav Henningsen in his classic *The Witches' Advocate*, he interviewed 1,384 boys and girls—boys between six and fourteen years old and girls who were twelve and under. Salazar found that their declarations were full of inconsistencies, and so he dismissed them. Also, under his mandate, 290 persons of all ages were reconciled with the church, 41 individuals guilty of lesser offences were discharged, and 81 people withdrew their original confessions.

Salazar interrogated the alleged witches on how they went to the meetings, where they were held, and what they did there. He required corroboration and unassailable proof regarding guilt or innocence. He found no clear evidence determining the location of the meeting places. There was contradictory testimony as to the means of travel. For Salazar, the alleged magical power of ointments and powders was sheer invention and deceit. (Animals could eat them innocuously.)

The skeptical inquisitor sought to convince both the accusers and the accused that it was all fabrication. There were people who claimed they had been to the Sabbath, while others denied the accusation. A woman who claimed she had had sexual intercourse with the devil was proven still to be a virgin. And so on. Salazar made note of 1,672 cases of perjury and bearing of false witness. He concluded: "And so, having weighed up everything with the proper objectivity and rectitude, I have come to believe, and shall continue to do so, that none of the acts that have been attested in this case, really or physically occurred at all."

SALAZAR AND others convinced the Inquisition that the whole phenomenon was essentially fantasy and hysteria. In 1614, the Inquisition issued strict guidelines demanding that the evidence in witch trials must be external, objective, and clear. But how can one positively demonstrate accused witches had a diabolical pact and engaged in intercourse with the devil, that they killed children and sucked their blood, that they flew to a witches' Sabbath, that they were the cause of bad harvests and heavy storms, and that the whole matter was not simply a fabrication?

The so-called Saintly or Holy Inquisition became the paradigm of prosecutorial and persecutory terror in Spain and elsewhere. (Still, thanks at least in part to Salazar, the Spanish Inquisition is considered to be the most lenient of all of the period's national ones, particularly after 1620.) In the 1630s, the European witch craze peaked. By 1650, there was growing skepticism; by 1680, the hysteria was pretty much over. Nevertheless, by then,

Witches

One of the most extraordinary chapters in Europe's Middle Ages concerns the history of witchcraft beliefs and practices. The Basque territories became a focal point in the Church's inquisitorial fight against witchcraft. From today's vantage point, the entire bizarre episode is a source of enduring puzzlement and a challenge to a coherent explanation as to how it could have happened at all.

Source: Ulrich Molitor, Vonden Unholden und Hexen *(Constance, 1489).*

somewhere between two hundred thousand and one million accused persons had perished.

How are we to understand the European witch craze? As Hugh Trevor-Roper argues, this is a "perplexing phenomenon," a standing warning to those who would simplify the stages of human progress. After the eighteenth century and the Enlightenment, the history of Europe was seen as one of progress. Despite some reversals and obstacles, ostensibly there were persistent advances. It was a story of the victory of light over darkness: the Renaissance, the Reformation, and the Scientific Revolution all supposedly signaled emancipation form the intellectual straitjacket and superstitions of the Middle Ages.

YET EACH "progressive" development is Janus-faced; light and darkness are intertwined. For example, the Renaissance experienced a revival not only of pagan letters, but also of pagan religion. The Reformation was a return to the New Testament Gospels, but also to the unedifying mindset of a rigid Old Testament. The Scientific Revolution also brought with it Pythagorean mysticism and cosmological fantasy as articulated in nineteenth-century Romanticism. Beneath the surface of an ever more sophisticated society, we find dark passions and inflammable credulity. The belief in witches was one such irrational force, and we are confronted with the fact that it was after the invention of printing and during the Renaissance that the witch craze really exploded. The years from 1550 to 1660 were worse than those from 1500 to 1550, and in the years from 1600 to 1650, the witch craze was even more pronounced and widespread throughout Western Europe.

In fact, the existence of witches was advanced by authorities of many stripes—cultivated popes of the Renaissance, the great Protestant reformers, the

Catholic saints of the Counter-Reformation, and the scholars, lawyers, and churchmen of the age of Bacon and Pascal. In this regard, if the sixteenth and seventeenth centuries were an age of light, the Dark Ages were more civilized, for although there was a belief in witches in the Dark Ages, there was no hysterical and punitive witch craze. What concerns the historian (and the anthropologist) is the organized, systematic demonology that the medieval church ultimately constructed out of those beliefs.

WHETHER BELIEVING or not in magical flights of witches and their secret sabbaths, the inquisitor projected a deeply ironic figure. If he credulously accepted at face value the confessions of his tortured suspects, then he shared their superstitious and demonological worldview proscribed by the church. If he did not, then he was judging them for acts that they admitted, but that he knew not to be true. In famous trials such as the one of Zugarramurdi, there were inquisitors of both minds, yet the process had to come down to a single, unappealable verdict. The inquisitors were confronted not only with the "facts" before them, but more primarily with their own belief system. In the final analysis, we are still left to wonder how the Holy Inquisition could fall into the grand delusion of its own making by actually coming to accept the extramundane reality informing the confessions of the alleged "witches." For inquisitor and accused alike, what was "real"—their ontologies—depended to a startling degree on what they "believed"—their epistemologies.

The European witch craze poses clear parallels (and lessons) for our own age. We are no more exempt from the effects of terrifying collective representations than were seventeenth-century Basque peasants. (In chapter 10, we discussed the current obsession with "terrorism.") A collective representation is a shared construct that categorizes some aspect of the human experience. It transcends, while informing, the belief system of the individual. It may become emotionally charged. It also tends to establish boundaries between believers (adherents) and non-believers (others). Not uncommonly, it is nourished by fear driven by perceived threat. In this regard, the European witch craze managed to feed on itself for several centuries. Although object of the auto-da-fé was to make public examples of exposed witches as a deterrent, the unintended side effect was to spur on the zealots to ever greater efforts to uncover the feared conspiracy in their midst. In short, in a real sense, the witch craze constituted the very phenomenon that it abhorred.

SOME ANALYSTS equate the witch craze with certain twentieth-century collective representations—the Third Reich's Jewish conspiracy in Germany and the Red Scare in the United States during the 1950s being prime examples. One might add the more virulent forms of racist and nationalist discourse, such as the "clash of civilizations" thesis and even the current "cultural wars" between so-called "religious fundamentalists" and "secular humanists." Historians and social scientists have tried to ascertain the origins of such stereotypes and how they are sustained. It seems fair to say that it is their greatest failure to date, in that we have but modest understanding of the forces in play.

Lesson nineteen

LEARNING OBJECTIVES
1. To survey the history of Basque and European witchcraft during the fifteenth and sixteenth centuries.

---

2. To analyze the role of witchcraft within Basque society and culture.
3. To apply these lessons to present-day events.

REQUIRED READING
Gustav Henningsen, *The Witches' Advocate* (Reno: University of Nevada Press, 1980), 1–36, 227–305.

SUGGESTED READING
Julio Caro Baroja, *The World of the Witches* (Chicago: University of Chicago Press, 1964).
Hugh Trevor-Roper, *The European Witch-Craze of the Sixteenth and Seventeenth Centuries and Other Essays* (New York: Harper and Row, 1956).

WRITTEN LESSON FOR SUBMISSION
1. What can we learn from European witchcraft about the role of collective representations in society?
2. What is the interdependence between reality and fiction?
3. What social and political logic generates the scapegoat?
4. What is the ironic role of expert knowledge.
5. Do you find in the daily press anything reminiscent of the phenomenon of medieval witchcraft?

20 · Believers and Visionaries

A S WE NOTED in chapter 7, since at least the late
Middle Ages, Basques have been Christians—Catholics. That remains true to this day. The vast majority of
Basques, both urbanites and rural dwellers, are baptized
Roman Catholics. Until the modification of the church
under the ecumenicalism of Pope John XXIII, the Basque
Country was a veritable seedbed of religious vocations. A
village of a thousand persons such as Aulestia was likely
to have not only a parish priest, but an assistant, as well.
Religious orders turned out missionaries who served in
such remote places as the Amazon Basin and the Congo.
Likewise, there were several orders of nuns involved in
charitable works, both at home and abroad. The Basque
Country ranked right along with Ireland as a bastion of
Catholicism and religious vocations.

Given the strength of the Basque Country's recent
religious heritage, perhaps it is not suprising that the
church's current crisis is felt more strongly there. The
late twentieth-century secularization of life throughout
the Catholic world, reflected in the dramatic decrease in
religious vocations and church attendance, is particularly pronounced in the Basque Country. Today, there
are many closed convents and monasteries, recruitment
for the seminaries is difficult, the former missionary
activity has all but dried up, many priests and nuns have
chosen to become secularized (some contracting marriage), and church attendance is down dramatically.

In Hegoalde, all of this has been accelerated by the
transition to democracy after Franco's death in 1975.
Since the dictatorship and the Catholic hierarchy maintained a close working relationship (Franco nominated
the candidates for bishop; the Spanish state paid the

Sanctuary of San Miguel de Aralar
Located in the Sierra de Aralar, the mountain chain separating Gipuzkoa from Nafarroa, this famous and sacred Catholic monastery (twelfth century) is in the very heartland of Basque pre-Christian legend and mythology.
Photo: Xabier Irujo

---

clergy's salaries; divorce and abortion were forbidden; instruction in Catholic doctrine was an integral part of the public school curriculum; books and films were censored or banned outright), democratization meant the secularization of life, as well. Thus, while still influential, the church no longer wields direct temporal power in the Basque Country.

IT IS THE purpose of this chapter to consider religiosity in the little community in the Basque Country—what anthropologists sometimes refer to as "popular" or even "folk" religion. At the outset, we would note that most "peasant" societies are incorporated to a considerable degree into one of the world's great religions (Christianity, Islam, Hinduism, Buddhism, Judaism). With but few exceptions, anthropologists have not studied the mainstream doctrinal and ritualistic expressions of the great religious traditions. Instead, the focus in work on the anthropology of religion in peasant cultural settings is on the ways in which "standard" doctrine and ritual are somehow filtered through local lenses and thereby modified or syncretized through both the subtraction and addition of certain beliefs and practices.

IN THE BASQUE case, our object of study is a popular expression of Christianity. Obviously, since the parish priest ministering to his flock is himself a product of a seminary, which, in turn, is tied directly into the Catholic Church's hierarchal and doctrinal mainstream, the church is already and always present within the little community. The sacraments of baptism, matrimony, the Eucharist, confirmation, and extreme unction, all so called rites of passage, are applied in Aulestia in much the same fashion as in Bilbao (or in New York, for that matter). In short, religion (like politics and the economy) demonstrates that neither peasant society nor the little community is truly a social isolate. However, it is also true that at another level, each of the "Christian" sacraments in rural Basque society has its local accretions—folk practices and beliefs. In Aulestia, for instance, until a baby was baptized, the mother was confined to her dwelling in the belief that she was vulnerable to evil spirits. In the event she had to leave the dwelling, she would place a roof tile on her head to signify that she was still at home. When Aulestia was threatened by an impending summer thunderstorm, the priest was expected to ring the church bells to ward it off.

Even more imbued with folk religion is the complex of funerary practices following a death. Death triggers both an intense cycle of funerary obligations among individuals and households lasting for a year (indeed, for several years, in the case of a widow as expressed in the wearing of black garments for the remainder of her life) while activating every significant social unit within the community (the *baserria*'s domestic group, the *auzoa*, the kindred, religious voluntary associations, and the village as a whole). In short, a death triggers an all-encompassing series of formal obligations among the survivors defined in terms of their genealogical proximity to the deceased and residential proximity to his or her *baserria*.

THE BOOK *Death in Murelaga* argues that it is through the medium of a death and all that it triggers that we can best understand the relations among the living, as well as between the survivors and the dead, in rural Basque society. When Douglass first conducted his research in Aulestia in the early 1960s, the parish priest, Don Emilio, was an extraordinarily progressive thinker. He delighted in the reforms of John XXIII (particularly the permission to say mass in the vernacular—in our case Basque—rather than Latin) and was an avid reader of such social-reformist novelists as the American Sinclair Lewis. To the chagrin of many villagers, Don Emilio renovated the church, removing many of its "antiquated" (in his view) features, particularly the *sepulturiek* (sepultures), rectangular spaces on the church floor, each corresponding to a *baserria* in perpetuity, where the household's female members sat whenever attending a religious service. For a year after a death in the family, someone was required to attend every religious service and light the many candles provided by kinsmen and neighbors. None of the foregoing is spelled out in the standard Christian liturgy, and Don Emilio believed that he was abolishing "superstitions" (he still rang the church bells to head off storms—but reluctantly). Laughingly (and tellingly), Aulestia's pastor would jibe to Douglass that he was "the enemy of the anthropologist."

Another realm in which standard doctrine and folk belief overlap or coincide, while still differing, is that of sainthood. The Catholic Church has a history of canonizing exemplars, who then either epitomize a human virtue or provide protection against a particular temporal ill. Parents are encouraged to confer at baptism a "Christian" (or certain revered Old Testament) name on their child. Catholic churches are likewise "christened" by being given a saint's name. Throughout much of the Southern European and Latin American Catholic worlds, it has also become common practice for whole communities to adopt a patron saint and then to celebrate on his or her feast day.

It is at this point that the folk edge of the religious sword comes into play. It is not uncommon for a particular saint's effigy to acquire a reputation for miraculous powers and therefore to become the object of the supplications of believers in search of cures or other favors. The church is at best ambivalent about such mystification and empowerment of saint's cults operating at the edge of official doctrine and institutional control. The festivals (as well as the celebration of Carnaval on the advent of the Lenten season) are perhaps even more threatening, given their potential for unrestrained licentious behavior.

ARGUABLY, WITHIN European Catholicism the strongest expression of a saint's cult is devotion to Mary. As Jesus's mother, she is both an anointed (chosen) holy figure and a potentially powerful intercessor with her son. In a multitude of guises (personal names, dedicated churches, as the patroness of communities), the Marian cult is widespread throughout Europe.

In Western Europe, there is a reasonably long-standing tradition of miraculous apparitions of the Virgin Mary, usually to shepherding children. It is perhaps the extreme expression of Marianism. One need only cite the renowned examples of Fatima and Lourdes.

COMPARATIVE ANALYSIS of the phenomenon suggests that the apparitions transpire at moments of considerable social and political tension. The Virgin Mary first appears in pristine (untroubled) rural contexts to innocents in order to confide in them instructions for the political leadership embroiled in some sort of monumental crisis, usually involving a war. The news spreads rapidly and easily triggers a contagion in which pilgrims flock to the site in the hope of seeing Mary themselves and possibly to obtain her intervention in the alleviation of some personal calamity.

There have been two notable apparitions of the Virgin Mary in the Basque Country. In the fifteenth century, she appeared to a shepherd tending sheep on a mountain above Oñati (Gipuzkoa). She requested that a church be built on the site, which came to be known as Aranzazu. (It is believed that, on first seeing the Virgin Mary in the midst of prickly brush, the shepherd remarked in Basque (Arantzan zu?—"You among thorns?"). But there is also the suggestion that the place, which is near many dolmens, was actually famed as an abode of Mari. Today it is the site of an impressive Franciscan monastery. Aranzazu has become a bastion of Basque culture— the architectural expression of its sacred charter, as it were. In this regard, for Basques, Aranzazu has symbolic import similar to that of the Monastery [of the Virgin] of Montserrat for Catalans.

Our Lady of Itziar, Gipuzkoa
There are many famed manifestations of Marian devotion throughout the Basque Country. This twelfth-century icon is still the object of veneration.

THE ANTHROPOLOGIST William Christian has studied the second and far more recent case of an apparition of the Virgin Mary in the Basque Country—the events at Ezkioga (Gipuzkoa) in the early 1930s, when Spain was engaged in an unaccustomed and ultimately unsuc cessful experiment in republican government

that culminated in civil war in 1936. The apparitions
were a major "happening." Over time, more than one
million people from throughout the Basque Country,
Spain, and Europe as a whole came to the site in the
hope of seeing the chosen children's periodic attempts
to reconnect with the Virgin Mary. The modern media's
dissemination of the ecstatic trances of the visionaries
and other believers transformed them into superstars.
Given the visionaries' access to the supernatural, the
faithful asked them to intercede on their behalf, particularly regarding the miraculous cure of hopeless medical
conditions.

The Catholic Church was ambivalent. On the one hand,
the church fathers were pleased by Ezkioga's capacity to
catalyze religious devotion. On the other, they saw a thin
line between fervor and hysteria. The behavior and messages of the visionaries threatened to spin out of control.
Then, too, there were the faint echoes of the ancient
witches' covens, not to mention the folk devotion to
Mari's sacred site.

As it turned out, the events at Ezkioga forced both
religious and secular hierarchies to draw lines between
reality and fantasy, religion and superstition, obedi-
ence to formal authority and personal religious ecstasy.
Ecclesiastical experts were asked to evaluate the apparitions and to determine their authenticity. In the final
analysis, they were dismissed as fake. When this verdict
failed to end pilgrimages of the faithful to Ezkioga, both
the religious and secular authorities took punitive measures. Ezkioga, for all of its contemporary buzz as a major
media event, has failed to leave its own Aranzazu legacy.

I N BOTH DON Emilio's attitudes and the official reac
tions to Ezkioga, we can observe a neat encapsulation
of the church's ambivalence regarding the practices of
folk religion. It is well known that Christianity accom-

modated non-Christian practices and beliefs in order to facilitate the proselytization of nonbelievers. While both are "Catholic," there is much that differentiates, say, Irish and Mexican Catholicism. On the strength of the foregoing evidence, it is possible to argue that there is a Basque Catholicism, as well—one that differs in some respects even from the neighboring Spanish and French variations.

Lesson twenty

LEARNING OBJECTIVES
1. To analyze the social centrality of religious belief and its existential challenges.
2. To analyze the apparitions of the Virgin Mary in the Basque Country.
3. To analyze the relationship between Marian apparitions and traditional Basque culture.

REQUIRED READING
William Christian, *Visionaries* (Berkeley: University of California Press, 1996), 13–65, 347–372.
William A. Douglass, *Death in Murelaga: Funerary Ritual in a Spanish Basque Village* (Seattle: University of Washington Press, 1969), 19–82.

SUGGESTED READING
José I. Tellechea Idigoras, *Tapices de la memoria: Historia clínica 279.952* (Donostia–San Sebastián Sociedad Guipúzcoana de Ediciones y Publicaciones, 1991).

WRITTEN LESSON FOR SUBMISSION
1. In your view, what are the most significant features of popular religion?

2. Discuss the connections between religious perception, symbolism, and belief.
3. Does the authentication of religious apparitions have anything to do with the sovereignty of states?

Part Four
The Contemporary World

B Y THE LATTER half of the twentieth century, anthropology's structural-functional approach—focused
on the little community, the tribal or island society as
holistic "ways of life"—was at least complemented, if not
challenged, by a more thematic approach to the study
of society and culture. In France, many embraced struc-
turalism, which in the hands of a Claude Lévi-Strauss
attempted to discern global cultural patterns that under-
pin certain universal categories of human thought. In
the United States, spearheaded by Clifford Geertz and
stimulated by interdisciplinary cross-fertilization, symbolic anthropologists sought to "read" cultures as texts,
the discriminating anthropological contribution to the
enterprise being the provision of "thick description,"
gleaned from lengthy participant observation of particular cultural complexes. Geertz's purview embraced macrostructural thematic topics such as politics in *Old Societies and New States* (1963) and religion in *The Religion
of Java* (1960), but it was his *Interpretation of Cultures*
that became the standard of a new interpretive anthropology. On the one hand, there emerged a plethora of
subdisciplines—such as economic anthropology, urban
anthropology, political anthropology, peasant studies,
the anthropology of religion, and psychological anthropology—each with its professional societies and journals,
while, on the other, the cumulative legacy of the substantial corpus of little-community monographs and the
proliferation of thematic research concentrated within
particular geographical regions together stimulated area
studies. That is, within the anthropological disciplines,
Africanists, Americanists, Europeanists, Asianists, and
Oceanists founded their own associations and journals.

Cane-cutters in Australia
Basque migrants adapted to the economic opportunities offered by the host country. In Argentine they became ranchers, in the American West sheepherders, and they cut sugar cane in Australia. Migration becomes crucial to an understanding of the Basque society and economy during the last several centuries.
Photo: William Douglass

Perhaps the most graphic expression of these developments was the fracturing of the previously monolithic American Anthropological Association into no fewer than seventeen sections—most defined by either a thematic or areal focus.

B ASQUE ANTHROPOLOGY is rooted in part, but only in part, within the Europeanist camp. We qualify this statement because, as noted in chapters 11 and 12, after five centuries of emigration, there are longstanding Basque diasporas on five continents. Therefore, a study of some aspect of, say, the Basque colony of Buenos Aires might contribute equally (or more) to Latin American studies, urban anthropology, migration studies, and diaspora studies as to Old World Basque studies per se.

In any event, whenever dealing with European subject matter, even if the purview is the continent's exoticized and marginalized peoples, it is particularly difficult to maintain the heuristic fiction of the all but isolated and self-contained little community. If there has remained a peasant dimension in European society, at least until quite recently, the continent also has been the womb of such sweeping macrostructural developments as the Enlightenment and the Scientific and Industrial Revolutions—the main forces in configuring what is sometimes called the First World.

TO THIS POINT in the course, our anthropological analysis has focused primarily on the little community and on certain traditional aspects of Basque culture. While each of us has conducted research in rural communities, subsequently, our interests have roamed far afield, both within and beyond Basque studies. Regarding the latter, whether studying tourism in the Basque Country (Douglass) or the world-famed Bilbao Guggenehim Museum project (Zulaika), we have attempted to analyze cutting-edge concerns within contemporary Basque society. We therefore turn now to the recent and present macrostructural economic, social, and cultural realities, particularly as reflected in the attempts by both the private and the public sectors to make Bilbao, Donostia, Gasteiz, and Iruña major players within the pervasive globalization of the new millennium.

In chapters 21 and 24, we will consider the attempts by both the public sector and the private sector to situate Bilbao as a major player within that world.

In chapter 22, we present an overview of the Basque economy, in part to counter any false impressions that we may have created thus far regarding the economic importance (or lack thereof) of both agriculture and fishing within the overall Basque economy. While our treatment is scarcely "anthropological" in the strict sense (it could just as easily have been written by an economist), we would argue that Basques have been both subjects and architects of European economic history and of the political variety, as well. Although Basques and certain facets of their culture have been "exoticized" and "ethnicized" by anthropologists (including ourselves) and by other scholars, it is equally true that they have been thoroughly immersed for at least the last millennium in the mainstream of Occidental civilization. The marginalization of Basques within the Spanish and French states is also quite relevant. Furthermore, if some might argue that Euskalherria has been "internally colonized" by both Spain and France (see chapters 7 and 8), it is equally true (as we have seen in chapters 8 and 11) that Basques were handmaidens of the Spanish (and to a lesser degree French) imperial ventures. There is therefore a sense in which a standard description of most aspects of Basque society, say of the economy, is at the same time emblematic of the new ethnography that focuses as much or more on the mainstream than on the margins and that does so in First World settings.

CHAPTER 23 deals with the internationally famed experiment with industrial cooperatives in the town of Arrasate (Mondrag n), Gipuzkoa, touted by many as a possible "third way" paradigm that is neither unfettered neoliberal capitalism nor socialism's command economy. Chapter 24, in turn, focuses on the infrastructural transformation and urban regeneration of Bilbao, on its recovery from the decline of its urban, industrial base. In chapter 25, we will then consider contemporary tourism in the Basque Country. Chapter 26 deals with the effect of frontiers, both internal and international, on the structure of contemporary Basque reality and the expression of Basque identity. Finally, chapter 27 examines the effects of all the foregoing on the traditional agricultural and fishing communities considered earlier.

21 · Bilbao

B ASQUE INDUSTRIALIZATION is inextricably tied
to Bilbao. Throughout history, it has been the cutting edge of the Basque economy. Fishermen, mariners,
shipbuilders, merchants, colonial adventurers, and
smugglers are some of Bilbao's colorful figures whose
livelihoods were dependent on the Cantabrian Sea. The
Nerbioi (Nervión) River, which passes through the city,
was the grand avenue to the Atlantic Ocean. As such,
it was the facilitator and symbol of Bilbao's maritime
traffic and openness to the world. The city was doubly
blessed with an important seaport and vast deposits of
mineral wealth. The Roman chronicler Pliny noted Can-
tabria's "mountain of iron," which was situated adjacent
to what would become Bilbao a thousand years later.

Founded in 1300 by Don Diego López de Haro, Bilbao's
charter guaranteed the nascent town exclusive jurisdiction over the Nerbioi's trade. By the mid-sixteenth century, the volume of exports (Castilian wool, Basque iron
implements) and imported European goods made the
Bilbao-Flanders run Western Europe's most important
trade route.

By this time, the medieval *villa*, the town of sailors
and craftsmen, had evolved into the commercial *villa*
capable of furthering and protecting its international
trade. (While excluded from direct participation in the
Americas run, Basque maritime interests established
a strong presence in Cádiz and Seville in order to participate.) The importance of Bilbao's maritime trade
persisted into the nineteenth century, during which it
actually increased. The port ranked tenth in tonnage
handled among Spanish ports in 1800 but, by the mid-
1860s, it was second only to Barcelona. Between 1847

and 1858, Bilbao's traffic increased from 30,000 to 68,200 tons, before declining to 50,772 tons in 1887. A decline in Castile's wool production and the loss of the city's status as a free port in the aftermath of the First Carlist War scarcely favored Bilbao's maritime commerce, but the setbacks were more than offset by the removal after the conflict of impediments to direct trade with Spain's remaining colonies (Cuba, Puerto Rico, and the Philippines) and the growing demand for consumer goods within the Spanish domestic market. By the mid-nineteenth century, 75 percent of Bilbao's import trade was with Great Britain (textiles, machinery, drugs, and chemical products), France (textiles), and Norway (cod). Bilbao exported grain, flour, wine, and iron ore—grain and flour alone constituting 72 percent of the total volume from 1858 to 1866.

Bilbao's third reinvention of itself transpired in the mid-nineteenth century, when it became a pulsating industrial city of the smokestack variety, with economic growth predicated on exploitation of the nearby iron-ore deposits for both export and processing locally into steel. The latter, in turn, fostered development of a major ship-building industry in the city.

BEGINNING IN the mid-nineteenth century, Bilbao also experienced a mining boom. After the invention by Henry Bessemer in 1856 of a converter that facilitated cheaper production of steel, Bilbao iron ore output went from a mere 5,000 tons in 1861 to 2,684,000 tons in 1880 and 6,496,000 tons by 1898.

During the late nineteenth century, Great Britain, the world's greatest imperial power at the time, imported two-thirds of its iron from Bilbao, or 65 to 75 percent of the city's annual exports. Foreign entrepreneurs came to Bizkaia not only as purchasers of crude ore, but also as investors in the exploitation of the mines.

International capital was crucial in the region's industrialization through its participation in the iron and steel industries, railroads, and harbor improvements. In fact, the two most important foreign companies, the Orconera Iron Ore Company and the Société Franco-Belge des Mines de Somorrostro, were multinationals. Although foreign companies extracted 40 percent of Bilbao's iron from 1880 to 1900, the exploitation of the mines provided a good symbiotic relationship between foreign and Basque capital that, in addition to profits, facilitated a healthy transfer of British technology. In effect, Bilbao became an appendage of the British world economic system. However, historians estimate that between 60 percent and 75 percent of the gains remained in the pockets of Bilbao's industrial elite.

Between 1879 and 1882, three modern steel refineries with powerful blast furnaces fueled by coke were established on the estuary's Left Bank: San Francisco, Altos Hornos de Bilbao, and La Vizcaya. By 1881, San Francisco's four blast furnaces alone were producing about 36,000 tons of iron, almost a third of the total Spanish production. The refineries' location on the Nerbioi River facilitated the import of British coal, the return freight for the ore exported to England. With the decline in the cost of coal, Bilbao began to dominate the manufacture of iron and steel in Spain. Its share of total production increased to 66 percent between 1880 and 1913. In addition to the new blast furnaces, the rapid expansion of Bizkaia's railroad lines, as well as proliferation of Bilbao chemical factories and shipyards, was further evidence of industrial modernization.

BILBAO'S SHIPPING industry attracted vast amounts of capital in the 1880s. During the mid-1890s, the Spanish government requested that three vessels be built in Bilbao's shipyards. (They were sunk in Cuba

Bilbao 2000
The new metro or subway system, designed by
British architect Norman Foster, is a highlight of
contemporary Bilbao.
Photo: Joseba Zulaika

---

during the Spanish-American War.) The port's fleet
increased from 90,000 tons in 1885 to 156,000 tons ten
years later. Sota and Aznar, Bilbao's biggest shipping
company, was formed in this period. Stimulated in part
by the maritime traffic created by the Boer War, Bilbao's
fleet increased another 50 percent by 1900—accounting
by then for about one-half of Spain's total tonnage.

Business investment in Bizkaia by 1901 was 483 million pesetas, which represented 55 percent of the Spanish total. Where did the capital come from? Historians such as Manuel Montero emphasize the importance of capital accumulation through mining and its investment in other industries; others, such as Emiliano Fernández de Pinedo, downplay the direct contribution of mining and instead stress international investments. As an example, 57 percent of the capital of Altos Hornos de Bilbao, the emblematic factory of the entire industrial complex, came from outside Bizkaia. Eduardo J. Glas concludes that mining profits can account for at most 60 percent of the capital investment. The rest had to derive from local savings or external investors. An overlooked source was the remittances of Basque emigrants from around the globe deposited in savings banks in the Basque Country.

BILBAO ALSO developed into a major financial center. In 1850, the important Unión Bilbaína insurance company was launched by forty of the city's wealthiest merchants. By 1861, there were seven insurance underwriters in the city. In 1857, the Banco de Bilbao was founded and secured the privilege of issuing legal tender. In 1890, the Bilbao stock exchange was established and continues to function to the present day.

By 1929, although Basques constituted a mere 3 percent of Spain's population, Basque capital represented 25 percent of Spanish banking resources, 38 percent of the investment in shipyards, 40 percent of the ownership of engineering and electrical construction firms, 68 percent of the assets of shipping companies, and 62 percent of the capital invested in steel plants.

Bilbao's prosperity underwrote urban renewal projects. Water conduits had to be built by the 1860s. The Bilbao-Tudela railroad was built, financed by local capital. The need for urban expansion, or *ensanche* (enlargement), became self-evident as Bilbao's population almost tripled in just thirty years, from 17,923 in 1857 to 50,772 in 1887. The first enlargement project was carried out in 1861. More than mere urban expansion, in the district that became know as the Ensanche' there arose an entirely new city. It was the urban space of Bilbao's industrial elite, with its new concept of social standing based on wealth. It marked the end of the closed urban structure of the medieval Casco Viejo (Old Center) focused on the Siete Calles (Seven Streets). The new city sprawled along the Left Bank, which soon prompted the annexation of the surrounding municipalities of Abando, Begoña, and Deusto. The new enlargement was also organized around an elliptical plaza and along the longitudinal axis of the Gran Vía. The Nerbioi River became even more central to the city's industrial resurgence. From Bilbao to the seacoast, a relatively level ten-mile stretch provided space for factories and contiguous proletarian housing. The residential houses of the wealthy were built on the Right Bank. Until recently (with the exception of the suspension bridge of Portugalete), there were no links between the two shores—thereby underscoring geographically the social chasm.

BY CENTURY's end, the financial institutions had moved to the Ensanche, the control center of Bilbao's economy. Further expansions of the city would eventually be necessary. The initial planning anticipated 70,000 residents but, by 1924, the population had surpassed 140,000. The housing problem created by Bilbao's industrial immigration could not be resolved within the restricted quarters of the original enlargement. The proletariat gravitated to the lower-class district of San Francisco, where, by 1915, there were 1,385

Bilbao 1960
In the mid-twentieth century, Bilbao's factories, ship-
yards and docks still functioned, making the city the
Pittsburgh of Spain.
Photo:William Douglass

---

inhabitants per hectare. (Along the Gran Vía, the ratio
was 190 per hectare.)

SINCE THE mid-nineteenth century, not only Basque
industry and finances, but also the distinctive configuration of the entirety of Basque society, politics,
and culture cannot be understood without reference to

Bilbao. By the sheer magnitude of its economic production and urban growth, its highly successful symbiosis
between international capital and local elites, and the
massive influx of migrant workers from the Basque
hinterland and Spanish regions, the city reshaped the
Basque Country, even threatening to make Basques a
minority in their homeland while relegating their language and culture to rural districts, as well as to the
lower end of the social scale. It also undermined the
social prestige of Basqueness. By 1887, 73 percent of
Barakaldo's population, 41 percent of that Balmaseda,
and 38 percent of Bilbao's residents were non-Basques.
Spanish became the language of commerce and culture,
easily eclipsing Basque as the city's vernacular by the
turn of the twentieth century. Politically, about this
time, Bilbao produced both the Basque Nationalist Party
(PNV) and the Spanish Socialist Party (PSOE), two of the
prime forces to this day in Basque and, in the case of the
PSOE, wider Spanish politics.

CONSEQUENTLY, if we consider the truly unique feature of Basqueness, the language, today, Bilbao is
the least Basque part of the Basque Country. Only about
10 percent of Bilbaoans speak Euskara, as compared with
35 to 40 percent of the inhabitants of Donostia. Such a
contradiction is at the very core of both the difficulties
and the dynamism of the Basque Country. This paradox
needs to be couched in the dialectics whereby local identities tend to coalesce in opposition to globalizing forces.
By attracting and absorbing non-Basque elements, Bilbao was at one and the same time redefining and antago-
nistically reinvigorating Basque history and culture, as
well as configuring their tenuous futures.

In sum, Bilbao has represented "the modern" in a
society whose traditional activities (pastoralism, farming, hunting, fishing, and seafaring) have been depicted

---

as emblematically Basque—not only by the natives, but in the narratives of visitors and anthropologists alike. The primary activities of peasants, fisherfolk, and globe-trotting seafarers are depicted as more virtuous and as reflective of a simpler Golden Age than is the economically constrained and socially demeaning lifestyle of the factory worker or that of the parasitical enterprises of urban merchants and financial speculators. The transition of Basque society from the rural to the industrial is portrayed by some as a kind of fall from grace. It is difficult to overstate the power of this myth.

Lesson twenty-one

LEARNING OBJECTIVES
1. To examine the statistics on Basque industrialization.
2. To appreciate the relevance of greater Bilbao in Basque industrial history.
3. To consider the role of Basque industry within the global economy.
4. To contemplate the effects of industrialization on Basque society and culture.

REQUIRED READING
Eduardo J. Glas, *Bilbao's Modern Business Elite* (Reno,: University of Nevada Press, 1997), 29–107.

SUGGESTED READING
Emiliano Fernández Pinedo, *Crecimiento económico y transformaciones sociales del País Vasco 1100–1850* (Madrid: Siglo XXI, 1974).
Manuel González Portilla, *La formación de la sociedad capitalista en el País Vasco* (Donostia–San Sebastián: Aramburu, 1981).

WRITTEN LESSON FOR SUBMISSION

1. What was the role of geography and natural resources in the industrialization process of Bilbao?
2. What was the relationship between local and international capital there?
3. What was the "culture" of the new industrial oligarchy in Bilbao?
4. Discuss the sociocultural effects of a globalized economy on the Basques.

22 · Euskadi's Economy

THIS CHAPTER examines the macrostructural features and trends within the Basque economy during the second half of the twentieth century. In chapter 27, we will consider their effects on the local farming and fishing communities. It should be noted that what follows focuses on developments in Euskadi to the near exclusion of Iparralde and Nafarroa. Iparralde has experienced little industrial growth. The lynchpin of its economy is tourism—bathing and casino gambling in the resort areas of the Côte Basque (Biarritz, Miarritze), agrotourism in quaint villages, and ecotourism in the mountains. There is also a considerable economic subsidy from France as a whole, since, historically Iparralde has received more governmental assistance than it paid in taxes. Nafarroa, and particularly Iruña, was targeted for industrial development during the Franco years, a program that added a new dimension to its previously agrarian-dominated economy.

During the latter half of the twentieth century, in stark contrast to the typically bucolic imagery of peasant farmsteads and quaint fishing villages, Euskadi became a heavily industrialized region. In 1955, 46.3 percent worked in industry, a figure higher than the average in the European Common Market.

In 1960, the per-capita income in Euskadi was 79 percent higher than the average in Spain. Bizkaia, Gipuzkoa, Araba (and Nafarroa) ranked first, second, third, and ninth among the Spanish provinces. After 1960, there was a rapid economic and demographic expansion for more than a decade. The annual growth of Euskadi's gross economic product and its industrial sector were estimated to be 7.7 percent and 10.1 percent respectively, a rate similar to that of Spain, but double that of the major European economies.

What distinguished Euskadi within the Spanish economy was specialization within a very few sectors. There was also perceptible dissemination of small and medium-sized industries out of greater Bilbao and into the hinterland. This expanding industrial base, in turn, attracted a new wave of job seekers from other parts of Spain. The non-Basque in-migrant worker therefore became increasingly ubiquitous throughout the Basque heartland.

THERE EMERGES, then, the portrait of an advanced industrial economy in Euskadi by this time. We might note the major shift away from the mining of the late nineteenth century, as well as the relative unimportance in the overall economy of two (traditional) sectors—agriculture (10.9 percent) and fishing (2.4 percent). Indeed, the figure for agriculture was generated primarily by commercial crops such as the viticulture of southern Araba's famed Rioja wine-growing district. The contribution of *baserri* mixed farming to Euskadi's economy was on the order of less than 2 percent. Between 1955 and 1973, 250,000 new jobs were created in Euskadi's economy, which attained a total workforce of 986,000, or an increase of 34 percent over the period. Seven out of ten new jobs were in industry, an increase of 65 percent over 1955, or a 2.83 percent annual increase (versus 1.59 percent in Spain and 0.6 percent in the European Common Market). By 1975, whereas in Euskadi, 52.9 percent of the total workforce was in the industrial sector (an increase of 6.3 percent in relation to 1960), in the European Common Market, the industrial workforce actually declined from 43.3 percent (1960) to 41.7 percent (1975). Inflation between 1960 and 1968 in Spain was 6.2 percent annually, and then 7.5 percent until 1973 (a 2.3 percent

Industrial ruins
Today most of Bilbao's factories and steel plants
stand idle—monumental ruins of an earlier era.
The Left Bank of the river that traverses Bilbao is the
site of all the iron mining and extraordinary industrial development that fueled the economic engine
of the entire region for more than 100 years. The several miles of rusted, silent, phantom-like, abandoned
factories and blast furnaces have become a unique
spectacle of ruined industry, derelict neighborhoods
and ecological devastation. There were about 450
industrial ruins in the region after the closure of Altos
Hornos. The soil of the 12 kilometer valley between
Bilbao to the Cantrabrian sea holds three times
more pesticides than the entire African continent.
Photo: Iñaki Uriarte

Percentage of Workforce in Agriculture, Industry, and Services, 1960 and 1975

	Agriculture		Industry		Services	
	1960	1975	1960	1975	1960	1975
Germany	13.8	7.4	48.2	46.0	38.0	46.6
France	22.4	11.3	39.0	38.6	38.5	50.0
European Common Market*	17.2	8.7	43.3	41.7	39.5	49.7
Spain	40.5	22.9	30.3	36.8	29.2	40.3
Euskadi	21.5	10.7	46.3	52.9	32.2	36.4

*The nine countries then in the European Common Market: Belgium, France, Italy, Luxembourg, the Netherlands, West Germany, Denmark, Ireland, and the United Kingdom.

positive differential in relation to the European Common Market).

DEMOGRAPHICALLY, in Hegoalde (Euskadi plus Nafarroa), between 1950 and 1975, there was an increase of 1,112,000 people, to a total population of 2,556,000, or 77 percent more than in 1950. During the first half of the twentieth century, there was an annual population increase of 0.93 percent; after 1950, the annual rate of increase was 2.31 percent. This is notably superior to other parts of Spain (with an annual average growth of 1.01 percent) and the European Common Market (a growth of 0.72 percent). Between 1950 and 1975, there was a direct increase of 387,000 people through inmigration. The high fecundity rates of migrants contributed an additional 53 percent of the increase.

It should be noted that much of this midcentury economic expansion and demographic increase was somewhat artificial in that Franco's Spain was treated as an international pariah and was subject to an economic boycott for the first fifteen years of its existence. As we has noted, largely thanks to support from the United States (in return for Cold War military bases), in the early 1950s, Spain was admitted to the United Nations and became the recipient of American foreign aid. It also accommodated European tourism and exported huge numbers of "guest workers" to other European countries. Revenues from tourism and rebates from its absent workforce were the twin pillars of Spain's foreign reserves.

It would not be until after Franco that Spain gained admission to the European Common Market (and then the European Union) and to NATO. In significant ways, the dictator sought to make Spain economically self-sufficient by imposing high tariffs on imports and thereby protecting inefficient domestic industries Over the short term, Euskadi was benefited by this, its mature (and hence obsolescent) industrial infrastructure enjoying privileged access to the Spanish domestic market.

FORMERLY agrarian Araba and Nafarroa underwent considerable industrialization at this time, stimulated in large measure by tax incentives and public subsidies, although again, the unusual political economy sheltered the fledgling industries from the full effects of competition from larger-scale, more technologically advanced European counterparts. On balance, Hegoalde's industrial boom of the 1950s and 1960s was fragile and contained the seeds of its own demise when eventually forced to compete in the global arena.

The Basque economy was severely affected by the international economic crisis of the late 1970s. Due to

its small size, due to its being heavily industrialized
and with scant diversification, and due its lack of com-
petitiveness, Euskadi's industrial economy was highly
vulnerable to external influences, particularly as a newly
democratic Spain sought entry into the European Common Market.

In 1977, Euskadi went through a profound economic
crisis reflected in declining productivity, a drastic fall in
investments, the collapse of many industries, and the
subsequent loss of employment. Clearly, many Basque
industries were simply unviable.

Between 1977 and 1981, there was an annual reduction of 2.1 percent in Euskadi's gross product, followed
by a slow recovery of 1.2 percent annually. The recovery
of the Basque economy lagged behind that of the rest of
Spain.

In 1975, the per-capita income in Gipuzkoa ranked second nationally, Bizkaia's third and Araba's fifth but, by
1985, their respective rankings were fourteenth, twenty-
first, and tenth. Unemployment has been the main
measure of the severity of economic crisis, experienced
by the youth and women in particular. Between 1973
and 1985 alone, 194,000 jobs were lost in Euskadi. In
1985, the total workforce consisted of 763,500 workers, or
fewer than in 1960, despite the fact that the population
had grown by 900,000 persons. In the late 1980s and the
first part of the 1990s, unemployment remained over
20 percent, double the European average, but similar
to Spain's. Since 1977, there has been out-migration of
workers from Euskadi.

AFTER THE 1980s, the economy of Euskadi has
undergone considerable structural transition.
Spain's entry into the European Common Market was
the death knell for antiquated Basque industries. However, some were able to effect reconversion, and new

ones were launched. Between 1972 and 1985, industry contracted from 47.9 percent to 41.8 percent of Euskadi's economy. More significantly, it became adapted to the global marketplace, in part stimulated by the Basque government's creation of a number of industrial parks concentrating on research and development in microelectronics and robotics.

Meanwhile, greater Bilbao's former heavy industries (steel making and shipbuilding) became a veritable rust belt of closed enterprises. Emblematic of the new economy, however, is the development of a superport near Bilbao, one of only two suitable sites in Europe for the offloading of the petroleum transported in supertankers.

CONSEQUENTLY, since the 1980s, there has been considerable (if uneven) growth in Euskadi's economy. Today's industries are competitive and healthy. By 2004, unemployment stood at 7.8 percent, versus 10.8 percent in Spain and 9.0 percent in the European Union. Compared with the economies of the twenty-five European Union countries, regarding both worker productivity and gross national product, Euskadi ranked fourth. In 2005, in terms of citizens' perception of the quality of their life, Euskadi ranked second in the world, behind Japan.

Emblematic of the new economy, which includes a tourism dimension as well, is Bilbao's famed Guggenheim Museum. The most spectacular component of a much more ambitious urban renewal effort, the museum is but a single feature of a strategy that includes a new airport, subway system, spectacular concert hall (the Euskalduna), shopping malls, and office complexes. Bilbao is now a truly globalized urban center. Donostia and Gasteiz seek to keep pace with impressive urban renewal and cutting-edge projects of their own.

The Bilbao headquarters of the BBVA
There are three important things about Bilbao, the
saying goes: the Mother Virgin of Begoña, the soccer team Athletic, and the Bank of Bilbao.

In the late twentieth-century, Bizkaia's two major
banks—the Banco de Bilbao and the Banco de Bizca-
ya—merged. Today, while its headquarters remain
in the Basque Country, BBVA has extended its operations throughout Spain, Europe and Latin America
and much of its activity is directed from Madrid.
Photo: Iñaki Uriarte

Lesson twenty-two

LEARNING OBJECTIVES
1. To analyze the basic economic structure of Euskadi in the twentieth century.
2. To survey the crises and transformations in Euskadi's economy since the late 1970s.

REQUIRED READING
Mikel Gómez Uranga, et al., *Basque Economy: From Industrialization to Globalization* (Reno: Center for Basque Studies, 2003), 18–62.

SUGGESTED READING
Servicio de Estudios, *Estructura socioeconómica del País Vasco* (Bilbao: Cámara de Comercio, Industria y Navegación de Bilbao, 1977).
Equipo de Trabajo, *Economía vasca: Informe 1985* (Bilbao: Caja Laboral Popular, 1986).
——, *Economía vasca: Informe 1992* (Bilbao: Caja Laboral Popular, 1993).
——, *Economía vasca: Informe 1998* (Bilbao: Caja Laboral Popular, 1999).

WRITTEN LESSON FOR SUBMISSION
1. Describe how Euskadi's economic boom of the 1960s and bust of the 1970s and 1980s are related to its industrial structure.
2. Examine the causes of Basque deindustrialization during the last part of the twentieth century.
3. What are the lessons of the evolution of industrialization for the Basques?

23 · Arrasate / Mondragón
Industrial and Agrarian Cooperativism

A RRASATE / Mondragón is a Gipuzkoan town of about thirty thousand inhabitants where a successful cooperative movement has taken shape since the mid-1950s. The movement's philosophy was established by its founder, the Reverend José María Arizmendiarrieta. His guiding principles were: "To act and not to win; to create and not to possess; to progress and not to dominate." He was an ascetic priest whose ideas belonged more to a monastery than to the competitive world of capitalist industry, more to the rural lifestyle of traditional Basque society than to urban elites of modern cities. He wanted to enrich the community, not the lone individual.

The basic principles of the cooperative movement specify that its workers will be its owners, will exercise control over and dispose of the profits, and that the suppliers of capital will have a fixed-interest return on their money. The cooperative movement is thus far more than an economic enterprise. It provides housing, education, banking services, and medical care to the participants. Some of these benefits, including the creation of a university, are based on cooperation among several individual cooperative enterprises.

In 1943, Father Arizmendiarrieta created in Mondragón his Professional School. Affiliated with and organized by the Catholic Action organization, it received support from various businesses of the town. Its curriculum was twofold: technical-professional, responding to the industrial needs of the area, and social, in that it inculcated a Christian view of life. Father Arizmendiarrieta prompted twelve students from Mondragón to pursue engineering by taking independent study courses

Father Arizmendiarrieta
The charismatic founder of the famed Arrasate / Mondragón cooperatives. The Mondragon cooperatives (MCC) is a group of manufacturing companies that began in the Basque Country in the 1950s and then expanded worldwide. They have become renowned as a paradigm of workers' self-management."

by correspondence. They became the professional brainpower behind a new factory, named ULGOR, which opened in 1955 and manufactured kerosene stoves. Initially, it was a private corporation, but it was transformed into an industrial cooperative society approved by the Spanish Ministry of Labor.

A NETWORK OF cooperatives would soon develop throughout the valley of Leniz, at the headwaters of the Deba River, in a rural milieu that includes the towns of Arrasate, Aretxabaleta, Ezkoriatza, Gatzaga, Aramaio, Oñati, and Bergara. Production focused on gas stoves and other kitchen appliances. Other cooperative ventures eventually included the creation of a savings bank (the Caja Laboral Popular), a social-security and health insurance cooperative (Lagun Aro), a consumer cooperative (Eroski), and an agricultural co-op. They were all loosely integrated into one system—the Mondragón Cooperative Group. The first cooperative in 1955 began with twenty-three workers; four decades later, Mondragón housed some 150 cooperatives that employed twenty-three thousand workers / partners.

Because the cooperatives are owned wholly by the workers who, through a general assembly, provide oversight, they have proven to be the best antidote against the unemployment that has periodically plagued the Basque and Spanish economies since the oil crises of the middle 1970s. When deindustrialization and the sale of local factories of multinationals became common in the 1980s, the cooperatives secured for themselves a central place in the production of machine tools and household appliances, two important sectors of the restructured economy. This made Mondragón-style cooperative ownership an alternative to capital flight.

For workers to become owners (a requisite for employment), they must contribute about one year's salary to the enterprise. (This sum can be borrowed at a low rate of interest.) The member opens an individual account with the Caja Laboral Popular, to which a share of the cooperative's yearly profits or losses is credited

or debited and which accrues interest at the standard
rate. The general assembly of each cooperative deter-
mines the distribution of the net profits. (There are min-
imums established by Spanish law.) Of these profits, at
least 10 percent goes to the social fund, used for education and housing. The reserve fund receives a minimum
of 20 percent. The remaining 70 percent is deposited
into the members' savings accounts at the Caja. In periods of crisis or business transformation, the cooperatives might invest half of their profits in the reserve fund.
The goal is always to create a balance between collective
and individual property that ensures collective operating capital while giving workers individual incentives to
contribute. Profits are distributed to members partly as
salaries in the form of *anticipos*, or payments, advanced
against the end-of-the-year distribution of profits. The
rest remains in the bank and available to the system for
reinvestment.

PAYMENTS ARE based on job ratings, which are
ranked depending on skill, responsibility, and attributes such as seniority and performance. Job ratings
increase from a low of 1.0 to a high of 3.0 by increments
of .5. Initially, the highest-paid manger earned 4.5 times
the salary of the lowest-paid worker. A consequence
of this was that managerial salaries were not competitive with those in the private sector, and the managers
argued that the cooperative should provide them greater
incentives to stay. In 1988, the Caja voted to increase its
salary for the managers' ratio from 1:4.5 to 1:6. When
the managers of other cooperatives called for a similar
widening of the salary spread, the workers resisted and
defeated the proposal, arguing that the lower ratio was
critical to a nearly egalitarian system.

The internal organizational chart of the cooperatives
is another remarkably democratic feature of the system.

The distribution of rights and responsibilities is regulated by the following organs.

A general assembly convenes at least once a year and includes the entire membership of each individual cooperative. On this occasion, votes are cast on the annual business plan, allocation of earnings, mergers and acquisitions, and admission and expulsion of members, as well as to elect a governing council

The governing council is made up of the president, vice president, and secretary of the general assembly, along with other members of the cooperative, all of whom are elected by the general assembly for four years. This body is a sort of board of directors, constituted solely by cooperative members. It is the responsibility of the governing council to present annual reports, prepare annual plans, propose the distribution of profits, appoint and oversee managers, and determine job classifications.

A general manager is appointed by the governing council for four years and is accountable to that body, as well as to the general assembly. The general manager presides over department heads—typically engineering, marketing, and personnel—who are appointed by him.

There is also a management council, advisory to the general manager, made up of department heads and other executives nominated jointly by the general manager and the governing council.

A SOCIAL COUNCIL is elected directly by the workers and represents them to management. It brings grievances on behalf of workers. It operates like a union in a private factory, but functions to exert pressure not only upward, but downward, as well, when conveying managerial decisions. The role of the social councils is a topic of considerable debate. There is ambivalence regarding their nature and functions, and critics consider them mechanisms for rubber-stamping decisions

already taken by management. In the view of William
Foote and Kathleen King Whyte, for example, the governing councils are primarily concerned with representing
the members as co-owners, while the social councils
represent the members as workers. Decisions are made
after balancing the interests of ensuring long-run profit-
ability versus improving present working conditions. In
one survey, however, only one out of four members of
cooperatives favored unionizing as substitution for the
social councils. Consequently, despite their critics, the
social councils remain popular with a majority of the
worker-owners.

FINALLY, THERE is an audit committee, which is a
watchdog body required under the Spanish laws
governing cooperatives. It is charged with approving all
documents brought before the general assembly.

Groups in new economic sectors, such as the kitchen-
ware and appliance producer Fagor, typically made up
of six to twelve cooperatives in similar lines of production, have their own juridical organization to centralize
management, marketing, and finance. The centralization
of the group structure provides flexibility in allocating
resources, but it does not promote democracy. There is
a feeling that important decisions are sometimes made
outside of the governing bodies of each of the individual
cooperatives.

This complex of enterprises has become world famous
as a possible "third way" between the capitalist and
socialist models of industrial production. As such, Mondragón attracts the attention of the international community of scholars, government planners, businessmen,
and even filmmakers.

Despite the vagaries of the Spanish economy over the
period of their existence, during which, at times, unemployment, has surpassed 25 percent of the workforce,

The children of cooperation
To work in a Mondragón cooperative is to become a
shareholder, a resident and participant in a cradle
to grave social experiment that is viewed by some as
an alternative to both socialism and capitalism.
Source: José Félix Diáz de Tuesta (et al.) Arrasate / Mondragón Images *(Arrasate: 2003).*

Mondragón's cooperatives have exhibited a survival rate
of 97 percent. Unemployment in Mondragón has been
dramatically lower than in private firms. A typical comparison (in a June 1985 survey) reported that unemployment in Mondragón was 6.9 percent (1,197 members),
three times lower than in the rest of the Basque Country.
Of the unemployed, a large portion (792) were temporarily reallocated to other cooperatives, and 301 were still
on the payrolls of their own cooperatives, leaving 104
members, or 6 percent, to receive support that would be

classified as unemployment insurance payments in the United States.

WHEN, IN times of recession, there is no work for all the members, the cooperatives assume primary responsibility for finding jobs. The individual cooperative and the entire Mondragón complex share the expenses of worker relocation. While unemployed, members receive 80 percent of their basic take-home pay and 100 percent of their social benefits. Members are entitled to early retirement when their cooperative is going through structural downsizing if they are fifty-eight years old or older. If they take early retirement, until they are sixty-five, they receive 60 percent of their regular pay and 100 percent of their social security. After age sixty-five, members receive a regular pension. After two years of employment, members are also eligible for an indemnification if they become unemployed. The responsibility for retraining laid-off members is assumed by the cooperatives. In sum, those who labor in a Mondragón cooperative are as much "members" as "workers" who enjoy cradle-to-grave social services. Working in a cooperative is therefore a lifestyle as much as an occupation.

Arrasate / Mondragón has become a much-admired model of the economic potential for creating worker-owned cooperatives. It has generated its own systems for stimulating entrepreneurship and providing technical assistance. By carrying out industrial research, effecting technological change, and intervening to aid failing cooperatives, collectively, the cooperative movement has been able to react sensitively and expeditiously to changing conditions and new challenges. Mondragón cooperatives now manufacture kitchen equipment, machine tools, electronic components, furniture, and other products. On balance, the enterprises compete successfully in the global economy.

The implications of Mondragón's experience have been felt worldwide. Its success has conveyed the message that workers' cooperatives are not simply a utopian ideal. Many scholars and public officials are studying Mondragón in order to learn practical lessons from it. As described by White and White, for example, Mondragón has had considerable influence on American legislation regarding workers' cooperatives and employee ownership.

INTERNATIONAL INTEREST in Mondragón is partly a response to the growth of employee-owned firms in Europe, the United States, Russia, and other countries in Eastern Europe. In the United States, for example, employee ownership was rare in 1976 but, by 1989, there were over ten thousand such firms with more than eleven million employees. The attraction of Mondragón's cooperative movement is related to concerns that arose during the world-wide economic crisis of the late 1970s. For example, although the scholarly and popular literatures portray cooperatives as apolitical and nonideological institutions, Sharryn Kasmir has argued that the depiction of the movement as apolitical is an industrial "myth" designed to promote cooperatives and participatory labor-management relations as a means of discrediting traditional trade unionism and working-class organization. They argue that workers' participation in management details is often more ideological than real.

Some claim that traditional practices predisposed rural Basque society for participation in the Mondragón cooperative experiment. The argument goes that the Basque *baserria* and *auzoa* displayed elements of traditional forms of economic cooperation. (As we have seen, the same argument could have been extended to the social and economic organization of fishing.) The *baserria* was

Urbanization of the Basque countryside
In rural Gipuzkoa modern apartments rise out of former fields dwarfing two aged baserriak while providing their inhabitants with industrial employment with an easy commute.
Source: José Félix Diáz de Tuesta (et.al.) Arrasate/Mondragón Images (Arrasate: 2003).

---

dependent on access to the resources of the village commons shared with other households, on the one hand, and participated in the projects of its *auzoa* on the other.

THE POINT, while not lacking certain elegance, is difficult to prove. On the one hand, the ostensibly "Basque" rural social practices can be found throughout much of "peasant" Europe in one form or another—but without leading to industrial cooperatives. More tellingly, there have been attempts to take the Mondragón-inspired cooperative model out into the Basque countryside, where, by the second half of the twentieth century, the *baserri*-scale agricultural economy was undergoing a genuine crisis. The idea was for several farms to pool their land, livestock, and labor to achieve both economies of scale in production and enhanced leverage when purchasing implements, machinery, livestock feed, and other goods and services. Management of the agricultural cooperative was under the guidance of a general assembly of representatives of each participating household. Periodically, it would elect a general manager, determine his salary and other benefits, and set policy.

Each cooperative developed its own statute and access to agrarian credits offered by both governmental agencies and private financial institutions. Normally, members received shares in the enterprise that were discriminated according to the assessed value of their contributions. Most cooperatives had a prescribed lifetime, and many respected the right of a participating household to withdraw at any time. In such event, the departing member would be reimbursed according to the number of shares held, shares whose value was prorated according to the overall worth of the cooperative enterprise at the time.

IN POINT OF fact, the agrarian cooperative movement has been an abject failure. Very few of the original ones survive, and there are no new ones coming on-line. One might then question the validity of the arguments that either primitive cooperativism in traditional Basque society provided the foundation on which Mondragón was erected or that Arrasate / Mondragón cooperativism has provided a viable model capable of being incorporated successfully into Basque rural life as it has confronted an agrarian crisis. In the final analysis, it seems that the individualism and privileging of a degree of household self-sufficiency manifest within the

---

baserri worldview has proven stronger than the cooperative links reflected within the *auzoa*. In this regard, the *baserria* may be viewed as more of a primitive capitalist enterprise than as a primitive socialist one.

Lesson twenty-three

LEARNING OBJECTIVES
1. To survey the history of Mondragón's cooperative movement.
2. To understand the organizational principles of cooperativism and their application to farmers' cooperatives.
3. To assess the new industrial ideology of apolitical cooperation.
4. To analyze the relationship between Mondragón and Basque culture.

REQUIRED READING
William Foote Whyte and Kathleen King Whyte, *Making Mondragón*, (New York: ILR Press, 1991), 239–300.
Sharryn Kasmir, *The Myth of Mondragón* (Albany: State University of New York Press, 1996), chapter 7.

SUGGESTED READING
Davydd J. Greenwood and José L. González, et al., *Industrial Democracy as Process: Participatory Action Research in the Fagor Cooperative Group of Mondragón* (Assen: Van Gorcum, 1992).
Pierre Servy, *Les coopératives de Mondragón* (Bayonne: Servy, 1981).
Joseba Zulaika, *Basque Violence: Metaphor and Sacrament* (Reno, University of Nevada, Press, 1988), 137–50.

WRITTEN LESSON FOR SUBMISSION

1. What are the guiding principles of Mondragón's cooperative movement?
2. How can we explain the success of Mondragón amid the economic crisis of the region?
3. Is Mondragón cooperativism embedded in Basque culture? If yes, how? If no, what might explain its emergence and survival?
4. Discuss the continuities and incompatibilities between the traditional forms of cooperation and the new industrial ones.
5. Are the Mondragón cooperatives a "traditional" or "modern" enterprise—argue both positions.

24 · **Reinventing Bilbao**
From Industrial Ruins to Urban Renewal

F IRST IT WAS a medieval *villa*, founded in 1300 by
Don Diego López de Haro, then it was a commercial
villa, engaged in international trade, then, since the second half of the last century, it was the regional industrial
city. But a new millennium was dawning, and in the
1990s, a new, postindustrial Bilbao was rising from the
ashes of its industrial ruins.

A massive infrastructural transformation and urban
regeneration process is under way to turn Bilbao into a
service-oriented and culturally attractive city. The flagship of the entire redevelopment, Frank Gehry's spectacular Guggenheim-Bilbao Museoa, has stunned the
international art and architectural worlds. But the goal is
more ambitious. The intent is to effect the postindustrial
reinvention of the city. As it undergoes the painful, yet
exhilarating metamorphosis from industrial ruination to
architectural rebirth, Bilbao presents singular opportunities for tourism-based industries, as well as presenting
unique challenges for students of Basque society and
culture.

The Guggenheim-Bilbao Museum exemplifies the
need to study contemporary culture in Basque society.
The museum has become for Basques the main text for
understanding what culture means in the contemporary
world, as well as for learning how to understand this
new sense of culture. Until recently, Basques have been
used to thinking of art and architecture as having to do
primarily with aesthetic forms within a concrete classical,
folkloric, or modernist tradition. An artistic institution
such as a museum was devoted primarily to identifying
and preserving great art. The extraordinary success of
the Guggenheim-Bilbao does not seem to rely simply

on such considerations. Other intangibles, having to do with the value of emblematic architecture, flagship urban renewal, cultural tourism, the international media, are as decisive as the value of the museum as museum. Thus, an exclusively artistic, or archival, or even economic, cultural, semiotic analysis of the phenomenon would miss crucial aspects of the success of the Guggenheim-Bilbao. Rather, all of the elements are in play, and the complexity of their interplay must be taken into account if we are to gain a full understanding of this momentous project.

A wasteland of industrial ruins is almost all that is left now of Bilbao's fabled industrial period. But the ongoing massive redevelopment is testimony to Bilbao's self-confidence. The city is far from having relinquished its tradition of international business. Its capacity for high-stakes risk taking remains undiminished.

T HE PERSPECTIVE of history as a process of decay and ruin is one that finds resonance in Bilbao's fin-de-millennium. The industrial and urban wasteland of the Left Bank includes kilometers of silent ruins, hundreds of buildings awaiting demolition, urban neighborhoods with deserted streets, and industrial sites with smokeless chimneys—entire valleys devastated by pollution, riverbanks contaminated beyond redemption. By 1995, Altos Hornos de Vizcaya, the smoke-belching "tall ovens" of fire that provided a livelihood to tens of thousands of families, the blast furnaces that were the proud emblem of the Left Bank's entire industrial complex, stood abandoned.

For historical, sociological, and financial reasons, it was impossible to reform the Basque economy without first revitalizing its main urban center—Bilbao. An economically agonizing and demographically imploding city sounded several alarms. (Bilbao's metropolitan

industrial area was home to a million people, almost
half of the Spanish Basque population). Throughout the
1980s, there already had been a massive effort to build a
new infrastructure—highways and bridges in particular.
But a radical new beginning was called for—a new image,
a new postindustrial economic base, in short, the entire
reinvention of an ancient, declining city.

ENTER THE architects as saviors. The staggering
architectural ruins of the Nerbioi's Left Bank legiti-
mized the presence of architecture's entire star system
in Bilbao. Frank Gehry, Cesar Pelli, Sir Norman Foster,
James Sterling, Michael Wilford, I. M. Pei, Federico
Soriano, Dolores Palacio, and Santiago Calatrava have
become household names there. The large parcels of
land that the demise of former industries on the Left
Bank's riverfront had left in a state of ruin were close
to the city's center and well-suited for major redevelopment projects. An ambitious $1.5 billion urban renewal
plan was soon in place. It focused on three areas: expansion and modernization of the port, the central artery of
Bilbao's commercial life; creation of new transportation
facilities that included a subway (designed by Norman
Foster—its first phase was completed in 1996), expansion of the airport (by Santiago Calatrava), and a central
transport hub for buses and trains (designed by James
Stirling, now espoused by Michael Wilford and still waiting to be built); and a new development on the riverfront. This included a one-million-square-foot office and
shopping-mall complex in Abandoibarra, designed by
Cesar Pelli, the Euskalduna conference and concert hall,
designed by Federico Soriano and Dolores Palacio, and a
museum of modern and contemporary art, the Guggenheim-Bilbao, designed by Frank Gehry.

Of all these major projects, two are emblematic of
the new Bilbao: Foster's sleek, costly subway, which,

Bilbao's Guggenheim museum
Architect Frank Gehry's emblematic building of universal renown that served as the cornerstone of the city's
renewal and revival.
Photo: Joseba Zulaika

---

besides its practical advantages, symbolized the city's
new infrastructure and its regained sense of modern
pride, and Gehry's voluptuous and optimistic Guggenheim Museum. The museum has overshadowed all other
projects by drawing to Bilbao the international attention
that it so desperately needed. Gehry's masterpiece has
become the undisputed emblem of a reinvigorated city

unwilling to fade away after the demise of its blast furnaces.

Gehry's work is an architectural triumph set amid the
city's postindustrial ruins. It has been likened to a whale,
a ship, an artichoke, a mermaid, a waterfall, a flower, a
fish, Marilyn Monroe, and a chopped-up Chinese paper
dragon. It has been hailed by the critics as *the* building
of the late twentieth century.

B ECAUSE BILBAO'S urban renewal and development
politics are informed by a desire to recreate a
service-oriented city that will appeal to tourists, what
matters most is how to situtate the city within the global
culture of travel and consumerism, bridging transatlantic distances, linking New York with Bilbao, and thereby
facilitating traffic in modern art, museum franchises,
tourism, and reformulated urban images.

The project of thus situating Bilbao in the newly imagined postmodern space of late global capitalism drew
heavily on the discourse of "urban regeneration."The
discourse of urban regeneration includes economic as
well as environmental, cultural, social, and symbolic
components. Leisure activities and so-called "cultural
industries" become most relevant in regenerating an
urban center. The distinctions between "art," "communication," "culture," and "entertainment" disappear. This regeneration of cities by leisure and cultural
industries has been attempted in various European
and American cities, but with uneven results. Nevertheless, the discourse regarding Bilbao reassures that the
city's new cultural industries benefit not only the yup-
pie tourist, but Bilbao's youth, its socially marginalized
migrants, and the unemployed in general. The argument
is that emblematic architecture is the condition for the
economic renewal that will bring back jobs and prestige

to the city. Bilbao's ruins thus authorized a discourse of entirely new beginnings.

In this discourse, architecture is *arché*—foundation. In classical aesthetic theory, architecture is the first art. Salvation by architecture is the cornerstone of the new regenerationist ideology in Bilbao. Due to its dependence on public funds, architecture tends to be used ideologically more than the other arts. Bilbao currently provides perhaps the grandest planetary example of architecture as both ideology and spectacle. The ideological use of architecture consists of the uncontested assumption that public power must invest massively in emblematic buildings conceived by star architects, buildings that are emblems of progress, culture, class equality, and peace.

Lesson twenty-four

LEARNING OBJECTIVES

1. To survey the industrial crisis and the reinvention of postindustrial Bilbao.
2. To contemplate the role of architecture in the regeneration of cities.
3. To understand the new tourism and service economies.
4. To analyze the intrusion of the local into global culture.

REQUIRED READING

Arantxa Rodríguez, "Planning the Revitalization of an Old Industrial City: Urban Policy Innovations in Metropolitan Bilbao (Spain)," in *Local Economic Development in Europe and the Americas*, ed. Christophe

Demaziere and Patricia Wilson (New York: Mansell, 1996), 73–91.

Hans Haacke, "The Guggenheim Museum: A Business Plan," in *Learning from the Bilbao Guggenheim*, ed. Ana M. Guasch and Joseba Zulaika (Reno: Center for Basque Studies, 2005), 113–23.

Video on Bilbao's Guggenheim Museum project

SUGGESTED READING

http://www.guggenheim.org (last accessed July 1, 2006).

Ana M. Guasch and J. Zulaika, eds., *Learning from the Bilbao Guggenheim* (Reno: Center for Basque Studies, 2005).

Coosje Van Bruggen, *Frank O. Gehry: Guggenheim Museum Bilbao* (New York: Solomon Guggenheim Foundations, 1997)

Joseba Zulaika, *Crónica de una seducción: El Museo Guggenheim Bilbao* (Madrid: Nerea, 1997).

WRITTEN LESSON FOR SUBMISSION

1. Analyze the ideological functions of architecture in Bilbao's urban renewal.
2. Are you convinced that cultural industries are essential for the economy of a region?
3. How do you relate the silenced blast furnaces (Altos Hornos) to the Guggenheim?

25 · Touring Euskalherria

TOURISM IS THE world's biggest industry. Unlike many other economic activities, it is nearly ubiquitous and certainly multifaceted, ranging from the sophisticated and urbane visitors who support the luxury hotels, gourmet restaurants, upscale shopping, museums, and monuments of a London, Paris, or New York and the entertainment attractions of Las Vegas and Orlando to adventure tourism in the Amazon and trekking in the Himalayas. Indeed, today, it is the rare country, region, or community contemplating economic (re)development that does not include the expectation (or at least the hope) of attracting tourists as a part of its plan. We have already noted the role of the Guggenheim-Bilbao Museum as the centerpiece of that city's urban renewal.

The yearn to wander—whether as a stranger or sojourner, explorer or traveler—to experience the other and the unknown, is deeply ingrained in human experience. Both Homer's *Odyssey* and Virgil's *Aeneid* have dimensions of travelers' accounts, as does Dante's divinely comedic journey to the afterworld. Within Occidental culture, the religious pilgrimage, whether to Jerusalem, Rome, Canterbury, or Santiago de la Compostela, was the quintessential expression of medieval Christian religious devotion, as is the Muslim's prescribed journey to Mecca.

Given the antiquity, ubiquity, and significance of "touring" in human traditions, it is surprising that its study within anthropology has gained credence only recently. It has been argued that the anthropologist, ever sensitive to the possible accusation that she was engaged in the study (that is, the pursuit) of exotica

Basque tourists and foreign Basques
During the pre-Lenten, Carnival parade in Etxalar, Nafarroa (1962), four local bachelors dress as stereotypical
tourists while the anthropologist (Douglass) dons traditional nineteenth-century rural Basque costume (much
to the delight of the villagers).
Photo: Fidel Cruz

---

in the far-flung reaches of the planet, sought to distinguish her project from that of the adventurer and
explorer, not to mention that of the the missionary and
colonial administrator, and most certainly from the
interests of that most shallow of travelers—the tourist.
Be that as it may, since publication in 1976 Of Dean Mac-
Cannell's canonical work *The Tourist*, there is now a subdiscipline of the anthropology of tourism that subjects
the tourist gazing upon the "natives" to anthropological
scrutiny and analysis.

Thanks to the seminal article by Davydd J. Greenwood, "Culture by the Pound," arguably the most frequently cited piece in the first volume of collected essays on the anthropology of tourism, *Hosts and Guests*, Basque-related research has contributed disproportionately to the anthropology of tourism. Nevertheless, the Greenwood piece reflects a certain critical stance in anthropology toward tourism itself, viewing it as in varying degrees exploitative of the cultures and communities involved and transgressive of their boundaries. In this view, which remains deeply ingrained in the work of some, though not all, anthropological studies of tourism, whether focused on the shallow and demanding visitor or the capitalist investor in infrastructure, tourism represents the penetration, exploitation, and corruption of cultural essences and authenticity for the titillation and / or economic gain of outsiders—and possibly a few select community members. While this is certainly a defensible viewpoint, it is not the only plausible one. It also incorporates certain negative premises (at times little examined) about the nature of "business" in the contemporary world. This point is elaborated further in the assigned readings.

And what of Basque tourism itself? It might be noted that within the European context, it is among the most ancient expressions of the touristic impulse. During the Middle Ages, the famed pilgrimage route to Santiago de la Compostela crossed the Basque Pyrenees and central and southern Nafarroa, giving rise to several way stations, inns, and convents for harboring pilgrims.

SUBSEQUENTLY, in the modern era, the physical attributes of Euskalherria, with its mild winters and moderate summers (at least by European standards), combined with a spectacular coastline sprinkled with picturesque beaches and quaint fishing villages, attracted a regular stream of visitors as early as the eighteenth century. As Europe entered the Romantic Age in the early nineteenth century, prompting growing dissatisfaction with Occidental civilization and a corresponding fascination with cultural exotica, the accessible and mysterious Basques, with their unusual origins and unique language, proved to be particularly attractive. There was therefore discernible "ethnotourism" in Euskalherria as early as two centuries ago. During the second half of the nineteenth century, the spread of a railroad network throughout the continent, as well as the inauguration of casino gambling in Miarritze (Biarritz), established Iparralde as one of Europe's prime tourist destinations, particularly during the winter months.

Similarly, there developed elitist Spanish tourism to Euskadi's quaint coastal villages and spectacular beaches. This tourism was equally seasonal and weather-related, but was the obverse of Iparralde's tourist complex. It was concentrated in the summer months, during which Madrileños sought relief from the searing summer heat of the Castilian plateau, the *meseta*. Francisco Franco, for example, was a notable regular summer visitor to Donosti.

IT IS THE NATURE of tourism to market a local feature or features to outsiders. This projection of imagery is of particular anthropological interest. It raises such questions as a group's conscious formulation of identity and its projection as an "attraction," the corresponding process whereby potential visitors, through their expectations, impose certain stereotypes on their hosts,the equity and consequences of the usually unequal distribution of tourism's economic benefits, and the effect of vending cultural attractions and staging performances based on a culture's "authenticity."

The Basque Country attracts both serious scholars and casual visitors in search of cultural exotica about equally. In addition to the bucolic imagery of quaint fishing and farming villages set in the truly spectacular verdant foothills of the western Pyrenees, there is the culture's rich folk heritage. Literally hundreds of villages possess their own folk costume, used only on ritual occasions at present, and even their own unique folk dance. Most celebrate an annual patron saint's festival. Indeed, during the summer, there is a veritable festival cycle in which no week is without its celebrations—all of which are now touristed. In chapter 17, we considered the most famous of all—Iruña's week-long San Fermín festival, whose tourist dimension was popularized by Ernest Hemingway's works *The Sun Also Rises* and *A Moveable Feast*. The novel *The Summer of Katya*, by "Trevanian" (the pen name of Rodney William Whitaker) describes vividly one such village celebration in Iparralde.

Two new and rapidly growing forms of Basque tourism merit mention. While Euskalherria's mountains are too low to support a quality ski industry, they are sufficiently spectacular to attract the ecotourism of trekkers and rock climbers. Even more vigorous and promising is agrotourism. Euskadi, in particular, has a structured program whereby *baserri* families are encouraged to offer farm visits of the home-stay variety. In order to qualify, the hosts must undergo a short course and certification in the provision of tourist services.

BASQUE TOURISM therefore has a dimension of antochthonous empowerment, or at least potentially so. Central to the discussion is the capacity that tourism provides to project one's identity. It may be argued that in the case of Euskadi, with its relative political and economic autonomy within Spain, the Basque government has taken the initiative, most notably with the

Guggenheim Museum, to project a culturally avant-garde and benign image both to combat the negative international stereotype of Basques as violent terrorists and to lay claim to a privileged place within the globalized contemporary world.

IN CONTRAST, tourism in Iparralde is dominated more by a French national tourism campaign directed from Paris that seeks to attract visitors to the French Basque area by emphasizing its quaintness (the peasant villages of a bucolic countryside), its physical attractions (beaches and mountains), and, particularly, the ancient cultural uniqueness of the Basques as the "Indians of Europe."

In any event, tourism has proven to be good business. For instance, visits to Euskadi were up 10 percent in August of 2005, compared to the same month the previous year.

Lesson twenty-five

LEARNING OBJECTIVES
1. To evaluate the role of tourism within contemporary Basque society and its economy.
2. To trace the history and complexity of tourism in the Basque Country.

REQUIRED READING
Davydd J. Greenwood, "Culture by the Pound: An Anthropological Perspective on Tourism as Cultural Commoditization," in *Hosts and Guests: The Anthropology of Tourism*, ed. Valene L. Smith (Oxford: Basil Blackwell, 1978), pp. 129–138.

SUGGESTED READING

Julie Lacy and William A. Douglass, "Beyond Authenticity: The Meanings and Uses of Cultural Tourism," *Tourist Studies* 2, no, 1 (2002): 5–21.

Trevanian, *The Summer of Katya* (New York: Crown, 1983).

WRITTEN LESSON FOR SUBMISSION

1. As a window on a particular culture, does tourism illuminate or distort?
2. Is tourism a benign or malignant activity? Argue both positions.

26 · Borders

I N RECENT years, within both anthropology and
cultural studies, there has been considerable interest in the related issues of the nature and influence
of international boundaries on frontiers, the political,
economic, cultural and social borderlands that they
create, and transnational issues, whether in the form
of globalization or in form of the ongoing interactions
between emigrant diasporas and their homelands of
origin. As we have seen, for nearly half a millennium,
the Basque Country has been traversed by a major international frontier (the Spanish-French border) and has
been a prime European sending area for transatlantic
emigration. Consequently, these "new" concerns or topics within the social sciences have been germane within
Basque sudies for a long time.

To complement the reading assignments, we will
underscore recent developments within both the Basque
borderlands and between the Basque Country and its
diaspora, developments that are attributable to two fundamental modifications of Spanish / Basque and European political institutions. First, there are the effects of
the Spanish constitution that, in effect, federalized Spain
without declaring it to be a federal republic. Divided
today into seventeen "autonomous" regions, Spain is
arguably Western Europe's most decentralized state.
Furthermore, as of this writing, several of the regions,
and most notably those of the Basques and Catalans, are
pressing Madrid for even greater concessions of political independence. Second, there is the European Community project, which, despite the recent reversals when
the proposed new European constitution was rebuffed
by the French and Dutch electorates, has gone a long

way toward obliterating the continent's internal borders while giving most of its member states a single currency—the euro.

Perhaps ironically, these two macropolitical developments are, in some respects, at cross purposes, or are at least capable of producing certain incompatibilities. Regarding the Basque nationalist agenda, it is fair to say that decentralization and transnationalization have weakened some internal divisions while strengthening others. When, for instance, in the late 1970s, the Basques were debating the proposed Statue of Autonomy that ultimately led to creation of Eusko Jaurlaritza, there was a concentrated effort to include Nafarroa. This was opposed by the province's Carlists and their political allies, for whom Basque nationalism was anathema and Spanish nationalism was the only acceptable patriotism. These proponents of keeping Nafarroa out of the Basque Autonomous Community were able to argue successfully for Nafarroan exceptionalism, predicated on the historical legacy of the ancient Kingdom of Nafarroa. Today, Nafarroa constitutes its own autonomous region, complete with president and parliament. In a real sense, then, while the Basque Statute of Autonomy conjoined Bizkaia, Gipuzkoa, and Araba into the single overarching polity of Euskadi, it also helped to reinforce an internal border between Euskadi and Nafarroa.

DEVELOPMENTS regarding Iparralde have evolved rather differently. In the last decade, particularly when faced with a degree of political violence in Corsica, Paris has paid lip service to the devolution of at least some political power to certain of the regions. In the Basque case, the evidence of actual transfers remains scant, however. Nevertheless, it is equally true that pro-Basque nationalist sentiment amongst Iparralde's citizenry, as reflected in electoral results, remains in the

Coat of arms of the Nafarroan monarchs
Some of Nafarroa's monarchs are entombed in Nájera
(Rioja) that was once part of their kingdom. Note the
Nafarroan symbols of chains and the fleur de lis.
Photo: Xabier Irujo

---

single-digit range. Even if they were permitted a referendum regarding, say, some degree of political integration
with Hegoalde, it seems inconceivable that the measure
would be approved by a majority of the French Basque
electorate.

There are, however, ways in which developments within the European Union have facilitated transnational cooperation between Basques on opposite sides of the French-Spanish border. While the EU is constituted by states, it also accommodates "regions" defined ethnically or culturally. Indeed, the first draft of the constitution that was recently rejected contained considerable language accommodating both respect for and institutional expression of the rights of Europe's "peoples-without-states." All such references were expurgated systematically from the text at the insistence of the Aznar government as one of the conditions for Spain's participation in the exercise. At this writing, the EU's constitutional process is stalled, however, it is clear that should it be revived, the debate regarding the continent's regional (versus statist) makeup will be revisited. Meanwhile, it should be noted that in the recent past and at present, French and Spanish Basques interact and even coalesce over certain common interests within the forums of Europe's existing regional institutions.

CERTAIN ACTIVITIES of Eusko Jaurlaritza over the past quarter of a century are also relevant. For the most part, Eusko Jaurlaritza is on the defensive in its relations with Madrid and experiences considerable frustration over the fact that approximately thirty competencies that were to have been transferred under the terms of the Statute of Autonomy from the central government to Gasteiz have not been handed over. However, there is one exception—foreign affairs. Despite the fact that the statute clearly reserves foreign policy and foreign relations to Madrid, Eusko Jaurlaritza has its Ministry of External Affairs. It regularly organizes international visits of the *lehendakari*, or president, which usually entail the attempt to meet with the host country's head of state. There have been several international trade missions.

Eusko Jaurlaritza also maintains a kind of embassy in
Brussels to argue the Basque case in the halls and within
the deliberations of the EU. Furthermore, Eusko Jaurlaritza supports the United Nations' appeal for underdeveloped countries and expends a higher percentage of
its gross domestic product on foreign aid than most of
the UN's member states. Many of these activities have
incurred the ire of Madrid over the years, and particularly that of its Ministry of Foreign Affairs.

Finally, Eusko Jaurlaritza has elaborated a policy on the
Basque diaspora. It has an official in charge of diaspora
relations. It devises means of providing financial assistance to Basque clubs and associations of clubs, such
as NABO in the United States and FEVA (Federation of
Basque-Argentinian Entities) in Argentina. It subsidizes
the tours of Basque performing artists, academics, and
exhibitions throughout the diasporas. It regularly sends
out delegations of political figures (including at times
the *lehendakari*) and entrepreneurs to explore ways to
strengthen ties between the diasporas and the homeland.
Every four years, Eusko Jaurlaritza hosts and subsidizes
a week-long congress in Gasteiz of the Basque Collectivities in the World. It is currently publishing the histories
of individual Basque diasporic communities, of which
more than fifteen have appeared to date. Finally, the
Basque government has a program called Gaztemundu
(Youth World) that facilitates visits to the homeland of
young Basques born in other countries.

IN SUM, WHETHER dealing with the Spanish national
scene, transnational (Iparralde-Hegoalde) relations,
the Europe of the regions, the influences of globalization
(best reflected in the emblematic Bilbao Guggenheim
Museum project), foreign relations at the level of the EU
and the UN, or the ties between the homeland and the
diasporas, Basques today provide a veritable laboratory

in which to study such processes as identity formation, its political expression at the local, regional, state, continental, and international levels, transnationalism, and globalization

Lesson twenty-six

LEARNING OBJECTIVES
1. To analyze the effect of frontiers on Basque culture and society.
2. To trace how the Basque borderlands have evolved over time.

REQUIRED READING
Zoe Bray, *Living Boundaries: Frontiers and Identity in the Basque Country* (Brussels: P.T.E.—Peter Lang, 2004), 19–39, 157–205.
William A. Douglass, "Borderland Influences in a Navarrese Village," in *Anglo-American Contributions to Basque Studies: Essays in Honor of Jon Bilbao*, ed. William A. Douglass, Richard W. Etulain, and William H. Jacobsen, Jr. (Reno: Desert Research Institute, 1977), 135–43.

SUGGESTED READING
William A. Douglass, "A Western Perspective on an Eastern Interpretation of Where North Meets South: Pyrenean Borderland Cultures," in *Border Identities: Nation and State of International Frontiers*, ed. Thomas M. Wilson and Hastings Donnan (Cambridge: Cambridge University Press, 1998), 62–95.

WRITTEN LESSON FOR SUBMISSION

1, Is there any longer a historically relevant Basque homeland? Argue both for and against.
2. How do you see the future of "Basqueness" in the world?

27 · Small Community
Twentieth-Century Effects

MACROSTRUCTURAL considerations such as we have been examining—economic, political, and cultural globalization—fail to capture fully the concrete effects of twentieth-century modernization, consumerism, and globalization on the rural Basque household economy. To illustrate the point, we might consider several developments in Aulestia. At the beginning of the twentieth century, the typical Aulestia *baserria* conformed to the mixed-farming model in which the emphasis was on self-sufficiency and minimal dependence on the marketplace. By midcentury, however, there were clear signs of crisis and change. Exposure to desirable, yet expensive consumer goods, particularly motorized transportation (initially motor scooters and then autos), labor-saving domestic appliances, and television required cash income that it was far beyond the traditional *baserria*'s capacity to generate. The youth became increasingly less willing to remain in agriculture, particularly if it meant caring for elderly parents as a condition of inheriting the *baserria* or remaining perpetually unmarried and under the authority of one's sibling, the heir or heiress.

The traditional avenue of escape, emigration, remained open to everyone. Given the series of economic crises in the several Latin American countries forming part of Aulestia's diaspora (particularly Argentina) few opted for those destinations. During the first three decades of the twentieth century, it became increasingly difficult to access the American West, and, once there, to establish one's own sheep outfit. However, by 1950, there was a contract sheepherder program in place that provided a man with certain employment and a salary paid in dollars. The highly favorable exchange rate and the fact that a herder's room and board were covered made it possible for a man to accumulate savings over the term of a couple of three-year contracts sufficient to acquire a farm or small business back in Bizkaia. Between 1950 and 1975, many young men from Aulestia did so. Australia was another favored destination. In fact, by the 1920s, the Mendiolea family from Aulestia was established in sugar farming in North Queensland and also ran a Basque boarding house in Ingham. Until about 1970, the Mendioleas were key sponsors of intending Basque immigrants, including facilitating the entry of many from Aulestia.

B Y 1960, THE Spanish economy had entered an expansive phase. This triggered massive migration to the established industries of greater Bilbao and also stimulated construction of smaller-scale factories in regional centers such as Gernika, Durango, and Eibar. The prospect of wage employment in the industrial and service sectors, with a fixed salary, set working day, and weekend leisure time (in contrast to the seven-day, dawn-to-dusk work schedule in *baserri* agriculture) proved irresistible to many of Aulestia's young persons. In some cases, they were able to commute daily to jobs in nearby towns. In others, working for wages meant relocation. Then, too, by the 1960s, there were three local nonagricultural employment options. An arms manufacturer in Eibar set up a small branch in Aulestia to employ a few young men, as did a fish cannery from Lekeitio that provided jobs to several women. A cooperative industrial marble quarry, in which most households purchased shares (a condition for employment there), also began operation.

Over time, agriculture became the evening and weekend activity of salaried males. It also became both

Morning mist
These stunningly picturesque baserriak in Etxalar, Nafarroa, emerging from the mists of a cool October morning
underscore the bucolic nature of the Basque countryside.
Photo: William Douglass

feminized, with the wives of workers assuming more
of the daily burden, and more the concern of the very
young and very old, the activity of children in their after-
school hours and of ostensibly retired persons. Such
changes in their available labor force prompted many
households to modify their traditional agricultural pattern, cutting back on the amount of potentially arable
land plowed and planted each year, on the one hand, and
the number of livestock maintained, on the other. Typically, over time, a *baserri* would get rid of its sheep flock,
stop raising a pig for annual household consumption,
and reduce its number of milk cows from, say, five to
three. Its cereal lands (the most labor-intensive) might

be converted to meadow and / or alfalfa, with its former meadows and mountain lands planted with pine saplings.

The introduction of pines had profound economic and social consequences. In the early twentieth century, it was found that *Pinus insignis*, a pine variety from California, was especially well adapted to Bizkaia's climate and soils. It was possible to produce a grown tree within about twenty-five years. A stand of mature pines had unprecedented cash value. As Aulestia (and much of rural Bizkaia) converted former village commons and privately held mountain lands to pine production, Bizkaia's chestnut, oak, and beech forests disappeared. The deciduous varieties had produced a nut crop critical in both the human and livestock diets. With their decline, as well as with the intrusion of pines into mountain meadows, the available pasturage (public and private) for both sheep and pigs contracted to insignificant levels, thereby undermining mainstays of the traditional *baserri* economy.

BY THE MID-TWENTIETH century, the conversion of the rural economy had progressed to the point that the practice of selecting a single heir to the *baserria*, with the conditions of continuing in mixed farming while caring for the household's retired generation, began to lose its attraction and significance. Once the former deciduous forests, meadows, and cereal lands of a farm had all been converted to pines, the *baserria* was more of a holding company than a viable agricultural enterprise. It therefore became increasingly common to divide the land equally among all of the offspring, with each owner then felling his or her stand of pines and replanting it for the next generation. Alternatively, once the integrity of the original *baserria* was shattered, the moral opprobrium against dismembering it lost relevance. The land became more of a commodity than a repository of an ancient agricultural and social system. Land is now sold readily, whether to those who wish to expand their holdings in commercial tree farming (it should be noted that the timber industry now provides Aulestia with yet another source of wage employment) or for other forms of development. It has become common for successful urbanites in greater Bilbao to purchase and renovate an abandoned *baserria* or acquire a parcel in towns such as Aulestia for the construction of chalets. This development, in turn, has provided work to local tradesmen and custom to weekend and summer businesses such as taverns.

Aulestia is not entirely devoid of an agricultural economy. Some farms continue to supplement their income by raising a couple of dairy cows, and a few have expanded dairy production to a commercial level. Some of the very best fields, the flat river bottom adjacent to the town nucleus, are now farmed intensely by truck-gardening operations producing vegetables grown during the winter months in greenhouses.

In sum, today, Aulestia presents a "prettified" version of its former agricultural self. Most of its original structures are intact, albeit better maintained. The new construction is by and large respectful, or at least evocative, of former *baserri* architectural styles. Aulestia continues to project the image of a traditional Basque "peasant" community—however, it is now more one of virtual bucolic cows than of real, pungent cow manure.

IT SHOULD BE noted, however, that irrespective of the abandonment of some *baserriak* and the redefinition of others, the *baserria* continues to possess paramount symbolic value within Basque cultural and political life. When Javier Arzalluz, longstanding leader of the Basque Nationalist Party, found a particularly promising young

Koblakariak (choralers)
On the feast day of Saint Agatha (February) it is customary for impromptu choirs to go from house to house serenading while collecting money for charity.
Source: José Félix Diáz de Tuesta (et al.) Arrasate / Mondragón Images *(Arrasate: 2003)*.

---

politician, he exhorted the young man with the words "Zu, etxerako"— "You for the house"—which was immediately understood to be the political equivalent of the time-honored tradition of the rural pater familias conferring succession of ownership of the *baserria* on his eldest son.

THERE HAVE been dramatic twentieth-century developments within the Basque maritime economy, as well. The Basques' longstanding seafaring tradition continues down to the present. There is a Basque commercial fleet, based primarily in Bilbao and engaged in international trade throughout the world. Until recently, the greater Bilbao area was also a serious player in the shipbuilding industry. At present, Basque officers and seamen serve in several non-Basque merchant marines, often the products of schools of navigation and seamanship located primarily in Bilbao.

During the twentieth century, Basque fishing communities enjoyed steady prosperity and a degree of growth—although nowhere nearly as marked as that of industrial areas. Improved forms of transportation have opened up new markets for the catch and, today, the lion's share goes directly to Madrid and other Spanish cities. This expansion of fishing implies other developments, such as the construction of shore-based fish processing and the growth of the transportation industry. Consequently, towns such as Ondarroa have more than doubled their populations since the turn of the century.

DURING THE late twentieth century, Spain ranked as one of the top three countries in the world in terms of size of its fishing fleet. In 1975, in Gipuzkoa and Bizkaia, there were 14,345 persons engaged in fishing—or about 10 percent of Spain's fishermen. Iparralde was a significant factor within France's fishing fleet. In 1976, there were 1,179 fishing vessels registered in French Basque ports.

There are now three modalities of Basque fishing: the nearby coastal or shallow-water form, or *bajura*, the deep-sea variety, *altura*, and major deep-sea fishing, *gran altura*, in distant waters. Coastal fishing is a cottage industry, with each owner usually having but a single boat. *Bajura* is overseen and regulated by the *cofradías*, such as that of San Pedro in Lekeitio that we considered in chapter 13. The main quarries for the *bajura* fleet are anchovies, from April to September, and bonito and striped tuna during the summer. Deep-sea fishing, or altura, transpires to the south of England and Ireland and to the west of France. The catch is mostly merluza (hake). In major deep-sea fishing (gran altura), the boats are large trawlers (more than fifteen hundred tons) with freezers. They fish for tuna off Dakar (Africa) and farther south, for sardines in Moroccan waters, and for cod off Newfoundland. They even range into Asian waters.

Altura and gran altura are highly industrialized, but it should be noted that the bajura fleet itself is capable of going as far afield as the coasts of Africa for extended periods of time. In altura, the boat is usually owned by an investor who does not go to sea. Rather, he pays a captain and crew to work for him on salary. The crew also keeps some of the species that are caught. According to one well-placed official who worked as an attorney for the Basque fishing industry, in the 1980s, some of the men in altura made as much as a million pesetas ($9,000) a month for the six-to-eight-month season. The official figure, based on their declared income, is much lower. The altura fleet goes out for an eleven-day period and averages about twenty-five days at sea per month. The owners, officers, and mechanics tend to be Basques, while the crewmen are usually non-Basques living in Basque fishing towns. The owners of the boats net about 7 percent of the catch as their return on investment. At times, the altura fleet employs a drag net, or arrastre, which has become very controversial, since it catches everything in its path. There has been increasing concern that European waters are being overfished with this highly efficient technology.

IN THE bajura fleet, the boats are smaller and carry a crew of twelve men. The owner may or may not participate. Fifty percent of the catch goes to the owner. The crew from top to bottom is Basque, and in the 1980s, the men averaged about $1,800 per month during the season.

There are still some boats that cross the Atlantic to fish. In the 1980s, twenty-four vessels from the port of Pasaia traveled to Canada in search of cod. There are also the tuna factories stationed out of the Canary Islands that fish from the African coast to Asian waters. These enormous floating factories seldom return to home port. They fish year round and freeze their catches as they go. They are worth several million dollars each and employ the most modern technology, including helicopters to search for schools of tuna. Of the thirty-two tuna boats registered in Spain in the 1980s, twenty-two were from the Basque fishing village of Bermeo alone. The men who manned them flew back and forth from the Canary Islands to spend time with their families.

BY WAY OF contrast, we might consider the fishing complex of Hondarribia. The town has sixty-five small boats, each with a crew of four and a clearly defined fishing area within easy reach. Each boat is crewed by a household or men from two or three related ones. Sons replace fathers in the enterprise. The boats are owned by the fishermen themselves. Fishing is done with six poles each with twelve hooks per line. The main quarry is hake and sea bream, and there is great concern not to overfish the area. On an extraordinary day, a boat can catch 100 kilos of hake and make $900, but as little as $45 is equally possible.

The men fish year round, but only from Monday through Friday, thereby resting the fishery over the weekend. The boats leave at 4:00 A.M. and return at 8:00 P.M. The fishing grounds off Hondarribia have been declared off-limits to net fishermen and to those who use long lines with hundreds of hooks. At the same time, by the late twentieth century, the fishing industry was in the midst of a genuine crisis, and the numbers of men and boats had declined drastically. In 1967, 15,000 men were employed in fishing, by 1984 there were but 6,500 fishermen working on 566 boats. This represented only 1.2 percent of the total workforce of the Basque Autonomous Community. About one-fourth of the men worked in *altura arrastre* fishing. Slightly more than one-half worked in *bajura*, and the remainder in *gran altura*.

The main town engaged in *altura*, and particularly *arrastre*, has been Ondarroa. It alone accounted for more that half of the income of the Basque fishing fleet. Despite the general decline in the industry, the Ondarroan fleet had expanded, and its fishermen were extremely aggressive, irritating both their fellow Basque fishermen and European Common Market authorities. For instance, one boat from Ondarroa deigned to fish Hondarribia's grounds with nets during the weekend period when they are supposedly to be rested. Enraged locals threatened to go to Ondarroa to set fire to the offending vessel. (Shades of the eighteenth century conflict between Lekeitio and Ondarroa discussed in chapter 13.) The Ondarroans were often referred to in the European press as "pirates." The name of the town became synonymous with lawlessness in European governmental circles. We might consider some of the factors that have contributed to this reputation.

IN THE YEARS immediately prior to Spain's entry into the European Common Market (1986), Spain's fishing fleet, and its Basque fleet in particular, was under considerable pressure to reduce its activity and its catches. Arguably, at the time, the Spanish fishing fleet was Europe's most aggressive. As it depleted its own coastal fishing grounds, it was infringing increasingly on those of EC countries, particularly in the area known as the "Irish Box" off southern Ireland and England and in a

The new agriculture
By the 1960s in Aulestia pine plantations had replaced
the former deciduous forests and plow land was being
converted to pasture.
Photo: William Douglass

---

portion of the French-controlled sea, as well. The two
main means of regulation were annual quotas of permitted catches and boat licensing.

BETWEEN 1977 and 1983, the EC reduced the Basque
fleet's authorized annual catch in Common Market waters from 43,800 to 28,546 metric tons and the
number of boats licensed to operate there from 266 to
126. In 1984–85, the limits were lowered again to 14,100
metric tons of fish and 106 boat licenses. The response
of Basque fishermen was illegal entry and resort to such
subterfuge as the sale of a part of their catch on the high
seas to EC-licensed vessels. Common Market authorities responded with enhanced surveillance and patrols.

In 1984, the French navy began detaining and fining
Basque boats regularly and in March sank a vessel operating in French waters. In April 1985, the French fired on
thirteen Basque boats off Ondarroa, and in July, the Irish
fired on an Ondarroan vessel fishing in Irish territorial
waters.

ACCOMMODATION of the Basque fishing fleet, then,
was the prime acerbic problem during the final
negotiation of Spain's entry into the EC. The compromise was to assign the fishermen a quota of 45,000
metric tons for each of three years beginning January 1,
1986. The Basques were given an additional 4,500 metric
tons, subject to periodic review of the health of the fish
stocks. The quota represented about 30 percent of all
fishing within EC waters, but was deemed inadequate by
Basque fishermen, who claimed already to be harvesting
(illegally) considerably more fish.

Regarding boat licenses, Basques were assigned 300
(of six months' duration each year), of which no more
than 150 vessels could be operating simultaneously in
EC waters. Basque vessels were not to be permitted into
the Irish Box until 1996. While both Spain and the EC
viewed the provision as generous, it was denounced by
Basques, since it imposed the considerable reduction in
their *altura* fleet mentioned earlier.

The Spanish-EC accord prompted an internal struggle
within the ranks of the Basque fishing communities. The
two major ports, Ondarroa and Pasaia, were immediately
at loggerheads over EC licenses. In 1981, the Spanish
Fishing Ministry had licensed 74 boats in Pasaia and 64
in Ondarroa. By the time of Spain's EC entry, the Pasaia
fleet was down to 51 vessels, yet its fishermen contended
they should retain the 74 licenses, which would permit part of the town's fleet to fish EC waters for more
than the six months allocated by a single license, since

Pasaia had removed antiquated boats from service and thereby had modernized. Meanwhile, Ondarroa had 96 boats contending for its 64 licenses, and argued that the surplus represented the town's own recent successful modernization of its fleet. According to Ondarroans, they were being treated unfairly if the former Spanish allocation of licenses carried over to the EC arrangement. Representatives of both towns lobbied Madrid, which tried to stay out of the conflict, and Brussels took the position that a final plan had to be submitted by April 15, 1986, a deadline that was not met. In late April of that year, the EC's fisheries ministers met in nearby Santander. More than one hundred fishing boats from Ondarroa blockaded the city's harbor in protest.

In May, Ondarroans began blockading fishing ports as far away as Galicia to disrupt the industry. Pasaia responded by opening its port to all boats denied access to their home ports. Ondarroans began threatening truckers for moving the catch from EC waters inland and tried to prevent crews from reaching their boats. The Spanish police had to separate rival groups of picketers and demonstrators from the two towns. In May, Spain's Ministry of Fishing reaffirmed the 1981 allocation of licenses, thereby ending the conflict, but without convincing the disgruntled Ondarroans.

MEANWHILE, IN 1986, there was an equally acerbic second crisis regarding Basque fishing. It seems that through an oversight, the EC had failed to deal with Basque access to a small area within its jurisdiction known as the Eskote fishing banks. Most of the area is within Spanish waters, but a 600-square-kilometer portion regularly accessed by the Basque fleet was French. In February, the French navy began expelling Spanish Basque boats from the French Eskote. Meanwhile, Spanish Basque fishermen from Pasaia and Hondarribia

denounced the detrimental fishing practices in the
Eskote employed by the French Basque fleet from Donibane-Lohizune and Hendaia.

Both Spain and France took the position that the
Basque fishermen should work through the issues themselves. Nevertheless, when a French court ruled in favor
of the Spanish Basque fleet's right of access to the whole
Eskote, the French navy continued to expel its boats
from French waters. Consequently, on May 19, 1986,
270 Spanish Basque boats blockaded the mouth of the
Bidasoa River for several days, preventing French Basque
fishermen from leaving port. On June 9, they blockaded
the port again, and thousands of fishermen and their
families demonstrated at the border crossing to prevent
French trucks from bringing fish into Spain.

After unsuccessful deliberations to resolve the crisis at
the EC level, Spanish Basques again threatened to block-
ade the Bidasoa, and the French navy sent eleven war-
ships to the area. In late June, at a joint meeting between
the Spanish president, Felipe González, the French president, François Mitterand, and the French prime minister,
Jacque Chirac, it was decided that the respective delegations of the two countries should assume responsibility
for resolving the problem. Meanwhile, the French Eskote
remained off-limits to Spanish Basque fishermen.

In sum, the first year of Spain's EC membership
proved disastrous for the Spanish Basque *altura* fishing fleet. Its total catch was down 40 percent from 1985.
Compared with 1977, by 1986, the number of boats in
altura was down from 251 to 118 and their crews from
4,010 fishermen to 1,738.

Different developments affected the *gran altura* fleet.
In 1972, there were eighty-six Basque boats fishing off
Terranova (50 percent of the Spanish fleet). By 1980, the
number had declined to thirty-five vessels due to deple-

tion of the fish stocks leading to low profit margins, the extension at that time of jurisdictional coastal waters (i.e. the portion of the ocean subject to territorial jurisdiction by the nearest country) from 12 to 200 miles, and high fuel costs. Also, Canada has imposed a codfishing ban throughout its eastern seaboard as a response to the nearly total depletion of its fish stocks.

An overview of the trends in Basque fishing industry is revealing. By the 1980s, on the eve of Spain's entry into the EC, the Spanish Basque fleet numbered 748 vessels with 7,950 fishermen. By 1992 the numbers had shrunk to 584 vessels and 6,546 fishermen. There has been further decline since then. While regulatory developments, both within EU waters and globally, are partially to blame, the issue of economic unviability due to overfishing is equally evident. In 2005, the anchovy catch within the Bay of Biscay was so poor that part of the fleet remained in port, and a total ban of uncertain duration was under active consideration. Clearly, the Basque fleet is not insulated from the complex issues facing commercial fisheries throughout the world at present.

Lesson twenty-seven

LEARNING OBJECTIVES
1. To assess the continuities and discontinuities between traditional and contemporary rural Basque lifestyles.

REQUIRED READING
William A. Douglass, *Echalar and Murelaga: Opportunity and Rural Exodus in Two Spanish Basque Villages* (New York: St. Martin's Press, 1975), 150–77.

SUGGESTED READING

Davydd J. Greenwood, *Unrewarding Wealth: The Commercialization and Collapse of Agriculture in a Spanish Basque Town* (Cambridge: Cambridge, University Press, 1976).

WRITTEN LESSON FOR SUBMISSION

1. Analyze the psychological and cultural challenges to the *baserria* (agriculture) and *bajura* (fishing) ways of life posed by globalization.
2. Compare and contrast the lifestyle of the eighteenth-century and twentieth-century Basque commercial fisherman.
3. Contrast the effects of five centuries of "traditional" Basque emigration with the twentieth-century abandonment of farmsteads.

Part Five

Basque Cultural Studies

IT IS TIME to situate our anthropological treatment of Basque culture and identity within the contemporary discourse known as cultural studies. Several comments are in order. First, within both anthropology and the other social sciences, studies of identity, whether specific to an ethnic / racial, gender, or sexual orientation, are currently ascendant, if not predominant. The common theoretical perspective informing all of these developments is that identity is in at least many significant ways a construct, rather than a given, within human affairs. Indeed, for many contemporary cultural critics, to regard identity as fixed and structural, rather than processual, is to fall into "essentialism"—that is,to treat race as biologically based, ethnicity as a largely immutable historical precipitate, and gender and sexual orientation as determined by nature. It seems fair to say that much of the anthropological literature, which seeks to describe a "culture" as a structural-functional whole or even as a comprehensive symbolic system, both of which are predominantly conservative and synchronic perspectives, is a prime target for the cultural studies critic. Much of our treatment to this point could be regarded as varying degrees of "trait listing" in order to define and then reify a concept of "Basque culture."

Second, there is no little irony in the history of anthropology's relationship with cultural studies. As we have noted, Clifford Geertz, in founding an alternative to structural-functionalism within his discipline, advocated that cultures need to be read as "texts," but deeply or profoundly. For Geertz, the anthropologist's penchant for lengthy field research, usually conducted in the relevant native language(s), both defines and privileges the anthropological perspective. At about the same time, cultural studies was emerging as an interdisciplinary effort, but primarily out of the ranks of the literary critics. One of the major thrusts of that initiative was the deconstruction inherent in questioning the very possibility of "true" textual analysis, perhaps best exemplified in the work of Jacques Derrida. While a full discussion of the resulting tensions that are both internal to social anthropology, on the one hand, and inherent in its relations with the other social sciences and the eclectic field of cultural studies, on the other, is well beyond the scope of this course, the foregoing may serve as an introduction to a vital dimension of contemporary Basque studies—the analysis of identity or "Basqueness" as a shifting reality (or realities) that is ever a work in progress. The specific themes range broadly across the continuum of Basque social and political organization and cultural expression. Feminism and gay activism, ethnicity and ethnonationalism, borderlands and frontiers, film and television, popular music, art, architecture, and the virtuality proffered by the Internet are all examples of topics now considered by cultural studies. We have already touched on some of these concerns. In this section, we will contemplate others, albeit not all.

CONSEQUENTLY, chapter 28 seeks to situate treatments of Basques within the historical and contemporary debates regarding race and ethnicity. Chapter 29 considers gender issues within Basque studies, chapter 30 focuses on Basque language policy and sociolinguistics, the former as a prime arena in which to formulate (or inhibit) Basque identity and the latter as a prime context in which to observe its expression. Chapter 31 discusses the Basque *bertsolaria*, or versifier. Chapter 32 introduces the new Basque music of the late and post-Franco period as social and political commentary.

With chapter 33 and its focus on the work of the writer Bernardo Atxaga, the focus shifts to analysis of the formal cultural production of contemporary Basque society. Chapter 34 examines recent Basque film as both a universal and a particular expression that situates Basques in the planet's globalized cultural scene while underscoring their distinctiveness within it. Chapter 35 considers the contributions of two Basque titans of twentieth-century art—the sculptors Jorge Oteiza and Eduardo Chillida.

FINALLY, CHAPTER 36 seeks to underscore, through the biography of a fictional woman from Gernika, at least some of the many complexities and subtleties at play in contemporary Basque society regarding personal and collective identity formation.

28 · On Cultural Essentialism
Racism and Ethnicity

B ASQUES PRESENT an extraordinarily rich context in which to study the relationship between biology and culture. There is an extensive body of literature regarding unique Basque biological features and their interpretation. For example, Basques manifest blood-group frequencies that are markedly different from those of any other European population and particularly different from those of their immediate neighbors, the French and the Spanish. Basques have the lowest frequency in Europe of blood type B and the highest of blood type O. With respect to the Rh-negative blood factor, they have the highest frequency of any population in the world, leading one geneticist to speculate that Basques may be the original human donors of the trait. Frequencies of it in other European populations are in the 8-to-15-percent range, whereas different studies of Basque population samples found incidences ranging between 30 and 40 percent.

It was during nineteenth century that linguistic and anthropological discourses practically reinvented "Basqueness." As we have seen, a convergence of archeology, paleontology, folklore studies, linguistics, and physical and cultural anthropology constituted Basques into an intriguing peculiarity. Linguist Wilhelm von Humboldt visited the Basque Country and wrote about the language and people in sympathetic terms, even arguing that the Basques constituted their own de facto "nation," thereby anticipating Sabino de Arana by nearly a century. Other top-ranking linguists from various European countries followed: Theodor Linschmann and Karl Bouda from Germany; Prince Louis Lucien Bonaparte, Julien Vinson, Henri Gavel, and René Lafon from France; Willem J. Van Eys and Christian Cornelius Uhlenbeck from Holland; Hugo Schuchardt from Austria, Edward Spencer Dodgson from England; and Fidel Fita, Julio Cejador, Antonio Tovar and Ramón Menéndez Pidal from Spain. All were attracted by Euskara, whose non-Indo-European nature and, indeed, seeming total uniqueness within the world's languages were both well established by the mid-nineteenth century.

By this time, both physical and social / cultural anthropology were emerging as scientific disciplines. Both were racialist in that they sought to arrange humankind within hierarchies of peoples according to their physical and cultural worth. Racial and cultural inferiority / superiority were deemed to go hand in hand, and this assumption informed classificatory schemes in which dark skin, kinky hair, stature, facial physiognomy, cranial capacity, and so forth were said to correlate with varying degrees of intelligence, primitiveness, barbarism, and civilization. Since the exercise was carried out almost entirely by Europeans and their colonial settlers, it is scarcely surprising that Caucasians were said to represent the "civilized" or "superior" apex of the hierarchy of human societies and cultures.

From the outset, however, the Basques occupied an anomalous position within the exercise. As it became evident that they, unlike most Europeans, were not descendants of the Indo-European-speaking invaders from Asia who populated most of the European continent, it seemed possible to treat the Basques as not quite European, or at least as not within the European mainstream. If one nineteenth-century British physical anthropologist was able to posit the existence of twelve races on his island, it was scarcely a leap of the imagination to regard the Basques as their own race, as well. On the other hand, as it became increasingly evident that

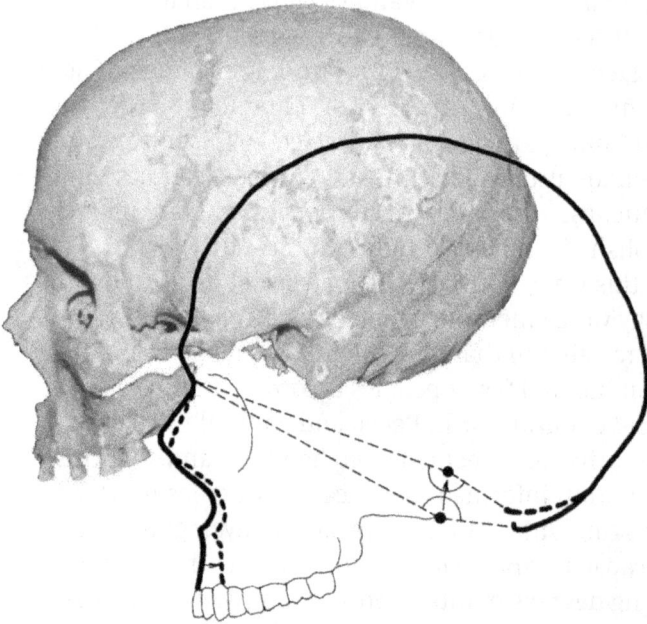

Famous skull from Urtiaga, Gipuzkoa
Anthropologists Telesforo de Aranzadi and José Miguel de Barandiaran excavated a series of supposed Upper Paleolithic skulls that led to speculation that proto-Basques were direct descendants of Cro-Magnons. The subsequent invention of Carbon-14 dating techniques determined that the skulls were far more modern than thought previously.
Source: Jesús Altuna, Lehen euskal herria *(Bilbao: 1975).*

Basques were in situ in their Pyrenean homeland prior to the invasions of most Europeans' ancestors, it was also possible to regard them as the quintessential Europeans. In this view, they were the possible key to understanding proto-European racial and cultural essences.

Consequently, by the 1850s, Paul Broca, the mid-nineteenth-century founding figure of French anthropology, was fixated on both the linguistic and biological study of Basques in the belief that they might well be the most pristine proto-Europeans and hence be key to an understanding of Europe's social and cultural foundations. The Swedish investigator Anders Retzius weighed in, as well. In 1860, the French anthropologist René Collignon published a book on "The Basque race," which was becoming more the scientific invention of Paris and Stockholm than of Bilbao or Baiona. The roster of nineteenth-century anthropologists who pondered the Basque case included such luminaries as Paul Topinard, Dominique Joseph Garat, Georges Hervé, and Alfred C. Haddon. As recently as 1923, the doyen of American anthropology, Alfred Kroeber, treated the Basques and their culture as exemplary of the interdependence between race and language.

Telesforo de Aranzadi (1860–1945) was the main figure in the development of Basque archeological and racialist studies. He corrected and then adapted many of the theories produced by European racialist anthropology about the Basques during the second half of the nineteenth century. Aranzadi also became known for his pioneering research on human hybridity, positing the argument that few, if any, human populations are racially "pure."

ARANZADI'S MAIN student was José Miguel de Barandiarán, who, as we have noted, conducted many archeological digs and created a group of researchers who gathered enormous amounts of folkloric and mythographic information. Despite its dated ethnographic premises, this corpus still provides crucial data for Basque anthropology. More questionable is his attempt to equate Basque prehistory with life in the rural Basque Country at the beginning of the twentieth century with reference to hearth forms, dress, hunting practices, the spatial orientation of dwellings, offerings to the dead, and mythical beliefs.

ARCHEOLOGISTS analyzing skeletal (primarily cranial) remains developed the hypothesis of Basque autochthonous evolution in situ. Barandiarán first formulated the hypothesis in his article "Antropología de la población vasca" (1937). The paleontologist Jesus Altuna expounds the biological continuity thesis thus:

> The deposit of Urtiaga is important among other things because in it there appeared a series of skulls that illustrate to us the origins of the Basque race. The oldest of them pertains to the end of the Upper Paleolithic [about 13,000 B.C.] and shows great similarity with Cro-Magnon Man, even if he has already initiated his evolution toward a present-day Basque. The Azillian skulls of the same deposit [9,000 to 6,000 B.C.] are intermediate between the Cro-Magnon type and the Basque type. Finally, the skulls of the Bronze Period [2000 B.C.] of the mountainous part of the country are mostly of the Basque race. This race therefore was not formed outside the country, coming subsequently to settle in it, but was originated right here, in the western Pyrenees, through an autochthonous evolution starting with Cro-Magnon Man.

This hypothesis marks the zenith of the archeologist as hero. Even if it was only a "hypothesis," the political implications of such foundational discourse were enormous. Later findings have invalidated the prehistoric dates on which the hypothesis is based. Jesús Altuna and Concepción de la Rúa, in "Dataciones absolutas de los cráneos del yacimiento prehistórico de Urtiaga," (1989) provide the following summary after reviewing the controversy:

> There are a great deal of contradictory statements concerning the stratigraphical and chronological position of some human remains exhumed by Aranzadi and Barandiarán (1935, 1936) from the Urtiaga cave. ... A dating of these skulls was made by the U-series disequilibrium method (U / Th and U / Pa) and the Accelerator radiocarbon technique. Through the dates offered by C14 ... we assign these skulls to the Bronze Age period. This is a burial, so that the Chalcolithic and the Bronze Age material could have slipped into more ancient levels. These results justify the doubts regarding the hypothesis about the Basque anthropological ... origin in Paleolithic times due to the scarce anthropological knowledge of this prehistoric period in the Basque Country. (23)

NEVERTHELESS, prestigious geneticists such as Cavalli-Sforza still characterize the Basques as the descendants resulting from the interbreeding between a population of Mesolithic aboriginals (overwhelmingly Rh-negative) and Neolithic farmers. By studying the geographic distribution of genetic patterns of present-day European populations, they perceive a genetic gradient that fits loosely with the long-established theory of Basque uniqueness derived from archeological and linguistic evidence. Jaume Bertranpetit and Luigi Luca Cavalli-Sforza have produced synthetic genetic maps for the Iberian Peninsula, concluding that "most probably, Basques represent descendants of Paleolithic and / or Mesolithic populations."

Jeremy MacClancy is critical of these results. He sees a methodology framed by its own limitations and replete

with questionable assumptions, such as that there have
been no significant changes in Basque genetic markers
over the last thousand years or so or that there is not
much genetic variation within the Basque population.
He also underscores the problematics in linking language with race.

IT MIGHT BE noted that this study of "race" is only
recently reemerging within anthropology (and then
primarily in terms of the mapping of humankind's
genome) after having been thoroughly discredited on
social and scientific grounds by the twentieth-century
excesses of the eugenics movement and, particularly, the
Holocaust. During the second half of the twentieth century, to the extent that racialist studies persisted, they
did so under the guise of the study of ethnicity, rather
than race. Furthermore, their thrust was informed more
by the notion of cultural relativism, the idea that every
human society possesses its own intrinsic worth and
may be appreciated or understood only in its own terms,
than by a desire to classify peoples and then arrange
them within a hierarchy of ultimate comparative value.
Even so, the reemergence of racialist study, spearheaded
primarily by geneticists, has triggered considerable
debate among physical anthropologists, given that the
various human genome projects could potentially under-
mine the standard anthropological antiracist discourse
that all humans partake of a single genetic continuum
and that genetic variability within supposed human
"races" is greater than that between them.

The critical point for our purposes is perhaps less the
ultimate scientific validity of racialist claims regarding
the Basque population than their (mis)applications. The
prime example in the Basque case was the racist xeno-
phobia manifested by Sabino de Arana in some of his
writings. His claim that Basques are racially superior to

Castle of Xabier, Nafarroa
Birthplace of St. Francis Xavier, famed Catholic sixteenth-century missionary to the Orient. Today Xabier is the object of an annual pilgrimage and considerable year-round tourism.
Photo: Xabier Irujo

Spaniards was not based directly on the conclusions of nineteenth-century anthropologists such as Broca, Collignon, Jacques, and Aranzadi (Arana was a journalist, not a scholar) but, by his time, their configuration of a unique Basque race had made its way into the popular press and the Basque worldview. It required little effort or imagination on Arana's part to convert this "evidence" into a claim of Basque racial superiority as part of the prelude to the demand for full Basque political sovereignty.

Consequently, it is fair to say that Basque ethnonationalism was born to a significant degree in a racialist and
racist discourse, and that one of its greatest subsequent
challenges has been to transcend this intellectual legacy.
Although in the Basque case (as in much of the rest of
the contemporary world), the concept of "race" has been
replaced by the seemingly more benign notion of "ethnicity," it is important to note that it, too, can just as easily lend itself to essentialist discourse.

SUCH HOLISTIC or encompassing concepts are neces
-sary in the social sciences, whether referring to
"states," "societies," "cultures," or "institutions," but
none have unlimited utility and hence should never be
accepted uncritically. In the early twentieth century, for
example, Max Weber was already questioning the suit-
ability of "ethnicity" as a critical analytical concept. He
warned that it "dissolves if we define our terms exactly."
Part of the problem is that Basque, or Hopi, or any other
ethnic identity has multiple sources. It is a historical
precipitate, rather than a structural given. It emerges out
of opposition to the other, that is, in opposition to one
or more other ethnic identities. Furthermore, as noted,
it readily informs and manipulates other discourses and
is, in turn, informed and manipulated by them. Consequently, statements (or clichés) about Basques and
Basqueness—for example: "Basques are hardworking,"
"Basques are honest;" "Basques are stubborn"—should
always raise the questions "Compared with whom?"
and "For what purposes?" Finally, there is the danger of
reduction and oversimplification of Basque as an identity that masks enormous heterogeneity. All "Basques"
are not hardworking, honest, and stubborn. Neither do
all who speak Euskara subscribe to the ethnicnational-
ist agenda, whereas many Basque ethnonationalists are
monolingual Spanish speakers—and so forth.

In sum, ethnic identity is always processual and problematic. At the same time, while a creation, it is not created ex nihilo. By this juncture in the course, we hope we have provided sufficient evidence for our contention at the outset that there is sufficient substance to justify considering Basques and Basque culture in their own terms, just as one might similarly study Spaniards and Spanish culture or Americans and American culture.

Lesson twenty-eight

LEARNING OBJECTIVES
1. To analyze the logic by which supposed interdependencies between culture and biology are naturalized and essentialized.
2. To survey the anthropological search for the "Basque race."
3. To analyze the extent to which Basque culture tends toward essentializations.

REQUIRED READING
Luigi Luca Cavalli-Sforza, "The Basque Population and Ancient Migrations in Europe," *Munibe* 40, no. 6. (1988): 129–37.
Jeremy MacClancy, "Biological Basques, Sociologically Speaking," in *Ethnicity: Biological and Social Aspects*, ed. Malcolm Chapman, (Oxford: Oxford University Press, 1993), 92–139.

SUGGESTED READING
Jesús Altuna y Concepción de la Rúa, "Dataciones absolutas de los cráneos del yacimiento prehistórico de Urtiaga," *Munibe*, 41 (1989): 23–28.

Jesús Azcona, "'Notas para una historia de la antropología vasca': Telesforo de Aranzadi y José Miguel de Barandiarán," *Ethnica* 17 (1981): 64–84.

José Miguel de Barandiarán, "Antropología de la población vasca," in *Obras completas*, vol. 12 (Bilbao: La Gran Enciclopédia Vasca, 1978), 149–68.

Luís Barandiarán Irízar, *José Miguel de Barandiarán: Patriarca de la cultura vasca* (Donostia–San Sebastián: Real Sociedad Bascongada de los Amigos del País, 1976).

William A. Douglass, "In Search of Juan de Oñate: Confessions of a Cryptoessentialist," *Journal of Antrhopological Research* 56, no. 2: 137–65.

William A. Douglass and Joseba Zulaika, "'Creating Basques': Anthropological Narrativity and European Cultural Exotica" (manuscript).

Angel Goicoetxea Marcaida, *Telesforo de Aranzadi: Vida y obra* (Donostia–San Sebastián: Sociedad de Ciencias, San Sebastián, 1985).

Joseba Zulaika, "Culture as Essence and Riddle" (manuscript).

WRITTEN LESSON FOR SUBMISSION
1. What can we learn about the disciplines of archeology and physical anthropology from the Basque case?
2. Evaluate MacClancy's criticisms of the findings of geneticists regarding a Basque race.
3. What kind of temporality are we dealing with in prehistory?
4. Consider the mythical power of the hypothesis of Basque autochthony.
5. What contemporary political implications and consequences might be expected from a foundational discourse of essentialist identity?

W E BEGIN WITH a discussion of a particular gender issue within the traditional Basque society of our earlier anthropological account. In this course, we have identified prime examples of institutionalized lengthy absences of sojourning males (the emigrant sugarcane cutter in Australia and the sheepherder in the American West), usually drawn from the *baserri* world, and the frequent extended fishing expeditions of the *arrantzaleak*. In all of these, the active female head of the household becomes the compensating authority figure, with corresponding social diminishment and marginalization of her male consort's familial role. There is a sense in which without such an adjustment, the circle of domestic life would remain permanently incomplete and "abnormal."

Similar compensation for the lack of gender complementarity and fulfillment is evident in the constructions of social reality effected by the male sojourners themselves. In *Terranova: The Ethos and Luck of Deep-Sea Fishermen*, Joseba Zulaika employs feminine discourse when describing the "motherly" concern of the cook for the crew's well-being aboard a fishing boat. The cook is "the soul of the ship." "He is like our mother," he was told, dispensing not only nourishment, but nurture. The cook listens to a fisherman's complaints and consoles him when he is down. The galley therefore functions as hearth and home, "the territorial and functional unit most loaded with emotional meaning." As such, it is the prime site of conflict, as well. In sum, the shipboard role of the male cook is at least partially maternal.

Echoes of such gender role reversal are evident in the cane barracks of northern Australia, as well, where each

Contemplating the future
According to recent UNESCO statistics, Basque and Japanese women share the distinction of the greatest longevity in the world's population (80.7 average age and growing by four months annually). Today five out of six widowed Basques are women. There are evident social, political and economic implications of these trends for the Basque society of the future.
Photo: Xabier Irujo

"gang" had its male cook whose unstated duties went beyond simple food preparation to that of lending a certain air of domesticity to an otherwise sharp-edged male universe. Similarly, the successful camp tender in the American West understood that it was as important to provision his herder (who was otherwise alone for days at a time) with human interaction as with food and reading material. The wise camp tender attempted to draw his charge into animated conversation, often engaging in sexual banter and humor. He might also assume temporarily (for the couple of hours spent together) the herder's "domestic duties," cooking their meal and possibly giving the herder a haircut.

Sandra Ott provides the most elaborate description of the gendered role-reversal process when detailing the summer sojourn of French Basque sheepherders with their flocks in the high-mountain pastures of Xiberoa. Several households pool their animals and then provide a male member to a team of six shepherds who live together in an *olha*, or stone hut. Their responsibilities are ordered hierarchically, and each of the men discharges a particular role for twenty-four hours at a time before rotating into another. The most prestigious role is that of the *etxekoandere*, or "woman of the house," and the least prestigious was called the *neskato*, or "female servant." The *neskato* is responsible for menial domestic chores such as dishwashing and works under the supervision of the *etxekoandere*. This "male housewife" is responsible for preparing the meals and for making cheese out of that day's ewes' milk.

EACH DAY, A newcomer arrives from a participating household in the valley and relieves the man who had completed the six-day cycle. The newcomer begins his first day as *neskato*, then passes on four successive ones through the ranks of the four shepherd roles, culminating in that of *artzain-nausi*, the master shepherd,, before becoming the *etxekoandere* the day before descending to the valley.

Herding sheep is itself framed in a maternal metaphor. The good shepherd has to display the same patience and affection toward the sheep as a "woman toward her children." This same attitude is required during the cheese making itself. Human conception is likened to the curdling of the milk in response to the rennet. Men differ in their cheese-making skills, a talent that is then equated to male sexual prowess. The cheese maker works with his hands beneath the surface of the milk, forming the sediment into a round mass. Upon proudly extracting his newly made cheese from the kettle, one proud shepherd displayed it to the anthropologist with arm's extended and the announcement "Ene niri txipi!"—"My little baby!"

UNTIL THE 1980s, anthropologists dealt with women's issues mostly in terms of cultural patterns, family roles, and public / private domains. This was the period in which theories about a "Basque matriarchy" were very popular. Based on the prevalence of projective images such as the flying witch Mari, several writers hypothesized the presence of a matriarchal complex in traditional Basque society. Johann Jacob Bachofen's theories on matriarchy and Jungian archetypes were influential in these hermeneutic approaches to culture. These matriarchal interpretations reified "Woman" as the all-powerful figure in the realm of myth or the unconscious, but demonstrated no interest in examining the concrete power relations in which the lives of contemporary women were embedded.

In 1981, the Basque parliament commissioned a study of women's educational, employment, health, and legal circumstances. A survey of 400 women from each of

the three autonomous provinces of Araba, Bizkaia, and
Gipuzkoa was conducted. It concluded that Basque
women were subject to an ideology that restricted their
lives to marriage, child care, and domestic work. It also
found their social prestige to be minimal, that they
depended on their husbands' support, and that they participated but little in public life.

CHARLOTTE Crawford's pioneering dissertation "The
Psychological Context of the Basque Mother"
(1982) is a study of women's roles. She concentrated
her research on the relationship between personality
and child-rearing practices. One of her salient findings
concerned the implications of sleeping arrangements
for personality development. According to Crawford, and
contrary to general belief, a study of 219 Basque mothers
yielded high correlations between the prolonged presence of infants and children in the parental bedroom
and higher personality integration and self-confidence.
It was conducted in the rural municipalities of Aia, Err-
ezil, Amezketa, and Ataun, in the fishing communities of
Orio, Getaria, and Mutriku, and in the urban centers of
Donostia, Oñati, Tolosa, and Eibar.

It was the creation of the Seminar for the Study of
Women under the direction of anthropologist Teresa del
Valle that made a real difference in raising awareness
of feminist issues. A group of researchers carried out
a systematic study of gender relations among Basques.
Their first collaborative publication in 1985, entitled (in
translation) *Basque Woman: The Image and Reality*, is
a comparative study of women's circumstances in rural,
fishing, and urban environments. It was carried out in
eleven municipalities.

The research applied the usual methods of the social
sciences in actual ethnographic contexts: participant
observation, in-depth interviews, and the gathering of

biographies and oral histories. Three hundred women completed a survey. The study had two main goals: to examine the conclusions regarding Basque women in previous studies and to investigate the diverse realities of women in the Basque Country. It analyzed everyday life, power relations, value systems, women's participation in Basque nationalism, and social change.

The conclusions went against the usual unitarian vision that Basque anthropology had provided in the past, that is, idealized women (*etxekoandreak*) enjoying an egalitarian and complementary existences vis-à-vis their male counterparts (*etxekojaunak*) in the traditional rural society. On the contrary, the study found important differences among women depending on place of residence, age, employment, and marital status.

The 1987 joint publication by the members of the seminar initiated new paths of investigation. Far from endorsing a monolithic view of "the" Basque woman, the research privileged diversity in the female experience. Differences in the socialization of boys and girls in various contexts was also given special attention.

ONE SPECIFIC concern was the gendered nature of the various social contexts of work, play, and domesticity. The doctoral dissertation of María Carmen Díez Mintegui, "Gender Relations in the Donosti Area and the Nafarroan Ribera, 1993" (our translation), addressed the conditions of mothers and wives in the workplace in two different areas—Donostia and southern Nafarroa. She focused on the conflicts generated by women's maternal responsibilities and career opportunities and described the changes that have transpired in these respects between 1970 and 1990. These have to do with departures from the long-established dichotomous model of the domestic space as the primary domain for women's lives versus the working space as a domain

Alternate generations
Basque girl dressed in typical grandmotherly folk costume.
Photo: Xabier Irujo

controlled by men. Traditionally, the various contexts of family, work, leisure, and social and political engagement have been largely conditioned by such a primary dichotomy. Díez found that, beginning in the late 1960s and 1970s, in the two areas she researched, there was a clear generational shift to the presence of women below the age of forty in the workplace. This tendency was more accentuated in Donostia. Nevertheless, unemployment was more prevalent among women than men. As to the hypothesis that socialization predisposes women primarily for domestic tasks, Díez found that, although it was still an "ideal" in some quarters that women remain at home, in fact, social change allowed for both alternatives, and many women had decided to work outside the household. Díez also found that the urban context provided better opportunities for women to realize personal life goals. She found that feminist ideology had had a positive effect on the women who were changing their attitudes.

In various articles, Lourdes Méndez has examined artistic production from a feminist perspective. Issues of body imagery, cultural representations, and power relations are central to her work. In several publications, Teresa del Valle has delved into the relationship between gender and urban space, particularly the male-biased gendering of public symbols such as monumental public statues and the naming of streets and parks.

Common to these feminist approaches is the genealogical search for gender differences and asymmetries. They are not content with describing "what" the case is, but "why" it has come about and "how" it could be modified. These investigators do not shy away from active involvement in generating such change.

PRIMARY OBJECTS of feminist critique are the essentialized or naturalized versions of "Woman" as a universal category. Rather than talking about "the family," or "the culture," or "Woman," critical feminist approaches seek diverse models of families, cultures, and feminine experiences. Women's social realities, their everyday experiences and strategies, and the differences and similarities that can be found between them and men are some of the main areas of study.

The concern with gender gathered strength in the 1980s. Gender is not the same as sex. Gender implies thinking about men and women in a systemic way—as a specific relation found in a particular place and time and embedded within a concrete system of power relations. The study of diversity in women's experience has to do with such social contextualization, that is, with understanding how race, ethnicity, class, and gender conjoin to constitute difference. At the same time, and reflective of the times in which the feminist research agenda was framed, there is a sense in which it situates Basque women squarely in the middle of Occidental, First World gendered issues. Many of the conclusions of the researchers are equally applicable to American or French women of the period. In this regard, Basque feminist research is one more example of the influence of globalization on Basque society and its position within the modern and postmodern worlds.

WHILE IT IS clear that Basque women share with their sisters throughout the developed world subtle, albeit real gender discrimination such as the "glass ceiling" in the workplace, it is also true that there has been extraordinary progress in this regard. In the spring of 2005, in anticipation of pending elections, the Basque parliament passed its *Ley igualataria*, or Equality Law, legislation that required that women constitute at least half of the slate of electoral candidates presented by every political party. As a consequence, today, the Basque parliament is the only one on the planet with a majority of female members.

Lesson twenty-nine

LEARNING OBJECTIVES
1. To understand the centrality of gender in Basque cultural studies.
2. To trace the history of feminist studies.
3. To undertake a critical analysis of matriarchalist interpretations.
4. To understand the role of feminism and in transformation of Basque society.

REQUIRED READING
Margaret Bullen, *Basque Gender Studies* (Reno: Center for Basque Studies 2003), 279–322.

SUGGESTED READING
Teresa del Valle, "Women's Power in Basque Culture: Practice and Ideology" (manuscript).
———, et al., *La mujer vasca: Imagen y realidad* (Barcelona: Anthropos, 1985).
———, et al., *La mujer y la palabra* (San Sebastián: Baroja, 1987).
Begoña Aretxaga, *Los funerales en el nacionalismo radical vasco* (San Sebastián: Baroja, 1988).
Lourdes Méndez, *Antropología de la producción artística* (Madrid: Síntesis, 1995).
Linda White and Cameron Watson, eds., *Amatxi, Amuma, Amona: Writings in Honor of Basque Women*. (Reno: Center for Basque Studies, 2003).

WRITTEN LESSON FOR SUBMISSION
1. Power relations are crucial to feminist critiques. Is "power" a univocal concept? How do you measure it? How do you compare it in diverse contexts?

_____

2. Discuss social changes that have affected gender relations dramatically among the Basques.

30 · Speaking Basque, Being Basque

THE SOCIAL anthropologist Jacqueline Urla studied the situational usage and social implications of speaking Basque in the early 1980s in the Gipuzkoan town of Usurbil. The title of this chapter is borrowed from her dissertation. Urla's work anticipated the impending concern with identity in both anthropology and cultural studies, particularly with identity as reflected in its sociolinguistic manifestations. Over the years, she has also become increasingly concerned with the political implications of language capacity and use. In the assigned reading published in 1993, Urla discusses the ways in which conducting a census always implies employment of somewhat arbitrary criteria and is always in the service of political agendas. Trying to quantify the incidence of Basque speakers and plot their distribution is never easy, nor is it politically neutral. In her 2003 article, Urla considers the ways in which Spain's central government, under José María Aznar and the Popular Party, sought to cripple the Basque-language movement by closing down its main newspaper and imprisoning the editorial staff under Spain's antiterrorism laws. The allegation was that the publication was a mouthpiece of ETA. The charge has never been substantiated properly and failed to convince most observers, including many who are opposed politically to the Basque radical Left. Perhaps the closure may be placed in context by noting that, at the same time, there appeared a series of articles in the Spanish press denouncing the *ikastolak*, or Basque-language primary schools, as seedbeds of Basque nationalism and future ETA activists and supporters. In sum, the campaign during the post-Franco era to recuperate and foster the use of Basque as both the vernacular and as the language of commerce and government, a campaign furthered by both private initiatives and Eusko Jaurlaritza's Ministry of Culture, is a politically charged issue, whether viewed from Madrid or Gasteiz.

The anthropological or sociolinguistic uses of language may be considered at several levels. Historically, by the last decades of the nineteenth century, use of Basque was diminishing and it was largely disparaged. It was spoken by few urbanites and was identified with the fisherfolk and peasantry. Even in the rural context, many parents discouraged their children from learning Basque, justifying their stand with the statement that "with Basque, you can't even get to Bilbao" or that "Basque is the language of the stable."

Sabino de Arana, a native of a Bilbaoan upper-middle-class family, was himself an *euskaldun berri*, or new Basque speaker. He learned the language as a young adult, published his own grammar, and sought to purge Basque of its many foreign (primarily Spanish and Latin) loan words by inventing neologisms. For instance, in place of *kafia* for "coffee," he proposed *akaita*. Many of his suggested forms persist in contemporary Basque, while others are ignored.

IN ANY EVENT, Arana's contemporary, the philosopher Miguel de Unamuno, prognosticated around the turn of the twentieth century that Basque could be extinct within fifty years, and it is fair to say that prevention of such an eventuality was one of Sabino's prime motives in founding the Basque nationalist movement. The preservation and recovery of the language has ranked high on the Basque nationalist agenda for more than a century.

During the Franco dictatorship, the public use of Basque was proscribed, driving the language into the

Intellectual baggage
Sample text of a Basque grammar composed by political refugee Bingen Ametzaga during his passage from the Basque Country to Uruguay. The trip should have taken about three months but lasted for more than a year because of the impediments posed by the German occupation of Europe and the Second World War.
Photo: Xabier Irujo

---

inner recesses of the home, where it served as the medium of intimacy. There was an official effort to denigrate Basque. Teachers punished schoolchildren caught using the language. The infamous example was the practice of the ring. It was given to a child caught speaking Basque at school. He or she then passed it on to a schoolmate who committed the same offense. At the end of the day, the child holding the ring was punished. Other draconian measures included the attempt to obliterate Basque names. Parents could not name their child

Josu or Miren, but instead were required to register him or her as José or María. Basque street names and those of towns and provinces were all changed to Spanish. In some cases, Basque inscriptions on tombstones were removed and replaced with Spanish ones.

D URING THE post-Franco era, with attendant empowerment of Basque institutions—including the creation of Eusko Jaurlaritza, the founding of a public university system, the proliferation of Basque-language media (including Euskal Telebista), and the legalization of the *ikastolak*—the circumstances and prospects of the language have shifted dramatically. It is now possible to acquire one's entire education, including a university degree, in coursework taught exclusively in Basque. Even for those students opting for primary schooling in Spanish, instruction in Basque as a second language is a requirement. Tens of thousands of non-Basque-speaking adults have attended *gaueskolak*, or evening classes, in order to gain at least some familiarity with the language. All official publications are bilingual. The capacity to speak Basque is now a competitive advantage for employment in the private sector and confers "points" upon an applicant seeking a public post.

Consequently, while the society of the autonomous Community of Euskadi is not entirely bilingual, it is certainly more diglossic than during the Franco years and before, to a degree beyond the expectations of many of the language's proponents. However, it is equally true that while every Basque speaker knows and employs Spanish, the converse is far from true. Consequently, Spanish still predominates in everyday interactions— whether causal conversation, commerce, or dealing with officialdom—particularly in the urban areas. Ironically, there is also a sense in which the recovery of the language is more conscious in the urban context (where it was all but lost), whereas in the rural areas Basque continues to erode. As one prominent *bertsolaria* commented recently, "I can now perform in Bilbao, but when I go to the villages, I hear young people speaking more Spanish than during the days of Franco!"

NOT SURPRISINGLY, given the political gridlock between Basque and Spanish nationalists, both the philosophy and the results of the government's language policy are objects of continuous scrutiny and debate. Few would deny that gains in the recovery of the Basque language have been made only at great economic and even social expense. The opponents question the worth of the exercise, framing their criticisms in terms of a dubious prognosis regarding the present utility and future viability of a seemingly unnecessary minority language, whereas for its proponents, the language is the symbol and repository of Basque identity itself. The debate is further exacerbated by being conducted against the backdrop of the realization that English is the language of an increasingly globalized world. Consequently, the Ministry of Education of Eusko Jaurlaritza has adopted a policy favoring trilingual instruction and curricular development.

Evaluating results always entails a degree of subjectivity, whether persons are pigeonholed by interviewers or invited to self-evaluate their language skills. For many reasons (modesty, hubris, political correctness, indifference, etc.), the responses to questions regarding the ability to comprehend, read, and speak Basque can vary enormously. Yet the aggregated statistics regarding fluency have immediate and serious political consequences as Basque parliamentarians debate the enormous costs of the language policy. The old adage of viewing the glass as half full or half empty is clearly applicable according to one's political predilections.

Given all of the foregoing realities—the quotidian expressions of language choices by speakers, on the one hand, and both the official policies and the institutional expressions of Basque langauge policy on the other— contemporary Basque sociolinguistics provides rich grist for the anthropological mill. An event as seemingly mundane as a private dinner party attended by both Basque and non-Basque speakers will likely be replete with nearly effortless code switching. The hostess may try out her halting English on the guest anthropologist, address her friend from Paris in better French (she once worked there as a domestic), and interact in Spanish with her brother-in-law from Galicia while addressing her daughter exclusively in Basque as part of her personal language policy to teach the language to her children. Such a gathering is but a microcosm of the linguistic interaction characteristic of contemporary Basque society.

TERESA DEL Valle's study of *korrika* reflects the anthropological interest in official expressions of language policy. *Korrika* translates as "foot race" or "marathon" and refers to an event that is organized periodically within Hegoalde both to underscore the importance of Basque and to garner support for AEK, a private linguistic initiative founded by the Basque radical Left. The event underscores both the unity of pur-pose of the Basque-language movement and its internal tensions. AEK is an NGO (nongovernmental organization)that competes with HABE, the official agency of Eusko Jaurlaritza's Ministry of Culture charged with implementing language policy. In short, AEK and HABE share the goal of fomenting Basque while contesting the means of doing so . During *korrika*, a baton containing a compartment with a secret message in Basque is carried throughout Hegoalde (and to the French-Spanish border that divides it from Iparralde) by volunteers—each of whom runs for one kilometer. At one level, it is a fundraiser for AEK; at another, it consciously protests the "internal" borders that divide Basques—whether the political ones erected by France and Spain or the more cultural separation between Euskadi and Nafarroa. The route is chosen to encompass those areas of the Basque Country where Basque is presently insignificant or absent. At the same time, *korrika* underscores the divisions between the mainstream Basque nationalists and the radical Left. Some of the former boycott it, while others participate with the caveat that their support is for the language, rather than for AEK's particular agenda.

Lesson thirty

LEARNING OBJECTIVES
1. To discuss issues of language loss and revival.
2. To examine the politics of language planning and education.
3. To reflect on the use of language for collective identity.
4. To analyze the relationship between language and nationalism.

REQUIRED READING
Jacqueline Urla, "Being Basque, Speaking Basque: The Politics of Language and Identity in the Basque Country." Ph.D. diss., University of California, Berkeley, 1987, 100–166.
Teresa del Valle, *Korrika: Basque Ritual for Ethnic Identity*, (Reno: University of Nevada Press, 1994), 1–37.

SUGGESTED READING

Jacqueline Urla, "Cultural Politics in the Age of Statistics: Numbers, Nations and the Making of Basque Identity," *American Ethnologist* 20, no. 4 (1993): 818–43.

———, "Euskara: The Terror of a European Minority Language," *Anthropology Today* 20, no. 4 (2003): 1–4.

WRITTEN LESSON FOR SUBMISSION

1. Do you believe that Basque has a future?
2. Discuss the practical versus the symbolic importance of the Basque language in the contemporary world.
3. What is the relationship (if any) between "speaking Basque" and "being Basque"?

31 · *The Bertsolaria's* Song
Orality, Literacy, and the Polis

W E ARE CONCERNED here with "the word"—the spoken word, as well as its imaginary and intellectual dimensions—and the transition to writing. It is useful to think of cultures in terms of how they arrange the sensorium. (See chapter 17 for the importance of smell in hunting, for example). It is commonly thought that the ancient Hebrews and Greeks differed in the value they ascribed to the visual and the auditory. For the Hebrews, understanding was a form of hearing, whereas, for the Greeks, it was a way of seeing. Similarly, some cultures are more tactile, while others emphasize taste. The Korean language has many more concepts referring to taste than does English. Walter Ong found it tempting to reduce religion to a particular condition of the sensorium: We are religious when the sensorium has a certain type of organization and no longer so after it changes. In such a view, religion would have to do with the invisible and the earlier oral-aural worlds. Yet a shift from one emphasis to another does not necessarily exterminate the former. Christian revelation, for example, has survived vast changes in the sensoria. Writing shifts the balance of the senses away from the aural to the visual, favoring a new kind of personality structure. In the modern world of electronic media, there is new emphasis on the auditory, but without a return to the past.

In the history of linguistic anthropology, there is a much-debated theory known as the Sapir-Whorf hypothesis, after the linguistic anthropologists who proposed it, Edward Sapir and Benjamin Lee Whorf. It states that language significantly organizes cultural ethos, and therefore one's mental frame of reference, while providing some of its most pronounced dynamics. The hypothesis was subjected to experimental tests—such as whether peoples from different cultures and languages perceive colors differently. The results were negative, and the hypothesis fell into disrepute. But some anthropologists, such as Paul Friedrich, have criticized such experimentation regarding the hypothesis and defended the position that in spirit it is insightful. In a nutshell, the hypothesis underscores that language is not just a vehicle of thought, but rather its very genesis. Poetic language, in particular, is a major aspect, function, dimension, and potentiality of every language. The Sapir-Whorf hypothesis takes issue with the folk dichotomy of science versus art and the privileging of scientific paradigms that overemphasize cognition and referential semantics. It questions the linguistic assumption of basic meaning, that is, the view that a word or symbol "basically really means only one thing." Such an assumption ignores much of the richness of linguistic and cultural symbolism. As an example, Friedrich found that in the Tarascan language, a word such as "mouth" would lose 90 percent of its meanings if taken to refer only to a body part. Much of meaning in language and culture is not "basic," as usually defined. Tropes are ambiguous. In much conversation, it is not clear what is fundamental as opposed to derivative. There are many instances of semireferential meaning.

THE KEY appreciation of the contrast between oral modes of thought and written ones comes from literary studies, particularly from the work of Milman Parry and Albert Lord, later supplemented by Eric Havelock and others. They made us aware that there are basic differences in the ways of managing knowledge and verbalization between primarily oral cultures and ones profoundly affected by literacy.

What is new in our understanding of orality is perhaps best expressed in the history of the so-called "Homeric Question." The *Iliad* and the *Odyssey* are the most exemplary and inspired classical poems in the Occidental heritage. For two thousand years, scholars have been interpreting them. Parry devised the fundamental axiom regarding the dependence of the choice of words and word forms on the shape of the orally composed hexameter line. He proved that virtually every distinctive feature of Homeric poetry is due to the economy enforced upon it by the constraints of composition. While poets are not expected to use prefabricated materials, Homeric poems were made up of elaborate clichés. Only a tiny fraction of the *Iliad* and the *Odyssey* are nonformulaic.

IF HOMERIC poetry was nothing more than standardized formulas relating standardized themes, how could it be so excellent and enduring? The answer is that in Homer's oral culture, knowledge had to be formulaic in order to be conserved through constant repetition. By the time of Plato, however, knowledge began to be stored in written texts, rather than in mnemonic formulas. This freed the mind for more abstract thought. Plato excluded poets from his ideal republic essentially because he found himself in a newly styled poetic world in which "mere" formulas had become outmoded and counterproductive. Thus, there was deep antagonism between the Homeric and Platonic views—a disturbing situation for a Western culture closely identified with both.

Given our dependence on literacy, it is difficult for us to conceive of an oral universe of communication, except as a variant of a literary system. Literacy begins with writing, but also involves printing as a later stage. Nevertheless, of all the many thousands of languages—possibly tens of thousands—spoken in the course of human history, only 106 have ever been committed to writing

Singers of the song
Photo taken after a performance of the two bertso-
lariak Martin Goikoetxea (third from left) and Johnny
Curutchet (second from right), in November of 2006 at
the San Francisco Basque Cultural Center.
Photo: Xabier Irujo

---

to a sufficient degree to have produced "literature," and
most have never been written down at all. Of the some
three thousand languages spoken today, only some 78
have a literature.

THE BASIC orality of language is therefore ingrained.
But writing—commitment of the word to space—en-
larges the potential of language almost beyond measure,
restructures thought, and, in the process, converts a few
dialects into "grapholects." Thus, standard English, for

example, has a recorded vocabulary of at least a million
and a half words, including hundreds of thousands of
still accessible, yet anachronistic and little-used, forms.
A simple oral dialect commonly has recourse to but a few
thousand words, and its users have virtually no knowledge of their etymologies. Still, literary language can
never dispense with orality, but verbal expression can
exist without writing, and mostly has done so. Words are
grounded in oral speech, but writing them down tyran-
nically locks them into a visual field forever. A literate
person always has some image of the spelled-out word
and is therefore unable to think of it solely in terms of
its sound, let alone appreciate the word's sensual effect
on an illiterate audience.

ACCORDING TO some scholars—those who privilege
texts—human consciousness cannot achieve its full
potential without writing. The development of science,
history, philosophy, and the critical understanding of literature and of any art would all be unthinkable without
writing. As noted earlier, Greek philosophy required the
restructuring of thought as facilitated by writing. Oral
cultures are traditionalist. Students of orality have found
that traditional societies must invest great energy in
repeating what has been learned through the ages. This
produces a highly conservative mindset that inhibits
intellectual novelty. Nevertheless, oral cultures produce
powerful and beautiful verbal performances of high artistic and human value, some of which are no longer possible once writing informs the psyche.

Basque culture has inherited from tradition the
extraordinary poetic institution of the *bertsolaria*, the
singer of improvised *bertsoak*, or verses. Typically of
humble (usually *baserri*) origins and semiliterate at
best, the *bertsolaria* spontaneously improvised and sang
verses for weddings, village festivals, or simply at male

get-togethers in taverns. Normally the "performance" was a running commentary on the event itself, including humorous and at times barbed commentary on those in attendance. If two or more *bertsolariak* happened to coincide, commonly a "competition," frequently in the form of an exchange of humorous personal insults, might ensue. In these guises, *bertsolaritza* was generally a lower-class phenomenon and the object of neglect, when not of disdain, among the cultured (literate and urban) social classes.

While the *bertsolaria* sings his verses, there is little premium placed on "music" per se. Occasionally a musically talented performer tries out a new melody, but most verses are framed within a familiar musical repertory. Having a good voice is an advantage, but only a slight one. The *bertsolaria* is judged primarily on his or her capacity for the nearly instantaneous composition of clever verses. In formal competitive contexts, there will likely develop an organic narrative in which each answers the other's last point.

THE HISTORICAL antecedents of *bertsolaritza*, or impromptu versifying, are shrouded in mystery. Some trace the phenomenon back to the "time immemorial" of former pastoral settings in the Neolithic era. During the fifteenth century, there is reference to female improvisers who sang elegies. There are also explicit prohibitions on mourning for a dead person by "singing lamentations," as well as denunciations of "shameful" women, or "profaners" who "make couplets and songs in an infamous and libelous manner." It is not until the late eighteenth century that we have recorded *bertso* songs, most of them written down for a given occasion, rather than improvised.

The debates surrounding the Homeric Question (the nature of Homer's poetry) illuminate formal aspects

The champion
Master bertsolari, Johnny Curutchet, in performance.
He took his place in the San Francisco Versifiers Hall of
Fame in 2006.
Photo: Xabier Irujo

---

of Basque impromptu versifying, as well. *Bertsolaritza*,
like the *Iliad*, relies on formulaic clichés, but without
sacrificing poetic power. It might be noted that the
use of formulas allows the *bertsolaria* in a competition to anticipate the drift and likely conclusion of an
adversary's verse, providing an opportunity to begin to
frame a reply to it before actually having to perform. An
additional facilitator of the flow of nearly instantaneous
composition is the nature of the Basque language itself.
As an agglutinative one, it employs many suffixes and
therefore lends itself much more to rhyming than does
English. In the reading, Gorka Aulestia examines the

extraordinary restrictions in rhyme and rhythm that the *bertso* singer has to honor. The singing itself creates very special social contexts of communication.

IT IS THE combination of verbal art and performance, textual creativity and social voice, that grants *bertso-laritza* such cultural relevance. As does any performance, it has the dual sense of artistic verbal action (the singing of the *bertso*) and artistic event (the performative setting that implicates the performers, the audience, the art form, and the venue itself). The performance sets up an interpretive framework within which the messages being communicated are to be understood as and become constitutive of the domain of verbal art.

Oral communication passes from mouth to ear to mouth. Hence the importance of veracity in the spoken word. Validation rests on personal knowledge. In oral societies such as the traditional Basque society, mastery of the word becomes an essential skill. Hence the significance of sayings, puns, and stories. Frequently, it is more important how something is said than what is said. Creation consists of restating the cultural heritage. There might even be an elaborated ideology whereby, for example, manhood and the word "man" define each other. Thus, "the man of his word" becomes a description of the ideal person. Nonambiguity (transparency) is crucial to this type of "word." There is an element of essentialism to it, as well. Deal makers and negotiators are seen as deceivers. Economy and precision in speech are valued. Its primary aim is not loquacity or eloquence, but commitment.

What is the meaning of improvisation in *bersto* singing? Improvisation has to do with time—with instant or immediate elaboration. The time limit is determined by the rhythm of the melody. Each time limit is nonrepeatable, and so is each *bertso*. Thus, improvised texts are unfixed. As Lord pointed out, it takes a vast cultural change to develop the new poetics of writing. Writing implies "writing down" one patterned text out of the many possibilities. In a written poem, the author has to provide the title, the theme, and the text.

Manuel de Lekuona concluded that the *bertsolaris*'s medium was one of vivid images rather than of profound ideas. This is manifested in four features: a relative abundance of elisions and "pregnant" constructions, absence of rhetorical-grammatical means of linkage between thoughts, careless logical-chronological order, and a lack of relation or logical cohesion between the images and the theme of the song. There is thus a jux-taposition of images within a formal frame. The song provides a unified field of meaning for the succession of images. Ellipsis becomes a condition of expressiveness.

DURING THE twentieth century, *bertsolaritza* under-went a radical change that has affected all of its artistic and social aspects. During the last three decades, *bertsolaritza* festivals and events of all kinds have multiplied. The topics have become more diverse, the techniques have become more complex, and the social relevance and prestige of the phenomenon have grown enormously. Traditionally, the themes the *bertsolaria* would sing about were taken from the everyday life. Nowadays, references to fictional persons, literature, cin-ema, and world affairs are common. Currently, the best-known *bertsolariak* are young and are mostly university students—all literate, some of whom publish poetry, as well. Traditionally, despite the references to women sing-ers in the fifteenth century, *bertsolariak* have mostly been men. Recently, the presence of female *bertsolariak* has become common.

As to the social relevance of *bertsolaritza*, suffice it to say that in a linguistic community of some six hundred

thousand Basque speakers, a survey in 1993 found that
15 percent of the people declared themselves to be "great
lovers of *bertsolaritza*," 35 percent said they were "aficio-
nados," and 28 percent stated that they were "attracted"
by it to some degree—a total of 78 percent who closely
follow or are influenced by the phenomenon.

ACCORDING TO Joxerra Garzia, Andoni Egaña, and Jon
Sarasua the main venues of *bertsolaria* singing are
public performances, contests and championships, *bertsolaritza* workshops, and *bertsoak* performed as informal group entertainment, in statutory education, and in
the media. Public performances occur in both open and
closed arenas, such as festivals, with a presenter who
assigns the topics, in unmoderated recitals (two or three
bertsolariak without a presenter), in dinner-table recitals, in after-dinner performances, in complimentary performances such as at funerals, inaugurations, weddings,
political events, homages, and other social occasions,
and in novel experimental formats such as the inclusion
of *bertsolaritza* performances within a theatrical play. In
all, there are some twelve hundred contracted *bertsolaritza* performances annually. A minimum of two and a
maximum of eight *bertsolariak* take part in each. There
are about a hundred "professional" *bertsolariak*, aged
between their early twenties and early seventies.

In contests and championships, the *bertsolariak* compete by performing before a jury that decides (by using
a point system) the worth of a strophe. The winner is
given a Basque beret, or *txapela*. The contests are age-
graded (juvenile, adult) and by geographical distribution
(regional, provincial, national). Every four years, there
is a major competition to determine the best *bertsolaria*.
Such competitive performances have become an important dimension of *bertsolaritza*, particularly in their
capacity for introducing new performers to the public.

Bertsolaritza workshops or informal group entertainment take place in the tradition of the gatherings in cider houses, taverns, and *baserri* kitchens. Today there are so-called *bertso-eskola*, or *bertso* schools, in which a group of friends gathers to practice improvisation simply as entertainment. It is the most spontaneous expression of versification. There are about a hundred such workshops annually in which more than thirty thousand people take part.

In addition, during the last two decades, *bertsolaritza* has been introduced into the primary and secondary curricula as a complement to other literary and artistic courses. It is believed that *bertso* improvisation helps students develop personal skills, engage with their cultural heritage, and enhance their musical competence.

Finally, *bertsolariak* perform on weekly television and daily radio programs. Annually, there are about thirty hours of television *bertsolaritza* performances and about five hundred hours of on the radio.

THE PARTICIPATION of the audience—in terms of applause, laughter, silence, attention—is obviously crucial to the entire performance, since improvisation makes every sung word an unpredictable creation. Today, the audience is typically a cross section of Basque society, reflecting a wide range of ages, occupations, and cultural interests. Although, traditionally, *bertsolaritza* was mainly the expression of the rural lifestyle, nowadays it is even more so the expression of an urban and industrial society. But in the final analysis, the power of the *bertsolaria*'s performance resides in the fact that, while engaged in one of the many varied topics for elaboration, he or she sings about the totality of the human experience.

Lesson thirty-one

LEARNING OBJECTIVES

1. To investigate the relevance of orality in traditional culture.
2. To analyze the relationship of the Homeric Question to the *bertsolariak*
3. To assess the relevance of improvisational troubadorial singing in the Basque tradition.
4. To discover the sources of verbal play and textual creativity among the *bertsolariak*.
5. To analyze the social contexts and functions of versifying.

REQUIRED READING

Gorka Aulestia, *Improvisational Poetry from the Basque Country* (Reno: University of Nevada Press 1995), 16–40.

Joxerra Garzia, Andoni Egaña, and Jon Sarasua, *The Art of Bertsolaritza* (Donostia: Bertsozale Elkartea, 2001), section 3, 81–133.

SUGGESTED READING

Samuel G. Armistead and Joseba Zulaika, eds, *Voicing the Moment: Improvised Oral Poetry and Basque Tradition* (Reno: Center for Basque Studies, 2005).

WRITTEN LESSON FOR SUBMISSION

1. Compare and contrast the improvisational oral communication with the written text.
2. Discuss performance as a frame of behavior that changes ordinary meanings and transforms social contexts.

3. Is formulaic improvisation (as discussed in the Homeric Question) of equal aesthetic value with the painstakingly pondered and revised literary creation?

32 · The New Basque Music
From Political Protest to Hip-Hop

MIKEL LABOA begins one of his records (*Mikel Laboa 14*, 1994) by singing softly, almost hesitantly, words written by the fugitive poet (a convicted ETA activist) Joseba Sarrionandia, accompanying himself with the bare notes of a Spanish guitar, creating an evocative and intimate mood, one of the many songs that his Basque public will savor endlessly.

> Errant birds
> have perched
> on the window
> at the frontier between light and darkness
> on the window
> have perched
> errant birds.

The record concludes with another of his classics, "Our landscapes," also by Sarrionandia:

> I love
> our places
> when the fog conceals them
> when it doesn't allow me to see
> what is hidden
> for it is then that I begin to see
> the concealed ...
> the marvelous places
> that open up within me.

Laboa's subdued and richly evocative voice produces a feeling that is as distinctive as the recurrent *sirimiri* or light rain of the verdant Basque landscape. The song—an intimate evocation of native place and space, overflowing with the melancholy of habitual rain and green lush Basque valleys, drenched in contemplative emotion—was forbidden by Franco's censors.

Yet poetic calm and aesthetic contemplation were not precisely the distinguishing hallmarks of what came to be known during the 1960s as "the new Basque song." As Raimon, the best known among the founders of the Catalan *nova cançó*, used to scream during the dark years of Francoism in his raging song "Al vent" (To the wind):

> all the colors of green
> *gora! gora!* [arise! arise!] fiercely cry
> the people, the land, and the sea
> there in the Pais Basc.

The war cry of the moment among Basque nationalists and antifascists was "Gora Euskadi!" (Euskadi Arise!), but this was a forbidden expression, so Raimon substituted "gora! gora!"

IT WAS MUSIC in the heroic mold of political resistance that the "new song" introduced to the social landscape during the middle 1960s, as made explicit by Raimon's lyrics:

> It's so beautiful and deep-rooted,
> as ancient as time the suffering of that people,
> it's so beautiful and deep-rooted
> as all the colors of green
> in that month of May.

This new figure of the protest songwriter came on the heels of internationally acclaimed singers such as Bob Dylan, Pete Seeger, and Joan Baez in the United States,

The new Basque Song: Mikel Laboa
Errant birds
have perched
on the window
at the frontier between light and darkness
Cover of CD Mikel Laboa: Euskal Kanta Berria *(1990).*

Jacques Brel and George Brassens in France, and Ata-
hualpa Yupanki and Violeta Parra in South America.
The protest song became a major vehicle for expressing
political resistance and spreading the ideals of freedom
and democracy. The first such Basque singer emerged in
Iparralde in 1961. It was then that Michel Labéguerie, a
medical doctor from Cambo and subsequently a mayor
and senator, as well, released his first record, which contained eight songs.

ACCOMPANIED by a guitar and with no display of
musical sophistication or commercial manner-
isms, Labéguerie's stark messages, delivered in a low
voice similar to that of Leonard Cohen, had a huge effect.
Until then, there had been the music of Basque classical
composers, such as José María Usandizaga, Jesús Guridi,
Pablo Sorozabal, and Francisco Escudero; there was academic polyphony; there were opera singers, as well as
choirs, and *ochotes*, or groups of eight male singers. But
Labéguerie's music, given its poetic tone and quiet emotion, was utterly different. The words of one of his songs,
based on personal experience (he had impregnated a
woman, was forced to marry, and then their child was
stillborn), were emblematic of his mixing of social realism and political allegory:

> The flowers in the spring
> bloomed early
> that year it happened
> before Palm Sunday.
> They forced us to get married
> you loved me so little
> they forced us to get married
> I didn't love thee.
> If there is heaven anywhere
> our child is an angel

An angel in the heavens
but no child in the nest.
The heart is trembling cold
wondering about the future
let the spring come
let the flowers bloom.
When birds in love
will start singing again
I will open the window
love will come in.
They forced us to get married
now we have to live together
They forced us to get married
we have to love each other.

The forced and loveless union allegorizes the dilemma of the Basque vis-à-vis Paris and Madrid. There are no heroic theatrics here, no idealization of the motherland, no sentimental outbursts. Another of Labeguerie's themes, sung in the same low-key tone and influenced by French songwriters such as Brassens, was the painful situation of Basque national collapse as expressed in a lullaby in which the mother tells the baby to sleep while invoking the absent father who will one day return "to make us free."

DURING THE early 1960s, Mikel Laboa was a medical student in Barcelona, where the rebellious *nova cançó* had irrupted with the force of a hurricane. He was also greatly influenced by Yupanki's song to his Basque mother using a traditional Basque melody. Laboa released his first single in 1964. A second one came out in 1966, based on lyrics by the poet Gabriel Aresti.

In 1967, Julen Lekuona and Lourdes Iriondo released records, as did Benito Lertxundi and Xabier Lete in 1968. Josean Artze, Jose Angel Irigarai, Jose Mari Zabala,

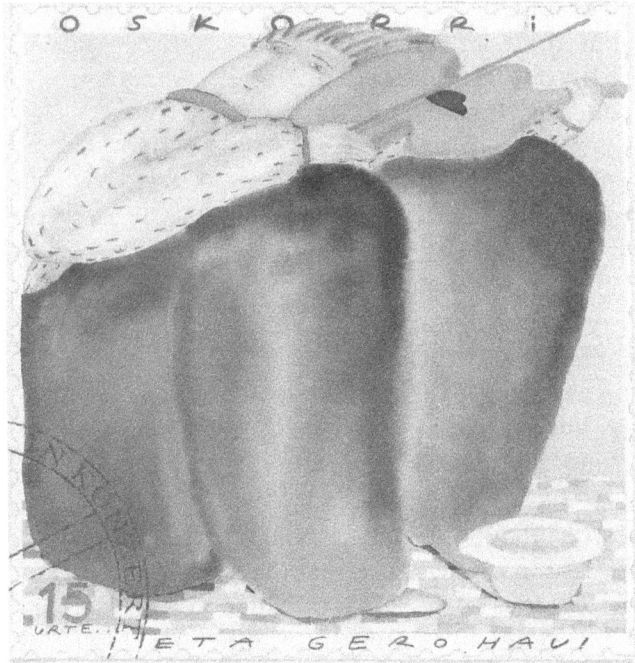

Local songs, international music
The folk group Oskorri embellished the repertory of
traditional Basque songs by incorporating into it international influences. The name of the group means "Red
Sky" and alludes to its left-wing politics, following the
lead of its initial lyricist, the poet Gabriel Aresti.
Cover of CD Oskorri: Hamabost Urte eta Gero hau!
(1987)

and others were also members of the group. Initially, Lourdes Iriondo, the only female in the group, had the greatest influence. One of her songs became emblematic of youthful defiance:

> Young, we are young
> and we are not happy
> we want to create
> a better world
> we are against lies
> we want no injustice
> young, we are young
> we are not happy.

NOTHING COULD be further from the new song-writers than the traditional romanticizing of rural life in such well-known folksongs as "Ikusten duzu goiz-ean" (You see in the morning) or "Uso txuria" (The white dove). Julen Lekuona, the avant-garde priest of Ez Dok Amairu, expressed their philosophy:

> We could in no way start now by singing the sad story of the white dove, for there are far sadder stories than that one. The white dove was long ago blackened by the smoke of the chimneys of our Basque industrial towns. We cannot live a romanticized life. We can-not—as Bertold Brecht said—just sing pretty things. I believe that singing has an enormous power to arouse people from the situation that they are in. And for that we have to confront our country with the real problems it is undergoing.

Some of the songs were about Vietnam, Martin Luther King's murder, and workers killed in Chicago. State censorship of the lyrics was constant, because each performance required a permit from the Ministry of Information and Tourism. One of Letxundi's songs was entitled "Detroit 67"; the words alluded to the fate of black Americans in the United States, and it was prohibited by Franco's censors. Then Lertxundi changed the title to "Don't Sing, Negro" and the same officials permitted its performance. Laboa's song with the words "I love our places when the fog conceals them" also suffered censorship. God alone knew what was concealed by the fog! Metaphor became a way to avoid censorship and fines. To refer to the deportation of eight hundred Basques in 1968, they sang of "the storm." An ETA operative might be called "the man of darkness," and so on.

This was all new at the time. ETA provoked a storm with its political demands from the activist underground, and the sculptor Jorge Oteiza had created a stir with theories of a new aesthetics and his repeated calls for a Basque School of Contemporary Art. The Ez Dok Amairu group thus was the voice of the awakened cultural resistance. Oteiza, who chose the "They Are Not Thirteen" title for the group and who became a father figure for its rebellious cultural activists, proclaimed: "there is no thirteen, we will break all cultural limits, we will break with the maleficence of the thirteen, and we will continue our own way."

ALTHOUGH THE initial goal of the group was to research, publicize, and renovate Basque traditional music, soon it was immersed in new experimental forms that had never been tried before. They went beyond song and popular music into dance, poetry, and theater. They created an integral art form that combined all those genera. This was done in the midst of renewed political agitation, and rather spontaneously. Frequently they were harassed by the Spanish police and forbidden to sing. They performed outside of the Basque Country, as well.

One of the experimental pieces by Ez Dok Amairu was entitled *Baga-biga-higa* (One, two, three) based on two traditional onomatopoeic lyrics, hardly intelligible words, that were believed to be spoken by witches in their ritual gatherings. Laboa thus started a series of experimental songs that combined the most traditional and most avant-guard music, his voice becoming at times a mere guttural sound expressing naked primeval feelings. He called these songs "Lekeitio" in honor of the fishermen's words, expressions, and screams that he heard as a refugee child in the port of Lekeitio during the Spanish Civil War. *Baga-biga-higa* was conceived by the aesthetic director Arze as a *sentikaria* (a place for experience) rather than an *ikuskaria* (spectacle).

THE PERFORMANCE began with a traditional dance, followed by a recital of poems, songs, the traditional *txalaparta*, or percussion planks, *tobera* instruments, the *alboka* horn, a slide show, and a conclusion with Laboa's singing of "Baga-biga-higa" accompanied by the *txalaparta*. Laboa explained: "We want to be an expression of Basque society by representing a spectacle based on contemporary themes—even if it has traditional roots—so that the society progresses in the manner we do in terms of ideas and music."

The spectacle was performed in various parts of the Basque Country, as well as in Barcelona, Pau, and the Bretagne. The handout in Barcelona read:

This is not your usual concert. Today we are experimenting with new forms. Until now, the concert presented one singer after another. This is one way of doing a recital, and it is a valid one, we won't deny that. We believe we have to go deeper, and this is what we will attempt. Today we are in need of creating something that is based on the past, but that belongs to the

future. We believe that nowadays, a group performance
can be as interesting as one by a single performer
alone. That is our performance's guiding idea: a creation that emerges spontaneously and attempts to
realize one's personality within a collective work. We
believe this is the best way. We have the *txalaparta*
at the center, an old instrument, an expression of the
contemporary working man, grounding for the work
of the group. Having thus central the carnival of history—old songs, old musical instruments, our songs,
poems, dances—we'd like to perform this spectacle of
feeling realized by means of our full experience. And
with the participation of everyone, we'd like to go on
fulfilling and enriching history.

THERE WERE other singers, as well. Bittor Egurrola,
Maite Idirin, Estitxu, Natxo, and others began singing in Bizkaia during the late 1960s. Peio and Pantxoa,
Manex Pagola, Etxamendi and Larralde, Borda and
Sarasola began singing in Iparralde. The group Oskarbi
was created in 1967. Another group, Oskorri, produced
a record with Gabriel Aresti's poems in 1976; six of the
songs were censored. Other familiar names were Gont-
zal Mendibil, Ibai Rekondo, Jon Bergaretxe, Urko, Maite
Aranburu, Iñaki Eizmendi, Txomin Artola, Maite Zubiria,
and Gorka Knorr. Bernardo Atxaga´s poems found a distinctive and original voice in Ruper Ordorika´s songs.
   Many of these songwriters took traditional folkloric
melodies and themes and modernized them. A folk
group such as Oskorri, formed in 1971, developed a
rich musical repertoire and made it known throughout
Europe. Being a folk group in no way means that they
were given to romanticizing the Basque Country or its
cultural heritage. To the contrary, their message was
clearly left-leaning and called for an ideological rupture

Songwriters, plugged and unplugged
Ruper Ordorika, a representative of the new generation
of songwriters.
Cover of CD: Ruper Ordorika

---

with basic tenets of traditional Basque conservatism.
Some of the songs sounded provocative, such as "On the
Donkey," which they took from Labeguerie and which
begins "Our donkey Balaan has gone to the church," the
donkey being an animal metaphor for mindless people,
a clear criticism of churchgoing practices. The relationship between the leader of the group, Natxo de Felipe,

and the cutting-edge poet Gabriel Aresti, who wrote most of their lyrics, is crucial to an understanding of the group's reception. The name of the group means "Red Sky," a clear allusion to the rupturist overtones of their lyrics. The last years of Francoism were marked by deep ideological polarization at all social levels that echoed ETA's various splits between Marxist-Leninist currents and nationalist puritanism. Ez Dok Amairu and Oskorri suffered the consequences of this polarization, because they were forced to choose among various ideological orthodoxies. In the end, it was the musical quality of its compositions and the novel mixing of traditional and international themes and instruments, including the electric guitar, the violin, and the saxophone, that provided Oskorri with a large audience among the Basques, as well as in various European countries.

A SINGER WHO trod the difficult path between cultural nationalism and ideological leftism was Imanol. In 1969, as a political refugee in Paris, he produced his first record under the pseudonym Michel Etchegaray. There he made friends with Paco Ibáñez, who had became very popular among the younger generation during the student revolts of the 1970s by singing the most uncompromising poems of the Spanish poets. Paco, who embodied the rebelliousness of antifascist protest in Spain, had spent his childhood as a migrant in the Basque Country, speaking Basque while living on a *baserria* in a small village. Imanol became the face of the Basque protest song in the early 1970s. His second and third records, produced in Paris and accompanied by Paco Ibáñez playing the guitar, were entitled *The Steps to Freedom* and *Now in Times of Struggle*. The song that reflected best Imanol´s ideological stance, an unprecedented song praising Basque migrants in Castile, was entitled "In Euskadi as in Castile":

My grandfather from Segura [a Basque town]
when he needed bread
he used to go to Castile
as a laborer
as a servant.
They say that he was very able with his sickle,
yes, of course yes!
he had ten children hungry at home
yes, of course yes! The laborers of Castile
when they need bread
they go to Goierri [a region in Gipuzkoa]
as laborers
to the factories.
They say that those foreigners are skillful workmen,
yes, of course yes!
the offspring are hungry at home
yes, of course yes!
If my grandfather and the Castilians
were owners of Castilian lands
and of the chimneys of Goierri,
their children, well fed
would not have to escape any longer,
not to Castile, not to Euskadi.

DURING THIS period, Imanol released two other albums, entitled *The People Will Not Forgive* and *To the Four Winds*, in which revolutionary and proletarian themes are predominant.

In 1979, he released the album *Propelled by Feelings*, in which the first and most popular song, with words by the poet Mikel Arregi, strikes a far more personal note:

I am a mediocre poet
and in blue colors.

ITOIZ

musikaz blai

Cover of Itoiz's CD Musikaz Blai (1984).

Endless rock 'n' roll

Itoiz was a highly successful rock group that combined hard rhythms with more symphonic ballads, commercial soft-rock and new wave elements. The young generations of the 1980s and early 1990s identified with this music. Some of its hits are still very popular—"Four roofs on top/ the moon in between/ and you looking to the sky…/ and again we will be happy/ in the fiestas of some town." *Cover of Itoiz's CD* Musikaz Blai *(1984).*

I write at night
slippery desires
they escape blind
to night's caves
the world upside down
I turn it all inside out.

In the 1980s, he made eight albums, including the
superb *Erromantzeak* (Romances), a collection of
Basque traditional lyrical and epic romances. In 1994,
Imanol, always with the great accompaniment of Karlos
Jiménez at the piano, released a haunting record with the
lyrics of Saint John of the Cross's "Spiritual Canticle:"

Where have you gone hiding,
lover, and left me sighing?
Wounding me
you vanished like a deer;
I rushed out shouting for you,
and you were gone.

In 1999, Imanol released *Remembering*, a collaboration
with Paco Ibáñez, both singing traditional Basque songs.
The cover design is by Oteiza. In the same year, he produced his first record of songs in Spanish, *Absence*.

BUT AT THE end of the 1970s, in the new Spanish
post-Franco democracy, much of this music of cultural resistance and ideological interpellation suddenly
became dated. A rebellious message with simple guitar
accompaniment was no longer sufficient. A sense of
crisis for the so-called new Basque song became discernible. It was a time for the influence of electric guitars and
rock and roll to be felt. In the early 1980s, a new music
called "Basque radical rock" took over. In December of
1980, the youth of Itziar, including former ETA activists,

organized a Basque music competition in their discotheque, Mandiope, that included radical rock groups.
Groups such as Zen and Zarama (Garbage), from the Left
Bank of Bilbao's Nerbioi River, participated. Zarama won
a prize with the song "I Am Afraid," a direct allusion to
police repression. The song "In the Midst of the Garbage" points to the desire to escape from the Left Bank's
environmental pollution:

> In the midst of the garbage
> I am always asking
> how can I get away from here.

Gabriel Aresti's best-known poem is entitled "I Will
Defend the House of My Father"; Zarama's first recorded
song began with the following words:

> I will escape
> from my father's house
> and if some poet wants it
> let him go to defend it.
> Heads are burning
> watching TV
> at night on the streets
> nothing but shadows of dogs
> and the old songs of drunks.
> The poets are silent
> nobody pays them any attention.

Another song, entitled "The Left Bank," provides a bleak
picture of the by then ruinous postindustrial situation of
the area:

> The flowers disappear
> in the land of the rats

the factories don't produce
the sun does not warm
workers of sad gesture
devoured by problems in dirty trains
this day is the worst in years
and who knows what it will be tomorrow.

Another group, Barricada, also from the Left Bank,
screeched in song: "We Are Rats from Bizkaia."

SOON, AN ENTIRE panoply of groups was to follow:
Jotakie, La Polla Records, Kortatu, Mak, and (in Iparralde) the rocker Niko Etxart became successes. Their
heavily metallic music with irreverently radical lyrics
became a social phenomenon in the youth festivals of
the 1980s. Ertzainak (The Police), from Vitoria / Gasteiz,
created in 1982, became one of the most representative
groups of the new radical music. They combined punk's
anger, ska's gaiety, reggae's warmth, and the spirit of
rock and roll. As provocateurs, they wanted to turn
everything upside down. Their first song, with echoes
of Jimi Hendrix's "Hey, Joe," was "He, txo"—"Hey, you,
you've been waiting for too long." The trope of "tropical
Euskadi" became popular. Other titles were "Until They
Leave Us in Peace," "Drugs," "Kill Your Father," and (in
English) "No Time for Love." One of their best-known
songs, "Confession," is accompanied by a violin:

The best of times are not forever
in the end we are just humans
after the lull comes the storm
there is no new spring for us
time always moves forward
and we cannot hold on to what we were
we have fallen into a routine
dear, let us become free as soon as possible.

They disbanded in 1993.

Basque radical rock was suited for extremist political messages of opposition to the status quo, including the politicization of daily life, equally for both Basque and Spanish nationalists. A culture of heavy drug consumption accompanied the new musical trend. In some Basque nationalist quarters, this began to be perceived as a "depolitization" of the youth and a deliberate effort on the part of the Spanish police to be permissive with the new culture of *pasotismo* (let it pass, or don't give a damn about anything). A discotheque such as Mandiope, which had been created within Itziar's tradition of rural cooperativism and intense involvement in nationalist politics, was suddenly suspected of corrupting the youth with its new drug culture and radical rock music. ETA placed a bomb in Mandiope, which ironically was established mainly by former militants or sympathizers of ETA.

One of the groups that performed in Mandiope while it was still a dance hall, to raise funds for the local *ikastolak* of the nearby villages, was Itoiz. Itoiz's idols included Led Zepellin, The Who, Genesis, and hard rock in general, as well as jazz and folk. It combined rock with pop, caustic rhythms with more symphonic ballads. The success of this so-called "symphonic rock" was enormous. Itoiz produced music that was far from radical rock. Its lyrics were not social protests, but rather more personal, intimate, and poetic. They sang of the sadness of the urban night—the drug addicts and prostitutes. As Pako Aristi put it, "where the radical rocker sees the police hitting a protester, Itoiz sees an old prostitute calling for the yellow taxi because she is cold and out of work." The hit song from their first record (1978) was "Lau teilatu" (Four roofs):

Vibrant, sentimental

The virtuoso accordionist from Bilbao, Kepa Junkera, took the small diatonic accordion, known as trikitrixa, and made it into an international success by incorporating a variety of rhythms and mixing it with other instruments and traditions.

Cover of the Kepa Junkera CD Bilbao 00:00 *(1999)*

Four roofs on top
the moon in between
and you looking to the sky.
The smoke in your hands
is moving away
it will reach me / and again we will be happy
in the fiestas of some town.

THROUGHOUT the 1990s, new musical expressions
would surface in music that was both traditional
locally and linked to international currents. Basque hip-
hop is one of the most interesting musical phenomena
to emerge from international influences. Jacqueline
Urla shows how the rap group Negu Gorriak has been
attuned to Basque cultural politics and how it has helped
create a political imaginary. Hip-hop is, besides music,
a multifaceted global youth culture that is frequently
implicated in the construction of local identities. As
Urla points out, people "find in hip-hop a language, a
set of resources, and knowledge with which to articulate
similar, but not identical struggles and concerns." She
shows how a subaltern group may use hip-hop culture
as an alternative political discourse, rather than more
overt methods of protest, thus providing a compelling
case for hip-hop's politicizing effect in the articulation of
a Basque identity. The tradition of Basque radical protest
has once again taken advantage of an international musical culture. Like other hip-hop artists who protest racial
or ethnic oppression (in Kurdistan, Liberia, Ireland ...),
Basque hip-hop musicians have proven that this applies
to their issues, as well.

Finally, in the tradition of Basque folklore, invoking
its roots while expanding on them, there is the accomplished accordionist Kepa Junkera. His 1998 recording
Bilbao 00:00 brought him international fame. He is from

Bilbao, and the passion and virtuosity of his music has come to represent the force of the new city energized by architect Frank Gehry's masterful Guggenheim Museum. As Xabier Recalde wrote in the CD's booklet,

> Some cities are like cakes, others seem to be decorated hangars for emergency lodging, others still are breathing units that flourish and crumble according to the mood of their inhabitants. Bilbao is among the breathing ones because it has grown out of the curls of everyday life. My city is a door to the sea; it is framed in iron, and its streets are bordered by concrete blocks, carved stones, and uncovered bricks ... . Bilbao is a city with music: the music springing from its soil, a Basque soil, and the music brought by the maritime language that keeps adding new words to its vocabulary. Lately Kepa Junkera is the embodiment of its sound; a Basque-speaking palpitation that recognizes itself in other airs and makes itself understood among foreign aromas, because this is the kind of image the mirror casts back at him when he looks out into other geographies. Kepa had already shared a table with fellow accordion players from Scotland, Ireland, and every corner of the Western world, but now he allows himself to be stained by different cultures to infuse new life into all that is common in their variegated music.

AND WHAT HAS happened in the meantime to the old guard of the "new" Basque songwriters? Many of them stopped singing long ago. Others, such as Xabier Lete and Joxean Artze, continue writing poetry. Jose Angel Irigarai, after a long silence, released a new record in 2004. A few, such as Benito Lertxundi, have remained productive and have flourished. Other new singers appeared along the way. Some, such as Labeguerie or

Estitxu, died. Imanol, boycotted by the Basque nationalist community because of his political leanings, left the
Basque Country at the turn of the 1990s and died in Ali-
cante, Spain, in 2004, at the age of fifty-seven.

LABOA SINGS infrequently, but his songs have lost none
of their appeal to the generations who grew up listening to his undramatic voice and crystalline emotion,
the most traditional songs returned to the glory of their
simplest forms, the most experimental ones laced with
guttural shrieks, and the unforgettable masterpieces
such as "Stardust." These are Lete's inspiring words:

> From stardust, one day, life began
> and from that matter unexpectedly we emerged.
> And that is how we live endlessly recreating our deci-
> sions
> without respite: by working we advance
> we are all tightly bound to that chain ... .
> Man's task is knowledge, to discover and transform
> to become one with nature and establish relations,
> and taking our energies back to their deep roots
> to get nourishment from this earth;
> turning the struggle of negation into positive affirma-
> tion
> by the law of contradiction always moving forward ... .
> From the same tree from which we were born will
> emerge new ones,
> new branches that will deny death,
> who will continue walking and becoming masters of
> their destiny
> by falling and rising up,
> who by the power and light of the real facts
> will realize with clear arguments our dream.

This is the voice of the poet who turned into song the dramatic social changes and political tragedies of the second half of the twentieth century.

THE SENTIMENTAL education provided by these poets and songwriters, rooted in the traditional culture, yet open to the international currents of the day, is crucial to an understanding of the recent transformations of Basque culture and politics.

Lesson thirty-two

LEARNING OBJECTIVES
1. To assess the musical and poetic expressions of cultural resistance and political protest during the last years of the Franco regime.
2. To analyze the relevance of popular culture in acquiring new artistic forms while recreating new forms of identity and a new political imaginary.
3. To survey the local Basque adaptation of international musical trends—from the *nova cançó* to the folklore revival, and from rock and roll to hip-hop.
4. To analyze the extent to which these new cultural creations are rooted in the Basque traditional culture expounded throughout this course.

REQUIRED READING
Sharryn Kasmir, "From the Margins: Punk Rock and the Repositioning of Ethnicity and Gender in Basque Identity," in *Basque Cultural Studies*, ed. Wiliam A. Douglass, Carmelo Urza, Linda White, and Joseba Zulaika (Reno: Basque Studies Program 1999), 178–204.
Jacqueline Urla, "We are All Malcolm X!: Negu Gorriak, Hip-Hop, and the Basque Political Imaginary," in *Global Noise: Rap and Hip-Hop Outside the USA*, ed.

T. Mitchell, (Middletown, Conn: Wesleyan University
Press, 2001), 171–93.

SUGGESTED READING
Jacqueline Urla, "Kafe Antzokia: The Global Meets the
Local in Basque Cultural Politics," *Papeles del CEIC*,
Universidad del Pais Vasco, http://www.ehu.es / CEIC /
pdf / 10.pdf [accessed July 27, 2006].

WRITTEN LESSON FOR SUBMISSION
1. How would you describe the relationship between
sociopolitical changes and expressions of Basque popular culture in the 1960s and 1970s?
2. Would you argue in favor of or against the premise
that the new forms of popular culture are rooted in
traditional culture? In which ways are they continuous
with or discontinuous from former cultural expressions.
3. Examine how rap and hip-hop music became an
alternative political discourse for Basque music in
the 1990s. Do you believe that such musical forms are
compatible with Basque traditional forms of singing,
such as *bertsolaritza*?
4. Would you agree that Kepa Junkera´s music and new
cultural institutions such as Kafe Antzokia represent
new strategies of Basque cultural politics? Explain.

33 · Atxaga and the Literary Imagination

BERNARDO ATXAGA (b. 1951) is the best-known living Basque writer. His book *Obabakoak* (Those of Obaba) won the Spanish National Prize for Literature in 1989 and has since been translated into more than twenty languages, a most exceptional accomplishment in Basque literature.

Atxaga was brought up in Asteasu, a rural village of Gipuzkoa, and any Basque can easily visualize many of the images and situations evoked in *Obabakoak*'s narrative: the hundreds of bends in the forested road to Obaba, its proximity to the sea, the town festival, the open-air dance in the square, the loitering on the steps of the old church while drinking beer, the passage of the cyclists, and so forth. Yet Atxaga's tender description of villagers, including marginal and solitary persons, is far removed from the typical bucolic treatment of the *baserri* lifestyle in earlier Basque literature. The characterizations are extended as well to marginalized urbanites undergoing identity crises.

Obaba is an imaginary village, a mythical place not unlike many small rural Basque communities. The first part of the book is devoted to stories related to Obaba. There is then a novella set in a small Castilian village named Villamediana. There then follow narratives widely dispersed in place and time, including Hamburg, China, Amazonia, medieval France, Castile, Baghdad, and the Himalayas.

Employing such diverse settings, different historical periods, and an array of literary topics, Atxaga masterfully recreates an imaginary world that is both per-sonal and universal, local and cosmopolitan. In the third part of the book, the protagonist, who is also the narrator,

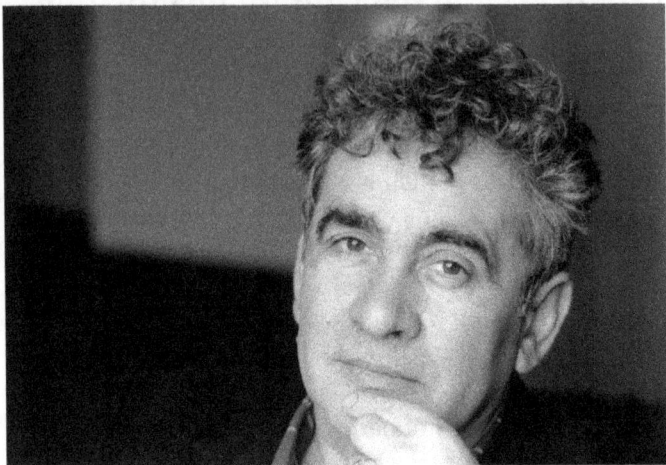

And the hedgehog woke up
The works of Bernardo Atxaga, the Basque poet and novelist, has been translated into twenty-eight languages. His highly acclaimed *Obabakoak* won the Spanish National Prize for Literature in 1989.
Photo: Basso Cannarsa

---

departs "in search of the final word"—which turns out to be an impossible quest. Time and again, different stories delay his search, while reality and fantasy mingle in an ingenious combination of universal and particular themes. Love, jealousy, vengeance, religion, and war are some of the topics reflected in these stories, told fondly by the protagonist, his friend, his uncle, and a "Mr. Smith."

ATXAGA'S LITERARY sources include Basque oral tradition and modernist literature. Some of his plots are borrowed from detective stories. There is a strong presence of South American authors such as

Jorge Luis Borges, Gabriel García Márquez and Julio Cortázar, including a strong strain of magical realism, however, above all, Atxaga is a consummate storyteller. Metaliterature is a prominent concern in his work. He writes stories about stories. Plagiarism is privileged, and the references to intertextuality are many. Another of his works, *Bi anaiak*, (Two brothers), employs the magical realism of a human story narrated by animals while retelling John Steinbeck's *Of Mice and Men* set in a Basque village.

FROM BORGES, he borrows the techniques of inserting one text within another, of mixing reality and dream, and the literary power of producing perplexity in the reader. For example, even if the possibility of a lizard crawling into the albino Maria's ear is at first refuted by the narrator, by the end of the day, Atxaga makes us believe that the story is true. To prove its veracity, the author introduces the names of various scientists (all fictional), along with invented scientific treatises regarding the species *"Lacerta viridis."* All this apparent "science" furthers our acceptance of the lizard story. The goal of the writer is therefore to create an aura of verisimilitude that questions the very status of reality while demonstrating through fiction the impossibility of capturing it in linguistic form. This is actually consonant with the history of science, since it demonstrates that scientific "discoveries" are arbitrary and conjectural. We cannot really apprehend the universe and its laws, but rather indulge in a discursive pattern constructed by human beings and their laws. What we can know is produced in and through our discourses.

Rather than a novel, *Obabakoak* is a collection of stories. Walter Benjamin's characterization, in his well-known essay "The Storyteller" applies to Atxaga as "the man who could let the wick of his life be consumed

completely by the gentle flame of his story." This is
echoed by the remarks of one of Atxaga's protagonists:
"all [my friends] agreed that I would do absolutely
anything just to get a chance to read them my stories."
Unlike the novel, which depends on literary tradition,
storytelling relies on oral sources. In Benjamin's words,
"The storyteller takes what he tells from experience—his
own or that reported by others." Not only is Atxaga a storyteller, through his characters, he reclaims the task of
storytelling.

THE STORY about lizards in the Obaba story "In
Search of the Final Words" is a good example of the
influence of the oral sources on Atxaga's literary imagination. Indeed, some of the passages that deal with the
dangers posed by lizards can be found in Resurrección
María de Azkue's collection of Basque sayings, *Euskalerriaren yakintza*, and in José Miguel de Barandiarán's
Mitología del pueblo vasco—both ethnographic collec-
tions of Basque folk stories and traditions.

Atxaga is well aware of the power of orality for invoking and enhancing the memory of the reader. In the
original Basque version, the presence of the spoken language is even stronger, as is made obvious by the use of
ellipsis and the lack of the conjugated verb. Some of the
short stories—"Maiden Name, Laura Sligo," "Wei Lie
Deshang"—have the evident rapid pace and musicality
of orality more than the style of a contemplative written
text. Similarly, the use of repetition, such as "the story
about the lizard and the final word can wait," "the journey toward the final word will continue later," "Once
again, the final word will have to wait" at the end of
the chapters are also drawn from the oral tradition.
Such redundancy keeps the writer and the reader on
track while sustaining anticipation. Traditional Basque
sayings find their way into Atxaga's book, as well. For

example: "[My father] said that in heaven there's a huge cake reserved solely for men who've never once regretted getting married. The cake's never been touched."

ORALITY EMPLOYS situational, rather than abstract or categorical, thinking. Atxaga's fable of the lizard crawling inside the child's head reflects the point well. It sums up every possible danger of childhood. Since these characters are anything but colorless, they facilitate oral mnemonics. The weird story of Sacamantecas in Atxaga's piece is, once again, a clear instance of his debt to orality. Most rural children of Atxaga's generation could remember having being told this frightening story. Folktales are told to discipline children, and Atxaga takes advantage of these storytelling devices for his literary purposes.

Death appears in Atxaga's work with striking regularity. Indeed, it is the unifying motif of the stories. As Benjamin puts it: "Death is the sanction of everything that the storyteller can tell ... it is the natural history to which his stories refer back." He goes on to say that the "meaning of life" is to the novel what the "moral of the story" is to the story—entirely different historical coordinates may be discerned from them. Life and time can be separated in the novel to the point that the entire novelistic action can be seen as the struggle against the power of time. In contrast, the story carries the unity of life out of the past, which is compressed in memory.

Fear is also central to Atxaga's work, as shown by the interpretation given to the story of the lizard by the main character's uncle. The story of Sacamantecas and the arrival of the train are similarly fashioned out of the fear that children might disappear. As Atxaga puts it, "Fear is everywhere, fear causes a great number of behaviors, fear creates fantastic characters."

Obabakoak concludes that all the good stories have been recorded. (The bad ones were ignored and forgotten.) Originality is therefore impossible. The "final word" cannot be found, because everything has been said already. Therefore, the only avenue open to the writer is plagiarism: This is particularly the case for the writer in Euskara, forced to have recourse to world literature for inspiration, given the paucity of the language's literary tradition. Nevertheless, although everything has already been said, the creative process may recombine the known elements—as happens in Borges's vast "Library of Babel."

SINCE BASQUE politics throughout the twentieth century have been dominated by the ethnonationalist challenge, it is scarcely surprising that most Basque writers have, through their works, commented on it. Again, given the artistic fascination with the extremes in human affairs, it is scarcely surprising that many Basque writers (and filmmakers) have addressed the topic of ETA and its capacity for drama. Atxaga is no exception. His successful novel *Gizona bere bakardadean* (*Lone man*) deals with the dilemmas of the inner musings and the daily existence of an ETA operative.

Lesson thirty-three

LEARNING OBJECTIVES
1. To analyze the writer as storyteller and the links between oral traditional themes and Atxaga's work
2. To analyze the cultural-political context of literary fictions
3. To analyze the relations between peripheral cultures and the global literary market

REQUIRED READING
Bernardo Atxaga, *Obabakoak* (London: Hutchinson, 1992).

SUGGESTED READING
Maria Olaziregi, *Waking the Hedgehog: The Literary Universe of Bernardo Atxaga* (Reno: Center for Basque Studies, 2005).

WRITTEN LESSON FOR SUBMISSION
1. From your own knowledge of Basque culture, is Atxaga a "Basque" writer, or is he, as one critic put it, as Spanish as paella?
2. How would you explain the international acclaim obtained by *Obabakoak*?
3. Can you think of other parallels to Obaba in contemporary literature?

34 · Basque Cinema
and the Ethnographic Imagination

A SALIENT CULTURAL development during the post-Franco democracy was the emergence of a new, vigorous Basque cinema. Filmmakers born in the Basque Country, such as Imanol Uribe, Alfonso Ungria, Arantxa Lazkano, And Diez, Pedro Olea, Alex de la Iglesia, Juanma Bajo Ulloa, Daniel Galparsoro, Helena Taberna, Montxo Armendariz, and Julio Medem began producing works that mirrored the extraordinary changes taking place in the social and political arenas. Some of the films reported historical events or were heavily ethnographic. Collectively, the cinematic body of work presents descriptions and analyses that are crucial for an under-standing of the day-to-day experience and transformation of Basque society.

In its initial period, the new Basque cinema was obsessed with the past. In our treatments of Basque prehistory, history, and ethnography, we have already noted the propensity to look toward the past as a ploy for defining Basqueness in the present. One such search for historical foundations is Ungria's film *The Conquest of Albania*, based on the military campaign of the Great Company of Nafarroa that, in the fourteenth century, set out to conquer that remote country. The troops from Nafarroa land in Albania and start their search for an "invisible" enemy that is nowhere to be found. The mood is reminiscent of that in Werner Herzog's *Aguirre, the Wrath of God*. Unlike Herzog's film, Ungria's story fails to build dramatic tension. In Casilda de Miguel's commentary, "The tale often reaches a metaphysical register, especially when it takes place amid an arid and unfriendly territory wherein the enemy always remains invisible and attacks by treachery, thus progressively sapping the spirit and the resolution of the Basque expedition."

Other historical films are José María Tuduri's *Chronicle of the Carlist War, 1872–1876* (1989), José Antonio Zorrilla's *Lauaxeta: To the Four Winds* (1986), and Imanol Uribe's *Escape from Segovia* (1981). Lauaxeta was a Basque avant-garde poet and political activist who, during the Spanish Civil War, forsook the pen for the gun. The day after the bombing of Gernika by German aviators in the service of Franco, and while showing the damage to a foreign correspondent, he was arrested. Months later, he was executed by Franco's troops. Zorrilla himself explains:

In *To the Four Winds*, everything told is real, although I did not try for excessive historical accuracy. I did not know the poet, as is the case with almost everybody else, but his figure allows me to explain many dramas that were lived during the Civil War. The film responds to the historical memory of the vanquished, of those who lost the war. My family, however, belonged to the side of the winners. I am a "regenerated" one who assumes willingly the historical memory of the vanquished.

LAUAXETA WAS considered to be the Basque Federico Lorca—whom he translated and with whom he was friends. Both were assassinated by Franco's forces and became symbols of antifascist resistance.

Uribe's *Escape from Segovia* narrates the real historical event of a group of ETA prisoners escaping from a prison in the Spanish province of Segovia. In the nascent Spanish democracy of the early 1980s, Basques were still confronted with the ghost of ETA and its unsolved armed struggle. As de Miguel observes,

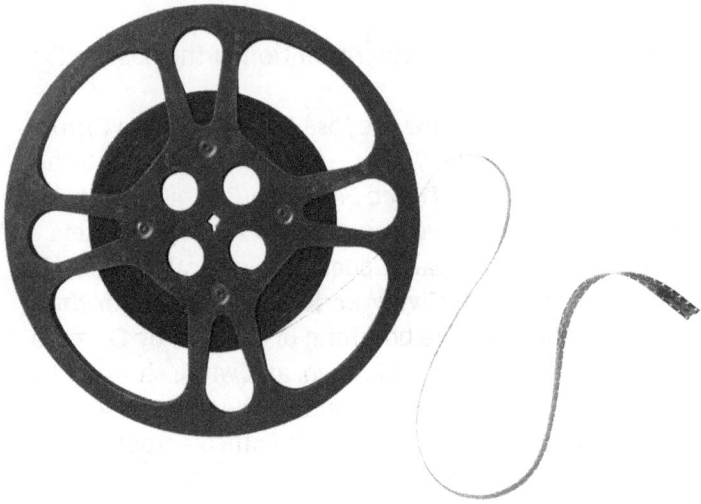

New Basque cinema
The period of post-Franco democracy ushered in a vigorous new Basque cinema which presents a crucial window
upon the current transformations of Basque society.
Photo: Photodisk, Inc.

Basque cinema in the eighties offers one of the most
visible manifestations of the narrative change of the
concept of "nation," a change, on the other hand,
quite visible in the social order. While in the Spanish
state most directors chose literary adaptations in order
to get government grants, here we find that more than
half the films were made with original scripts based on
real or historical facts ... . Moreover, Basque cinema
was in search of its own identity and chose to offer a
nationalist vision of history that had been absent from
the dominant discourse for quite a long time.

But what is most remarkable from the perspective of
this course is the ethnographic content of some of the
films. They present arguments that are closely linked to
the anthropological perspectives developed here. One
of these dimensions has to do with the rural setting of
some of the films, such as Armendariz's *Tasio* (1984)
and Medem's *Vacas* (1992).

THESE FILMS represent traditional family life and a
cyclical passing of time situated in a Basque geographical context. Tradition and modernity clash, creating spurts of violence of both the domestic and political
kind. Both films are centered in the traditional *baserria*
or farmstead described in chapter 14. It is on the *baserria* that the lives of the characters take shape and where
they experience love and violence. The views of the rural
country expressed in the two movies do not coincide,
however, even though both portray the inner world of
Basque traditional life. Their depictions of neighborly
auzo relations stress different aspects, Medem's representation underscoring its violent rivalries. Their representations of gender relations are also markedly different in that Armendariz reduces women's role to that of
subordinate mother and wife, whereas Medem empha-
sizes the focal female role in sustaining the *baserri*
household. But neither attempts cinematic realism: "I
was not looking for a realistic photography. I wanted to
create an atmosphere and a mood that seemed realistic," Armendáriz's has said. Medem speaks in similar
terms: "I did not want to make a film to show the rural
world. *Vacas* is an imaginary world, one of madness. It
shows the inner world of a character. It invents a place
in between life and death at which the protagonist has
arrived after a traumatic experience."

As to their main male characters, Medem's Manuel Iriguibel is a cowardly woodchopper, and Armendariz's Tasio is a fearless and independent charcoal maker and furtive hunter. As Jaume Martí-Olivella comments, "it's reasonable to conclude that *Tasio* betrays a male-gaze attitude, despite its subtle treatment of sex and violence," whereas:

> In *Vacas*, on the contrary, there is a self-conscious and metafictional attempt to deconstruct the traditional male gaze. Structurally, Medem's film is organized around the metonymic (con)fusion of the eyes of the cows with the camera eye and the (burning) hole of the tree trunk located in the midst of the forest. From a feminist perspective, however, Medem's attempt seems to fall prey to what Julia Kristeva termed "the power of the abject."

WHILE *TASIO* is patriarchal and celebratory of the waning rural experience, *Vacas* is a postmodern deconstruction of the idealized view of the rural life.

It is worthwhile to concentrate on how the critically acclaimed *Vacas* provides representations of the pre-modern life of Basque traditional society by using post-modern aesthetics, since contemporary filmmaking is an urban phenomenon, and the very selection of a *baserria*, with its traditional chores and lifestyle, as a setting for a modern film, is in itself highly unusual. The movie's historical period runs from the Carlist War of the 1870s to the Spanish Civil War of the 1930s. It is divided into four episodes having to do with the Carlist War, life on the *baserria*, love and the birth of a child, and migration to America and return as a photojournalist covering the Spanish Civil War. This fragmentary narrative structure allows Medem to create a plot in which the characters

are not fully developed and can be presented as archetypes. We are not given psychological reasons why the
characters act the way they do. In critical moments, the
characters are seen through the viewpoint of a cow's
eye—the cow serves as a witness to the stories taking
place. The *auzo* relationships and rivalries that are at the
core of Medem's plot, the daily activities of the *baser-
ritarra*, such as scything and stacking the hay or deliver-
ing a calf, and the intimate relationship between people
and animals provide the setting for the universal themes
tragically played out by the characters. The bucolic landscape of the farmstead becomes the setting for display-
ing the passions of the protagonists.

As is underlined by Javi Cillero, there are many
intertextual references to other films in *Vacas*. The
battlefield scenes of the Carlist War make obvious references to other movies covering this period, as well to
the literary work of Pio Baroja and a vast historiography.
The initial images of the woodchopper, Manuel Irigibel,
and his cowardice manifested in his trembling before
engaging in combat, are reminiscent of many Hollywood
Westerns and war movies, such as John Houston's *The
Red Badge of Courage* and William Wyler's *Friendly
Persuasion*. The cowardly woodchopper paints his face
with the blood of his comrade and feigns being dead,
thus escaping certain death: This, too, is a typical ploy
in war movies and goes back to Odysseus's escape from
Polyphemus in the cave. Manuel is lying naked on the
grass, feigning to be dead, when a cart full of corpses
rolls over and crushes his knee, leaving him lame for the
rest of his life, a clear allusion to the myth of Oedipus
and to war movies in which the returning maimed soldiers have to adjust to normal life.

Later in the movie, while passing through the forest
in a cart filled with dead soldiers, Manuel jumps from

the cart and sees a cow standing unemotionally behind him. Then the story moves forward to the twentieth century, and an older Manuel is sitting on a stool next to the *baserria* and painting a cow. In Luis Buñuel's and Salvador Dali's 1929 surrealistic film *Un chien andalou*, the opening sequence consists in slashing an eye with a razor. In Medem's film, the camera goes inside the cow's eye and sees the events from the animal's perspective. A noted Basque writer, Jon Mirande, had also written a story about a conversation between a man and cows in a field in which the cows only gaze back at him. The same year that the movie came out, Bernardo Atxaga published a book entitled *Memories of a Basque Cow*.

THERE ARE ALSO references to a children's literary classic, the story of Txanogorritxo or Little Red Ridinghood, as Manuel tells his little granddaughter to be careful of the wild boars in the forest when she starts out in pursuit of a stray cow. In another scene, there is a pursuit by an unseen intruder, the classic ghost chase in horror movies.

The wood-chopping contest is reminiscent of a Western competition. A wood chip from one of the competitors, Ignacio Iriguibel, Manuel's son, flies into Catalina's clothes, presaging their later affair. The proud loser refuses to extend his hand to the winner, Ignacio, as in many Westerns. The encounter between Ignacio, who is married, and the sexually attractive Catalina as femme fatale has innumerable connotations in many films, some of the recent examples being *Fatal Attraction* and *Basic Instinct*. Later in the film, Peru, the child born out of wedlock to Ignacio and Catalina, is walking in the forest and playing with a wild-boar trap, situations that are intertextually linked to, for example, Truffaut's *Enfant sauvage*, or *Wild Child*, as it was called when released in the United States.

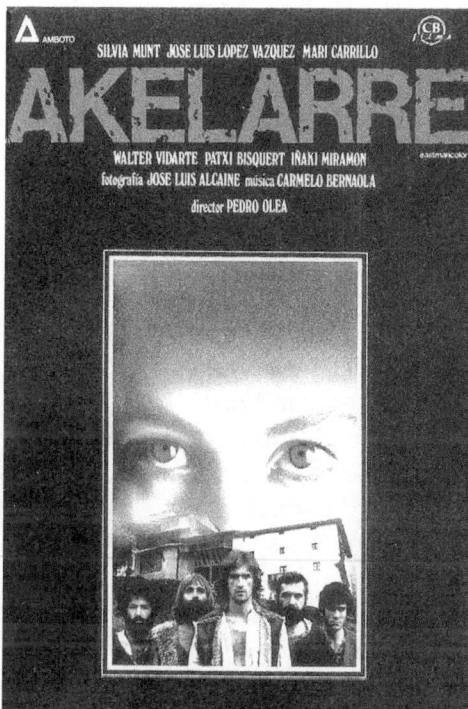

The eyes of history
Akelarre, by Pedro Olea, focuses upon the historically
resonant drama of a witch hunt in a Basque village amid
clashes among opposing social groups.
Source: Basque Film Archives

Medem portrays Ignacio and his group in a car on
their way home after winning a woodchopping competition. The introduction of the theme of the car into
a rural setting is reminiscent of the Old West / New
Frontier opposition in contemporary films. The tragic
events between the lovers Ignacio and Catalina are

played out around the car theme, a symbolism that recalls the gangster movies of the 1930s and 1940s.

THE YOUNG photographer returning from America in the last part of the movie reminds the viewer of Hemingway during the Spanish Civil War. Like Gary Cooper in *For Whom the Bell Tolls*, he is a sympathizer of the Republic. Hemingway's *The Sun also Rises*, with its depiction of the San Fermin festival, was also turned into a film. The photojournalist evokes the image of the photographer Robert Capa during the Spanish Civil War. Capa had taken pictures of Basque soldiers in the forest that have to do with war scenes in *Vacas*. The Civil War story also links it to Ken Loach's film on the anarchists at the Catalunyan front, *Tierra y libertad*, and to all sorts of war movies throughout the world.

Finally, the confrontation in the woods between the cow and the horse is intertextually linked to Picasso's *Guernica*, his masterpiece, a universally recognized emblematic representation of war. The allusion is reinforced by the grandfather having painted two cows facing each other, a painting entitled *War*.

As Cillero concludes,

In our view, *Vacas* can be constituted as recreation of film scenes typical of different movie genres or literary sources. This way of approaching *Vacas* allows us to discover many links and references to cultural icons. Once it is closely analyzed, Medem's story recalls many moments in classic filmmaking and literature that add different textures to the film. The result is an interaction of narratives, this so-called intertextuality with many plays and movies, a way of narrating a story that has to do with postmodernist aesthetics.

Just as Bernardo Atxaga's work (see chapter 33) is the most accomplished literary representation of the ethnographic culture described by anthropologists, Medem's and Armendariz's works can be seen as equally compelling creations that elaborate on the same cultural themes. In Atxaga's novels and short stories, particularly in his mythical place Obaba, reminiscent of Gabriel García Márquez's Macondo in his *One Hundred Years of Solitude*, ideas of nature, rural life, the wildness, and the forest, as well as all sorts of animal metaphors, are intrinsic. There is a strong intertextuality between the imaginary world constructed and popularized by Atxaga and the screen images of these filmmakers. Such aesthetic relationships became an actual collaboration when in 2005 Armendariz produced the film *Obaba*, based on Atxaga's celebrated novel *Obabakoak*.

BASQUE FILMMAKERS, while denying that their works have anything to do with something called "Basque cinema," have delved into the various aspects of their urban society and culture, explored contrasting fictions and allegories of their history, and examined the intricacies of radical otherness and migrancy in contemporary Basque postmodern life. Thus, Daniel Calparsoro's *Leap into the Void* places at the center of his narrative, and in the context of Bilbao's postindustrial ruins, someone of a different race. The leader of the gang is a Brazilian immigrant, loved by a young woman who is interpreted by the actress Najwa Nimry, the daughter of a Basque-Jordanian family. It was in the midst of Bilbao's ruins on the Left Bank of the Nerbioi River, where Gehry built his magnificent Guggenheim Museum, Calparsoro situates his powerful film, as if invoking Benjamin's "Theology of Hell": not the nostalgia of long-gone riches and empires, but the critical consciousness of the fragility of

Una producción **Elias Querejeta**

Tasio

Tasio adulto	**Patxi Bisquert**
Tasio adolescente	**Isidro José Solano**
Tasio niño	**Garikoïtz Mendigutxia**
Paulina, mujer de Tasio	**Amaia Lasa**
Hermano de Tasio	**Nacho Martinez**
Amigo de Tasio	**José Maria Asín**
Guarda, enemigo de Tasio	**Paco Sagarzazu**
Padre de Tasio	**Enrique Goicoechea**
Madre de Tasio	**Elena Uriz**
Fotografía	**José Luis Alcaine**
Música	**Angel Illarramendi**
Director	**Montxo Armendariz**

Subvencionada por el Departamento de Cultura del Gobierno Vasco Con la colaboración de TVE S.A.

Traditional life, modern times

Montxo Armendariz's film *Tasio* celebrates the waning of the rural experience—farmers, woodchoppers, charcoal makers, hunters, fishermen. It narrates the story of Tasio, who lives at the foot of the Urbasa Mountains with his wife and daughter and works as a charcoal maker. It depicts his adventures with his arch enemy—the forest warden.

Source: Basque Film Archives

a capitalist social order that requires one catastrophe after another in order to perpetuate itself.

Such migrant mutations are also at the center of Olea's *Akelarre* and de la Iglesia's *The Day of the Beast*. *Akelarre* deals with the theme of witchcraft that we studied in chapter 19. Olea himself described his film in these terms:

> In *Akelarre*, I tried to defend the position of the witches because I believe that their pagan ways had a lot to do with the Basque matriarchy that has always existed. What I showed in *Akelarre* was the struggle between a pagan way of life confronted by a Catholicism that is imposed from without; this confrontation expresses in my view the opposition between woman-cave-uterus and man-religion-church. It is the struggle between patriarchy and woman's secular power, a fight that is at the origin of all the problems shown in my film.

As for *The Day of the Beast*, it is a satanic comedy whose protagonist is Angel Berriatua, a professor of theology at the University of Deusto, who is described in these terms in the film's press release: "Angel has spent half of his life deciphering the prophetic message concealed in the sacred pages of 'Revelation.' His endless drive has led him to a terrifying conclusion: The Antichrist will be born in Madrid, in the predawn hours of December 25, 1995, in a secret place. There is barely time to do anything to observe the signs that indicated the coming of the Son of Satan to Earth." De la Iglesia chooses farce to present the uncanny return of the repressed in the Basque and Spanish imaginaries when confronted with the hellish social realities of the modern city. Angel mutates from being a monk with the spiritual pursuit of deciphering the Bible to an evildoer in search of the Antichrist. Just as Galparsoro used Bilbao's industrial and urban ruins as a setting for his film, de la Iglesia uses Madrid's postmodern KIO towers and their inverted V shape as an emblem of the satanic forces. *The Day of the Beast* is a parody of witch hunts and religious intolerance, a theme that is present in other movies, as well.

IN SUM, THERE has been a considerable confluence of both Basque film and literature during the post-Franco era, informed by many of the retrospective anthropological and historical issues that we have raised in this course. In the recent filming of *Obabakoak*, whereby a nearly contemporary novel is turned into a film, we see a maturing of both the films and literary expressions of contemporary Basque culture into what might be regarded as a new Basque high-cultural tradition capable of standing on its own.

Lesson thirty-four

LEARNING OBJECTIVES
1. To examine the diverse filmic representations of Basque historical and cultural realities during the post-Franco democratic era.
2. To analyze the connections between Basque film and the overall Basque anthropological culture.
3. To assess the varieties of Basque cultural experience as depicted in these films.

REQUIRED READING
Jaume Martí-Olivella, "Invisible Otherness: From Migrant Subjects to the Subject of Immigration in Basque Cinema," in *Basque Cultural Studies*, ed. William A. Douglass, Carmelo Urza, Linda White,

and Joseba Zulaika (Reno: Basque Studies Program, 1999),205–26.

———, "(M)Otherly Monsters: Old Misogyny and / in New Basque Cinema," *Anuario de Cine y Literatura en Español* (1977): 89–101.

Viewing of the film *Vacas*.

SUGGESTED READING

Jaume Martí-Olivella, *Basque Cinema: An Introduction* (Reno: Center for Basque Studies, 2003).

Javier Cillero, "Intertextual Elements in Julio Medem's *Vacas*," *Journal of the Society of Basque Studies in America* 17 (1977), 35–58.

WRITTEN LESSON FOR SUBMISSION

1. Describe Medem's use of postmodern intertextual aesthetics to represent a premodern rural world in *Vacas*.
2. How are *Tasio* and *Vacas* similar, and how are they different? What narrative elements do they have in common? How are gender relations portrayed in both films? In what ways does *Tasio* constitute a patriarchal and idealized reconstruction of a bygone rural country? Compare it with *Vacas*.
3. Assess how the problem of violence is represented in the various films discussed in the chapter, particularly in *Vacas, Lauaxeta,* and *Escape from Segovia*. How would you compare them and their attempt to become Basque foundational narratives?
4. Discuss in what ways Basque cinema is about various kinds of migrancy.

35 · Modernist Art: Oteiza and Chillida

MODERNITY AS A form of experience refers to
the social and cultural condition brought about
by modernization. Modernism is the deliberate reflec-
tion and representation of such a new condition. At the
turn of the nineteenth century, Paris was the center of
modernist art. The main "isms" of the period—Post-
Impressionism, Fauvism, Cubism, Futurism, Expression-
ism, Surrealism—were most evident there. For Basque
painters, the pilgrimage to Paris became a tradition:
Darío de Regoyos, Adolfo Guiard, Francisco Iturrino,
Juan de Echevarria, Ignacio Zuloaga, and others made
it. But ethnographic and / or folkloric realism was also a
major presence in the works of some of the best Basque
painters: Aurelio Arteta, Ramón de Zubiaurre, Ricardo
Baroja, Julián Tellaeche, Elías Salaverria, Alberto Arrue,
and Jesús Olasagasti, to cite but a few.

In the postwar period of the 1940s and 1950s, two towering figures emerged in the Basque / Spanish art world:
Jorge Oteiza and Eduardo Chillida. Oteiza (1908–2003)
was born in Orio, a small fishing village in Gipuzkoa.
He spent his childhood and adolescence in Donostia. In
1927, he moved to Madrid to study medicine, but two
years later decided to devote his life to art. Early in life,
he abandoned religion; art was going to supplant it with
an equally absolutist aesthetic vigor. In 1931 and again
in 1933, he won the first prize for sculpture in Donostia
and began to exhibit his work in the company of a group
of young artists.

As an avant-garde sculptor, Oteiza was influenced by
the contemporary aesthetic movements of Europe—
Cubism, Russian Constructivism, Neoplasticism, De
Stijl, and the Bauhaus. The 1930s were difficult times
for European artists. The crisis of Surrealism, the Nazi

takeover of the Bauhaus, the Russian poet Vladimir
Myakovski's suicide, the second thoughts regarding the
heroic mission of contemporary art—all made the life
of the artist anything but serene. In 1935, Oteiza emigrated to South America, where he would spend fourteen
years. He traveled extensively there and met with local
artists and intellectuals, as well as with groups of Basque
migrants and exiles from the Spanish Civil War. He was
close to both Communists and Basque nationalists.

THE STATED reason for his visit to South America
was to study the "fantastic statuary left by an
unknown people" in the Columbian city of San Agustín.
He subsequently wrote a book-length essay on these
imposing prehistoric statues in the Andean mountains
of Columbia at the headwaters of the Magdalena and
Cauca Rivers. Oteiza's existential attitude toward art is
nowhere more clearly stated than in this essay. What he
discerns in this statuary is a "matrix culture" created by
"the original American people." He embarked on nothing less than a utopian search for the primordial expression in such a "matrix" of the original state of art and
the ultimate uncontaminated vision of reality.

In 1957, Oteiza was elected to represent Spain at the
Sâo Paulo (Brazil) Biennial, considered at the time to
be the most prestigious international art competition.
He accompanied his works with a text entitled "An
Experimental Proposal 1956–57," which examines the
development of his artistic process. This manifesto lays
out Oteiza's filiations in contemporary art and presents
his ambitious reconfiguration and conclusion of that
tradition in a manner that is still baffling and provocative. At the time, Oteiza was engaged in highly abstract
experimentation in his sculpture. The cryptic text, while
intended as an explanatory caption for his sculpture,
presents a formulation of his aesthetic ideas and goals.

In the modernist tradition, for Oteiza, art was the greatest spiritual adventure, but he was searching for a rigorously "Objective Aesthetic."

Oteiza's approach has to do essentially with the decomposition of basic Euclidean forms, a process we see in Cubism, Constructivism, Surrealism, and other aesthetic movements. For Paul Cézanne, in nature, everything is modelled according to the sphere, the cone, and the cylinder, and he argued that by learning to paint these fundamental forms, everything was within the artist's reach. The history of modern art is basically one of deconstructive modulations of these Euclidean forms. Pablo Picasso's decompositions of them are the most familiar. The sculpture of Henry Moore, a significant influence on Oteiza, is another example. Oteiza compares the energy liberated by Moore's work to "nuclear fission" through perforation of an existing solid sculpture, whereas he likens his own energy more to fusion, or the conjunction of light elements.

THE QUIXOTIC goal, then, of Oteiza's "Experimental Proposal" is to achieve a final decomposition of the cylinder, the cube, and the sphere. As a harbinger of his formal experiments and scientific methods, his first sculpture, executed in 1931, an archaic figure in a rounded stone, was entitled *Adam and Eve: Tangent S equals A divided by B*, and was accompanied by algebraic calculations to explain the formal inner relations of the work. But it was upon his return from South America, in 1948, that he began playing with the idea of a new cylinder by working with hyperboloids. Thus his *Unidad Triple y Liviana* (Triple and light unity) is a vertical superposing of three hyperboloid units whose marked convexities invoke the surrounding space as a container; space that becomes the true agent of the statue. This led, in 1957, to the work *Disoccupation of the Cylinder*.

Breaking the cosmos
The stark work of Jorge Oteiza plays with the disoccupation of space--the void. It made the Basque sculptor one
of the world's most influential during the latter part of
the twentieth century. The work "Disoccupation of the
Sphere. Version B for Mondrian (1958)" stands in front
of Bilbao's city hall.
Photo by Iñaki Uriarte.

Oteiza was closest to the Russian Constructivists and the Dutch movement known as De Stijl. He frequently quotes Wassili Kandinsky and Piet Mondrian, but Kasimir Malevich is the figure that Oteiza saw as his immediate precursor. Malevich was the Russian artist who launched the movement known as Suprematism and for whom abstraction was the revolutionary art essential to the new socialist society. Malevich wrote: "I have transformed myself *in the zero of form.... Things have disappeared like smoke.*" Russian Constructivism's political and theoretical progressive radicalism fitted well with Oteiza's temperament. It developed a so-called "laboratory art," an austere form of formal inquiry elaborated further by Oteiza in his well-known "laboratory of chalks."

OTEIZA CREATED a matrix he called the "Malevich Unit," one that follows horizontal as well as diagonal structural trajectories that are incomplete and reach out for further relationships. In this fashion, Oteiza created a new vocabulary of units that could be flat, curved, left vacant, positive-negative, endowed with curved aperture, and so on. He also investigated the possibility of a tridimensional unit. Subsequently, Oteiza went on to play with series of binary and ternary units, experimental works that did not require conclusions and in which error was an intrinsic part of the creative process. He created these series with materials such as chalk, tin, and wire.

His "disoccupation of the sphere" addresses the problem of mobility in sculpture, an issue that is central to Oteiza's aesthetics. He was unconcerned with natural types of movement, such as flotation, suspension, or other psychological or kinetic effects that are external to the statue and not intrinsic to its structure. Oteiza's first work in this series—*Par Móvil* (Mobile Pair)—illustrates his procedure. He disoccupies the sphere by taking two semicircles and opposing them perpendicularly through their central point. The result is an unbalanced structure that expresses the sphere's intrinsic instability; the sculpture's two points of support can never guarantee its stability and, while searching for another fulcrum, it creates a continuous structural mobility. But this is still a "centered" structure—Oteiza abhored centering in that, traditionally, it organizes closed circles around itself. In order to open the sphere's forms, he opposed the semicircles, broke the anticipated circuits, and decentered and complicated the forms in an unpredictable series so as to unveil an inner structure.

AT THE END of Oteiza's "An Experimental Proposal" manifesto there is a section entitled "Funerary Stelae" that will appear cryptic to a non-Basque reader, but that conceals a paradigmatic dimension of the apotheosis of this sculptural experiment. These funerary stelae, of which there are thousands in Basque cemeteries, are typically three to five feet tall, upright stone pillars with a very definite form: on top of a trapezoidal "shoulder" rests a completely circular disc with an irradiative center. These funerary stelae are iconic representations of a pre-Copernican world, aesthetically controlled by the premises of circularity, enclosure, irradiative centers, and the formal implications of the void. Oteiza's experimental proposal attempts literally to break down this pre-Copernican finite world by decentering and opening up its archetypal aesthetic axes, expressed formulaically in the stelae. Thus, it is far from accidental that Oteiza refers to these stelae in his programmatic text.

In the same fashion, it was no coincidence that Eduardo Chillida's first abstract sculpture in 1951 was entitled *Ilarik* (Funerary stela), a work that can be traced directly to deconstructing the stela's primary axes. Both

Comb of the winds (1977)
Chillida's heroic sculpture on the famed Concha or
Bay of San Sebastian is now emblematic of his home
city. This is one of the three spectacular pieces of steel
anchored in the rocks that receive the brunt of the Atlantic's crashing waves. The sculpture "combs" the Cantabrian gales. Here the sculptor visits his creation.
Photo: William Douglass

Oteiza and Chillida sculpted dozens of works entitled
and / or shaped after funerary stelae, a clear acknowl-
edgement that for them, this religious statuary is a
primordial reference. For both, the stela is an aspect of
the traditional "Wall," another of Oteiza´s persistent
ideas, whether he is dealing with prehistoric art, Mexican muralists, or his postsculptural forays into architecture. "The new Wall," states Oteiza in his Sâo Paulo
manifesto, "must turn out to be, always, a fragment of an
open system, of an unstable, broken equilibrium, which

gradually reestablishes itself from the outside." From this perspective, Oteiza and Chillida's entire oeuvres can be summed up as titanic efforts to transcend the centered and closed spaces of the pre-Copernican aesthetic legacy. This is obviously not simply developing a tradition. Rather, in formal and aesthetic terms, it is a radical break with tradition, recomposing it at a different level of formal complexity.

THUS, IN THE sculptural and theoretical works of Oteiza and Chillida, not only the latest avant-garde art, but also the presence of the forms and ideas of traditional aesthetics were decisive, as well. Notions such as the "void," "circularity," "closure," and "limit," essential to traditional semantics, and thematic forms such as those deriving from the funerary stelae, became increasingly present in their works. The idea of the "void," for example, played a crucial role in the debates over pre-Copernican and modern conceptions of space and was even elaborated by various religious traditions. It is also central to Basque traditional ideas of ritual and aesthetics. The vacuist premise of *huts* (void, empty, zero) is employed generally in the traditional culture to represent such imageless notions as "cure," "grace," "freedom," "beauty," and "simplicity." Many of the titles of Oteiza's and Chillida's works and writings invoke *huts*. The centrality of this aesthetic in their works can therefore be discerned in both avant-garde discourses and Basque cultural concepts. The many associations between the artist's work and his native Basque culture are made explicit in the Chillida video *Portrait of an Artist*.

Chillida (1924–2002) also left his native Donostia for Madrid to study architecture. Soon his interests shifted to sculpture, and in 1948, he went to Paris. Chillida's initial works were sculpted in stone and blocks of plaster;

his carvings of male and female torsos were influenced by Greek sculpture. In search of his own style, in 1951, he returned to the Basque Country and began working with a blacksmith. Chillida found himself through forging iron. As Gaston Bachelard wrote of him, "Eduardo Chillida wanted to know muscular space without fat and heaviness. The world of iron is all muscles. Iron is the straight, the certain, the essential force."

Chillida's first abstract sculpture, as noted above, was a simple funerary stela's tridimensional geometric configuration, with planes and angles that change as the viewer looks at it from various angles. This work was followed by others in which iron is forged in sharp, angular forms that are reminiscent of fishhooks, scythes, pitchforks, and anchors. They convey a sense of struggle and irradiative energy. Some of the titles of these sculptures are *From Within, Vibration, Silent Music, In Praise of Fire,* and *In Praise of Air.*

THE GALERIE Maeght in Paris held Chillida's first one-- man show in 1956. He became known in the American art world by winning the Graham Foundation Prize in 1958, the year in which he also received the International Grand Prize for Sculpture at the Twenty-Ninth Biennale in Venice. In 1979, he received the Andrew Mellon Prize and was featured at the Carnegie Institute, together with Willem de Kooning.

Chillida liked to effect variations on a general theme, working in series. Thus, he made twelve variations of his extraordinary series *The Anvil of Dreams.* The "anvil" alludes to the forger's fiery tradition of violently hitting and shaping the incandescent iron, whereas the "dream" evokes the intensely poetic and spiritual purpose of his artistic work. Another series was named *Trembling Irons.* Chillida gave much thought to the notion of limit, which in its temporal version was for him the indefinable moment of the present, while spatially he saw it as the enigmatic trace whose "rumor" creates form. His series *Rumors of Limits* bends and sprawls in all directions.

CHILLIDA'S best-known series is the one entitled *Comb of the Winds*. A group of three sculptures installed on the rocky promontory constituting the western parameter of Donostia's famed Concha beach has become emblematic of his native city. He began the series in 1952–53, but it was his second wind comb in 1959, an iron hand of six outstretched diagonal fingers, that showed the extraordinary potential of the theme. Chillida made many etchings of his hands, fist, and fingers. The hand was his main working tool, as well as the metaphor for space, power, and society.

Working in the tradition of the aesthetics of the void prevalent both in contemporary avant-garde and in native semantics, Chillida created the series *Around the Void*, in which the central space is encircled by densely compacted angular blocks. The interplay of positive and negative forms creates a sense of potential energy, with the stresses of the bent iron serving as visible reminders to the viewer of the energy expended in forging the iron blocks. "The requisite of the void," the critic Peter Selz argues, is central to Chillida's vision, as it is in Oteiza's work as well.

While iron was Chillida's main medium, in the mid-1960s, he discovered alabaster and its translucent quality. His first alabaster work was *Homage to Kandinsky* (1965), the artist who wrote *Concerning the Spiritual in Art*. The alabaster pieces display an architectonic quality, although they are not models for larger projects. Some of Chillida's series in alabaster are *House of Light*, *Homage to the Sea*, and *Homage to Goethe*. In Octavio Paz's words, "The alabaster sculptures ... are blocks of transparencies in which form becomes space, and space dissolves in luminous vibrations that are echoes and rhymes, thought." Later, in 1977, Chillida discovered fireclay, or the highly oxidized *terre chamotte*, which, when fired to a very high temperature, has a solid and rugged surface. He made of this material many *Lurra* (Earth) pieces, blocks with incisions and crevices that point to an unknown inner space and that share the organic quality of the Earth.

Lesson thirty-five

LEARNING OBJECTIVES

1. To analyze the commitment to avant-garde modernism by Basque artists.
2. To understand primitivism and other experimental propositions.
3. To analyze modernism's involvement with and over-coming of traditional aesthetics.
4. To examine the local and international contexts of Basque art.

REQUIRED READING

Jorge Oteiza, "An Experimental Proposal," "The End of Contemporary Art," and "The Basque Cromlech as Empty Statue," in *Oteiza's Selected Writings*, ed. Joseba Zulaika (Reno: Center for Basque Studies, 2003), 220–44, 259–64, and 323–30.

Peter Selz, "Chillida's Place in Twentieth-Century Sculpture: The Requisite of the Void," in Peter Selz, *Chillida*, (New York: Harry Abrams, 1986), 113–17.

View video on Chillida, *Portrait of an Artist*.

SUGGESTED READING

Margit Rowell, "A Timeless Modernism," in *Oteiza: An Experimental Proposition*, (Barcelona: Fundación Caja de Pensiones, 1988), 16–24.

Peter Selz, *Chillida* (New York: Henry Abrams, 1986).

Kim Bradley, "Basque Modern," *Art in America*, June 1998: 89–121.

WRITTEN LESSON FOR SUBMISSION

1. How would you relate the work of Oteiza and Chillida to other Basque cultural manifestations, such as ritual, folk curing, religion, or politics?
2. Are Oteiza and Chillida "Basque" artists? Argue both for and against the premise.
3. Describe some of the concepts central to Oteiza's aesthetic theories.

36 · Mirentxu's Puzzle

W E BEGAN this course with the treatment of Basque prehistory, so it is fitting, or perhaps ironic, that we conclude with consideration of what some deem to be Basque posthistory—the likely or at least plausible submersion of Basque culture and identity into both a globalized world culture and the wider European Union polity.

These twin concerns—a posited emergence of a homogenized global culture and the erosion of the sovereignty of even recognized states, let alone of the political aspirations of substate nations—(e.g., Scots, Kurds, Catalans, Basques, Quebecois, etc.)—are currently prominent within the research agendas of the various disciplines of both the social sciences and the humanities. There seems to be ample evidence for the defenders of the theses that the worlds' cultures are becoming increasingly diluted into a kind of world culture and that global politics are becoming increasingly "postsovereign." One need only contemplate the spread of First World, and particularly American, influence throughout the global economy (McDonald's, Wal-Mart, etc.), the proliferation of English as the world's predominant scientific, artistic, and financial medium, and the global interconnectivity afforded by the Internet. Similarly, the increased international importance of NGOs, the emergence of multinational entities such as NAFTA, MERCOSUR, and ASEAN, not to mention NATO and the European Union, have all arguably undermined the former powers of existing states. Similarly, the global reach of today's multinational enterprises defies the capacity of individual states to tax, let alone to control, their activities. Then, too, today, there is not a single developed country that

remains unchallenged by some combination of considerable in-migration of legal and illegal aliens and the out-
sourcing of jobs to underdeveloped parts of the planet.
In some sense, the recent riots in France and the debate
over construction of a fence along the U.S. border are
linked phenomena.

NEVERTHELESS, the prognostication of a globalized, postsovereign world does not go unchallenged
by either scholars or current events. A phenomenon
such as the Internet is as capable of empowering the
expression of the *particular* as it is of imposing the *general*. In the political arena, it is possible to discern not
only the erosion of nationalism and of state sovereignty,
but, during the post–Cold War period, their proliferation.
Indeed, while some discern a "clash of civilizations" in
the current conflict between parts of the Occident and
parts of the Islamic world, in fact, the majority of the
planet's political conflicts are still of the local variety in
that they regard control of a particular power center (for
example, Liberia) or seek to carve a new sovereign polity
out of an older one (Darfur, Aceh, or Eritrea). The proliferation of new states has been furthered as well by the
fragmentation of old ones (Yugoslavia, the Soviet Union,
and Czechoslovakia).

Basque culture, society, and politics are subject to all
of these contending pressures and possibilities. While
analysts of disparate viewpoints debate recent Basque
history and the nature of contemporary realities, their
one point of agreement might be the impossibility of
prognosticating the immediate future. If one considers
recent developments in Spanish domestic politics—the
replacement of José María Aznar by José Luis Rodríguez
Zapatero, the increasing militancy of Catalan nationalists, and an emerging political axis between Catalans and
Basques—one could make a plausible argument that

Euskadi will have greater political autonomy in the short term. Nevertheless, it is equally possible to envision a reaction by Spanish nationalists in which the Spanish political parties forge a common front to combat a perceived threat to the unity of the state. Under such a scenario, it is scarcely far-fetched to imagine the severe diminishment or even the abolition of the region's powers within a future Spain. Then, too, there is the issue of the European Union and of Spain's place within it, as well as that of its constituent regions—particularly those such as Euskadi and Catalonia, with their active ethnonationalist challenges to central authority. In this regard, Spanish sovereignty is challenged not only from Barcelona and Bilbao, but from Brussels, as well.

WE HAVE summed up and given concrete form to the effects of these contending forces on Basque identity by constructing a representative, if fictional, biography of a contemporary Basque woman. She was born in 1973 in Gernika. Her given name is María Asunción Quintero, but her family and friends all call her Mirentxu, the Basque diminutive for "Little Maria." Her father, José Quintero, came to Bizkaia from Galicia in 1963 to work in a domestic-appliance factory. It was there that he met his future wife, Edurne Jayo, who was raised on a *baserria* in Aulestia. At home, the family spoke Castilian almost exclusively, although during the three years that Mirentxu attended grammar school in an *ikastola*, Edurne tried to speak to her in Basque, but eventually gave up when her native Bizkaian failed to jibe with the schoolroom Batua. Mirentxu also tried to watch Euskal Telebista, but except for a cartoon show, she found it to be less interesting than the available Spanish alternatives. Then, too, her father would silently change the channel of their only set whenever he wished to watch the nearly ubiquitous soccer coverage. In fact, José never

Boys drumming

Children parading during the annual festivities in honor of the patron saint, St. John the Baptist, of the town of Arrasate. If they celebrate the past, they personify the present and future in the core community of the cooperative movement. While situated in the Basque cultural heartland, Arrasate's population is increasingly cosmopolitan and includes people from throughout Iberia and the world. The town also boasts a new university, symbolic of its commitment to universal ideas.

Photo: José Félix Diáz de Tuesta (et al.) Arrasate / Mondragón Images *(Arrasate: 2003).*

actively opposed Edurne's efforts to teach Mirentxu and Juan, her brother, Basque, but he withheld his approval.

During her *ikastola* years, Mirentxu belonged to a parish youth group and learned to perform several Basque dances. The priest was a strong advocate of Basque nationalism and readily blurred the line between folklore and politics. She faithfully attended the annual patron saint's festivities in Aulestia, the main occasion on which she interacted with her Basque cousins. She had others in Donostia, where José's brother Manuel resided. On several occasions, she had attended the festivities there organized by the city's Galicians in order to celebrate their heritage. In fact, Mirentxu preferred the sonorous *gaita*, or bagpipe of Celtic legacy, to the more strident strains of the Basque *txistu*, or flute. Nor was she entirely alienated from her Spanish heritage. She was a closet fan of the Real Madrid soccer team, particularly when it played against Bilbao's Athletic, which paradoxically was her father's favorite. Perhaps it was the filial revenge of a daughter deprived of her cartoons. But in fact, it had persisted and became her own personal protest against the frustrations that she experienced within a deeply divided and conflicted society.

JOSÉ'S TWO concessions to his children's Basque heritage were his acquiescence in addressing his daughter as Mirentxu (a privilege withheld from Juan), which he deemed to be intimate, quaint, and benign, and his silence regarding Basque and Spanish politics, although his sentiments lay with the latter. José's biggest disappointment in life, in fact, was the fact that Juan was living now in France or possibly Latin America, a fugitive from Spanish justice after having been identified as an ETA operative. No matter how hard he tried, José was simply incapable of understanding his son's political commitment. Juan's present predicament was indeed almost too painful for José to contemplate and added a palpable bitter edge to his accustomed silence.

Mirentxu was not really all that surprised. She had watched Juan's seemingly inexplicable transformation from vocal member of the town's most politicized *cuadrilla*, or social group of drinking buddies, to quiet loner. He would while away the afternoons behind the closed door of his bedroom, listening to the same patriotic Basque music over and over again. In their infrequent conversations, he was critical of her indifference to politics and her *pasote* routine. "You are just wasting your life hanging out at the discothèque all night long with those druggie friends of yours," he would say. And then he began to disappear for days at a time without warning, providing some sort of obviously lame explanation after the fact.

E TCHED IN her memory forever was the afternoon Juan burst through the front door in a panic and began packing his suitcase, while José followed him about his room asking repeatedly, "Son, what's happening?" Juan had kissed Edurne and embraced Mirentxu wordlessly, as if for the last time, and then bolted. An hour later, their street was cordoned off, and the stern lieutenant was demanding that Juan give himself up. Edurne became hysterical, sobbing with fear and periodically shouting incoherent pleas. She was terrified by the memory of her neighbors' fate a few years earlier. The couple had been reputed to harbor ETA fugitives from time to time and were shot to death in their home during a police search. When their parish priest had denounced the killings from the pulpit, he had received death threats and a police search of his own house—he had fled to America out of fear for his personal safety.

Mirentxu's life dilemmas were of a different sort. She was unemployed and had recently experienced her own

Zubizuri (white bridge)
A woman (Mirentxu?) crosses the new bridge that links Bilbao's left and right banks (the twin symbols of the city's class differences) while providing international visitors access to the Guggenheim Museum. Zubizuri is therefore a bridge from the past to the future as well as between localized and globalized worlds.
Photo: Inaki Uriarte

frustration and bitterness after having failed the test in Euskara that would have given her the preferential points to secure the civil-service job she had coveted. She supported the Socialist Party and, while favoring the Statute of Autonomy, opposed the Plan Ibarretxe. Two of her less-talented friends had just been hired within the bureaucracy of Eusko Jaurlaritza, mainly through personal ties with influential members of the Basque Nationalist Party. So she now questioned whether she even had a future in the Euskadi of her birth.

AND THEN there was her secret. Now thirty-two and still living at home, she was under not so subtle pressure from Edurne to find a serious boyfriend. References to unborn grandchildren were becoming frequent. Yet unbeknownst to her parents and most of her friends, Mirentxu was a homosexual. Her only serious lesbian relationship (during a two-year sojourn in Madrid) had proven to be supremely guilt-ridden and ill-fated. Despite Mirentxu's claim that she had come to Madrid to escape the rancorous political discourse and sporadic violence in Euskadi, her Castilian lover had blamed her Basque temperament and sympathies for the breakup of their relationship. Try as she might, Mirentxu could not quite shake the feeling that maybe there was some truth in the accusation, particularly when she recalled her demand that Mariasun accompany her to a meeting of the Madrid Basque Club and her insistence that they go to a Basque restaurant whenever dining out.

Mirentxu's sexual predilection had distanced her from the church that had been so much a part of her upbringing and had entrapped her in a daily web of little lies. Yet she simply lacked the courage to declare herself, ostensibly because it might be some sort of last straw for her father. In reality, her greatest trepidation was Edurne's probable anger, given her blatant homophobia and scornful comments whenever the subject of homosexuality was broached.

This morning, Mirentxu had e-mailed her friends Arantxa and Joseba, the only confidantes privy to her secret. While not married, they were working and living together in Copenhagen. Mirentxu had considered writing to her uncle, Edurne's brother Agustín, in Boise, since he had once volunteered to help her emigrate to the United States, and she knew that her adjustment there would be facilitated by the large Basque presence in Idaho. However, such a move would scarcely liberate her from family pressure and probable opprobrium were she to act upon her sexual predilection.

As a citizen of the European Union, there were no longer frontiers impeding Mirentxu from moving to Denmark. Arantxa had recently visited her parents in Gernika. It was then that she described to Mirentxu the ease with which the couple had found good jobs in Copenhagen, the city's tolerance of its gay community, and even the growing support network there of transplanted young Basque workers. Then, too, it was only a day's drive away from "home." Mirentxu opened the city guide to Copenhagen that she had just purchased with the decisive gesture that signaled that her mind was made up ...

IT IS THE purpose of the foregoing fictional family sketch to illustrate the processual and conflictive nature of identity formation and its many situational nuances in contemporary Euskadi. From a social-scientific analytical point of view, even regarding something as seemingly "essential" as ethnicity, most persons have access to multiple identities that can be asserted or denied, ignored or manipulated, according to circumstances. Douglass's "Robert Erburu and Becoming a

Postmodern Basque." is meant to illustrate this process from the perspective of individual actors.

Some final comments are in order regarding ethnic identity. First, ethnicity assumes different meaning in an ethnic homeland as opposed to a diasporic context. In Mirentxu's case, being Basque in Euskadi differs in certain critical fashions from being Basque in Boise or Buenos Aires. Without becoming ascriptive, it is certainly more of a given in the former and a project in the latter. It is simply not the same to embrace, assert, or deny one's Basque identity in a social context, Euskadi, where the definition of Basqueness is openly contested economically, socially, and politically on a daily basis in the media, public institutions, and the street, versus the diasporic ethnic enclave embedded within a society that is largely ignorant of and certainly indifferent to Basque cultural uniqueness. In sum, the manners and means of maintaining and expressing Basque ethnicity vary considerably from one context to another according to both unique historical processes and contemporary social, economic, and political realities.

SECOND, THIS distinction operates not just between the homeland and the diaspora, but is evident as well when comparing the several Basque diasporas. It is simply not the same today to be Basque in San Francisco, Boise, Sydney, Manila, and Mexico City.

Third, as noted in Mirentxu's story, there is now a new Basque diaspora emerging, facilitated not only by the mobility of Basques within the Spanish and French states (there are now particularly impressive Basque clubs in Madrid, Barcelona, and Paris, for example), but also by their mobility within the European Union. Thus, there is now a Basque presence in most Western European metropolises, notably London, Milan, Rome,

Brussels, and Amsterdam. Indeed, we may well be witnessing the formation of a "Euro-Basque" identity.

FOURTH, HAVING noted that all of the foregoing differ
entiators producing axes of variation within Basque
identity, we should also note the overall unifying influence provided by the Internet. Today, Basques of the
homeland and the several diasporas are able to participate in an overarching discourse regarding Basqueness—a kind of a Basque virtual reality that exists in
cyberspace. It is a world in which the descendant of
Basque immigrants residing in Buenos Aires is able to
access an enormous body of information regarding his
or her heritage, and even undertake a virtual journey to
the Basque homeland, while at the same time maintaining lateral contacts, as it were, with fellow ethnics in
other Basque diasporas.

Lesson thirty-six

LEARNING OBJECTIVES
1. To understand some of the challenges that Basques
   face at this juncture in world history.
2. To appreciate the dilemmas, subtleties, and opportunities afforded by cultural identity and its many manifestations.

REQUIRED READING
Andoni Alonso and Iñaki Arzoz, "Basque Identity on
   the Internet," in *Basque Cultural Studies*, ed. William
   A. Douglass, Carmelo Urza, Linda White, and Joseba
   Zulaika (Reno: Basque Studies Program, 1999), 295–
   312.
Manuel Castells, "Globalization, Identity, and the Basque
   Question," in *Basque Politics and Nationalism on*

the Eve of the Millennium, ed. William A. Douglass, Carmelo Urza, Linda White, and Joseba Zulaika (Reno: Basque Studies Program, 1999), 22–33.

William A. Douglass, "Robert Erburu and Becoming a Postmodern Basque," in *Portraits of Basques in the New World*, ed. Richard W. Etulain and Jeronima Echeverria (Reno: University of Nevada Press,), pp. 230–56.

SUGGESTED READING

Begoña Aretxaga, Dennis Dworkin, Joseba Gabilondo, and Joseba Zulaika, eds., *Empire & Terror: Nationalism / Postnationalism in the New Millennium.* (Reno: Center for Basque Studies, 2004).

William A. Douglass, Carmelo Urza, Linda White, and Joseba Zulaika, eds., *Basque Politics and Nationalism in the New Millennium.* (Reno: Basque Studies Program, 1999), pp. 208–28.

———, *Basque Cultural Studies.* (Reno: Basque Studies Program, 1999).

———, *The Basque Diaspora / La Diáspora Vasca.* (Reno: Basque Studies Program, 1999).

WRITTEN LESSON FOR SUBMISSION

1. Discuss Mirentxu's ethnicity. Is it dominated by any one of her ethnic credentials?
2. In your view, how will Mirentxu likely respond to a curious Dane asking about her ethnic origins? Discuss.

Conclusion

IT WOULD be elegant and satisfying to be able
to conclude this course with an integrative and comprehensive summary. Alas, that is impossible, since
Basque anthropology has both evolved and fragmented
mightily since the mid-twentieth century, when the term
antropología referred to physical anthropology, and an
eclectic such as Father Barandiarán moved effortlessly
among what today would be called prehistory, cultural
anthropology, physical anthropology, and folklore studies.

From the standpoint of intellectual history, Basque
anthropology has assumed the guises of its other Iberian
and European counterparts without becoming Ameri-
canized. Thus, the referent of the term *antropología* has
shifted from physical anthropology to the social / cultural variety, while physical anthropology itself, prehistory, and linguistics constitute their own separate disciplines and departments within the Basque academy.

Of particular interest for present purposes are the
developments within the fields of social and cultural
anthropology. It has been stated frequently in the
anthropological textbooks that the discipline is more, or
at least as much, a methodology as a theoretical perspective. Since the times of Franz Boas and Bronislaw Mal-
inowski, the defining characteristic of anthropology has
been conducting prolonged fieldwork among the subject
populations. Indeed, the field study of a minimum of a
year's duration was the discipline's rite of passage from
about the 1920s until quite recently. The extent to which
fieldwork is integral to the anthropological study, therefore, might provide us with a useful way of discussing

the present state of affairs within Basque social and cultural anthropology.

First, there are those who remain in the ethnographic / folkloric tradition of Telesforo de Aranzadi, José Miguel de Barandiarán, and Julio Caro Baroja. For them, the paramount challenge is to document the remnants of traditional culture—beliefs, customs, and crafts—before they disappear. In this regard, perpetual fieldwork is not only central, but is the sine qua non of the anthropological enterprise. Theorizing rarely transcends speculation regarding the distribution of particular cultural traits. Not surprisingly, such initiatives contain a strong archival dimension. At the outset, we discussed the influence of the enthusiastic weekend archeologist and antiquarian in the formation of Basque anthropology. They continue to be drawn as participants to this particular kind of investigation. At the same time, it may be said that this entire intellectual enterprise has moved from the center to the margins of Basque anthropology, in terms of both the number of practitioners and the effect of their findings.

THE SECOND brand of Basque anthropology is that practiced by most of the scholars cited herein. The investigator has conducted at least one prolonged field project during his or her career, usually within the little community or regarding a particular social institution. Sandra Ott worked in Santi Grazi, Davydd J. Greenwood in Hondarribia, Joseba Zulaika in Itziar, Sharryn Kasmir in Arrasate, Jacqueline Urla in Usurbil, Charlotte Crawford in Bermeo, Marianne Heiberg in Elgeta, and William Douglass in Etxalar and Aulestia. At the same time, both Zulaika and Teresa del Valle, to cite but two, have conducted research in Bilbao. It should be noted that space limitations and language considerations have prevented our detailing the works and careers of a whole generation of Basque social anthropologists who were the products of the new university system created in the Basque Country during the post-Franco era. This is an egregious oversight in one sense, but is also a result of the fact that practically none of their work is available in English—the language of this course.

Finally, there is a new kind of anthropologist, prepared through coursework in the discipline, as well in as the other social sciences, history, and philosophy, whose dissertation work is conducted in the library, rather in the field, and whose fieldwork experience is either limited or nonexistent. It might be noted that this development is not unique to Basque anthropology. Rather, it is increasingly common throughout the discipline, because many of our former (colonial) field venues are off-limits for Western anthropologists, "primitive" societies in general have disappeared, and some of the world's "native" peoples are increasingly reticent to being "studied" by outsiders and / or have developed their own anthropology. In any event, there is now a cadre of Basque investigators who publish social criticism, ranging from newspaper columns to lengthy monographs, focused on Basque identity, particularly as reflected in ethnonationalist politics. For these intellectuals, the line is readily blurred between their academic research and their political activism. De facto, they have tended to be highly critical of Basque nationalism and certainly of ETA, to which some once belonged.

WE WILL conclude this course by harking back to what we stated at the outset regarding the discipline of anthropology in general. We noted that by definition, it is the study of everything human. It is therefore scarcely surprising that its Basque variety, like all others, harbors a plethora of trends and tendencies, both methodological and theoretical. Yet despite such eclecticism, the twin premises of this course are that "Basqueness" is sufficiently distinctive within the world's cultures to warrant study in its own terms and that there is sufficient coherence among the various attempts to do so to warrant our describing a discipline that we have chosen to designate as Basque anthropology. At the same time, we refrain from proscribing any of the foregoing anthropological investigations of Basque cultural realities, nor would we prescribe some sort of proper future agenda for the discipline. Rather, it is our view that each of the various trends and tendencies should be evaluated in their own terms and not according to some sort of scale regarding more and less worthy kinds of Basque anthropological research.

Pictures

Jesus Altuna: 33, 50, 55, 58, 58, 382
José Miguel de Barandiarán: 102
Basque Film Archives: 461, 464
Jill Berner: 82
Basso Cannarsa: 448
Fidel Cruz: 348
William Douglass: 14, 152, 215, 218, 260, 304, 314, 363, 371, 474, 200
Albrecht Dürer: 87
María Elena Etxeberri: 186
Gordejuela: 183
Jim Harter: *Transportation: A Pictorial Archive from Nineteenth-Century Sources*. Dover, New York 1984: 170
Johann Georg Heck: *Heck's pictorial Archive of Art and Architecture*. Dover, New York 1994: 111
Alberto Irigoyen: 197
Xabier Irujo: Cover, 79, 99, 137, 167, 178, 208, 223, 234, 240, 245, 248, 270, 240, 356, 385, 392, 397, 404, 413, 416
Itoiz: 436
Kepa Junkera: 441
Mikel Laboa: 425
Richard Lane: 160
Joyce Laxalt: 127, 230
Francisco Letamendia, *Euskadi: pueblo y nación*: 140, 145
Ruper Ordorika: 433
Oskorri: 428
Photodisk, Inc. Seattle 1995: 456
Picture Book of Devils, Demons and Witchcraft. Dover, New York 1971: 275, 285, 288,
Craig Rairdin: 90

Donald R. Rice: *Animals, a picture sourcebook.* Van Nostrand Reinhold Co, New York 1979: 256

José Félix Diáz de Tuesta (et al.) *Arrasate / Mondragón Images* (Arrasate: 2003): 333, 336, 336, 483

Iñaki Uriarte: 320, 325, 471, 486

Jennifer Thermes. World Views. Artville, Madison, 1997, 26

Joseba Zulaika: 311, 343

Index

Note: Illustrations are indicated with italicized page numbers.

A

Douglass, William
  anthropological studies, 192, 493
  attends San Fermin festival, 264–65
  credentials, 7
  participates in *marmitako*, 232–33
  research in Aulestia and Etxalar, 17
doves, 259–60
Dürer, Albrecht, 87
Durkheim, Emile, 54

E

Echevarria, Juan de, 468
Edict of Union, 103–4
education, 86–87
Edward III, 85
EGI, 128
el Fuerte, Sancho, 81
Eleanor of Aquitania, 84
Elizalde, Joaquín, 181
Elkano, Juan Sebastian de, 177, *178–80*
emigration
  early, to Australia, 184–89
  effect of U.S. immigration law on, 161–69
  from Aulestia, 361–62
  modern-day, to Australia, 189–90
  to American West, 155–58
  to Latin America, 150–53
  to Philippines, 181–82
Emilio, Don, 232
England, middle-age rule of, 84–85
ensanche, Bilbao's, 312–15
Eroski, 329
Errobi, 22
Ertzainak (The Police), 439–40
Escudero, Francisco, 426

Zorrilla, José Antonio, 455
Zubiaurre, Ramón de, 468
Zulaika, Joseba, 7, 18, 192, 493
Zuloaga, Ignacio, 468
Zumalacarregui, Tomás de, 113
Zumárraga, Juan de, 151, 281

Colophon

This book was edited by Bud Bynack and indexed by Ron Strauss. It was laid out and produced by Gunnlaugur SE Briem, who also designed the typeface, BriemAnvil.

It was printed and bound by Fidlar Doubleday of Davenport, Iowa.

The Basque Studies textbook series